I enjoy sharing my books as I do my friends, asking only that you treat them well and see them safely home

Delores Friesen

Foundations of
Family Therapy

FOUNDATIONS

OF

FAMILY THERAPY

A Conceptual Framework for Systems Change

LYNN HOFFMAN

Basic Books, Inc., Publishers

NEW YORK

The author is grateful for permission to reprint material from the following sources:

W. Robert Beavers, *Psycotherapy and Growth*. New York: Brunner/Mazel, 1977. By permission of the author and the publisher.

E. Wertheim, "Family Unit Therapy and the Science of Typology of Family Systems," *Family Process* 12 (1973). By permission of the publisher.

Lynn Hoffman, "Deviation-Amplifying Processes in Natural Groups," in Haley, J., (ed.), *Changing Families*. New York: Grune and Stratton, 1971. By permission of the publisher.

Lynn Hoffman, "'Enmeshment' and the Too Richly Cross-Joined System," *Family Process* 14 (1975). By permission of the publisher.

Lynn Hoffman, "Breaking the Homeostatic Cycle," in Guerin, P., (ed.), *Family Therapy: Theory and Practice*. New York: Garner Press, 1976. By permission of the publisher.

Lynn Hoffman, "The Family Life Cycle and Discontinuous Change," in Carter, E., and M. Orfanides (eds.), *The Family Life Cycle*. New York: Gardner Press, 1980. By permission of the publisher.

Library of Congress Cataloging in Publication Data

Hoffman, Lynn.
   Foundations of family therapy.

   Includes bibliographical references and index.
   1. Family psychotherapy.   I.   Title .
   RC488.5.H6   616.89'156   80-68956
   ISBN: 0-465-02498-X   AACR2

To My Family

Martha, Joanna, Livia, and Ted

Contents

Acknowledgments

A great many people were part of the long journey that resulted in this book. I want to express my appreciation to Don Bloch, Director of the Ackerman Institute, who very generously bestowed on me an unofficial grant, by giving me the space and time to complete the manuscript. At the Ackerman Institute, an atmosphere of collegial and creative enterprise was provided by Olga Silverstein and Peggy Papp, of the Brief Therapy Project, and by members of my current research team, Gillian Walker, Peggy Penn, John Patten, Joel Bergman, and Jeffrey Ross. I owe many of my ideas to the stimulating discussions I have had with these important colleagues.

Peggy Penn and Carl Bryant read early drafts of the manuscript and offered sound advice and enormous encouragement, for which I am most grateful. At a later stage, the manuscript was carefully read by Paul Dell and Carlos Sluzki, whose excellent suggestions are incorporated into the text.

As for colleagues less involved in the final process but whose intellectual energy and personal support constituted an invaluable contribution, I would like to thank Mara Selvini Palazzoli and her associates in Milan, Giuliana Prata, Luigi Boscolo, and Gianfranco Cecchin, who have given me unfailing encouragement. I am also most grateful to other colleagues, who have taught me, inspired me, and believed in me: among these are the late Don Jackson, Virginia Satir, Jay Haley, Dick Auerswald, Salvador Minuchin, Harry Aponte, Carl Whitaker, Monica McGoldrick, Carrell Damman, and Harry Goolishian.

For understanding and appreciating my work and helping make it known to colleagues in England and Europe, I am indebted to John

Byng-Hall, Philippe Caillé, Rosalind Draper, and Mia Andersson.

At Basic Books, I want to thank my editor, Jo Ann Miller, who believed in the project from the beginning and who helped me push and pull the manuscript into final shape. It is rare to find an editor who will involve herself so unstintingly and creatively in all the details that give spit and polish to a book. Project editor Julia Strand worked patiently and diligently during every stage, transforming the manuscript into a finished book. I appreciate, too, the efforts of Leo Goldberger, who led me to Basic Books.

Finally, I must express my gratitude to the staff and faculty of the Ackerman Institute for providing me with a respectful yet challenging environment in which to work, and for the many helping hands they held out to me in matters both large and small. To these people, and to my family, who have put up with me during the whole long process, and to many others to whom I owe much but do not have the space to mention, my thanks.

LYNN HOFFMAN
February, 1981

Foreword

In this volume Lynn Hoffman undertakes an eagerly awaited display and integration of the theory and technique of family therapy. Her vision is panoramic; she possesses that relevant and encyclopedic fund of information that could have come only from long and thoughtful observation of the best of her colleagues at work, from having struggled with teaching and doing family therapy herself, and finally from having encompassed the now voluminous pertinent literature. The attempt is daring; it is aptly titled "foundations."

It is safe to say that this is the earliest time at which this book could have been written; equally so, that it has been written none too soon. We are at the end of the second great cycle of growth in the field. It is necessary to take stock, pull together the loose threads, and consolidate the gains that have been made. This volume does that superbly; it will provide a solid base for the future growth that is to come.

Attention to family as a clinical entity and as a fruitful area of theoretical concern developed in a tiny but portentous fashion in the third decade of this century. Clinical psychiatry during that period, and the more important years following World War II, was dominated by psychoanalysis, itself already struggling with revisionist movements. Psychoanalysts like Sullivan, Horney, Thompson, and Fromm-Reichmann, among others, were enlarging the perspectives of their science to include insights from field theory, linguistics, and cultural anthropology. Thus, as psychoanalytic theory constructed ever more intricate models of intrapsychic sequences and structure-functions, "news of a difference" was beginning to be heard more insistently. The difference was context—first, that context, in linear terms, had an effect; later, that context *was* the effect. Clinical concern with family followed most naturally, and the first great growth cycle began.

As Hoffman makes clear, the systemic evolution in psychotherapy was contemporaneous with profound shifts in the perspectives of the natural and the other behavioral sciences. As a single instance, the Society for General Systems Research was organized in 1954 and began publication of its estimable yearbook series two years later. I have just opened the second volume of that series at random and come upon Anatol Rappaport's critique of Lewis F. Richardson's "Mathematical Theory of War." Under the heading "Etiology of Deadly Quarrels," we find, "The temptation to look for lineal cause-effect relations, especially where events vital to our survival are involved, always persists." Indeed it does, and Hoffman takes precisely this issue as her departure and termination points.

Hoffman begins her integrative effort by jumping right into the epistemological struggle: "The central concept of the new epistemology—both the homeostatic and the evolutionary paradigms—is the idea of circularity." She lingers over linearity but a moment and moves along quickly with a description of her personal intellectual journey. The essence of that journey, it seems to me, lies in the effort to understand creation, genesis: "I was . . . intrigued by the idea that deviation, or deviance, per se, was not the negative thing it was thought to be, once one abandoned the point of view of those who wanted it corrected." The associated epistemological riddle of morphostasis-morphogenesis provides the central thread of *Foundations of Family Therapy* on which the works of theorists and clinical innovators of the family therapy field are hung like so many sparkling jewels. Bateson is the centerpiece: Hoffman's consideration of his early work, *Naven,* and the concept of schismogenesis provides the foundation for her discussion of "these curious self-reinforcing cycles" that ultimately are the concern of the family psychotherapist.

I imagine some of the scholars, investigators, and clinical innovators whose work is described in this volume may be miffed at the inevitable abridgement of their work. But look at the extraordinary array of talent: All the stars of the first magnitude are included, and, with rare exceptions, all of the lesser luminaries. Hoffman has paid attention, is graceful and inclusive. I am impressed with the payoff of her years of careful observation; she knew who was good and, even more, who was going to be good.

I want to endorse her choices wholeheartedly and unequivocally. The work of the authors cited here is the basic reading list in this field. Serious students might begin right now to educate themselves by systematically following the path Hoffman has traced out: Bateson, Haley, Buckley, Wertheim, Watzlawick, Jackson, Ackerman, Minuchin, Rabkin, Selvini Palazzoli, Auerswald, Wynne, Whitaker, Satir, Weakland, Paul—Hoffman has absolute pitch for the good ones—Prigogine, Elkaim, the list goes on and on.

It is important to remember that family psychotherapy is a clinical science. The test of the goodness of its theories is that they generate (or rationalize) actions leading to change in a direction taken to be desirable (by someone who will pay the bill). We may wish as well for the theories to be elegant, parsimonious, and isomorphic with other good theories; we should like for them to be empirically verifiable (witness Bateson's impatience with efforts to empirically verify the double bind hypothesis). But the clinician will always buy bad theory that works, will willingly be effective rather than rigorous if that works. The miracle of family therapy has been that the shift to a systemic perspective—"I need to meet with your family in order to assist you"—is an effective intervention in and of itself. Conscientiously adhered to, from an open and non-blaming stance, the assembling of a family in order to study and modify the pain or malfunction of one of its members is enormously facilitating. I have commented elsewhere that all clinicians should now be obligated to explain why they have chosen *not* to begin their involvement with a problem by this route.

There are two rivers of ideas flowing through the volume. The first, as I have noted, builds on Bateson and is concerned with assembling the elements of a unified theory of family function and family therapy. Hoffman might well have limited herself to that monumental task and to those authors whose works are most relevant. But the pioneers, the iconoclasts, and the great originals also have much to say to us. Where, in fact, a unified theory does not yet fully exist—surely this volume is helping to birth it—a strategic choice for Hoffman is how to deal both with the one truth and the many truths.

Of course all the authors cited are both foxes and hedgehogs, knowing both many truths and only one (but knowing that one well). Yet the great naturals and the pure truth seekers need different treatment. Compare, for example, Ackerman and Minuchin, Satir and Jackson. Both pairs originated and worked in the same general setting: Satir and Jackson at the cybernetics-oriented Mental Research Institute in Palo Alto, California; Ackerman and Minuchin having their roots in the east coast world of psychoanalytic child psychiatry. All four have powerful personas, and there is no doubt that they make a strong impression; they are distinctive and individual, no one would mistake one for the other. Yet Ackerman and Satir need to be preserved as people if their genius and special contributions are to be properly noted. Hoffman is to be credited for her awareness that this is so and for her ability to accomplish the task. She has a curious and beneficent eye, a mode of inquiry that asks not only, "What is going on here?" but "What is going on here that is good?" The results of her inquiry are set forth lucidly and felicitously. It has been my good fortune to know all the folks with whom Hoffman deals in this volume: I can attest that she is highly accurate in her selection of their essential ideas and, where personal description is called for, a word painter with a complex palette that she uses well.

Consider her sketch of Virginia Satir. Satir has been enormously influential; she was one of the original group at the Mental Research Institute in Palo Alto, the founding mother of the field of family therapy. Over the years she has energized multitudes of patients and colleagues. Yet it is fair, I think, to say that Satir is *sui generis,* as is Milton Erickson, in Hoffman's view and mine. Magnificent exemplars, they teach by being. Their genius sharply contrasts with the cookbook techniques of Jay Haley, master dramatist that he is, who eschews all "use of self" and forces his students to be circumscribed and explicit about what is to be fixed and how to do it.

But it is Hoffman's anecdote about Satir to which I wish to direct the reader. It takes place in a first interview. The identified patient is a young man who has impregnated two young girls. The family is consumed with shame; the boy sits isolated in a corner of the treatment room. And there is Satir's marvelous opening line, ". . . we know one thing for sure: we know you have good seed." In one sentence we have positive connotation, reframing, a masterful power rebalancing—and likely enough a "deep" interpretation of the history and dynamics of the event. We must be grateful to Hoffman: She was there (it took place in 1963), she knew it was significant, she remembered it and has told us about it.

This volume is crowded with such anecdotes, drawn from direct observation and from a sensible reading of the literature. Above all there are Hoffman's original ideas, worked into and interpreted with the other material she presents. As a single example, her linking of Ashby and Minuchin in her classic paper, "'Enmeshment' and the Too Richly Cross-Joined System," will provide nourishment for clinicians and theorists for many years to come. I would have liked the book to be longer, and mean by that to praise it with a faint damn. The constraints of space limitation should be noted by the reader, particularly the tyro, who should take this volume as a prodigious homework assignment. Readers will need to return to it again and again—as good a reason for buying a book as any I can think of.

DONALD A. BLOCH, M.D.
February, 1981

Foundations of
Family Therapy

Prologue

Behind the Looking Glass

This book is a journey to a newly discovered kingdom, the world behind the looking glass. For me, the advent of the one-way screen, which clinicians and researchers have used since the 1950s to observe live family interviews, was analogous to the discovery of the telescope. Seeing differently made it possible to think differently. And new ways of thinking have led to an epistemological revolution, one that touches all the sciences and that challenges many traditional concepts, from the belief in linear causality to theories of individual motivation.

Family therapy, although not a behavioral science per se, is in the odd position of being one of the few areas of behavioral research and practice to be influenced by this epistemological shift. It is therefore more than just a novel therapeutic technique; it is based on new assumptions about human behavior and human interaction that have far-reaching implications. To really understand it, we will have to go back several decades and explore the diverse themes and concepts around which the family movement has evolved.

A Bicameral Model

Let us start with the technological invention just described: the screen. The late anthropologist Gregory Bateson speaks in *Mind and Nature* of the advantages of a bicameral format—the jump to a new perspective or emergence of new possibilities that follows the placing together of two eyes, two hands, two chambers of the brain.[1] This format applies also to the one-way screen. The screen turned psychotherapy into a bicameral interaction that offered a similar chance to explore a new dimension. One had two places to sit. One could take a position, and have somebody else take a position commenting on or reviewing that position.

It is not strange, then, that the screen became a stake-out place from which to view the fauna of a realm that had always been before us yet never truly seen. One of the early discoveries made by those who first viewed families with schizophrenics was that what were thought to be mental illnesses belonging to individuals might not be illnesses in the medical sense. In fact, they might not be disorders at all. Rather, they could be seen as orderly manifestations that had meaning in the families or other social settings in which they occurred.

Not only the process of assessment but the process of therapy profited from the two-chamber framework. The use of the two rooms to divide the tasks of therapy—regardless of how this division was described—led to a new and more powerful way of organizing systems change. With this format it became possible to abandon what was becoming for many an outmoded concept: the concept of the therapist as a free-standing agent acting upon a free-standing subject, the client or family.

Why was this concept becoming outmoded? To explain, I will have to enlarge the field of vision and describe a cluster of ideas that has been rocking our Aristotelian universe for a long time. The shift to these ideas is linked very closely, first, to developments in such fields as physics, biology, mathematics, and second, to the cognitive sciences that have emerged from computer technology. The figures who seem to have had the most impact on the family field in its infancy were, oddly enough, not so much psychotherapists but such scientists as information theorist Claude Shannon, cyberneticist Norbert Wiener, and general systems theorist Ludwig von Bertalanffy. One must add to this list Gregory Bateson, whose synthesizing genius showed how ideas from such divergent sources could be useful to the understanding of communication processes, including those associated with psychopathology. Bateson was also one of the first to introduce the idea that a family might be analogous to a homeostatic or cybernetic system.

Unfortunately, however, for those who like simplicity, the family field did not develop in a straightforward fashion from the ideas of these early thinkers. There are now two distinct generations of thought in family therapy. Building on the cybernetic model, theorists like the late psychiatrist Don Jackson, at the Mental Research Institute in Palo Alto, California, emphasized the equilibrium-maintaining qualities of symptomatic behaviors in families, as if they were literally analogous to homeostatic elements.[2] Recently, theorists like University of Texas psychologist Paul Dell have developed an evolutionary rather than a homeostatic model.[3] Deriving his evolutionary epistemology from the work of a group of scientists who came to prominence during the 1970s, such as physicist Ilya Prigogine, or biologist Humberto Maturana, Dell conceptualizes families, as well as all living systems, as evolving, nonequilibrium entities capable of sudden transformations. Dell applies this evolutionary paradigm to a consideration of family systems, in contrast to the homeostatic paradigm of the earlier family thinkers.

Circular versus Linear Thinking

The central concept of the new epistemology—both the homeostatic and the evolutionary paradigms—is the idea of circularity. In the field of mental health there has been a growing disenchantment with the linear causality of Western thought. Mental illness has traditionally been thought of in linear terms, with historical, causal explanations for the distress. Efforts to explain symptomatic behavior have usually been based on either a medical or a psychodynamic model. The former compares emotional or mental distress to a biological malfunction or illness. Treatment consists of finding an "etiology" of the so-called illness (a typically linear construct) and then instituting a treatment, such as administering drugs or devising other means of altering or blocking those bodily processes which are considered responsible for the patient's state. The people in charge of this treatment would of course be doctors, and the settings would often be hospitals.

The psychodynamic model is influenced by nineteenth-century discoveries about such forms of energy as electricity and steam. As with the medical model, etiology is conceived of in linear terms. Symptoms are said to arise from a trauma or conflict that originated in the patient's past and that has for a variety of reasons been relegated to the unconscious. Treatment consists of helping the patient to recover the memory of the repressed event, which could also be a fantasy or an unacceptable wish, and to reexperience the emotions that were buried within it. Once the secret material becomes known to the patient and the buried emotions are "worked through" within the safe confines of the therapeutic relationship, the patient will presumably no longer need the symptom.

Thus these two models typically see symptomatic distress as a malfunction arising either from biological or physiological causes, or from a repressed event in the past. In both models the individual is the locus of the malfunction, and the etiology is connected with an imperfection in his genes, biochemistry, or intrapsychic development.

After decades of strict adherence to these models, a new conceptualization began to emerge. Evidence provided by the watchers behind the screen supported the growing disenchantment with the linear, historical view. If one saw a person with a psychiatric affliction in a clinician's office, it would be easy to assume that he or she suffered from an intrapsychic disorder arising from the past. But if one saw the same person with his or her family, in the context of current relationships, one began to see something quite different. One would see communications and behaviors from everybody present, composing many circular causal loops that played back and forth, with the behavior of the afflicted person only part of a larger, recursive dance.

Of all those writing about the shift to a circular epistemology, it is Gregory Bateson who most persistently tried to capture this elusive beast. In *Mind and Nature,* he makes a distinction between the world of physical objects and the world of living forms.[4] The physical world, the world of Newton, assumes a billiard ball model in which causality is linear and forces act unidirectionally upon things. Bateson objects that the world of living forms is poorly explained by comparing it to a billiard table. In the world of living forms not just force but information and relationship become important.

The classic example of this viewpoint is the difference between kicking a stone and kicking a dog. In the case of the stone, the energy transmitted by the kick will make the stone move a certain distance, which can be predicted by the heaviness of the stone, the force of the kick, and so forth. But if a man kicks a dog, the reaction of the dog does not depend wholly on the energy of the man, because the dog has its own source of energy, and the outcome is unpredictable. What is transmitted is news about a relationship— the relationship between the man and the dog. The dog will respond in one of a number of ways, depending on the relationship and how it interprets the kick. It may cringe, run away, or try to bite the man. But the behavior of the dog in turn becomes news for the man, which may modify his own subsequent behavior. If, for instance, the man is bitten, he may think twice before kicking that particular dog again.

Therefore, Bateson would argue, we need a new grammar, a new descriptive language, to depict what is going on in the living world. What characterizes this grammar? First, as we might expect, it objects to "thing" language, which grows out of linear notions of cause and effect, in preference to a recursive language, in which all elements of a given process move together. "The man used a scythe to mow a field" is thing language and is linear. It suggests that one marked-off segment (a man) took another marked-off segment (a scythe) and used it to chop up another segment (a field). One gets the linear progression: A, using B, acted upon C, to effect D. Here is a recursive, circular description of the same process by Mary Catherine Bateson, the anthropologist's daughter:

A man with a scythe is constrained by the form of the scythe; indeed his own body motion is informed by the curves of his tool, a concrete proposition about the interlocked movement of man and tool through deep growing fields across the generations; as time passes, his own musculature will become a record of the scythe's teaching, first in stiffness, then in emerging grace and skill. We need time to understand this system, to get beyond seeing it as simply instrumental.[5]

In the case of living systems, it is not possible to assign one part a causal influence *vis à vis* another, or to put in any linear markers at all. As Bateson says, a brain does not "think." What "thinks" is a brain inside a man who is part of larger systems residing in balance within their environment. One cannot draw a line indicating one part that thinks and another that is profiting by the thinking. "What thinks is a total circuit."[6]

Similarly, in describing the evolution of the horse, Bateson talks about the relationship between horse and grass in which each reacts back upon the changes of the other. To speak of the horse "evolving" and the brain "thinking" as if they were not part of an ongoing, self-reflexive process that includes other elements would be to ignore the laws of relativity for living forms. Newtonian descriptions classify an item according to inherent attributes and characteristics. Recursive descriptions define an item in terms of its relationship with other items. To quote Bateson again:

I was utterly fascinated, and still am, with the discovery that when you use language rightly to describe a flowering plant you will say that a leaf is a lateral organ on a stem which is characterized by having a bud, namely a baby stem, in its axil. So the definitions became: a stem is that which bears leaves, and a leaf is that which has a stem in its angle; and that which is in the angle of the leaf is a baby stem, and so on.[7]

Ideas like these have extraordinary implications, not least when applied to the field of psychotherapy. The therapist can no longer be seen as "impacting" on the client or family through personality, craft, or technique. The therapist is not an agent and the client is not a subject. Both are part of a larger field in which therapist, family, and any number of other elements act and react upon each other in unpredictable ways, because each action and reaction continually changes the nature of the field in which the elements of this new therapeutic system reside. A circular epistemology forces the therapist to take account of the fact that he or she is inevitably part of this larger field, an inextricable element of that which he attempts to change.

The Beginning of the Journey

At the time this book was conceived, what we can now call the homeostatic model of the early family therapy researchers was in its infancy, and the evolutionary model based on recent ideas from physics and other scientific fields hardly born. In 1970 I wrote a paper on deviation-amplifying processes, originally entitled "Beyond Homeostasis,"[8] which contained ideas that now seem to me an attempt to bridge the two positions, or move the first one forward. It was published simultaneously with a similar essay, Albert Speer's "Family Systems: Morphostasis and Morphogenesis," which also broke the confines of the homeostatic model.[9]

This book arose out of a compelling need to build a framework that would explain where the concepts flowing into both models came from and how these models fit together with the many other ideas and models that are still bubbling up out of the family therapy field. (Family therapy was, and still is, a wondrous Tower of Babel; people in it speak many different tongues.) In addition, I have tried to integrate other research in the social and behavioral sciences that can back up the observations of clinicians working with families.

My fascination with social fields and with describing them systematically also played a part in the explorations that resulted in this book. My experience resembles that of those early meteorologists who realized that weather systems could not be understood locally, that one man's downpour could be another man's drought. In studying weather systems one might encounter complex redundancies in the way various elements intersected: wind, vector currents, clouds, moisture, cold and warm fronts, time zones, latitudes and longitudes, the pulls of lunar gravity, or the flares on the sun. Above all, there would have to be some way to account for the changing *differences* among these variables. To grow and evolve, the science of meteorology had to find a kind of crow's nest from which it was possible to observe patterns and sequences moving the same way or differently through time, rather than seeing only particular pieces of weather that happened to occur in this or that place. In short, what had to be discerned were the larger configurations that make up our modern weather charts. Satellite photographs, taken from literal sky-borne crow's nests, now show the spirals of these weather systems, graphically portrayed in cloud formations circling the earth.

The study of human behavior has undergone similar changes. As long as one stood on earth, so to speak, and experienced rain one day and sun the next, one had to invent a demonology that controlled these different manifestations. Similarly with unusual behaviors. A demonology explaining irrational behaviors was invented time and again by human groups to explain the variable weather of the soul. In some periods, powerful spirits were believed to act upon a person from without; at other times, powerful impulses were seen to control the person from within.

Only recently has it been recognized that just as weather can be seen as large, moving systems, so perhaps human behaviors may derive from large relationship configurations moving through time. To say, "This is a schizophrenic," that is, a person with a supposed mental disorder, makes as much sense as to state, "This is a rainy day." The so-called schizophrenic can just as well be described as a manifestation of a larger weather system in human affairs. The next step is to find an imaginary satellite from which to view the patterns and sequences that will give us weather charts for such behaviors, at least within small, reasonably stable groups.

That, of course, is the problem. Behaviors cannot be studied apart from the fields in which they occur, but the fields must be integrated enough to allow study. How much easier it is to understand the movements of ants or the dances of bees. If only large human structures—nations, societies, cultures—were as homogeneous or predictable. The family is one system that transcends the limits of the single person yet is small and clearly bounded enough to serve as a researchable unit. In the family, as in weather, once one leaves the individual and surveys the family as a systemic entity residing within even larger fields, one begins to see clear redundancies and distinct patterns.

Thus it is not hard to see the powerful lure family research held for one eager to explore social fields from a systemic view. I first stumbled upon family research in Palo Alto in 1963. There, at the Mental Research Institute, I began to see from the studies that had come out of Gregory Bateson's 1952–1962 research project on communication that a change in a family depended very much on the interplay between deviation and the way deviation was kept within bounds.

I was also intrigued by the idea that deviation, or deviance, per se, was not the negative thing it was thought to be, once one abandoned the point of view of those who wanted it corrected. Deviation (including symptomatic and irrational behaviors of all kinds) could be highly important for a group. Although homeostasis was a central concern of the Palo Alto family researchers, when I read their writings I found myself more interested in what worked *against* homeostasis; what introduced variety, strangeness, novelty. It seemed to me paradoxical that families with symptomatic members were thought to be pathogenic since I began to suspect that only when someone or something deviated from the family norms could the family derive new information and evolve new structures. Without some chink through which variety might enter, there seemed no possibility for a system to achieve basic structural change. Most families must reorganize as the generations are born, grow old, and die. If a family could not achieve that kind of change, it would most likely not survive.

Families with symptomatic members thus became illustrious material for study, since in those families the issues of change would be most intensely highlighted. Therefore I began by asking what were the properties of family fields in which new information, and hence change, entered with difficulty if at all. Were there explanations for the stability of these fields? They seemed to remain relatively the same despite the need for periodic reorganizations that every family must face. Was there research in other fields that might throw light on these mysteries? Was there even a language in which to express these concerns, since our old language seemed designed by its very structure to obscure them? These were the kinds of questions to which I sought, if not answers, at least indications that would tell me where to look.

Organization of the Book

This story unfolds with the detective work of those early family researchers who first gazed into the murky depths of families with schizophrenic members and recorded what they saw. Much early research on schizophrenia and the family, as Dell points out in a recent essay, merely sought to provide a new theory for its cause, whether that was the family, the "schizophrenogenic mother," or some other agent.[10] I will focus on the research that does not primarily offer a new etiology but moves us along the epistemological path I am tracing.

In Chapter 2 I move to the cybernetic model suggested by Bateson's seminal ideas on schismogenesis. This term, though ponderous, nevertheless contains a blueprint for the way social groups cohere or split, stay viable or reorganize. It is also a concept that can be applied to many escalation processes, especially those found in social interaction.

Early clinicians had been fascinated by the tendency they perceived in families to maintain the status quo, and posited that something akin to homeostatic mechanisms were responsible. What interested me was the contrary process whereby antihomeostatic processes might take over. The implications of these processes for systems change is the subject of Chapter 3. Some small deviation could get out of hand and create a "runaway" or positive feedback chain. It was anyone's guess whether the original organization of the system would change, be destroyed, or stay the same. But it seemed to me that in the grand scheme of things, deviation was a source of new information essential to the survival and evolution of social groups, and that the early family theorists had not emphasized this aspect sufficiently.

In Chapters 4 and 5 I begin to investigate in more detail the issue of family typology. At first, family researchers tried to link symptomatology to family types: the schizophrenic family, the alcoholic family, and so on. But this kind of typology is hard to establish, especially since a family may contain persons displaying a number of different symptoms. I also explore other attempts to create typologies: bipolar ones, in which families are ranged along a continuum with each end representing an opposite form of organization; process models, with families organized according to different types of sequences; grid models, representing more than one dimension; and developmental models, showing a continuum from "pathology" toward "normalcy." However the typology is arranged, different categories of families are usually linked to different classes of disorders. At the same time there is the possibility that the whole question of typology may be either premature or a dead end, and that a focus on family "paradigms," or system-wide formulas for processing information and change, may be more useful.

In Chapters 6, 7, and 8, I try to put under the microscope the tissue of one particular kind of family: the family that produces severe psychiatric disorders. Researchers had found in this one type of family, at least, distinct patterns of organization either different from, or more intense than, similar forms in seemingly normal families. The application of coalition theory by members of the Bateson group to the structures typically found in "disturbed" families led me to a broader look at coalition theory and its first cousin, structural balance theory. Of all the areas of social psychology that I explored, the theory of structural balance (though originally intended to explain cognitive, not social, fields) was the only theory that was in any way predictive for the formal interaction sequences one could see operating in families with symptomatic members.

Consequently, in this group of chapters the focus is directly on the characteristics of triangles one can expect to see in "disturbed" families. These triangles obliterate generation lines, confuse appropriate boundaries between family subgroups, and subvert the family hierarchy as prescribed by a given culture. At the same time, we find that they are associated with families so rigidly organized as to make any change in organization problematic, especially changes associated with the growing up of the children. Research, both in families and in organizations, suggests that one possible reason for the persistence of these inappropriate triangles is that the child (or other third party) presents a problem that keeps covert difficulties or conflicts in important executive pairs from surfacing.

At this point we move from an emphasis on family theory to an emphasis on theory of change. The book becomes far more clinically oriented and process variables rather than structural variables come into view. The idea that living systems often make sudden evolutionary shifts at natural transition points in the family life cycle is the subject of Chapter 9. The appearance of symptoms at these times may indicate that a particular transition is perceived by the family as problematic, even dangerous. Not all families are able to negotiate these transitions on their own. When a symptom develops, it can be seen as a constant reminder, in symbolic form, of the need for change, while at the same time apparently blocking it.

Chapter 10, "The Thing in the Bushes," explores the target most therapists seem to be gunning for in terms of repetitive cycles or sequences. These sequences are presented not as dysfunctional but as having a logic and a meaning at the family-system level, even though they may be experienced as painful or stressful by individual family members. Chapter 11 examines how this type of sequence is broken or disrupted by therapists working in four different models.

Although this book is not intended to be a historical overview, it seems to me that the practice of therapy is a form of live research, a notion I illustrate in the subsequent chapters on family therapy pioneers and major schools. The clinical work of successful pioneering therapists is a prime source of information on families and family therapy. The experienced clinician intuitively recognizes the shape of common symptomatic configurations and knows how to go about changing them. The schools I describe are singled out because they represent consensus positions: a consolidation of practical and theoretical issues following the trails blazed by the first explorers.

I then move to an examination of an important new development: the systemic approach of Mara Selvini Palazzoli and her colleagues in Milan. Originally influenced by the early formulations of the Bateson group, the Milan Associates continue to work more and more closely within a Batesonian framework of circular causality. In both their theory and their therapy they have taken a leap toward an idiosyncratic and original model that is very different from that of their current Palo Alto colleagues. Chapter 15 describes their present work.

The last two chapters are speculative and raise more questions than they answer. Chapter 16 is a discussion of the therapeutic double bind, and of various theories about why it works. Chapter 17 describes issues that are now coming to the fore and that lead to a consideration in the closing chapter of the implications of the new evolutionary epistemology to which we have been alluding throughout the book.

On a more personal level, this evolutionary epistemology can be applied to my own journey. Looking back on the thought and study that led to this book, as well as to other work in the field, what may seem like blind spots and dead ends also represent stages in a necessary process. The very logic of an evolutionary model prohibits throwing away trials that are unsuccessful. The only prohibition is against continuing to repeat such trials.

With this proviso, let me turn back to the 1960s, when I first became acquainted with the work and writing of the early systems thinkers, clinicians, and other pioneers of the family therapy movement, and try to convey the enormous impact their discoveries made upon my own thinking and writing and upon the development of the family field.

Chapter 1

Early Research on Family Groups

Live Observation

It was when people with symptomatic behaviors were first observed in their natural habitat—the family, rather than a clinician's office—that the family movement began. One can say that there is such a thing as an epidemiology of ideas. Paralleling its use in the growing field of animal ethology, live observation began to be used with human families in formal or informal research during the 1950s. At the same time lone clinicians were stumbling onto family therapy and then stumbling onto each other as they sought to validate the information they were getting.

However, the rules of the psychoanalytic establishment banned the contamination of therapy by the inclusion of relatives. As a result, "treatment" occurred mostly in the guise of research. An at-home anthropology developed in which clinicians took the lead, with the family context of psychiatric disorders becoming visible for the first time. As the Chinese say, "Only the fish do not know that it is water in which they swim." Humans also have an inability to see the relationship systems that sustain them.

There was no father or mother of family therapy, and no first family therapy interview. Like Topsy, the movement "just growed." The major impetus for its growth came out of the work of researchers like Nathan Ackerman in New York; Murray Bowen in Topeka and Washington, D.C.; Lyman Wynne and Margaret Singer at the National Institutes of Mental Health in Bethesda; Carl Whitaker in Atlanta; Salvador Minuchin and E. H. Auerswald at the Wiltwyck School in New York State; Ivan Boszormenyi-Nagy, James Framo, and Gerald Zuk in Philadelphia; Theodore Lidz and Stephen Fleck at Yale; and Gregory Bateson, Don Jackson, Jay Haley, John Weakland, Paul Watzlawick, John Bell, and Virginia Satir in Palo Alto, to mention only a few. These people, their core-searchers, and many others in cities across the country became the backbone of a new and engrossing movement of practice and ideas.[1]

Most of these researchers focused on investigating the properties of the family as a "system." By "system" they usually meant any entity whose parts co-vary with each other and which maintains equilibrium in an error-activated way. Their emphasis was on the role played by symptomatic behaviors in helping to balance or unbalance that system.

However, the family movement represents more than a different approach to therapy. It is a different way of looking at behavior, and it can be described as a kind of communications research focusing on the face-to-face relationships of people in ongoing groups. This position has been summarized in Watzlawick, Jackson, and Beavin's classic *Pragmatics of Human Communication,* a book that was also the first attempt to popularize the seminal ideas of Bateson and his group.[2]

The Bateson Project and "Learning to Learn"

In the 1950s, Gregory Bateson was leading a remarkable research project that attempted to classify communication in terms of levels: levels of meaning, levels of logical type, and levels of learning.

Among other areas of interest—such as animal behavior, paradoxes, hypnosis, play—the group looked at patterns of schizophrenic transaction. They wondered whether these patterns might arise from an inability to discriminate between levels of logical type— between the literal and the metaphoric, for example. People who are thought of as crazy will use figures of speech literally, or talk in metaphors without acknowledging it. The Bateson group hypothesized that a person with this kind of difficulty might, in Bateson's words, have "learned to learn" in a context in which this difficulty was in some way adaptive. If this learning context could be understood, the mysteries of schizophrenic speech and behavior might be understood. Because the family is the primary learning context for humans, they reasoned that the family of the schizophrenic might have shaped his peculiar ways via the peculiar communication requirements that were imposed upon him.

At the same time, psychotherapists who were independently watching schizophrenics in the context of the family observed that if the patient got better, someone else in the family usually got worse. It was almost as if the family required the presence of a person with a symptom. Not only did the Bateson group find evidence for this assumption, but it was impressed by the extent to which the family encouraged, even demanded, that the patient show irrational behavior.

Noting the obstinacy with which change was resisted, even when it meant the improvement of a loved one, Jackson coined the term "family homeostasis." He described family interaction as "a closed information system in which variations in output or behavior are fed back in order to correct the system's response."[3] Haley elaborated on this, comparing the family to a servomechanism with a "governor":

Granting that people in on-going relationships function as "governors" in relation to one another, and granting that it is the function of a governor to diminish change, then the first law of human relationships follows: *When one person indicates a change in relation to another, the other will act upon the first so as to diminish and modify that change.*[4]

The Bateson group became identified with an idea of the family as an equilibrium-maintaining entity partly because so much of the group's research was done with families that had an extremely restricted range of behavior. A major question was whether a family could be said to behave as a "system" at all—whether all families had a greater patterning in their communications than one would expect if these communications were ruled by chance. This question seemed to be answered affirmatively in experiments showing a greater rigidity of communication patterns (for example, in order of speaking) in families in which somebody had a symptom than in families in which nobody did.[5]

However, the Bateson group showed in their clinical work a clear awareness of the importance of deviation in leading to a new setting for the family system. Jackson often observed what he called a "runaway" while working with families. This referred to any amplifying feedback process that escalated rapidly, leading to a breakdown, a blowup, or some violent result. Jackson often said that he preferred to work with a family in which this kind of movement was taking place. With a very immovable family, especially one that included a chronic schizophrenic, he would sometimes try to start a runaway as a therapeutic gambit.[6] This could be done by "prescribing the symptom"—that is, increasing the angle of deviance of the patient from the rest of the family. Alternatively, the therapist could reinforce any family member's behavior, pushing it to continue in the same direction in a kind of *reductio ad absurdum*. Such interventions would presumably threaten the homeostasis of the family and thus lead family members to grasp the therapist's suggestions more readily, in the hopes of establishing a new balance or to come up with a new balance of their own.

The Double Bind

What is strange is that during the early phases of the Bateson group's study of schizophrenic communication, nobody thought of observing schizophrenics with their families at all. Instead, interviews were held with hospitalized patients at the Palo Alto Veterans Administration Hospital, where Bateson was a consultant. As a result of these interviews, and many conversations between members of the group, the double bind hypothesis began to take shape. In 1956, the now famous paper, "Toward a Theory of Schizophrenia," was published and the double bind concept was finally born.[7]

"Double bind" describes a context of habitual communication impasses imposed on one another by persons in a relationship system. Under some circumstances these impasses seemed to elicit the responses known in their aggregate as schizophrenia. A double bind was in essence a multilevel communication in which an overt demand at one level was covertly nullified or contradicted at another level. "Dominate me" is a relatively nontoxic example of the double bind. Here the person addressed can only "dominate" by obeying —which is the opposite of domination. Such a request is therefore impossible to respond to. Like any paradox, it has to be teased apart into its two levels: (1) the reported wish to be submissive, contradicted by (2) the implicit or explicit command that the listener obey the speaker. The "command" message is of a higher logical type than the "report" message, because it states who sets the rules for the subclass of allowable behaviors. The only way one can respond to such a request is to point out how impossible it is, to make a joke of it, or to leave the field. But when none of these courses is possible—and when the confusion between report and command levels imposes itself as a kind of confusion in the receiver's mind—then serious trouble can arise.

In the original double bind article, examples of this kind of impasse were given and formal conditions were set as prerequisites for its appearance in a toxic or pathogenic form. Here are the basic ingredients:

1. A primary negative injunction, "Don't do that."
2. A secondary negative injunction at another level which conflicts with the first: "Don't listen to anything I say" (perhaps conveyed by tone of voice or manner).
3. An injunction forbidding comment (usually nonverbal cues reinforcing rules that no longer need to be made explicit) and another forbidding the person to leave the field (often delivered by context, as when the person is a child).
4. A situation that seems to be of survival significance, so that it is vitally important for the person to discriminate correctly among the messages.

5. After a pattern of communication containing these elements has become established, only a small reminder of the original sequence is needed to produce a reaction of panic or rage.

As an illustration the article cites the example of a mother who is feeling bothered by a child, but instead of saying "Go away, I'm sick of you" says "Go to bed; you're very tired and I want you to get your sleep." If the child accepts this loving concern at face value and attempts to draw closer, the mother will probably move away. If he challenges the loving behavior or reacts negatively, she will probably get angry. If he comments on her anger, she may get even angrier. Thus he will be punished for discriminating accurately. He will most likely be too confused to comment on his predicament, and he will be unable, being a child, to leave the field. This would be a formal example of a double bind.

It is amazing to think that the double bind article was written without first-hand observation of the transactions described. But this omission is understandable if one considers the influence of traditional psychoanalytic thought. Most of the early family researchers had an analytic orientation, which not only held that a symptom was a sign of internal dysfunction originating in the past, but also forbade the therapist to see relatives of a patient for fear of contaminating the intense relationship with the therapist, or transference, that was seen as an essential ingredient of the therapeutic process.

Fortunately, a chance occurrence alerted Bateson and his colleagues to the importance of what was going on in the family in the present. Jay Haley, who met with patients at the VA hospital and audiotaped his conversations with them, found that one young man had severe anxiety attacks every time his parents visited him. To try to find out why the patient reacted as he did, Haley asked the parents to come to the next interview. Out of subsequent meetings with the young man, his parents, and his therapist came a serendipitous development: an audiotape in which an obviously adoring mother, in the space of a few minutes, turned a fairly rational son into a person who displayed confused thinking, contradictory statements, irrelevant remarks, and other communication patterns associated with the "thought disorders" of the condition known as schizophrenia.

The incident occurred shortly after Mother's Day. The young man's mother showed the therapist a card that her son had sent her from the hospital. The therapist read the legend: "To One Who Has Been Just Like a Mother to Me." The mother declared that she felt very hurt. The son defended himself, saying, "Look, Ma, I only wanted to sting you a little." The mother then put on a dazzling display of contradictory statements, defining herself as willing to accept any hurt if that would help him, placing herself in the category of the Virgin Mary who would do anything for her son, and at the same time declaring that all she and his father wanted was for him to stop picking them to pieces, because they were ordinary people who did not deserve that kind of treatment. The son backed down under this onslaught. First he claimed that he didn't even remember the card, then he blamed the commissary for selling cards like that, then he said that he hadn't been particular enough about the wording on cards since his illness, and finally he insisted that he felt that she had been a "good enough mother." When his father added helpfully, "A *real* mother," he repeated, "Yeah, a *real* mother —so that's all."[8]

We seem to be dealing here with a rather eerie cat-and-mouse game. Such games probably justify the initial reason Bateson became interested in schizophrenic communication: the apparent inability of the schizophrenic to distinguish between the literal and the metaphoric. This seemed to be translated into a virtual allergy to any "report" message that secretly encloses a "command" message indicating that the sender controls the relationship.

Seen in this light, some "thought disorders" may be redefined as maneuvers in a desperate struggle. The vague, amorphous, or disqualifying communications presented by the other parties in this struggle (always the mothers of schizophrenics in the early literature) may be equally well defined as maneuvers. One could see the logic of a resort to confused thinking if accepting the definition of the relationship implied by another person's statement would amount to giving the other person the upper hand.

For instance, a mother might say to a hospitalized son: "The way you're staring at me, you look ready to hit the ceiling." Son might counter this apparently innocent remark (implying hostility on his part, of course, and not so innocent) by saying, "I'm not tall enough to hit the ceiling," and follow this statement with silly jumps. Mother might then ask, "Have you taken your medication today?" (translated: You're sick, not mad at me—but I still control the definition of the relationship).

Using metaphor in a "crazy" way (without indicating that it is a metaphor) is another way to escape. An example of this comes from a filmed interview with the family of a schizophrenic girl. The father tells the girl that she is to say anything she likes to the doctor. The girl replies with a seemingly irrelevant remark: "It's a free country, but the prices are fixed." Translated from schizophrenese, this might mean: "Dad says I'm free to talk, but we all know that whatever I say will be used against me."

At any rate, once researchers and clinicians began to observe live family interaction, there was no going back to ivory-tower speculation. A torrent of articles describing the marvels of communication in families with schizophrenics began to pour out. Most of the articles written by researchers associated with the Mental Research Institute in the 1960s contained brilliant examples of strategies designed to establish or escape definitions of relationships by members of these families. These communications could be disguised as irrational, confused, amorphous, or irrelevant, but they were seen to be deadly nonetheless.

Many of these articles are reprinted in Jackson's two-volume Human Communication Series, *Therapy, Communication and Change,* and *Communication, Family and Marriage.* [9] Some of my favorites are Weakland and Jackson's "Patient and Therapist Observations on the Circumstances of a Schizophrenic Episode," Jackson and Yalom's "Conjoint Family Therapy as an Aid to Intensive Therapy," and Weakland and Frye's "Letters of Mothers of Schizophrenics." [10] A thoughtful and entertaining compendium of "double binding" communication has also been compiled by Sluzki, Beavin, Tarnopolosky, and Veron in their article "Transactional Disqualification: Research on the Double Bind. [11] For an exhaustive compilation and critique of the double bind literature, see Sluzki and Ransom's *Double Bind: The Foundation of the Communicational Approach to the Family.* [12]

The Infinite Dance of Shifting Coalitions

In spite of the fact that the work of the Bateson group furnished a focal point for students of nonpsychodynamic transactional thought, the communications approach had an inherent drawback: it tended to be essentially dyadic. Since conversations between three or more people were too complex to be analyzed on a microlevel, the unit of attention was usually the two-person exchange. The double bind theory was itself originally formulated in dyadic terms. There was a binder and there was one who was bound, although the reciprocal nature of the bind was acknowledged. The theory implicitly isolated a unit comprising two communicators, with the focus of interest the characteristic type of exchange between them.

As a result, a number of articles qualifying the original double bind theory began to emerge. Weakland was the first to break out of the dyadic mold, with a 1960 essay, "The 'Double Bind' Hypothesis of Schizophrenia and Three-Party Interaction," a brilliant prefiguring of later thinking in the field.[13] In 1962 the authors of the original double bind article offered a critique that downplayed the focus on individual behaviors or single sequences in favor of the theory's emphasis on circular systems in interpersonal relations.[14] The following year Watzlawick put up a stouter defense of the original paper than the authors had done, even while conceding that they should have made the mutual nature of the bind clearer, instead of presenting it as a one-way street.[15] Essays in the 1970s by both Weakland and Bateson suggest that this concept does not have to do with the etiology of schizophrenia at all, but is part of a larger attempt to establish an epistemology within which terms like "etiology" and "schizophrenia" would have no meaning.[16]

The first step in this chain of revisions, as Weakland's 1960 article makes clear, was to look at schizophrenic behavior in terms of triads instead of dyads. Members of the Bateson group were beginning to show an interest in coalitions, and although they did not specifically acknowledge the sources of this interest, it is instructive to note Bateson's contribution. He offered an analogy from game theory for a type of behavior that the group had noticed over and over again in families with a schizophrenic: the fact that no two persons seemed to be able to get together, whether to be close or to disagree, without a third person taking part. For this phenomenon Bateson used the phrase "the infinite dance of shifting coalitions."[17]

Bateson's argument was that this behavior was formally similar to the instability of a five-person game described by Von Neumann and Morgenstern in *Theory of Games.* [18] Von Neumann assumed that intelligent, gain-oriented players could be expected to form coalitions to maximize their profits. However, the situation changed when the number of players became five. Von Neumann describes a possible five-person game (equally applicable to a three-person game, according to Bateson) in which coalition possibilities became inherently unstable. Every time a winning arrangement formed, reasons of self-interest would force a new one to take its place. Thus, as Bateson put it, "There will always be a circular list of alternative solutions so that the system will never cease from passing on from solution to solution, always selecting another solution which is preferable to that which preceded it."[19]

Bateson thought that Von Neumann's five-person game offered a rough analogy to what went on in families with a schizophrenic. He added the proviso that in these families, three persons seemed to be a sufficient number to get the same result. In schizophrenic families, no two members ever seemed able to get together in a stable alignment. Either another family member would intervene, or the two who paired off would feel so uncomfortable about excluding the other person that they would dissolve the coalition themselves.

Though the original double bind described a two-person arrangement, Bateson saw a way, through the game metaphor, to translate the concept into a particular kind of family organization. He argued that the untenable predicament of the schizophrenic could arise from having to participate in the interactional equivalent of Von Neumann's game. A robot would be insensitive to the fact that every reasonable solution he arrived at was immediately proven wrong. But human beings are not this insensitive. In fact, they have an inflexibility bestowed upon them by their greatest asset, their ability to learn—that is, their ability to acquire automatic responses to habitual problems. Without this capacity, a person would be forever inventing solutions to each problem as if he were encountering it for the first time. This is why human beings have a commitment to the process of adaptation at the deeper level of habit. Bateson argued that in a system where adaptations are not allowed to persist at deeper levels, as in Von Neumann's unstable game, it is logical to assume that the individual involved will experience extreme disruption and pain. He will be caught in a perpetual sequence of double binds, situations in which there is always a penalty for being right.

The "Control" Theory of Schizophrenic Transaction

In a later paper discussing the evolution of ideas during the ten-year course of the Bateson project, Haley compares Bateson's interpretation of the double bind to his own.[20] Bateson had suggested this model for the behaviors in the family of a schizophrenic: "the schizophrenic communicates *as if* he expected to be punished every time he indicates that he is right in his view of the context of his own message."[21] Haley argues that there is an implicit assumption about motivation in this kind of thinking, similar to the traditional idea that people are driven by inner needs and desires such as fear of punishment, wish for love, and avoidance of pain.*

In *Strategies of Psychotherapy,* trying to move from an individual to a systemic level, Haley examined the effect of the double bind tactic on the larger interpersonal field of the family.[24] He started with the idea, shared by the entire Bateson group, that the disqualification of meanings is a recurrent feature of communication in a family with a schizophrenic. A disqualified message is a statement affirmed at one level and disconfirmed at another: "Of course I love you,"

---

*Paul Dell has pointed out that Haley is nevertheless in favor of ascribing something like motivation to the *system.*[22] In the paper cited above, Haley states that a power struggle may be expressed as a "need" of the system when individuals within it must struggle for control because hierarchical levels are not clearly defined.[23]

said in an angry tone of voice. Note that if one person in a family is disqualifying his own and others' messages, it will be hard for everybody else not to reciprocate. The only response to messages that conflict on different levels, Haley remarks, is more messages that conflict on different levels. Thus we are left with a vicious circle; once established, it keeps on going.

Now what, Haley asks, might one expect of persons caught in a situation like this? He hypothesizes that they will become inordinately sensitive to having their behavior governed by others. Disqualification of meanings is, after all, a tactic a person can use to control someone else's behavior. But it is a sword that cuts two ways. It can be used as a counterstrategy to prevent one's own behavior from being controlled. Thus a picture emerges of a type of family dominated by issues of control. One example of a covert battle for control of the relationship goes as follows (here a mother is talking to her grown son):

PATIENT: Did you bring my laundry?
MOTHER: How do you feel?
PATIENT: Do you have my laundry?
MOTHER: You look sad.
PATIENT: I'm O.K.
MOTHER: Are you angry with me?
PATIENT: Yes.[25]

Moving to the larger framework of the family as a cybernetic system, Haley remarks that just as the "governor" in a servomechanism controls the range of movements within it, so people in a family act to control the range of one another's behavior. The tragedy of a family that uses this tactic is that the struggle for control exists not only at the level of the particular rule, but also at the metalevel of "Who is to set the rules?" The Russellian Theory of Logical Types proposes that all messages consist of (1) a statement and (2) a statement about that statement.[26] The theory establishes a hierarchy of types or levels of abstraction and prohibits the joining of a higher level with a lower level. Therefore there is no such thing as a simple communication; every message is qualified by another message on a higher level. When these two levels of message are treated as one, as in the example of a signboard reading "All Statements on This Signboard are Untrue," we have a self-contradictory situation or paradox.

Basing his argument on Russell's Theory of Logical Types, Haley states that in the family control struggle, if rules on two levels of abstraction are jammed together, a similar communicational difficulty results, and there is no way to end the struggle. At Level One, each reports a statement. At Level Two, each attempts to define the relationship that acts as the context for that statement. But since any decision about behaviors (Level One) cannot be made without an agreement as to who is to decide what behaviors are to be allowed (Level Two), there is a constant denial and confusion about almost anything anyone in such a family tries to say or do.

In the dialogue quoted above, the son was trying to focus on concrete issues and the mother insisted on moving to issues that had to do with how he was feeling. If the son agreed with the mother about what was appropriate to talk about, he not only placed himself in a somewhat infantile position but gave her the right to decide what should be talked about. This becomes a good illustration of the "control" theory that Haley proposes as an explanation for the constant mode of disqualification observed in families with a schizophrenic member.

The Undifferentiated Family Ego Mass

At the same time the Palo Alto group was studying schizophrenic communication, researchers from a clinical rather than a communications background were working the same territory. As this book will not attempt to cover much of the important work in this area, readers are referred to Riskin and Faunces's exhaustive study, "An Evaluative Review of Family Interaction and Research."[27] However, one or two early figures deserve to be singled out for the boldness of their ideas and their willingness to break with the traditional language of psychodynamic theory.

Murray Bowen was one of the first psychiatrists to hospitalize whole families for observation and treatment. He had begun in the 1950s with the idea that schizophrenia was the result of an unresolved symbiotic tie with the mother. After working for about a year with mothers and their children in a milieu treatment setting at the Menninger Clinic, he began to feel that schizophrenia was a sign of a larger pathology in the whole family and tried to have as many family members as possible live on the hospital ward during treatment. Subsequently, he developed a three-generation hypothesis for schizophrenia. According to this theory, the grandparents of the schizophrenic child were relatively mature, but one child, very attached to the mother, remained extremely immature. Later, this child chose an equally immature spouse. The result of the combined immaturities in this marriage was a child who was so symbiotically tied to the mother as to be schizophrenic.

From this research came many of Bowen's ideas about the characteristics of emotional disturbance, applied both to families and to the individuals who lived in them. The ideas that are especially important for our discussion include the multigenerational transmission of emotional illness; the importance of working with the family of origin; and the concept of "differentiation." These areas and other aspects of "Bowen Theory" are fully described in Bowen's *Family Therapy in Clinical Practice*. [28]

One of Bowen's major contributions to family theory is his thinking on the part played by triangles in family interaction. Triangulation is a process that occurs in all families, all social groups, as twosomes form to the exclusion of, or against, a third. The triangle is an essential building block for Haley's theory of pathological systems and Minuchin's structural approach to family theory. Unlike Haley's and Minuchin's relatively static forms, however, Bowen's sense of triangles is a fluid one.

For Bowen, a two-person emotional system will form a three-person system under stress. For instance, tension might arise between the two, and the one who was more uncomfortable would relieve tension by "triangling in" a third person, perhaps by telling a story about that person. Then the tension would shift to the new twosome, relieving the tension between the original pair. But the outsider, once he becomes drawn in, may respond to the tension by accepting an alliance with one of the others, so that the outsider of

29

one moment becomes the insider of the next. For instance, a struggle between a son and a mother might erupt over his going to school, but become deflected when the father enters the scene and attacks the mother and defends the son.

In addition, the action may not remain localized within the original triangle but may activate other triangles, involving more and more people. Bowen describes how a family in distress can draw in more and more outsiders.

In periods of stress, the process can involve the entire nuclear family, a whole spectrum of more peripheral family members, and even nonrelatives and representatives of social agencies, clinics, schools and courts. In periods of calm, the process can remain relatively contained within a small segment of the family, such as the symbiotic relationship in which the emotional process plays back and forth between mother and child with the father isolated from the intense twosome.[29]

One may ask how the process Bowen describes can be seen to obey lawful movements. If no alliance remains static from one moment to the next, isn't this a recipe for chaos? This problem has dogged family observers for years, since the apparent confusion of behaviors in families with a high degree of pathology nevertheless seems to add up to a highly restricted set of choices. Bowen attempts an explanation by saying that no matter how chaotic triadic behaviors in a family may look, these behaviors are nevertheless passing along very limited and almost preordained pathways. He believes that when a family has been together for a long time, the process of triangling goes through such a fixed chain reaction that a skilled observer can often predict its stages and, by inserting himself into the sequence, even control it.

One problem Bowen talks about is the distinction between triadic processes in families with disturbed members and families that are presumably "normal." Bowen associates pathology with rigidity and suggests that, although all families create triadic patterns, these patterns will become more rigid when the family is facing a change or undergoing stress, and will be more flexible in periods of calm.

In addition, Bowen continually moved away from a linear definition of pathology as a condition transmitted through the nuclear family from one generation to the next. Instead, he became more and more fascinated by the evolutionary processes of the larger kinship group. When working with a family member, he will help that person trace back the lines of his singular destiny to relationship configurations that may have existed before he was born. A key to Bowenian thinking is the idea that if someone can achieve a more flexible position in one family triangle, even a distant one, this can have positive repercussions on other, closer ones and may even nullify injunctions from the past that constrict relationships in the present. Bowen sees networks of triangles as deeply linked and reactive to one another. As in a spider's web, a touch at any spot will vibrate right across the web. Thus, in a family, a change in one corner may activate unpredictable responses in another corner, and may help to free persons long caught in static and inhibiting positions, including the person initiating the change. This emphasis on the family of origin has had an incalculable influence on the development of the family therapy movement.

Bowen presents one particular attribute of families as an index of pathology: the concept of "differentiation." He noticed that families with a psychotic member exhibited an intense, clinging interdependence which he called the "undifferentiated family ego mass." This is such a ponderous phrase and calls up so many psychodynamic meanings that it can easily be dismissed. But that would be a mistake. Struggling to refine his concept, Bowen tried again: "a pre-existing emotional 'stuck-togetherness.'" Later on we shall find something similar in the idea of "pseudomutuality" that Wynne uses to describe the gluey quality of the family of the schizophrenic, and Minuchin's notion of the "enmeshed" family.

What all these observers are describing is a tightly coalesced triadic structure, and the problem is one of wording. A noun like "mass" suggests a lump of stuff all composed of one substance; the adjective "undifferentiated" suggests that this mass has no pieces or sub-parts. But "stuck-togetherness" comes a bit closer to the idea that what we are getting at is a set of interconnecting, mutually repercussive relationships. If they are "undifferentiated," they are so in the sense that none of the parts or pieces can move independently of the others or the whole.

For Bowen, at any rate, lack of differentiation or "fusion" was a sign of trouble in a family. By contrast, he postulated that when individual members maintain a high degree of differentiation, the family will do well and its members will do well. Differentiation, however, is not to be confused with "emotional cutoff," which is a defense against too intense fusion that may take the form of a family member leaving physically and staying out of contact but never really freeing himself psychologically. In that sense, emotional cutoff is really lack of differentiation in disguise.

Bowen has a superior feel for triadic processes in families and has put his finger on an essential aspect of the way they work. Part of this aspect has to do with the permutations of relationships as they shift from moment to moment, and the larger schema represented by the sequences they take. For example, one may find an unalterable pattern around the "bad" behavior of a child. Stage one: Mother coaxes, child refuses to obey, mother threatens to tell father (father-mother against child). Stage two: When father comes home, mother tells him how bad child has been, and father sends child to his room without supper. Mother sneaks up after father has left the table and brings child a little food on a plate (mother-child against father). Stage three: When child comes down later, father, trying to make up, offers to play a game with him that mother has expressly forbidden because it gets him too excited before bedtime (father-child against mother). Stage four: Mother scolds father for this; the child, overexcited indeed, has a tantrum and is sent to bed; and the original triangle comes round again (mother-father against child).

Although Bowen himself does not describe triadic sequences in such precise detail, his view contributes to a "process taxonomy" of family interaction. According to his writings, triangles in families shimmer through their preappointed changes like a light show. There is an inner, Euclidean logic to this view, and later researchers and therapists in the family field have justified Bowen's preoccupation with the triangle by continuing to expand and deepen it.

Pseudomutuality and the Rubber Fence

Lyman Wynne is another psychiatrist-researcher who started out with an interest in the thought disorders of schizophrenia and the influence of family communication style on these disorders. He, like the Bateson group, took a systems view of the family and not only noted the redundancies that seemed to be characteristic of families with a schizophrenic, but backed up Bateson's observations on shifting coalitions and Haley's on unstable dyads: "In the family of a schizophrenic, the structure of alignments and splits seems to shift in a bewildering rapid fashion but with one feature of great constancy: the meaning of any *particular* alignment does not clearly emerge."[30] Instead, he noted, these splits and alignments came across to the observer as unformed, fragmented, and separated from each other in a "psychological apartheid." The result was that the alignments did not seem like true closeness, but what Wynne called "pseudomutuality," and the splits did not seem like real hostility or distance, but "pseudohostility." Feeling that there were invisible laws governing the appearance of these displays, Wynne remarked, *"When an alignment has developed within a given family therapy group, look for an emerging split at another level or in another part of the group; if a split emerges, expect an associated alignment to come into view."*[31]

Wynne felt that these changes from splits to alignments, back and forth, had something to do with homeostatic maintenance processes in the family, although he did not explain how. He also believed that these processes took place in any family, but that in a family with a schizophrenic member they were particularly vivid and pronounced.

As an illustration, Wynne describes a sequence that took place with stereotyped regularity in a family with two daughters, one of whom had been diagnosed a catatonic schizophrenic and had been hospitalized. Betty, the patient, was eighteen; Susan was three years younger. Wynne and his cotherapist noted two features in the family structure that seemed to be closely related: first, an alignment between Betty and her father, and second, a split between the parents. The repetitious sequence that illustrated both observations

33

was this: During a therapy session the parents would start to quarrel, usually over one of Betty's symptoms, like her compulsive cleaning of the house. The father would take Betty's side, and Susan would characteristically come in on the side of the mother. As the argument heated up, the father would start to intensify his attentions to Betty. At these times he might move close to her, even touching her. If he did, she would often jump abruptly away, in a move of rejection. Instead of reacting back toward Betty, the father would turn to the mother and accuse her of being "vicious" and "mean." Oddly, the mother would refuse to rise to the challenge but would cut off this exchange with a flat remark like, "Well, that's all right." The father would lapse into silence and the sequence would usually be over.

Wynne does not detail Betty's symptoms during these sequences but says that in general Betty's most psychotic behavior followed her intense rejections of her father, and he remarks on the cyclical nature of these interactions. Any rejection of a parent by a daughter would set the parents bickering, especially a rejection by Betty. But no matter how loud the arguments became, they seemed to be more formal than real. The parents never got violent or threatened to divorce. More important, this pattern seemed to be kept going by everybody. For instance, even though the mother objected to the father-Betty intimacy, if it failed to materialize she might remind them that a father and daughter ought to be fond of one another.

We can see this cycle as a repetition of several interaction states. One is a form that polarizes the family, with Susan and mother aligned against Betty and father. Another would be the father-Betty coalition against mother, with father protecting and mother attacking Betty. Wynne's example thus gives a graphic picture of how the daughters' behaviors may have worked as a kind of counterpoint, mitigating the periodic escalation of hostilities between husband and wife. Evidence for this idea can be found in the sudden shift in the triad, as Betty violently rejects her father, shows psychotic behavior, and apparently triggers off a temporary truce between the parents.

A striking feature of this family cycle was the apparent agreement of all concerned to accept a "cutoff point." Animal ethologists use that term to describe the cessation of ritualized hostilities between two males engaged in fighting or aggression. The bickering of the parents in the sequence described by Wynne seemed to have the same ritualized quality, as did their mutual decision to break it off.

Wynne makes the point that the closeness of the mother to people outside the nuclear family, notably her own mother and her employer, frequently replaced Betty as the focus of argument between the couple. Thus, in describing a cyclical repertory for this family, one would have to place a mother-grandmother alignment next to the father-Betty tie. One would expect the cycle to involve a periodic drawing together of the wife with her mother (employer, other relatives, and so on). This closeness would presumably coincide with periods of distance between husband and wife. It is logical to think that this distance would start off the father-Betty coalition, or perhaps one of the daughters would trigger parental bickering with a rejecting remark. Either of these moves would bring mother back into the picture, and some version of the cycle described would follow.

Wynne's descriptive papers on families with schizophrenics show that two features struck him with particular force. One was the strangely unreal quality of both positive and negative emotions, for which, as we have said, he used the terms "pseudomutuality" and "pseudohostility."[32] The other was the matter of the boundary around the family. Wynne was the first to comment on its peculiar nature: an apparently yielding, but actually impervious, barrier against outsiders (especially therapists). Wynne called it the "rubber fence."[33]

Wynne's explanation of how these features operate in such families is that there is an intense wish by family members for mutual relatedness which excludes the ability to tolerate difference or dissent. The illusion of "pseudomutuality" reinforces the party line that all are linked together. The "rubber fence" forms a boundary around this illusion which protects the family from the perils of new information or potential change. Children in these families are thus caught in the dilemma of never being able to differentiate or disengage, because any attempt brings on expectations of disaster.

Wynne went on to speculate how the behaviors that produce and perpetuate these family features might, in a child, create the kind of thinking disorders displayed in schizophrenia and other affective disturbances. Denials of thoughts or feelings, inability to judge objective "out there" reality, blurring of differences of opinion, cryptic and fragmented utterances would all be logical ways to communicate in a family in which one had no basis for what was "real" except validation by other family members, and where the only "reality" validated would be intense loyalty and closeness. An attempt by one member at individuation might cause the family to focus all its fear and dislike of non-mutuality onto him or her, making that person into a scapegoat. This would reinforce the family's primary value of closeness and enslave the negatively perceived person just as effectively as if he had never tried to leave the fold.

No treatment of the work on schizophrenic communication should ignore the contribution of British psychiatrists R. D. Laing and A. Esterson, whose concept of mystification (closely related to the double bind) was illustrated by a series of studies of schizophrenic young women carefully observed in the context of their families. The evidence that the apparently distorted perceptions of these women were fed and supported by disguised communications from other family members is forcefully documented in the book based on these studies, *Sanity, Madness, and the Family.* [34] The behavior of the schizophrenic was adaptive; it was a logical response to an illogical situation.

To describe this behavior, however, most of the researchers we have discussed used a cybernetic analogy, since families with schizophrenics (or maybe all families) seemed to possess something like a homeostatic element that resisted change. Symptomatic behavior was considered an integral part of this resistance.

The writer who drew most brilliantly upon the cybernetic analogy was Bateson. Bateson's ideas about the patterning of social fields, and the cybernetic paradigm he developed to support those ideas, were to have a unique influence on the family researchers who were his disciples and those who followed after.

Chapter 2

The Dynamics of Social Fields

Bateson and the Grand Design

One of Bateson's central concerns was what he called "the pattern that connects." He believed that at some level of structure there is a congruence among the laws governing different types of events. Speaking of his father, a noted British geneticist, he said,

In this early—and as I think he knew—his best work, he posed problems of animal symmetry, segmentation, serial repetition of parts, patterns, etc. . . . I picked up a vague mystical feeling that we must look for the same sort of processes in all fields of natural phenomena—that we might expect to find the same sort of laws at work in the structure of a crystal as in the structure of society, or that the segmentation of an earthworm might be comparable to the process by which basalt pillars are formed.[1]

One of the elder Bateson's areas of study was the way parts of organisms differentiate. Some do so serially, down a hierarchical ladder, like the legs of a lobster; this is metameric differentiation. Others differentiate symmetrically, with each part exactly like the other, like the radial tentacles of a jellyfish.

What, one might ask, have lobsters and jellyfish to do with the structure of human society? The younger Bateson, looking for a grand design, thought they might have a lot to do with it. He needed what he called a "visual diagram," and the analogy of differentiation in biological structures provided him with the form that came closest to explaining one of the problems that fascinated him most when he started his career: the patterning controlling social segmentation.

It was around the time he was studying the Iatmul culture in New Guinea in the early 1930s that the problem began to haunt him. He had gone out like a good cultural anthropologist, equipped with the proper background (he had been a student of Franz Boas), using the right tools (notebooks and informants), following the usual procedures (immersing himself in the life of the culture), and generating appropriate themes through which to interpret his findings (concepts like "eidos" and "ethos").

However, he did one improper thing: He did not stay within the confines of the universe as defined by anthropologists of that day. A ceremony caught his eye that did not lend itself either to orthodox interpretation or to his ingenious categories. This was the *naven* ceremony, and the processes it expressed seemed to deal with social instability: that is, how conflicts and divisions within the group were handled. The main findings of Bateson's resulting book, *Naven,* contributed greatly to his subsequent thinking about social processes.[2]

The Iatmul of New Guinea were headhunting people living in villages of two hundred to a thousand inhabitants. Placement in the various phratries, moieties, and clans was determined by patrilineal descent, but the lines connecting each family with the mother's kin were emphasized in less formal ways. What struck Bateson most forcefully was the absence of hierarchy in this society. There was no governing body, no chief, no status structure of importance in any of the villages. If someone wronged someone else, there was no higher authority to whom disputes could be brought. Clan feuds might result, and retaliations would be exacted, either through sorcery or through more direct means, like killing someone. At the same time there was an intense emphasis on rivalry and display. The clans or initiatory moieties were constantly competing. What seemed to happen when rivalries became too intense or quarrels insoluble was that one of the feuding clans would split off and form a new village.

Here is where the visual diagram afforded by biological differentiation processes came in. In a later article discussing Iatmul society, Bateson explains:

Impressed by the phenomenon of metameric differentiation, I made the point that in our society with its hierarchical systems (comparable to the earthworm or the lobster), when a group secedes from the parent society, it is usual to find that the line of fission, the division between the new group and the old, marks a differentiation of mores. The Pilgrim Fathers wander off in order to be *different*. But among the Iatmul, when two groups in a village quarrel, and one half goes off and founds a new community, the mores of the two groups remain identical.[3]

Bateson never explored further his idea that hierarchical societies tend to produce heretical groups when they divide, whereas symmetrical groups produce carbon copies. What he looked at more thoroughly (and what is more germane to this study) is the mechanisms countering fission in the Iatmul, chief among which seemed to be the *naven*.

The *naven* was a ceremony, or group of gestures deriving from this ceremony, which affirmed the attachment between a child, a *laua*, and his mother's brothers, his *waus*. *Navens* might be performed at important moments in the child's life. They would take place when he changed from one status to another, or when he achieved certain culturally approved "firsts," (his first fish spearing or his first homicide). *Naven* gestures were also elicited by inordinate displays of pride or boasting by *laua* to *wau*. In these cases a *naven* behavior by *wau* would be in the nature of a chastisement, reminding *laua* that he was stepping out of line.

A really grand *naven* could draw in relatives from both sides of the family. The children's uncles on the mother's side would dress up like silly old women and treat the children like mock husbands. On the father's side, the female relatives would don male ceremonial attire and strut about caricaturing male warlike displays. Iatmul women enjoyed this all the more because they were normally subordinate to the men.

39

At first Bateson assumed that the *naven* operated like a sort of social glue, strengthening the ties to the mother's family of origin in this very patrilineal culture. But the visual pattern that began to dominate his thinking was of planes of cleavage crossing each other. The main split line was between brothers and brothers-in-law and the clans they represented. Thus any custom that strengthened the link between them, or counteracted its tendency to break, would be important.

Along with the effort to see the structure of Iatmul society statically, in the form of a design, came another effort to see it dynamically, in a state of movement. It was at this point that Bateson coined the term "schismogenesis." This word described the type of escalation found throughout the natural world and exemplified by the vicious circle and called by other researchers "mutual reaction processes," "deviation-amplifying mutual causal processes," "positive feedback chains," and the like.

Schismogenesis

Bateson applied his new term primarily to relationships between people, as opposed to mutual causal processes in general. He defined it as a *"process of differentiation in the norms of individual behavior resulting from cumulative interaction between individuals."*[4] These processes are distinguished by the fact that they develop by mutual reaction, exponentially. In Iatmul society Bateson observed the presence of self-reinforcing cycles in which the actions of A would trigger B's responses, which would then trigger an even more intense reaction from A, and so forth. These cycles could be broken down into two types. One of these types Bateson called "symmetrical" meaning that the escalating behaviors of A and B would be essentially similar, as in cases of rivalry or competition. The other type he called "complementary" because the self-generating actions would be different, as in cycles of dominance-submission or succoring-dependence.

Bateson cites several examples of schismogenic cycles. One is the self-reinforcing-relationship sequence that results in some types of mental illness. Bateson specifically mentions paranoia, in which the patient, being distrustful, triggers responses in others that have the result of justifying his fears and making him even more distrustful. Another example is the type of marital maladjustment that results when one partner is extremely assertive and the other very compliant, and these characteristics become progressively accentuated, the one partner becoming more and more compliant as the other becomes more and more assertive.

Bateson notes that these processes can occur in arenas other than interpersonal ones. He mentions the way culture contacts between two societies can lead to special arrangements that can be either symmetrical or complementary, the symmetrical spirals represented by arms races and the complementary ones represented by tensions between social classes.

Bateson also suggests that there are two aspects to these self-reinforcing processes. There is the exponential process that is self-stopping or gets stopped, and there is the exponential process that does not get stopped *but does not destroy the system.* Of particular interest is the escalation that passes beyond the limits of the previous arrangement, apparently rushing toward ineluctable doom, and then emerges with a transcendent synthesis nobody had foreseen.

In this chapter we will be addressing ourselves to the two types of exponential process described by Bateson and to the principles that govern not only self-stabilizing escalations but the ones that threaten to get out of hand. In addition, we will examine the ideas of other researchers who have puzzled over these curious self-reinforcing cycles and devised some useful theories about them.

Mutual Reaction Processes

Kenneth Boulding, in his *Conflict and Defense,* investigates the properties of self-reinforcing cycles using the term "mutual reaction processes."[5] He devotes a good part of his treatise (published in 1962) to an analysis of formulas presented by the British political scientist and mathematician L. F. Richardson in a 1939 study of armament races and international hostilities with the unusual title "The Statistics of Deadly Quarrels." Richardson had devised mathematical equations to express escalating hostilities between nations, dominance-submission patterns, and the like. Boulding translates these formulas into graphs, which he calls "Richardson Process Models."

Boulding is clearly talking about the same thing Bateson is talking about: processes in which a movement by one party changes the field of the second, forcing a compensatory move by the second party, and so on. In economics, Boulding says, this process is exemplified by the price war; the political scientist knows it as an armaments race; students of relationships find it in competitive clashes between husbands and wives; labor movement people see it in the struggles between union and management; and it is even found in the animal kingdom, in the relationship between predator and prey.

Boulding is mixing interpersonal and noninterpersonal processes here, and does not make use of Bateson's distinction between symmetrical and complementary differentiation, but he does show representative cases of both. One graph depicts a symmetrical escalation in which two parties intensify hostilities until they reach what Boulding calls an "equilibrium point," at which place the activity stops. According to Boulding, who has taken the idea from Richardson, this point represents an intersection where aggression is canceled by some increasing factor like war weariness or fatigue. In another graph depicting this situation, the escalation mounts indefinitely, but Boulding says this could not happen in real life because there would be some boundary which could not be passed without the system breaking down or the activity shifting to a new form: arms races to war, marital quarrels to divorce, and so on.

In the different case of a dominance-submission cycle, Boulding follows Richardson in graphing a situation analogous to the predator-prey relationships in sparsely inhabited terrain. In the Arctic, for instance, where wolves subsist on rabbits, an increase in the rabbit population means more wolves. But the increase in the wolf population begins to erode the rabbit population. This in turn reduces the wolf population until the rabbit population builds up again.

The same situation often holds true in human relationships, where one person is apparently dominated, the other the one who dominates. The dominant person will increase his power over the submissive one until the submission reaction becomes so extreme that it no longer stimulates a dominance reaction. The submissive person will then become increasingly assertive until the dominance reaction is triggered off again and the cycle repeats.

The terms "dominant" and "submissive" are unfortunate because they suggest a power struggle rather than a systemic sequence that neither person has the power to resist. The beauty of the concept of complementary escalation is that it avoids the tendency to see such struggles in terms of individual motivation. In fact, as Boulding points out, such arrangements tend to have a pattern of circularity, moving about a point of equilibrium. The graph which depicts them fittingly takes the form of a spiral. Although Boulding does not take up the question of complementary mutual reaction processes getting out of hand, examples can be imagined: parents disciplining their children to the point of injuring them or worse; "master races" exterminating "inferior" ones in the name of racial purity.

In a 1949 essay on Balinese culture, Bateson, too, contemplated the implications of Richardson's equations, which he saw were in some sense mathematical expressions of his concept of schismo-genesis.[6] For him, as with Boulding, the mysterious question was: What puts a stop to such processes, since their very nature is to escalate? We are back to an examination of contrary movements: a sequence with a rise and fall which is self-stabilizing, versus a sequence with an escalation that mounts until some breaking point is reached or some other event occurs that checks the rising curve. In other words: deviation-counteracting sequences versus devia-tion-amplifying sequences.

Pondering the Richardson equations, Bateson was dissatisfied with Richardson's assumption that if a symmetrical escalation reached an equilibrium point, or reversed itself, this would be due to some such factor as fatigue. Instead he posited another possible answer: the dual need for tension arousal followed by tension re-duction, which is characteristic of many organisms and is expressed in activities such as fighting or making love.

Bateson investigated other kinds of stops to schismogenesis, stops that were not physiological but based on external social constraints. He pointed out in *Naven* that one factor that prevents a "runaway" is to be found in the nature of the relationship between two parties. If there is enough mutual dependence between two complementary parties, one of whom is stronger than the other, differentiation will never proceed beyond the point where schismogenic tendencies are countered by mutual dependency needs. Similarly, a symmetrical escalation may be held in check by reciprocal arrangements based on the interests of both parties, like a barter agreement or—my own 1980s examples—the holding of hostages or nuclear warheads.

Bateson also discusses a variant in which one complementary process might counteract another. He takes as an example a marriage in which the tensions arising from a relationship based on assertion-submission are relieved by a shift to a relationship based on caretaking dependency.[7] The relationship is still complementary, but the values it represents shift from negative to positive. Symptoms like depression or a psychosomatic illness in a spouse may be a response of this kind, or may signal the cutoff point for an assertion-submission sequence that has gone too far.

There are larger, societal checks to schismogenesis. Bateson notes that participating in a national celebration may lessen interclass tensions; in the same way, a war may unite a country divided against itself. He also felt that the custom of headhunting among the Iatmul, which pitted the society against other groups, may have lightened the interior stresses due to rivalry and competition.

The anthropologist Fredrik Barth describes a different example of a social checking mechanism in his study of the way the fiercely warring Pathan clans of Afghanistan are prevented from totally exterminating one another.[8] He notes the deterrent effect of a minor chieftain whose support can always tip the balance between two more powerful chiefs. If a chief who needs a lesser man's support to win against a rival chief puts too much pressure on his rival, the rival can offer the lesser man enough concessions, including his own chieftainship, to get him to defect. Knowing this, the first chief will never threaten to wreak as much vengeance on his vanquished enemy as he might if the third party were not there.

These examples, however, do not suggest what laws or guiding principles may be governing these mysterious action/reaction processes, or the checks which arise to stop them. Bateson's contribution was a growing suspicion that there might be some inbuilt, self-equilibrating arrangement in social groups which kept schismogenic movements under control. In his study of the Iatmul he was already mulling over the idea that symmetrical and complementary types of schismogenesis might operate in a mutually counteracting way. For instance, he posited that a small dose of symmetrical behavior in a complementary relationship might act to check the tendency toward progressive differentiation. He took as an example the relationship of an English squire to his villagers, which is a complementary and not always comfortable one. If the squire played cricket with the villagers once a year, Bateson noted, this small action might be enough to ease the strain.

Later, discussing Richardson's formula for rivalry, which states that the intensity of A's actions is proportional to the degree to which B is ahead of A (B—A), Bateson observed that the appropriate formula for a *complementary* progressive change would be the opposite, since A's actions would be proportional to the degree to which B is behind A (A—B). Thus he says,

Notably this formulation is itself a negative of the formulation for rivalry, the stimulus term being the opposite. It had been observed that symmetrical sequences of actions tend sharply to reduce the strain of excessively complementary persons or groups. It would be tempting to ascribe this effect to some hypothesis which would make the two types of schismogenesis in some degree psychologically incompatible, as is done by the above formulation.[9]

But what made the greatest impact on Bateson's efforts to clarify his thinking about mutual causal processes was his discovery of cybernetics or the science of self-correcting systems like servomechanisms. In the 1958 Epilogue to *Naven,* he describes the influence upon his thinking of the Josiah Macy, Jr., Conferences which were held during the 1950s and at one of which, in Princeton in 1955, he was asked to speak.[10] It was during these meetings that he became seriously intrigued with the ideas of Claude Shannon, Norbert Wiener, and other cybernetic theorists and began to rethink his concept of schismogenesis in terms of the error-activated feedback cycles found in self-governing systems.

The analogy Bateson found most useful was that of a steam engine with a governor. The whole arrangement depends on a loop in which the more there is of something, the less there is of something else. In contrast, when the situation is such that the more there is of something the more there is of every other element, you have what systems engineers call a positive feedback chain or a "runaway." In a steam engine, if the governor were constructed so that the more the arms diverged the more the supply of steam increased, this would cause the engine to operate faster and faster, until it exhausted the available amount of steam or its flywheel would break. A third possibility would be some form of external restraint —for instance, representatives of the next system up (the engineers) might come in and prevent a breakdown by stopping the machine.

Bateson saw the potential of this model in explaining the behaviors he had observed while he was studying Iatmul culture. In particular he was now able to analyze the baffling *naven* ceremony as if it were a loop of behaviors keeping certain variables of the social system within bounds.

The Naven Ceremony as a Cybernetic Mechanism

Noting the forces in Iatmul society that promoted vicious cycles leading to either schism or war, Bateson asked what checks existed to prevent these outcomes. With self-corrective circuits as a model, Bateson believed an answer was now possible. Might there not exist in this society a system by which appropriate complementary behaviors would bring about a corrective decrease in symmetrical behaviors? Could not the system be self-corrective in a circular fashion? Bateson reviewed his findings on Iatmul culture in this light.

First of all, there was the overriding structural fact that the weakest links in Iatmul society were those among maternal relatives. These were broken when a group seceded from its community, since women went to live in the clan of the man they married.

Bateson quite naturally asked why, if the *naven* ceremony was to be understood as providing integration in this area, the emphasis was on strengthening uncle-nephew ties rather than the brother-

brother-in-law ones. He surmised that it was due to the importance of stressing complementary links as a corrective to symmetrical escalations threatening the stability of the group. Clan rivalry made the possibility of fighting or fission a constant threat, and the *naven* seemed to occur when the delicate balance between competing clans was about to tip. Thus Bateson observed that the *naven* ceremonial, which is a caricature of a complementary sexual relationship, was set off by overweening (symmetrical) behavior. When a *laua* boasts in the presence of *wau,* the latter exhibits *naven* behavior. But the full *naven* occasion takes place in the context of a step toward vertical mobility on the part of the *laua,* as when he becomes a successful warrior or hunter. This would be even more of a symmetrical escalation, not only as regards *wau,* but in relation to *wau*'s entire clan.

However, Bateson was not satisfied with a vague hypothesis of one schismogenic process intensifying until a corrective contrary process was set in motion. He wished to find a more specific way to explain the mechanics of this arrangement. This led him to cybernetics, and to the use of a concept that seemed to be crucial to an understanding of the way cybernetic systems worked.

First and Second Order Change

Up to now, Bateson and other researchers had seen two ways in which deviation processes might operate: a self-stabilizing sequence, which the *naven* typifies, and, alternatively, an escalation leading to destruction of the system. But there is a third possibility, which is that a runaway or escalation can set a leap in motion that may transform an entire system.

According to systems theorist W. Ross Ashby, this third possibility is explained by a two-level model for change. Living systems, Ashby noted, are not only able to vary their behaviors in response to minor variations in the field (as the body keeps within an optimum range of temperature by perspiring when it is hot and shivering when it is cold), but are often able to change the "setting" for the range of behaviors whenever the field presents an unusually serious disruption (as in animal species that developed the capacity to grow thicker fur when winters became colder, or worked out a pattern of migrating to warmer climates until spring).[11]

This type of "bimodal" feedback is useful, says Ashby, because it enables the entity or organism to survive both day-to-day fluctuations and drastic changes. He called the corrective responses to minor fluctuations "first order change" and the responses to drastic differences in the environment "second order change." The analogy most often used to illustrate this distinction is the homely house thermostat. The automatic shifts it makes to keep the room within a certain temperature range are first order changes. To make a second order change, however, as when the outside temperature falls precipitously, the householder must alter the setting of the thermostat.

Bateson was looking for factors that would control the potential runaways of schismogenesis, but he also realized that schismogenic processes could be useful in breaking up an inappropriate, outmoded, or unhealthy stability. In his Epilogue to *Naven,* he paid tribute to Ashby's formal analysis regarding change in steady-state systems.

Let us follow Bateson's lead in applying these ideas in detail to the workings of Iatmul society. For instance, one variable of critical importance to the society was intense rivalry. In the absence of any hierarchical structure for resolving conflict, the balance of power between clans had to remain relatively even. If one or another clan gained even a small advantage, it had to be counteracted before an escalation started that might get out of hand. The all-out *naven* ceremony may be seen as a first order change, one which would substitute symmetrical escalations for complementary ones. As the latter is incompatible with the former, this would effectively hamper the development of symmetrical runaways, and maintain the status quo.*

But what if a positive feedback chain were set off which the usual ceremonies were unable to control? I have surmised that it is possible that splitting is a second order change that comes about when

---

*Bateson, unfailingly circular, allowed also for the possibility that too much complementary behavior might trigger off symmetrical displays.

complementary themes are unable to check the escalation of mutual belligerence. Among the Iatmul, a group will go off to form its own village whenever tensions rise above a certain point. Bateson notes the tendency of the Iatmul to expand by a proliferation of small offshoots, each resembling the parent body but not connected to it. In this way Iatmul society survives.

Unfortunately, the deviation-counteracting effect of a self-stabilizing circuit that will create a first order change is, like a razor, double-edged. The *naven* ceremony confirms the group in its old, set ways, and thus has long-range implications for the weakening of the group due to loss of flexibility and risk of error. It is at this point that the biologists offer a comforting vista with their talk of "variety pools" and the role of deviance in forcing new solutions. To quote another systems thinker, Roger Nett:

Since the creative strength of a society must be sought in the capacity of individuals to evaluate, extend, correct, and ultimately to alter existing definitions and understandings (a process which is, in effect, deviation) the problem of ordering a society becomes one of utilizing the vital element —deviation—in social-organizational context.[12]

In the next chapter we will explore further what writers with a systems orientation have to say about the forces that promote differentness and those that promote sameness in living systems in general, not just human systems. The emphasis will be on what the sociologist Magoroh Maruyama calls the "Second Cybernetics." Since most theorists of family relationships have focused on the "First Cybernetics"—deviation-counteracting processes and negative feedback chains—Maruyama suggests that more attention be given to this "Second Cybernetics," which he sees as an essential aspect of change in all living forms.

Chapter 3

The Second Cybernetics

Morphostasis and Morphogenesis

Magoroh Maruyama believes that the survival of any living system—that is, any self-maintaining entity—depends on two important processes. One is "morphostasis," which means that the system must maintain constancy in the face of environmental vagaries. It does this through the error-activated process known as negative feedback. The other process is "morphogenesis," which means that at times a system must change its basic structure. This process involves positive feedback or sequences that work to amplify deviation, as in the case of a successful mutation that allows a species to adapt to changed environmental conditions.[1]

The phenomenon of positive feedback has usually been looked at from the point of view of its destructive effects on a given system. Norbert Wiener discusses it in terms of mechanisms like control feedback elements in antiaircraft guns, observing that if the feedback element is pushed beyond some optimum point, it will begin to overcorrect, making wider and wider arcs until the oscillation causes the machinery to break down.[2] Garrett Hardin, a biologist, analyzes the same process as it applies to social systems.[3] Describing a number of homeostatic models, both man-made and natural, he doubts that a true homeostatic system can ever operate freely in human affairs, because of the tendency for vested interests to build up. Social power, he observes, is inherently a process of positive feedback. And herein lies danger. All systems, according to Hardin, possess a "homeostatic plateau"—limits within which the system is self-correcting—but beyond the homeostatic plateau, at either extreme, lie positive feedback and destruction.

Both Hardin and Wiener have the bias of many thinkers who are grounded in communications theory: They equate any movement toward randomness or chaos with something undesirable. Maruyama, along with systems theorists like Walter Buckley and Albert Speer, believes such movement can have positive value. In addition to examples of destructive positive feedback cycles, he cites others that increase the survival potential of a given system. Thus he gives a cybernetic framing to an evolutionist theory of deviation that embraces change of any sort.

Another way to look at these two processes is in terms of what Buckley, following Ashby, calls "variety" and "constraint." Constraint is synonymous with pattern, structure, regularity. It goes away from a random state, toward what the systems theorist Erwin Schroedinger calls "negentropy."[4] No living system could survive without pattern or structure. On the other hand, too much structure, too much "negentropy," will kill it. This is why there must always be, as Buckley explains it, "some sources of mechanism for *variety,* to act as a potential pool of adaptive variability to meet the problem of mapping new or more detailed variety and constraints in a changeable environment."[5]

One good example of too much negentropy is described in a recent paper by family researcher David Reiss on family "paradigms" (blueprints, in effect, for facing new situations or making sense out of old ones).[6] Reiss speaks of one family that recently migrated from Europe to the United States and encapsulated themselves in an apartment encrusted with objects from the past, complaining about the difficulties of life in a dirty, crowded city. Because of their reliance on a strategy that did not carry within it the capacity to shift to meet new circumstances, they were unable to find new avenues for enjoying themselves. A contrasting family, which saw new and difficult events as an opportunity rather than a threat, solved the dilemma posed by traveling in a foreign land by insisting that one daughter, who knew the language, be with the family whenever transactions with the natives were required.

As described so far, the two types of feedback—that which welcomes and that which inhibits change—would seem to have opposite functions. Negative feedback is conservative and promotes the status quo; positive is radical and promotes newness. But this is far from the whole story. Buckley, in talking about the "vicious circle or spiral or escalation," says that "it is not at all certain whether the resultant will maintain, change or destroy the given system or its particular structures."[7] One can think of examples: the growth of monopolies might lead to such total inequity that social revolution would result, *or* it could inspire a movement toward antitrust legislation. The death of a religious or political heretic might reinforce the system he repudiated, *or* his martyrdom might lead to a revision of the entire social order. The death or suicide of a family member might close off possibilities for change in the family, *or* it might release unexpected potential for growth.

Maruyama paints an even more complicated picture. He points out that it is possible to have both positive and negative mutual-causal loops counterbalancing one another in any given situation (by "loops" he means a series of mutually caused events in which the influence of any element comes back to itself through other elements). As an example he offers a vector diagram showing forces and counterforces impinging on the growth of a city. Factors such as number of people, migration level, modernization, sanitation facilities, amount of garbage per area, bacteria per area, and number of diseases form a number of interrelated positive and negative loops that increase or decrease the population.

Maruyama does not, alas, make any suggestions about how to predict outcomes from this interplay of loops. He leaves us merely with the statement that "an understanding of a society or an organism cannot be attained without studying both types of loops and the relationships between them."[8]

Timing and Stages

But there is another way to look at feedback loops. What is important is not only the relative strength of these loops and the way they are combined but *timing*. In assessing a self-correcting system, a particularly important factor is the balance or unbalance of the system at any given time. This is, of course, what Jackson and other family therapists realized when they tried unsuccessfully to introduce changes into families that were not in crisis and why at times they would deliberately try to make the family "system" exceed its limits or create a runaway.

Family therapist Salvador Minuchin, for instance, describes the value of inducing a crisis in the case of a family with an asthmatic daughter. He decided to ask the father, who was usually careful to bow down to the expectations of the mother, to come home unexpectedly late one night. The father chose a Friday night before a weekend trip for his experiment, and the mother, a mild-mannered woman, went after him with a pair of scissors. After this, the focus of treatment moved to the parents and to the other brothers and sisters, and the asthmatic daughter began to improve.[9]

Another aspect of feedback processes which is related to timing is that they often occur in alternations or stages. Bateson calls attention to "inverse progressive changes," as when an increase in mutual hostility between a couple reaches some built-in limit and a shift toward mutual affection (also limited) takes place.[10] Such an oscillation usually implies an overall stability.

Maruyama describes a different sort of situation, in which a deviation-amplifying process can, over a period of time, change into a deviation-counteracting one. Here there is a drift toward increasing differentiation which at some point loses its somewhat adventitious nature and stabilizes. One example (my own) is the way many couples nowadays start living together under the comfortable impression that they can always leave. Sooner or later they find that time and habit have placed them in as binding a relationship as any marriage.

Naturally, the process can go the other way, with a formerly stable system moving into a period of disequilibrium. Deviation-amplifying chains characteristic of this sequence seem to divide along the lines of Maruyama's and Hardin's different ideas about the nature of positive feedback. There is a gradual process by which a variation takes hold, and the runaway that develops when a system's error-activating mechanisms break down. Of course the two types of positive feedback may *not* be related—for instance, a drift toward deviation may occur all by itself and not in connection with any systemic entity—but they may also be stages of a larger process. An example is the behavior of animal populations that live in an environment where there is an unlimited food supply and few competing species to act as a natural check to increase. These populations periodically start to overexpand in the manner of the first type of positive feedback. At a certain point they will suddenly adopt a self-destroying behavior—like the lemmings' famous march to the sea—as if a limit in the "plateau" regulating their numbers had been reached and triggered a runaway (literally) to destroy the excess.

But here a difficult question presents itself. Can this sequence really be said to go in the direction of a deviation-amplifying result? From the point of view of the lemming population as a whole, if not from that of the subgroup that gets destroyed, the entire series of events has operated to reinstate the status quo. But it is also possible that a deviation-amplifying process can bring about a leap toward a new and more complex state. At this point we must bring in the concept of levels.

Levels

So far, we have been looking at the effect of feedback loops on one particular system. What we need to consider next is that feedback processes in living systems must always be viewed in terms of *several levels of systems at once.* The fact that there is a hierarchy of living systems is not a new discovery, although it is not always related to cybernetic theory. To prevent confusion, let us make it clear that we are not talking about levels in a descriptive or epistemological sense (as in Levels of Logical Type) but in a structural sense, as in layers of living systems. The social scientist Herbert Simon has offered the thought that the complexity of natural phenomena could be better understood if we realized that we are always dealing with "layers" or "nests of Chinese blocks," in sequences of increasing inclusion, such as: individuals, primary groups, organizations, social systems; or, in biology: gene, cell, organ, organism. Any activity in one of these layers will obviously be operating simultaneously in at least one other.[11]

Bateson, always aware of levels, makes a similar point when he notes that the study of interaction always involves at least two pieces of information, "a statement about participating entities and a statement about that larger entity which is brought into being by the fact of interaction."[12] He then adds that an important source of destructive interaction can be a discrepancy between the goals of two systems on different levels:

For example, a self-maximizing tendency may lead to the destruction of some larger system which was instrumental and necessary to the existence of the self. In special cases, the self-destruction of the smaller entity is instrumental to the survival of the larger system.[13]

The struggle of social theorists to discriminate between an open aim and an unintended consequence in human events, embodied in terms like overt/covert and manifest/latent, may in many instances have to do with this same fact: that any action taking place in a social field will touch at least two contiguous systems. The sociologist Robert Merton comes close to suggesting this in an essay on manifest and latent function. Listing Durkheim as one of many thinkers who have, without realizing it, used a concept of latent function, he observes that "Emile Durkheim's similar analysis of the social functions of punishment is also focused on its latent functions (consequence for the community) rather than confined to manifest functions (consequence for the criminal)."[14]

Examples of behaviors that affect more than one system at a time are constantly cited by family researchers; in fact it was the surmise that the individual sufferer from mental illness could not be understood *without* looking at the consequences of his distress for the family group that started family therapy on its way. Following this line of thought, Haley observed the double consequence of symptoms of all kinds: the effect on the individual, which was to make him less responsible and more helpless; and the effect on his family relationships, which was to give him a lever for enormous control.[15] The Bateson group used the terms "overt" and "covert," to distinguish between openly acknowledged behaviors and those whose consequences were involuntary or denied.

Holding fast to this concept of structural levels, we can now see that any feedback may have deviation-amplifying and deviation-counteracting effects at the same time, depending on which system one is looking at. Tragic drama is suggestive in regard to this point. What the Greeks called hubris, translated as overweening pride and linked to the tragic hero's downfall, closely resembles our old friend the positive-feedback chain of social power. Once set in motion, this chain is deviation-*amplifying* from the point of view of the hero, whose deviance in relation to his group is increased to the point that he is eventually cast out, brought low, or otherwise destroyed. It is deviation-*counteracting* from the point of view of his society, in that out of the ashes of the hero's downfall supposedly rises a new social peace. An alternative explanation might be that the society uses the aftermath of the debacle to recalibrate the setting for its own equilibrium. Thus a tragedy may essentially describe a "morphogenetic" change (change *in* the homeostatic setting) rather than a "morphostatic" change (change *governed by* the homeostatic setting).

Whichever way we define what is going on, it is clear that without some such multilevel view, we will not begin to understand it. Such ideas allow us to think differently about the process that links the deviant and his group. The social typecasting of deviants thus emerges as an area where two streams of thought, one from general systems theory and one from sociology, begin to intersect.

The Typecasting of Deviants

Most studies of deviance read like contributions to the sociology of occupations, except that "occupation" is extended to cover delinquency, mental illness, and the like. However, a respectable few are concerned with the circular causal processes that increase the difference between a person and his group so that he is perceived unfavorably.

Leslie T. Wilkins, in "A Behavioral Theory of Drug Taking," explicitly applies Maruyama's mutual causal concepts to the typecasting process.[16] He explains how an addict "outlaw group" is created through the mutually reinforcing effect of social definition on self-image, and how the further step of placing addicts together in rehabilitation or detention centers amplifies their difference from the community (and likeness to each other) even more. Using this framework, Wilkins makes an intelligent criticism of systems of control that are directed toward changing the individual deviant rather than the process which creates him.

Family theorists have also developed a literature on deviance focused on the symptomatic member of a family—but they often use the concept of scapegoating rather than typecasting. This wording brings up an interesting problem. It is easily noticed that scapegoating is a mutual causal process, despite the implication that the scapegoat is the victim and everyone else is taking advantage of him. Nevertheless, the word is weighted in favor of the underdog and is hard to use objectively. Perhaps this is why most research on deviance does not employ it.

Nevertheless, Ezra Vogel and Norman Bell's "The Emotionally Disturbed Child as a Family Scapegoat" is an excellent contribution to this literature on family deviants.[17] According to the authors, emotionally disturbed children are invariably involved in tensions between their parents. The parents, by projecting their conflicts onto the child, maintain a reasonably harmonious relationship, but the cost to the child may be great. A major contribution of the article is a description of the way the child is selected and then inducted into his role. Some chance characteristic of the child—it need not even be an obnoxious trait so long as it differentiates him—will be singled out and then developed, increasing the contrast between himself and everyone else in the family. The authors do not see this as a mutual causal process in Maruyama's sense, but it fits the definition very well.

Most writing about typecasting and scapegoating has one of two emphases. The first is on behavior as it functions on different levels of systems. Researchers studying the family as a system and most of the contributors to the sociology of deviance write from this standpoint. The other emphasis, based on traditional, individual-oriented ideas, gravitates to concepts like "projections," "expectations" or "roles." Into this category falls much clinical writing on such behavior as delinquency and mental illness.

From the point of view of family therapy, the individual-oriented approach badly misrepresents the subject. For instance, to speak of the "role of the scapegoat" is to present the deviant as a *person* with fixed characteristics rather than a person involved in a process. "Scapegoating" technically applies to only one stage of a shifting scenario—the stage where the person is metaphorically cast out of the village. After all, the term originates from an ancient Hebrew ritual in which a goat was turned loose in the desert after the sins of the people had been symbolically laid on its head. The deviant can begin like a hero and go out like a villain, or vice versa. There is a positive-negative continuum on which he can be rated depending on which stage of the deviation process we are looking at, which sequence the process follows, and the degree to which the social system is stressed.

At the same time, the character of the deviant may vary in another direction, depending on the way his particular group does its typecasting. Which symptoms crop up in members of a group is itself a kind of typecasting. Thus the deviant may appear in many guises: the mascot, the clown, the sad sack, the erratic genius, the black sheep, the wise guy, the saint, the idiot, the fool, the impostor, the malingerer, the boaster, the villain, and so on. Literature and folklore abound with such figures.

It will thus make a difference in any study of deviance whether one chooses to depict one's subject in cross-section, by phase or type, or to trace it in terms of a shifting, longitudinally viewed career. One of the problems with early family research was the attempt to see a typology of families according to symptom: the "schizophrenic" family, the "delinquent" one. More recently it has been realized that what is needed are longitudinal studies that show the varying nature of the family deviant over time, or the use made of different family members in changing succession, as need arises and persons offer themselves.

The Meaning of Deviance for Social Systems

One view of the meaning of deviance is that it promotes cohesion. Most writers on the sociology of deviance agree with Emile Durkheim that the deviant's main function for the group is to promote solidarity and highlight rules and norms. A good summary of this position can be found in R. A. Dentler and Kai T. Erikson's "The Functions of Deviance in Groups."[18] Arlene Daniels, in an essay on scapegoating in a sensitivity training group, makes the further point that this morale-building function seems to come to the fore in groups in which expressions of anxiety and hostility are encouraged.[19]

Another view emphasizes the danger to society. In the same article Daniels remarks that the process of scapegoating may only serve to keep an unworkable system functioning long after it should have collapsed. Many an outmoded group or sect owes its longevity to this fact.

A third view of deviance emphasizes its *mediation* function in situations where people are in conflict. Family theorists have observed that the presence of a deviant may be vital to the management of conflict. Researchers studying or working with families of schizophrenics were amazed at the way the patient's symptoms would flare up when attention was focused on some crucial disagreement, particularly one between the parents. Jackson felt that this type of activity served a diversionary purpose and often termed it a "rescue operation."[20] Family therapy studies, as typified by the Bell and Vogel article, almost uniformly emphasize the way in which the parents of an emotionally disturbed child, who are often in serious, if unadmitted, conflict, can unite around their common involvement with the child. Thus the hostility between them is submerged and a surface harmony prevails.

Observations like this led to the belief that whatever else "schizophrenia" might be, it was always associated with a potential split in the family. Haley speculatively redefines schizophrenia as a "conflict of groups" and suggests that schizophrenia is a name for behavior that results from mediating in many warring family triangles.[21] In families where profound differences exist between the parents—which often means between whole kin groups—a need for family unity leads to rewards for ambiguous communication that keeps the peace. Certain persons will be singled out to handle this task. Such persons will not make sense to outsiders, and may even be thought mentally ill, but within the family context this ability not to make sense is encouraged, presumably because it helps the family to stay together.

Irresistible Runs

In talking about homeostatic mechanisms, writers like Hardin assume that if a homeostatic plateau is exceeded, a disastrous deviation-amplifying process will set in and destroy the system. Yet in families that come into therapy one finds constant small "runs"—positive feedback chains that look as if they might turn into runaways but never do.

These runs may be escalating arguments like those Jackson saw in his work with what he called (following Bateson) "symmetrical" couples.[22] Or they can take place in a marriage where husband and wife have defined their roles in a complementary manner, with one seeming to be "strong" and the other "weak." Such a pair, as Jackson says, "can be viewed as a mutual causative system, whose complementary communication reinforces the cycles of interaction between them."[23]

One can also see spirals of hostility between parents and a child. William Taylor cites such an interchange from Haley and Hoffman's *Techniques of Family Therapy* as an example of "recurrent states" in family interaction.[24] Runs like these are nearly irresistible, as anyone who has ever been caught in one or watched one knows, and they repeat and repeat like a broken record, never reaching any conclusion.

What are these forms and why do they occur? The answer may well be that they are a response to a system that is constantly threatening to exceed a variety of homeostatic limits. Why else would there be so many positive feedback chains that abort? It is even possible that the many redundancies of communication noted by researchers in families with disturbed members, particularly in the disturbed child/parents triangle, are all feedback chains of this type.

This explanation implies that there *is* something in family systems resembling homeostatic plateaus. Although no family researcher has, to my knowledge, used the idea of such a plateau in interpreting family behavior, the sociologist Robert Bales has used it in speaking of small-group behavior. Although he finds that a successful meeting need not necessarily have fewer negative than positive reactions by group members, he remarks that there seems to be a kind of optimum balance on which success depends. A departure to either side will bring trouble. Bales finds this most true when there is an excessive rate of disagreement: "Apparently, when ill feeling rises above some critical point, a 'chain reaction' or 'vicious circle' tends to set in. Logic and practical demands of the task cease to be governing factors."[25] In fact, says Bales, when they reach this point groups can hardly accomplish anything.

In the same way, there seems to be a certain range within which family functioning is maintained. In families in which a member is deemed "abnormal," this range may be an extremely narrow one. Dr. Richard Fisch, of the Mental Research Institute in Palo Alto, has used the term "the ten-foot pole" to describe the narrow range of closeness and distance that seems to limit the relationships of some of the couples who come to him for therapy.

Let us set up an example of the ten-foot pole in action. Assuming that the relationship between the parents is one of the most important variables in the family, the "setting" for closeness and distance between them would be very important. Suppose a husband is always exceeding the setting for distance from his wife because of a prior setting for closeness with one of his parents. One might then expect to find in the family a recurrent mutual causal sequence of some sort. This sequence may take the form of the bickering that Jackson noted, when each spouse, feeling the "victim" of the other, provokes the very hostilities that justify his or her own. Or it may take the form of an increasing withdrawal, with distant behavior provoking even more distant behavior in reciprocal fashion. Before such a run can become a runaway, with potential for productive change but also risking destruction of the system, a child or other family member will often move in to block the escalation—Jackson's "rescue operation"—and divert the hostilities and concern of the parents to himself. Thus he substitutes a safe deviation-amplifying process for one that threatens the family at its core.

One can think of still another sequence. If two parents who engage in a withdrawal contest go too long without contact, a child and one parent may get into a run of mutual hostilities which is blocked when the other parent moves in to defend the child. This action then serves to reestablish a connection between the parents, albeit an unfriendly one. One can imagine runs countering runs in this way in a kind of periodic seesaw, and observation of families confirms that at times this is exactly what happens.

"Pathological" Balance

The questions can still be asked: What keeps patterns like these so firmly installed? Why don't they break down? Perhaps the answer can be found in our concept of levels: The imbalance in the nuclear family is serving to correct an imbalance in the larger kin system, and is embedded in the equilibrium-maintaining mechanisms not only of that system but of its subordinate parts. These may be other nuclear families, dyads within families, single persons, or body parts belonging to those persons—and just as one cannot tamper with any one element in an ecosystem without affecting the whole, so one cannot change much in a family or a member of a family without affecting a larger field. This includes other social systems impinging on the family as well. Although we cannot say that such a "field" has a homeostasis as Jackson thought the family had a homeostasis, the combined effect of many systems leaning on or pulling against one another may add up to the kind of stability for which the ecosystem is such a good analogy.

To make this idea a bit more concrete, let us look at the interplay of feedback influences, both those amplifying and counteracting deviation, in the hypothetical case of a child whose irrational behavior seems to heal a parental split. First of all, the same process that amplifies the deviance of the child is deviation-counteracting in regard to the marital dyad. Moving to another level of system, one could say that the very consequence of having a "sick" member may be deviation-amplifying for the nuclear family if it interferes with important family functions. For instance, the family line may die out with that generation if the sick member is an only child who becomes unable to have a family of his own.

However, if one shifts to the extended kin group, a deviation-counteracting effect may reappear. The parents' inability to form a strong tie may be due to the fact that one or both of them are still being used to mediate relationships in their own families of origin. If so, they are stabilizing relationships in these other groups. Given this prior arrangement, it is possible that all the others have to follow. Whatever the case, it is clear that any intervention that tries to reverse the deviation-amplifying sequences here, without figuring out how to deal with the deviation-counteracting ones, will fare badly.

To sum up, we can say that a family which is off-balance in regard to its own system because it is maintaining the balance of other systems will perpetually be exposed to the destructive effects of positive feedback chains. In an effort to compensate, some of these will be used to counter others. Any form that prevents a disastrous split in the family, as when a child's behavior serves as a diversion, can be thought of as a corrective circuit for an escalating feedback chain. Alternative mechanisms might be for one of the spouses to develop a symptom and heal the split by becoming more dependent on his partner, or for the family to achieve a united front by scapegoating some outsider, or by mourning a departed member. Some families use an uneasy mix of all these strategies.

All families become periodically unbalanced; they have to, as power relationships between the generations shift. And all families experience the stresses that produce vicious circles in interpersonal relationships. What is different in families with members in the deepest trouble is the way these vicious circles continually repeat, without ever forcing the family to change in a morphogenetic direction, because a symptomatic problem or a pattern represented by a problem person is there to prevent such a change.

And that brings us to a further question: If family pathology can be so stable, what can finally cause it—as sometimes happens—to break down? In searching out the answer, we arrive at the place where the sociology of deviance—with its process of typecasting— and family theory—with its process of scapegoating—begin to suggest common conclusions.

When the Corrective Circuit Fails

The reasons why the circuits that keep family pathology in place sometimes fail have never been expressed satisfactorily. Many family theorists take the view that there are really two parts to achieving true mental patienthood: a long period of training in the "right" family setting, learning to mediate in many triangles, *and* the proper accreditation by an authorized psychiatric source. The two types of deviation-amplifying process alluded to before come to mind: (1) a condition of deviance gradually arrived at, and (2) a crisis that ushers in a runaway. Of course what constitutes a crisis in a particular family can only be answered in the specific instance. But one can surmise that any sudden shift in the arrangement of checks and balances in the kinship group and its subsystems will cause an upset that the family may be unable to handle. A very obvious threat of this sort would be the departure of a key person who seems to be helping to stabilize the family. Children who are performing in this way often erupt with disturbances when they reach adolescence, and the next system up—the community—is often brought in to restore equilibrium.

Is this a well-deserved end, then, to the pathological balance? Not always. The officials whom society empowers to act in these situations often authorize the family to go on using the person who is the key to their stability as before. But there is a difference. Previously, in our hypothetical family, as the distance between the parents would periodically widen, the child would produce the behavior that caused it to close up again. But—an important point—he was not yet your true scapegoat; he was not hated, feared, extruded. It is society that comes in and turns the "fault" that intermittently opens up between the family and the child into a permanent chasm. The scapegoating process—redefined here as a way of relocating the split in the family—is only made easier by hospitalization or institutionalization. The family is free to continue to have a symptomatic person without having to deal with his or her inconvenient protests.

Thus does society move in to take a deviation-amplifying role, replacing the family's relatively benign ceremonies with its own "degradation ceremonies," as sociologist Erving Goffman calls them. The person so honored is now stigmatized and placed outside the pale. But what promotes deviance on the level of one system can inhibit it on another. Society is the beneficiary of the deviation-*counteracting* effect produced by a deviant on his group, which is to reaffirm its solidarity, its belief in itself and in the righteousness of its ways. But herein lie the very seeds of its destruction (back to a deviation-*amplifying* aspect again!), not in terms of the present structure of the group but of its future ability to adapt and change. One could say that every single-deviant arrangement is one more coffin nail for the group.

Thus, this apparent conclusion only raises a new set of questions. Do these mechanisms for maintaining equilibrium also have the potential for disrupting it, and in such a case, how can one predict whether the result will be destruction of the social group or a leap to a new form? Are there laws governing these forceful cycles? Are they all the same, or do they differ? We are in much the same state as when the existence of electricity was discovered, but not until the principles governing this source of power were understood could it be harnessed and put to use.

In the next chapter we will move back to the mundane question: How can these principles be applied? We will be back on the clinical plane again, tracing the findings of researchers who have tried to describe a typology or continuum on which to range the families they were working with. Early attempts at typology placed families in categories defined by symptoms: the "schizophrenic" family, the "alcoholic" family, the "multiproblem" family. As Reiss points out, this ties the type of family to the type of problem one individual in the family is said to possess, and comes perilously close to traditional psychiatric classifications.[26] Researchers took an important step when they tried to place families in terms of structures or sequences rather than particular disorders. Jackson's interactional typology for couples, and Minuchin's structural typology for disturbed families, though bipolar, nevertheless begin to move our thinking away from a individual symptom-related orientation and toward a family-wide view.

Chapter 4

Typologies of Family Structure

Symptom Typologies

Out of the fascination with schizophrenic communication and how it might be fostered by family communication, a new branch of family research arose. This approach focused on microstudy of interactions, verbal or nonverbal, in an attempt to link communication style with the dominant type of symptom found in a family: in other words, to suggest a typology of families by symptom.

Early work in this direction came about in a rather circuitous way. We have already seen the uses of accident in the Bateson group's research. Now serendipity enters again. At Yale in the early 1950s, Theodore Lidz and his coworkers were attempting to map out the interior workings of the family of the schizophrenic. Since they had a psychoanalytic orientation, it did not occur to them to see the family as a whole. Their original plan was to obtain Rorschach protocols from each family member and to construct a portrait of the family from a composite of these materials. The team did once try to see a family with the patient, but this proved unworkable, and the experiment was not, at that time, repeated. Lidz subsequently became discouraged about the value of his Rorschach protocols and the project was temporarily discontinued.

It was during this period of discouragement that Wynne met Lidz and learned about the research with the Rorschach protocols and the disastrous family interview. Wynne had also been using an indirect method of family research, one even more inferential and roundabout. To study the family of the schizophrenic, he had devised the scheme of having a therapist interview each family member and, by analyzing the interlocking and reciprocal nature of the transferences, try to figure out what the family must be like. This, like Lidz's protocols, had proved unsatisfactory.

Wynne asked Lidz to send him a number of the Rorschachs, specifying that they should be from parents of young adult schizophrenics and "normals." A gifted coworker, Margaret Singer, analyzed these transcripts blind and was able to discriminate accurately between parents with disturbed offspring and those without. She then performed the even more unusual feat of taking protocols of disturbed adolescents with a variety of labels (Autistic/Schizophrenic, Neurotic/Withdrawn, and Delinquent/Acting Out) and matching these with the correct sets of parents.[1]

This early success in predicting symptomatic members from close analysis of family communication was never sufficiently replicated by other researchers to qualify as more than a brilliant, suggestive beginning. But at the time its impact on other researchers was great. The group in Palo Alto was also trying to isolate communicational variables associated with different kinds of symptoms. Studies like those of Wynne and Singer supported the idea that a typology of families based on symptoms was more than just a dream, and that the Rosetta Stone of family communication was about to be deciphered.

So it was that at the Mental Research Institute in the early 1960s a fascinating guessing game was played. A researcher would play back a piece of taped family conversation to a group of colleagues; for instance, a fragment of a structured interview between a mother and father. The assembled company would then try to guess whether these parents might have a schizophrenic offspring, an underachiever, a delinquent—and they were often correct. If the conversation was between parents with a young child, the group might speculate whether the youngster might be expected to have a psychotic break at, possibly, age twenty. Don Jackson and his fellow researchers were trying to perfect a predictive as well as postdictive methodology for analyzing communicational characteristics of families with symptoms. One of Jackson's major interests just before his death in 1968 was a study of families that produced members with ulcerative colitis. Once identified, he believed, patterns associated with specific symptoms could be "read" from samples of family interaction.

Interaction Typologies

Even though Jackson's "matching" experiments were not always successful, the notion would not die that different kinds of symptoms might be linked with different kinds of families. However, it began to be clear that it was not possible to be too specific about the symptom. The Palo Alto researchers began to play with a different kind of typology, one based on attributes or sequences. Jackson had already suggested a classification of relationships that crossed degree of marital satisfaction (or misery) with longevity: Stable-Satisfactory; Unstable-Satisfactory; Unstable-Unsatisfactory; and Stable-Unsatisfactory. This typology was dyadic and did not have a true family-wide application, but it served as a grid for a typology of couples.[2]

Jackson used another couple typology based on Bateson's categories for schismogenic relationships. In *Mirages of Marriage* Jackson defined three basic "modes of interactions": symmetrical, complementary, and a balanced mix of the two that he called reciprocal. Each had its own potential for pathology, but Jackson felt that the reciprocal mode was preferable, since it allowed for more flexibility and fitted the basically egalitarian ideals of American society.[3]

In *Pragmatics of Human Communication* Jackson and his coauthors recognized that symmetrical and complementary couple sequences may be found in normal, healthy interaction but may also become rigid and produce distress.[4] Symmetrical escalations, if taken to an extreme, amount to constant rejections of each self by the other. These escalations, when pathological, stop only when one or both partners become physically or emotionally exhausted, and then often only long enough to allow the partners to recover their breath. The authors analyzed the stereotyped arguments of George and Martha in Edward Albee's *Who's Afraid of Virginia Woolf?* as a particularly stunning example of this pattern.

The other type, the rigidly complementary sequence, is most dramatically shown by the sadomasochistic couple, although it is common in many kinds of marital misery. This form is felt to be more pathogenic than the other because of the constant disconfirmation of the two respective selves. Each partner must fit his own definition of self into one that complements the other. This arrangement works if one partner is sick or temporarily dependent on the other, but when it is rigidly invoked it does not allow for growth and change.

One of the most impressive illustrations of the use of microanalysis to isolate basic schismogenic patterns and to relate these patterns to symptoms is shown in a series of structured interviews asking, "How did you two meet and marry?" which were given to parents in clinical and nonclinical groups at the Mental Research Institute. *Pragmatics of Human Communication* uses three excerpts from these interviews to illustrate a couple that interacts in a rigidly symmetrical fashion, one that interacts in a rigidly complementary fashion, and one that does not fall into either category but responds flexibly. Naïve people are likely to choose the third excerpt as the most "pathological" because it appears to show more expression of conflict, popularly supposed to indicate trouble in marriage. The opposite is really the case, for the third couple is getting along very well. The "symmetrical" couple came into therapy because of their constant fighting, which was having a bad effect on their children, and because of sex difficulties. The "complementary" couple, although not in a clinical sample, was found to be emotionally distant, and the wife was extremely depressed.[5]

These studies try to decode interaction patterns in wider social fields. Unfortunately, they do not show how these sequences finish or top out, rather than leading to a runaway. Watzlawick in *Pragmatics of Human Communication* does bring up Richardson's fatigue explanation, and also refers to Bateson's idea that one kind of sequence acts to cancel the other, but these explanations do not go far enough.[6] In real life, rigid escalations of either type are usually associated with third-party interferences that block them off, as well as with "cutoff" behaviors (walking out in a huff, going to get a drink, and so forth) and "trigger signs" for starting up again. In none of these writings are the exchanges conceived as circularities; the snake does not have its tail in its mouth; and so the descriptions do not seem complete.

Structural Typologies

By the late 1950s the groundwork had been laid for the next step: a sorting out of organizational features of families that produced problematic members. Early family research had been with families of psychotics, but the families that began to be studied in the 1960s, poor and disadvantaged families, produced problem people who did not always have so much trouble with "what is real" as with "what is right" according to the mores of the larger society.

They also seemed to be organized somewhat differently. The route of inquiry was now reversed. Instead of being sidetracked by the idea that there might be an "alcoholic family" or a "schizophrenic family"—that families might differ according to symptom—the architecture of the family was looked at and categories of organization were established. Oddly enough, only then did it begin to seem that specific types of family structure might indeed be connected with certain categories of problems.

The first attempt at an organizational typology came from a research project designed by Salvador Minuchin, Braulio Montalvo, and others to study the families of delinquent boys, which was reported on in *Families of the Slums*.[7] These boys' families seemed to fall into two categories. One was characterized as the "enmeshed" family, the other the "disengaged" family. Since both types were found among poor families, it seemed that disadvantaged families could not simply be lumped together under the rubric "culture of poverty," nor did the label "delinquent" always point to the same kind of family organization. *Families of the Slums* attacked the myth that poverty was necessarily synonymous with disorganization, and upheld the principle of equifinality: that the same outcome did not necessarily mean the same origins, at least in reference to the context of symptomatic behavior.

In the disengaged family, there seemed to be a relative absence of strong connections, and relationship ties between family members were weak or nonexistent. The enmeshed family, by contrast, resembled an error-activated system with high resonance between the parts. The disengaged style gave the researchers the impression of

an atomistic field; family members have long moments in which they move as in isolated orbits, unrelated to each other. They act as parts of a system so loosely interlocked that it challenges the clinician's notion that a change in one part of a system will be followed by compensatory changes in other parts.[8]

The enmeshed family was characterized by a "tight interlocking" of its members. "Their quality of connectedness is such that attempts on the part of one member to change elicit fast complementary resistance on the part of others."[9]

Minuchin's definition of "enmeshed" has a quality reminiscent of Haley's "First Law" of human relationships, discussed in Chapter 2. Haley saw the homeostatic monitoring of behaviors as a normal state of affairs in any group with a past and a future, but found it present to an exaggerated degree in families that fostered psychopathology. It is possible to say that there is such a thing as too much homeostasis, and the term "enmeshed" seems to embody that idea.

One of the indicators of this state of affairs, according to Minuchin, is a lack of differentiation between individual family members. As noted in Chapter 1, this idea is similar to Bowen's "undifferentiated family," but "enmeshed" has the metaphoric edge over "undifferentiated" in suggesting a too-tight connection between parts rather than a gluey blob. A useful analogy for this hard-to-describe phenomenon is the situation of the boys in the Never-Never Land in Peter Pan, who all had to turn over in bed at the same time whenever one turned over.

Another effect of enmeshment, which Minuchin emphasizes in Families and Family Therapy, is to weaken the boundaries that allow family subsystems to work.[10] In brief, the boundary between the nuclear family and families of origin is not well maintained; the boundary separating the parents from their children is frequently invaded in improper ways; and the roles of spouse and parent are never clearly differentiated, so that neither the spouse subsystem nor the parent subsystem can operate with ease. Finally, the children are not differentiated on the basis of age or maturation level, so that the sibling subsystem cannot contribute properly to the socialization process.

In a more microscopic view of the interactions that characterize an enmeshed family, Minuchin comes up with observations that support much of what other family therapists and researchers have described. For one thing, he confirms the striking inability of dyadic transactions to persist in many disturbed families. In one family that included a child with a psychosomatic disorder, he noted that the family continually deflected conflict through the use of third parties. Whenever two persons disagreed and attempted to work out some problem, a third would intervene. In this family:

Dyadic transactions rarely occur; interaction is either triadic or group. It is characterized by a rigid sequence, which promotes a sense of vagueness and confusion in all family members. For example, if a parent criticizes one of the children, the other parent or a sibling will join in to protect the child, and then another family member will join the critic or the criticized. The original issue becomes diffused, only to emerge again later in a similar sequence and to be similarly unresolved.[11]

One could say that an inability of coalitions to remain stable would indicate a special kind of structure—one whose systems and subsystems are so entangled that, whenever there is a conflict of rules or interests, there will be a tug of war over which set of alignments will predominate. Since the outer limits of homeostatic plateaus of various subsystems will continually be overpassed, there will be many countering movements, or schismogenic reactions of the sort Bateson described in *Naven.* As a hypothetical instance, a wife has been talking for an hour on the phone with her sister. Her husband, who hates his in-laws, gets into a fight with the older son. The mother intervenes to try to protect the boy, but the father smacks him and the boy goes to his room and slams the door.

The fight moves to the couple, with the husband hurling insults at the wife's family and the wife screaming back. At this point a younger boy, who is asthma-prone, starts to have an attack. The wife goes to minister to the boy, who sometimes has to be taken to the emergency room. This time the attack passes. After the child is put to bed the father apologizes to the mother, who refuses to speak to him. However, she phones her sister in the daytime for the next few days.

We note that there are six escalating sequences here, each one breaking up the one before it. They alternate between a presumably symmetrical one (husband/wife) and various complementary ones (parents/children). The kin group, the marital pair, the parenting subsystem, and the sibling rescue squad are all participating units. This event, or one like it, takes place at least once a week.

The Too Richly Cross-Joined System

Ashby, too, focuses on the processes of equilibration in complex systems. In *Design for a Brain,* he writes:

Clearly, at any state of the whole, if a single part is not at equilibrium (even though the remainder are) this part will change, will provide new conditions for other parts, will thus start them moving again, and will thus prevent that state from being one of equilibrium for the whole. As equilibrium of the whole requires that *all* parts be in equilibrium, we can say (metaphorically) that every part has a *power of veto* over the states of equilibrium of the whole.[12]

Thus Bateson's phrase, "the infinite dance of shifting coalitions," seems applicable to any system composed of many parts and subparts, all linked together in an interdependent way. Systems of this type find it difficult to negotiate changes in their environment. But how then to account for a universe full of complex entities whose adaptiveness has been demonstrated by the fact that they have survived? Ashby addresses himself to this puzzle and suggests that there is an optimum degree to which parts of a system should be interdependent if the system is to adapt well, or at all. His thoughts on this are beautifully relevant to Minuchin's concept of the "enmeshed" family with its extraordinarily high resonance among parts.

In *Design for a Brain* Ashby investigates the possibility of using a cybernetic model for adaptive systems, in particular a system like the brain. The book is also a brilliant treatise on homeostatic principles and an application of these principles to the mechanics of natural selection and adaptive processes in general.

From the beginning Ashby insists on seeing organism and environment as a unified field, two interacting aspects of a whole. He bids us consider that the dividing line between organism and environment is essentially a mental artifact. Using the analogy of a mechanic with an artificial arm trying to repair an engine, he asks whether the arm is to be thought of as part of the organism that is struggling with the machine or part of the machinery with which the man is struggling.

To describe the totality Ashby chooses a term—the "state-determined system"—that includes organism, environment, and the invariant line of behavior that results when the interplay between the two is fixed and variables are constant. According to Ashby, the state-determined system has no randomness in it. If it is at a certain state and in certain conditions, it will do a certain thing, and it will do this thing whenever the state and conditions recur.

Ashby also discusses the attributes of a stable system—one that persists—and describes the familiar mechanism of negative feedback that, by correcting deviations, keeps the essential variables of the system within critical limits. Expanding this topic, he speculates on the attributes of what he calls an "ultrastable" system—one that not only remains steady in the face of small, continuous disturbances but can reorganize itself to adjust to a large change in the outer context. We have already given some consideration to these ideas, as they impacted upon Bateson, in Chapter 2.

Ashby surmises that a system with the capacity to handle both kinds of change would have superior adaptive powers. He further notes that the mechanism that governs such a shift in values would probably take a step-function form, meaning that it would respond to a drastic change in the value of some variable that would occur whenever an element reached a critical state. This second order type of feedback, which he calls a "step-mechanism," would differ from the first order feedback shown by the merely stable system in that it would operate only occasionally, when essential variables of the system overpassed their limits. At this point it would trigger off a search for a new value that would once more return the system to a stable state.

To test this idea Ashby constructed a simple, four-unit cybernetic machine, the "Homeostat," which demonstrated the presence of both levels of feedback. It not only corrected for minor disturbances but was able to arrive at a new solution after a gross displacement of one of its parameters. But, the Homeostat possessed a major defect: it was too richly cross-joined. The dilemma of the Homeostat brings to mind the lines written by the seventeenth-century poet Francis Thompson in musing upon the interconnectedness of all things in the universe: "Thou cans't not pluck a flower without troubling of a star." One consequence, in regard to the Homeostat, is ruefully commented upon by Ashby. He points out that a homeostatic arrangement like the brain, with millions instead of only four units, would take till infinity to reach a solution on a trial-and-error basis.

But the worst problem with the Homeostat was that the whole could not come to equilibrium until all its subparts did. Partial successes thus could not be retained. Ashby offers the following analogy:

The example *par excellence* occurs when the burglar, homeostatically trying to earn his daily bread by stealing, faces that particular environment known as the combination lock. This environment has, of course, been selected to be as difficult for him as possible; and its peculiar difficulty lies precisely in the fact that partial successes—getting, say, six letters right out of seven—count for nothing. Thus, there can be no progression toward the solution. Thus, confronted with an environment that does not permit use to be made of partial adaptation, human and Homeostat fail alike.[13]

What, then, is to be made of the fact that the world is full of organisms that are homeostat-like and yet have shown the power to adapt? Ashby suggests that this is possible in cases where the system is not fully joined, or not at all times, and he goes on to state:

"The idea so often implicit in physiological writings, that all will be well if only sufficient cross-connexions are available, is, in this context, quite wrong."[14]

It seems to me that this is also what the concept of enmeshment is about. The cross-connections between the parts and subparts of a family system can be so rich that efforts of any element of that system to find a new solution or to introduce the kind of random searching that is the essence of trial-and-error adaptation cannot succeed.

Consider in this light the predicament of a therapist trying to change a family that is enmeshed. He or she is in the position of the experimenter in the early days of the cathode-ray oscilloscope, a situation Ashby cites in another brilliant illustration of his thesis that too much joining is not good:

Adjusting the first experimental models was a matter of considerable complexity. An attempt to improve the brightness of the spot might make the spot also move off the screen. The attempt to bring it back might alter its rate of sweep and start it oscillating vertically. An attempt to correct this might make its line of sweep leave the horizontal; and so on. This system's variables (brightness of spot, rate of sweep, etc.) were dynamically linked in a rich and complex manner. Attempts to control it through the available parameters were difficult precisely because the variables were richly joined.[15]

What Ashby calls a "too richly cross-joined system"[16] can be treated or changed, he says, when enough communication is blocked so that the parts become temporarily independent of each other. The parts don't have to be actually severed. It is enough if one of the linking elements stands still and shows no change. The parts linked by this unchanging element are then separated by a "wall of constancies." Constancies, Ashby remarks, can "cut a system to pieces."[17] In this way he comes to the position that there are times when an increase in communication would be positively harmful.

This does not mean that the absence of communication is a good thing. Rather, there is a happy medium. If there were not enough communication between parts of an organism, or between it and the environment, it could not survive. For instance, the tongue has to be told to get out of the way when the teeth bite on a piece of meat. The fewer the joins between the reacting parts, the fewer the possible modes of action, but a good level of communication means that a large repertory of behaviors will be available. These benefits, among others, have to be weighed against the disadvantage that the richer the joins, the more difficult it will be to make new adaptations.

For family therapists, this last point is especially interesting. Whole schools of family therapy have been founded on the idea that the more the communication, the better off the family. Actually, much of family therapy consists of efforts to block communication, even when the rationale of "more communication" is ostensibly being followed. Ashby's statement that a system too much connected with itself will not be able to change easily parallels the growing belief of a number of therapists that many families improve merely because the therapist has blocked the usual pathways and forced them to search for new ones. But these ideas are also important for the close backing they give to Minuchin's observations about enmeshed family systems.

His observations that a family is not at its most efficient when its parts and subparts are too closely interlocked, and that a functional family is one in which there are status schisms between generations, age differentiations between children, demarcations between sybsystems enacted by the same persons, and a clear boundary around the nuclear family, seem to fall in with Ashby's general conclusion that a system needs to guard against too much cross-joining or else must be able to create a temporary independence of parts. Most family therapists agree that when a family displays too tightly connected coalition patterns, this is a recipe for symptoms and distress.

Bowen, too, describes a therapeutic gambit that strongly resembles Ashby's recipe for creating "constancies" or "cutting a system to pieces." At times Bowen singles out one family member and insists that he or she take a position on some family issue and maintain that position in spite of opposition by the rest of the family—which usually appears. This is a tactic designed to achieve what Bowen calls "differentiation of self," but he also describes it in a triadic context, saying that if one person in a three-person emotional system can remain detached, tension within that triangle will resolve itself. One assumes that whether this third person is the therapist or a family member, Bowen is still talking about what he calls "detriangling the triangle," forcing one of the elements in a chain of linked triads to remain still and not react.[18]

The Too Poorly Cross-Joined Family

This category, like the particles that physicists believe exist because theoretically they should, may be a figment of the mind. A too tightly connected family system argues for the existence of its opposite, a too loosely connected one. However, an argument can be made that if such a category exists, it is just as far from representing random behavior as that found in the so-called enmeshed family. The phrases used to describe such families suggest some kind of formlessness, some kind of chaos. More unfortunately, the word "disengaged," though well meant, suggests a quality of not caring. Minuchin's example of the difference between an enmeshed and a disengaged family is that in the former the parents get upset if the child skips dessert, and in the latter they may not notice if he does not eat all day. Yet in families with few routines or ceremonies, individuals can still show great caring toward one another.

A further confusion develops because one cannot classify a family on Minuchin's scale without reference to the larger context. A family as loosely structured as the "disengaged" family is said to be will quickly become locked in with social institutions that form a more enclosing kind of enmeshed structure, with agency personnel acting as surrogate parents. The danger of cross-generation joinings, linked by researchers like Haley to pathology in the family, is as applicable to this new format as it would be to a family group.

Thus one can argue that there is no such thing as a totally disengaged family. Usually one finds that families whose members do not become drawn away into jails and hospitals, or get official watchers assigned to them, have a great deal of structure, though not always in a conventional form. It is to the credit of Minuchin and his researchers that they identified the alternate family forms of the very poor: families with a grandmother and mother acting as parents for children of both women; and similar arrangements in which a mother is aided by a parental child. These families run into the same troubles as any other type. That is, symptomatic members appear in families in which a mother and grandmother are subverting each other just as often as in families where mother and father are subverting each other.

Perhaps it would be more useful to think of a continuum of possibilities rather than categories at two ends of a pole. One could never find a family at the far end of such a continuum because it could not survive under either set of conditions.

In addition, terms like "centripetal" and "centrifugal," first used by Helm Stierlin to describe organizing principles of families with adolescents, may be more useful than the terms "enmeshed" and "disengaged."[19] Concrete analogies might also help: bumper cars at a fair versus a roller coaster—each man colliding with others in the space of the rink, as opposed to people stuck tightly together by the force of the ride. I also sometimes think of "rubber band" or "sticky glue" families as opposed to "colliding molecules" families— "fused" families versus "fragmented" families—always with the proviso that these types do not present an either/or, but rather suggest extreme edges against which families might be measured.

In particular, I am partial to the idea that continual, random-seeming connectedness, whether through noise, touching, altercations, or overlapping conversations, can be a way of *being organized.* Lewis Thomas suggests this in a passage on termite behavior in *Lives of a Cell:*

Grouped termites keep touching each other incessantly with their antennae, and this appears to be the central governing mechanism. It is the being touched that counts, rather than the act of touching. Deprived of antennae, any termite can become a group termite if touched frequently enough by others.[20]

By contrast, if termites are isolated from each other, this activity stops and they become quiet and standoffish. If they are in a pair, they will actually abstain from touching each other, as if this poor shadow of the real thing were too painful a reminder. This is not to suggest that human beings are like termites, only to show that in the animal kingdom, patterns of organization may take a number of equally valid forms.

Following this same line of thinking, I would like to take styles of family interaction that seem fragmented and disjointed and show that they are not random but rich in configurations.

Redundancies in the "Disengaged" Family

Assuming for the moment that there really is a continuum from too tightly connected to too loosely connected on which families can be placed, let me take the position that what may look like loosely connected families are not without rigidities of their own. Research on families with schizophrenics has produced evidence to challenge the idea that these families are without structure. One could similarly question whether the so-called disorganized family is without structure. It may have elements as restricted and stereotyped as those of the enmeshed family, and for different reasons be just as resistant to change.

To start with, the model for the "disengaged" family was the multiproblem poor family that came to the attention of social agencies and clinics because it had, supposedly, "broken down." What are the features of this family as described in *Families of the Slums*, still one of the only books to take a systems view of poor families?

One finding was that most multiproblem families are headed by isolated mothers without resources. When there is a kin group that helps out, or a caring boy friend, or a strong grandmother, or an appropriately used parental child, the family may at times work badly, but it works, because the mother is not totally alone. It is when these supporting people are not available that problems get out of hand. As the authors state in *Families of the Slums:*

A prominent feature of disengaged families is the isolation of the mother, who seems unable to contact the external world and draw on extrafamilial sources of support. In the most extreme forms of this profile, one must look beyond the chronicity of incompetence in mothering to a family history usually lacking in anchorage points such as stable work patterns and stable relationships to a male, friends or other social groups. The mother is alone.[21]

Another feature seems to be a hiatus or gulf between the adult world and the sibling world. The parents and other grownups seem to dissociate themselves from responsibility for the children's behavior, unless it is personally upsetting to them or brings on unwelcome community attention. The siblings develop into a collusive subgroup, sometimes protective and supportive of each other, sometimes not, but functioning as a slightly wild pack or tribe, good at outwitting adults' attempts to control them.

When the family is headed by an isolated, overwhelmed mother, these attempts seem to be of a global, all-or-nothing kind. A mother may seem sunk into apathy, ignoring the most incredible amount of noise and confusion on the part of the children. But at some moment she will tolerate the situation no longer and will hit out right and left, often ignoring the major offender, who may be at the other side of the room, to strike a nonoffender who is near at hand.

Minuchin and Montalvo also comment on the skillful confusion tactics a group of children in such a family can use to provoke and annihilate adult authority. Not only parents but therapists are hard put to match wits with these children. There is a revealing example in an interview in *Families of the Slums*. Somebody had taken money from mother. One child accused another child, who after much prodding said that he got the money from a friend; more confusing information was fed in by other children; then the original accuser said that the accused thought the money was his bus fare, and added that he always thinks he can take money because the father used to hide money under the rug, but he is never scolded if he takes it even though the other children are. By this time the mother and therapist are lost. The "game" seems much like the proverbial children's clapping game: "Who took the cookie from the cookie jar?" and seems to end either in disruption and no closure, or else, after much confusion, a particular child, usually the family scapegoat, will be established as the guilty party.

What principle could unite these different observations, leading to a hypothesis that would explain the childrens' collusive mischief?

Minuchin and Montalvo give us a hint in commenting on the anxiety displayed by a group of children when the mother left the room, and their consequent noisy, disruptive behavior with much talk on scary, violent themes. The authors feel that this response represents the uncertainty caused by the disappearance of the one figure that acts as an organizing principle for these children. They describe the interaction in sequence form: The mother leaves, the children become anxious and act up, she then must come back in to reestablish control, they calm down again. A circular causality is operating.

This presentation is linear, since it describes only the way the cycle works for the children. A truly systemic view would point out how all the pieces fit and move together. An illuminating instance comes from a family interview by Harry Aponte. This interview, recorded on videotape, contains clues that suggest how the redundancies of multiproblem families like this one might be contributing to an ecological balance of sorts within the family.

The interview is with a poor black family that fully answers to the description "multiproblem." Everybody—the mother, six grown or nearly grown children, and two grandchildren—is at risk, from breakdown, illness, nerves, violence, accident, or a combination of all these factors. In addition, the family members are noisy, disruptive, and hard to control.

At a certain point Aponte asks the mother, "How do you handle all this?" The mother, who has been apathetic and seemingly unconcerned as the therapist tries to talk with the children, says, "I put on my gorilla suit." The children laugh as they describe just how terrible their mother is when she puts on her gorilla suit.

An incident occurs shortly after this conversation which suggests that a circular causal sequence is at work, one of those redundancies that may have to do with family balance. Mother is still apathetic and looks tired, and the therapist begins to ask about her nerves. At first the children are somewhat quiet, listening. As she begins to admit that she has bad nerves and that she is taking pills, they begin to act up. One boy pokes the baby; another boy tries to restrain the baby from kicking back; the baby starts to yell. The therapist asks the twenty-year-old daughter (the baby's mother) if she can control him; she says no. At this point the mother gets up and smacks her daughter's baby with a rolled-up newspaper, rising out of her lethargy like some sleeping giant bothered by a gnat. She sits the baby down with a bump, and he makes no further trouble. During this sequence the rest of the children jump and shriek with joy, causing their mother to reprimand them, after which they calm down and the mother sits back, more watchful now and definitely in control.

Looked at from one point of view, this is an example of disorganized behavior. The mother is abdicating her responsibilities; the children are badly behaved; and when the mother does try to control them, she overreacts and is only partly effective. But from another point of view, we may be seeing an ameliorative sequence. Let us assume, as in this case, that one is dealing with a family with an isolated, overwhelmed mother who gets into periodic depressions as a form of recuperation from stress. Let us assume also that the children become correspondingly anxious. A powerful antidote to both the depression and the anxiety would be disruptive behaviors by the children. The cycle goes thus: The mother's depression carried past a certain point triggers off collusive mischief in the children; once this mischief rises to a certain level, it will impel the mother to reassert her power; seeing the mother taking an active position relieves the children, and as she takes over they quiet down. Peace will prevail until the mother once more sinks too far into depression or acts apathetic, and the whole sequence will start again.[22]

This is a very global, primitive cycle, and it appears to be common in such families. It is also fairly limited in its usefulness, as all family members pay a price for learning the behaviors it requires. For one thing, these behaviors automatically get them into trouble in the outer world. Outside the home—in the classroom, for instance—one frequently finds the following scenario: Teacher writes words on the board for the children to copy down, then sits quietly at her desk marking papers. For a child who comes from a home where quietness by the adult in charge is a danger signal, this creates anxiety. The child may start making faces at another child or throw something or whisper an insult. There are children who become experts at instigating fellow children at such a moment, and other children who get caught and wind up being sent to the principal.

This is only one possible way to interpret the disorderly behavior of children in multiproblem families. It represents a sequence that contributes to the stability of the home, even though it is at the expense of the individuals who get caught in this machinery. We shall see in later chapters other circular causal cycles, different but equally difficult to see, which seem to work collaboratively to keep the balance (or *are* the balance) in "enmeshed" families.

The bipolar model we have been discussing has some serious drawbacks, however, in that it implies a too-simple dichotomy between random and rigid. Aponte's use of "underorganized" as a substitute for "disengaged" is an attempt to deal with this problem. However, underorganized still suggests an either/or continuum, as if we were simply talking about families having too much or too little structure or organization.

I am also dissatisfied with the continuum concept itself. It does not cover enough variables, nor is it rich or interesting enough. In the next chapter we will consider different, more complex models, both grid and process formats. In particular, we will address the growing tendency to think of family worlds on the total system level, calling upon a new and important concept: the "family paradigm."

Chapter 5

The Concept of Family Paradigms

The Metaphysics of Pattern

Using this apt phrase, psychologist Paul Dell has recently called attention to a profound difference between the transactional model of research on families of schizophrenics and the etiological one. Studies that try to establish an etiology different from the traditional individually oriented one have assumed a causal link between family structure and psychotic behavior. But to say that a particular condition is contingent on a given type of family organization, or to think that there is a direct connection, is to make the mistake of linear thinking.

The transactional view, according to Dell, is not concerned with etiology but amounts to a redefinition of what schizophrenia is. Transactional researchers take the position that behaviors labeled schizophrenic are part and parcel of the pattern of family relationships in which the behaviors are embedded, and that neither family nor afflicted individual can be singled out as the "location" of the disorder. As Dell says,

The behaviors of family members which together constitute the various aspects of the pattern are not linearly causal of one another but are co-evolutionary. Bateson (1960) and Wynne and Singer (1965a) speak not of causation but of how the family as a whole fits together. Thus, etiological constructions of the family theory of schizophrenia (e.g., Fromm-Reichmann, Lidz) as embodied in most research to date, neither grasp nor adequately test the transactional position.[1]

Dell places David Reiss in the transactional group. In his work Reiss is clear about the need to see a family-wide or systemic pattern, a "family paradigm," as an emergent property of family experience. It is not reducible to the perceptions or reactions of any individual member of the families. According to Reiss, studies that link family structure too directly to disorders of individuals, exemplified in such terms as "schizophrenic families" and "multiproblem families," violate that concept.

Building on the experiments of Wynne and Singer, among other influences, Reiss has tried to research a "metaphysics of pattern" of his own. In an earlier phase of his work he did indeed attempt to correlate family interaction styles with disturbances that might be expected to emerge in individuals in such families. In later thinking he seems to be broadening his concern with pattern to include a much richer application of key variables that account not just for families with symptomatic members but for the whole rich variety of families. In addition, he is beginning to suggest that such disturbances may have to do with the inability of the family paradigm, for whatever reasons, to process information when the outer (or inner) field changes too radically. At this point, the paradigm may break down, with the consequent possibility of extinction of the family or, in a more positive direction, paradigmatic change, which gives the family a new lease on life.

Let us start with Reiss's more clinically oriented work. In a research paper linking family interaction styles with individual thinking processes, he describes a problem-solving experiment that drew on three populations: eight families with offspring diagnosed "schizophrenic"; eight families whose members had "character disorders" (defined by Reiss more concretely as "severe solitary delinquencies"); and eight with offspring who had no known disorder.[2] The parents, the symptomatic child, and one sibling were included.

The problem design required a subject to sort a group of fifteen cards, each containing a patterned sequence of letters or nonsense syllables (PVK, PMVK, PMSMSVK). The experiment itself consisted of three parts: first, an individual task in which each person, sitting in a separate booth, was asked to sort the group of cards by himself; then a family task, with each family member getting the same series of cards to put in order; and a final individual card-sorting task. During the family task each member would start with two cards and when these were sorted would press a "finish" button and get another card, until all fifteen were sorted. Family members could communicate with each other by earphone, and were encouraged to share ideas and information. Whether to trade ideas or go it alone, to adopt a uniform strategy or to use different ones, to wait for enough cards to suggest an overall pattern or to settle for a sequence choice based on the first few, were all options a family or its individual members could choose, depending on family communication rules. The experiment was set up so that it was easier to arrive at a correct hypothesis for sorting the cards after they were all, or mostly all, in, but a rule for ordering them could be guessed at, and trial-and-error attempts were possible because later cards could verify that a given sorting arrangement was in fact correct.

This experiment suggested the existence of family mini-universes which were very different from each other, and which correlated closely to the clinical groupings. Reiss called these categories "consensus-sensitive," "interpersonal distance-sensitive," and "environment-sensitive," terms corresponding to the "schizophrenic" families, the "delinquent" families, and the "normal" families. The variables that differentiated these families were selected out by the test and were congruent with earlier family research findings, especially those of Wynne. Thus the experiment is not merely interesting in itself but represents a theory-building effort that goes back several decades.

The three major characteristics that seemed to mark off the groups of families were: first, family members' ability to use cues or suggestions from each other; second, their ability to use cues from the laboratory; and third, their ability to reach closure. The puzzle was constructed so that it could be solved most effectively when sufficient information was obtained and when this information was shared. It was important for all family members to coordinate their separate efforts to build useful hypotheses for sorting the cards, and to offer new suggestions or corrections. It was also necessary to pay attention to information from the environment, in the form of the cards that were continually being fed in. Clearly the experiment tested two sets of connections: connections between family members and connections between family members and the outer world.

The three types of families responded very differently to the tests, and the families with clinical problems did most poorly. Reiss found that families with schizophrenic members were very clued in to each other but very walled off from everything else. Their internal sensitivity did not help them with the test but hindered them. In Reiss's words, "In this kind of family, there is a joint perception that the analysis and solution of the problem are simply a means to maintain a close and uninterrupted agreement at all times."[3]

Reiss's explanation for the "consensus-sensitive" family's need always to be close and in agreement was that they experienced the environment as threatening and dangerous. The testing situation was a threat to be warded off; thus people in these families would reach a solution very quickly, before much information had become available, and hang on to this solution even when later facts or a better solution arrived at by another family member contradicted it. Consequently they would most often fail to find an adequate solution to the problem, not because of insufficient family communication but because of premature closure. They would rather be wrong than fight.

This syndrome picks out the family characteristics that Wynne called "pseudomutuality" and the "rubber fence." It also confirms the quality of "enmeshment" that Minuchin described and the tendency toward emotional fusion and undifferentiation that Bowen found. These researchers, being clinicians, tended to limit their descriptive models to families with problems. Reiss goes in a much-needed normalizing direction by extending his categories to include families that do not necessarily present problematic members. As a normative cultural variant of the consensus-sensitive family, for instance, he cites studies of southern Italian clans, with their code of family solidarity and their perception of the outside world as menacing and unpredictable.

Diametrically opposed to the families with schizophrenic members were the families with members who had "severe solitary delinquencies." These families attended very well to cues from the external environment but did not attend to cues from each other. During the tests family members behaved as though it would be a mistake to accept opinions or hypotheses from their relatives. There seemed to be an overpowering need to show that one could be independent, could master the environment on one's own. Taking a more general view, Reiss says that these individuals seemed to share "a perception that the environment was split into as many pieces as there were family members; each member had access to his own piece and therefore attended to environmental cues from his piece only."[4]

These families, the "interpersonal distance-sensitive" families, seemed to experience the laboratory and the externally given problem as a way to demonstrate individual mastery. Since the boundary between the world and members of the interpersonal distance-sensitive family is not governed by the principle of the protective stockade, their problem-solving skills tend to be better than those of the consensus-sensitive families. They have a better appreciation of "out-there reality," as opposed to the distortions called for by the family whose main idea is to remain close. But their stance as loners cripples them in another direction. They do not take well to the collective sharing of hypotheses, and may do poorly because an individual will persist in trying to solve the problem on his own and so prolong the test time, as well as being limited to his own resources.

Normative examples of the interpersonal distance-sensitive family are not well reported on. Reiss cites Minuchin's "disengaged" family as an example from a population with delinquent children; however, he singles out characteristics that are not necessarily pathogenic, notably the sense of isolation and distance people sometimes seem to experience in these families. He also comes up with an example of a middle-class interpersonal distance-sensitive family (the Littletons), described in sociologists Robert Hess and Herbert Handel's *Family Worlds,* who had a disconnected, individualistic style of interaction and tolerated a high degree of conflict and dissonance.[5]

The third category, the "environment-sensitive" family, represents the relatively problem-free group. People in these families hold both the values that Reiss emphasized in an optimal balance, indicating an ability to use cues from other family members and at the same time to accept and incorporate cues from the environment. Members of these families can make hypotheses individually or jointly, can delay closure until enough alternatives are explored to validate the conclusion finally arrived at, and can process and share new information. Unlike the consensus-sensitive family, they are not constrained by a need for cohesion at all costs, nor are they hampered by a philosophy of go-it-alone. This group has a surrounding membrane which is tight enough to provide support but not so impermeable as to block out fresh data. Flexibility about both degree of internal connectedness and connection with the outside world seems to be the distinguishing mark of the family that does best, at least on the problem-solving tasks in Reiss's study.

It seems odd to look for cultural models for families in this category, which is already normal by definition of not having come to community attention, but Reiss cites studies of eastern European *shtetl* culture as affording a world view that embraces a strong sense of family ties but allows for exploration and mastery of the environment as well.

Reiss has truly attempted a "metaphysics of pattern" in this description of family systems, even though this summary of his typology is static and has emphasized only three dimensions: internal connectedness, external connectedness, and closure. We shall see in a discussion of his later thinking on family systems that he breaks out of this model to one which includes variables that govern the ways in which a family changes paradigms. In the meantime let us look at the work of another researcher, Eleanor Wertheim, who has added the change variable in her own way.

A Grid Model for Family Topology

Wertheim's variables have to do with a process taxonomy—the way a system changes or remains the same over a period of time. In her article "Family Unit Therapy and the Science and Typology of Family Systems," Wertheim argues that one must take into account the change mechanisms of a family as well as its structural elements.[6] If a family is a rule-bound, change-resistant entity, two dimensions are important to check. One is the family's morphostatic (steady-state or homeostatic) tendencies, the other its morphogenetic (rule-changing) capacities. In the first dimension Wertheim distinguishes between Consensual Morphostasis (Mc), representing a balance between individual goals and family goals, and Forced Morphostasis (Mf), found in a family in which individuals are bound by rigid but covert rules that operate in the interest of the family. We might think of participatory democracy versus a more totalitarian form of rule, although the totalitarian society is different in that the rules are anything but covert.

The second dimension, the rules for changing the rules, incorporates what we have spoken of as second order change. If a family is high in Consensual Morphostasis, Wertheim thinks this automatically means that its rules can be changed in a flexible manner to meet changed circumstances, that morphogenic changes are built

Table 5.1

Classification of Family Systems and Their Predicted Response to Family Therapy (F.T.)

Induced Morphogenesis (I.M.)	Consensual Morphostasis (Mc)	Forced Morphostasis (Mf)	Type	Integration of System	Predicted Response to F.T.		
					Accessibility	Duration	Outcome
High	High	Low	Open	1 Integrated	—	—	—
		High		2 Fairly Integrated	Accessible	Short-Term	Favorable
	Low	Low	Partly Open (Extra-systemically)	3 Unintegrated	Accessible	Long-Term	Variable
		High		4 Pseudo-Integrated	Accessible	Short/Long-Term	Favorable
Low	High	Low	Partly Open (Intra-systemically)	5 Integrated	—	—	—
		High		6 Fairly Integrated	Resistant	Short/Long-Term	Favorable
	Low	Low	Closed	7 Disintegrated	Unmotivated	Failure	Unfavorable
		High		8 Pseudointegrated	Resistant	Long-Term	Variable

Source: Wertheim, E., "Family Unit Therapy and the Science and Typology of Family Systems," *Family Process* 12 (1973), 343–376.

into its regulatory capacities. Again, as in a democracy, there is machinery for a new vote to be taken and a new party with a potentially better program to be elected. One can assume that a family has this capacity if it appears to be flexible or makes morphogenic changes easily, like a horse that takes naturally to jumps.

If a family cannot find the means to alter its rules when change is called for, then we would look for a capacity to accept change from the outside, usually from agents of the system the next level up, meaning the wider community. Wertheim terms this property Induced Morphostasis (IM). Families that can use community resources, friends, ministers, doctors, therapists, or elders from their own kin groups to help them negotiate a morphogenic change are in this category.

Wertheim adds to her change variables a group of structural variables that have to do with boundaries, both internal and external. Thus she includes systems that are both internally and externally open; systems that are both internally and externally closed; partly closed systems that are open only internally; and partly open systems that are open only externally. Mixing the change dimensions with these structural dimensions, she develops eight family types from which she then derives eight clinical profiles, as in Table 5.1.

The resulting grid consists of two structures that operate with optimal flexibility, produce few problems, and are called "integrated"; two that are associated with mild neurotic problems and are called "fairly integrated"; two that are called "pseudointegrated," following Wynne's concept of pseudomutuality, and are associated with either acute or chronic psychotic disorders; and two that are, respectively, "unintegrated" (families producing social disorders) and "disintegrated" (families that can hardly be said to be families at all).

Wertheim compares her grid with Reiss's scheme and finds them compatible, with modifications. The environment-sensitive family she identifies with her "open-integrated" family; the consensus-sensitive family with her "closed pseudointegrated" type; the interpersonal distance-sensitive family with her "externally open-unintegrated" type.

A way to synthesize these categories is represented in Table 5.2, which uses Reiss's three categories for family structure but organizes them on the basis of degree and type of connectedness. The environment-sensitive families are both externally and internally well connected. The interpersonal distance-sensitive families are well connected externally but poorly connected internally. The consensus-sensitive families are well connected internally but poorly connected externally.

Within each type, then, there would be two versions, which would be differentiated according to Wertheim's mix of cybernetic elements: homeostatic (morphostatic) versus rule-change (morphogenetic) variables. The consensus-sensitive families would be high on Forced Homeostasis, being rigidly rule-bound, and, of course, low on Consensual Homeostasis. There would, however, be a difference between the consensus-sensitive family which was high on induced rule-change and the "rubber fence" family which rejected outside attempts at change. The latter would be the most resistant family, most likely to produce psychotic manifestations and least in touch with "reality."

For instance, families from religious sects that emphasize values or beliefs not shared with the surrounding society sometimes also

Table 5.2
Typology of Family Structure

		Forced Homeostasis	Consensual Homeostasis	Induced Morphogenesis
Environment-Sensitive Family	A	High	High	Low
(externally and internally well connected)	B	Low	High	Low
Interpersonal Distance-Sensitive Family	A	High	Low	Low
(externally well connected; internally poorly connected)	B	Low	Low	Low
Consensus-Sensitive Family	A	High	Low	High
(externally poorly connected; internally well connected)	B	Low	Low	High

↑ Structural Variables ↓

← Process Variables →

fall into this category. Groups can hold belief systems which, if held by an individual, might proclaim him psychotic: the ending of the world on a given date, or communication with beings from other planets. People in such groups are not necessarily thought of as crazy since they share their beliefs with others. But one can see that consensus about basic beliefs would be central to a group's ability to hold onto members and continue to exist. One could even say that the *more* unprovable or implausible a belief system was, compared to the beliefs of the outer society, the more effective it would be in protecting and walling off the group. There is a usefulness, a validity, to this kind of shared illusion that may make it easier to understand the reasons behind consensus-sensitive behavior in families with psychotic members.

The interpersonal distance-sensitive family would be low on either type of homeostasis, since it is poorly connected and does not possess a high degree of cohesiveness. But the family in this category with a capacity for induced rule-change would, by definition, be more amenable to help from the outside than one without this capacity. As Wertheim points out, the "disintegrated" family type may be a nonviable form and may not be salvageable. It is hard to come up with an interpersonal distance family in a pure form; perhaps none exists, but only strange amalgams. One such amalgam, a family with many "colliding molecules" characteristics and yet with some "sticky glue" as well, is the poor black family described earlier, in Chapter 4. In the videotapes of this family there is one sequence that seems to illustrate the interpersonal distance-sensitive principle of "every man's an island" (to misquote John Donne).

The three daughters aged twenty, nineteen, and seventeen, were describing their feelings of fear and insecurity at night after their mother had gone out to work. Instead of taking turns watching the apartment, so that the rest could sleep while one stayed up, all three stayed up together. It was as if this were not a shared situation but three personal and private situations that had nothing to do with each other. The mother, described by the children as not afraid of anything, was felt to have all the power, and when she was gone the daughters felt extremely vulnerable. The older boys displayed a different version of this unconnected go-it-alone stance. When the therapist asked, "Can't the boys take care of you?" the girls complained that the boys (including a twenty-four-year-old who was part in, part out of the house) didn't seem to worry or care. If the girls tried to wake them up at night, they would refuse to take the girls' fears seriously and go back to sleep.

The very permeable boundary around this family was graphically illustrated by the fact that people could easily get in and threaten their safety. They lived in a neighborhood of houses poorly locked, streets badly policed, and territories constantly threatened, but the situation had a correlate in the fragility of the family boundary and the structural deficits that kept it fragile. The children had not learned how to form protective groups, plan strategies, organize hierarchically.

To move on to the last category, the environment-sensitive family would be high on consensual Homeostasis and low on Forced Homeostasis, and, like those in the other categories, would differ only in the degree to which outside agents would be accepted as reinforcers for internal rule-change. Wertheim suggests that the family that accepts outside agents is more functional than the other one in this category, implying a value system in favor of therapy. It is equally possible that the version of the environment-sensitive family that rejects induced rule-change is better off than the other type. Spontaneous shifts may be preferable to induced shifts, as spontaneous labor, when possible, is preferable to induced labor.

Wertheim uses her scheme to predict types of problems likely to be found in each of her categories, and she has psychiatric profiles for all eight. The reduced set of categories represented by Table 5.2 merely distinguishes between the three possible structures described by Reiss, divided into two subversions of each, using Wertheim's change variables. It is probably too early to claim clinical profiles for these groupings; it is enough merely to have a grid from which to start researching such profiles in more detail.

Process Models for Family Organization

The problem with grids is that they are a self-contained and essentially static model for how families work. There is never any hint of how a family gets from one box of the grid to another, or even whether this is possible. If it is, then is there an order to the way families change? Are there levels of organization through which families, if they do change, must pass through, or can they move anywhere on the board?

These questions are at least addressed by Beavers's "cross-sectional process model."[7] Beavers's model has three levels of organization, from families at the bottom of the scale, extremely chaotic and confused, with poor boundaries and no hierarchy, to a second level, which is extremely authoritarian, to a top level that is flexible and adaptive, neither too loose nor too strict.

Beavers draws his model in the form of a sidewise A, with the end of each bottom leg representing, respectively, "centripetal" families on the one hand, and "centrifugal" on the other (see Figure 5.1). The centrifugal group is said to produce sociopathic behaviors while the centripetal group produces psychotic disturbances. Confused communication, unclear boundaries, and avoidance of power issues characterizes both these poorly functioning groups. In the mid-section of the A, where the two styles begin to meet, there are behavior disorders on the centrifugal side and neurotic behaviors on the other. However, the model allows for a "continuum of competence," and the midrange also begins to show evidence of hierarchy, even though the structure is dictatorial. At the top of the A, the structure presumably allows for even better functioning by family members.

This model implies a passage from less to more workable structures. Beavers argues that it is only a step from chaotic to authoritarian forms, and that a flip from one state to another is common and may also be therapeutically useful. Haley is close to Beavers here when he advocates in his recent book, *Leaving Home,* a therapeutic approach based on getting the parents of "crazy young people" to behave like virtual tyrants.[8]

Another process model, one slanted more toward normal families, is Kantor and Lehr's typology of open, closed, and random structures.[9] The model is different from Beavers's because it does not conceive of dysfunctional families as belonging to different groups or levels but as flawed variations of normal types. Kantor and Lehr assume that families can be categorized according to a choice of different homeostatic ideals, or ways to approach equilibrium and

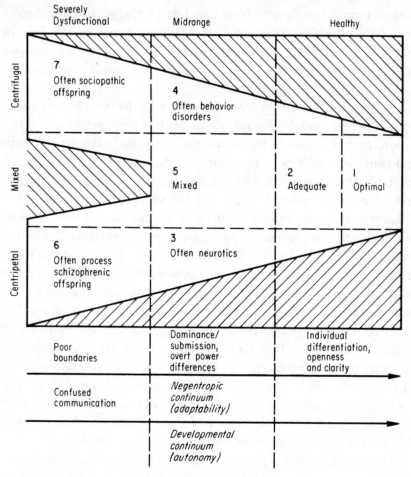

Figure 5.1
Beavers's Cross-Sectional Process Model

SOURCE: R. Beavers, *Psychotherapy and Growth*. New York: Brunner/Mazel, 1977, p. 96. (This figure has been modified by Beavers; it will appear in other, as yet unpublished, articles.)

change. The family structure derives from the type of homeostatic arrangement adopted and is not an invariant piece of architecture. The flawed forms also derive from that ideal, and differ accordingly.

Kantor and Lehr's three family types resemble the familiar political categories of authoritarian, anarchistic, and democratic regimes. The closed family is highly structured, hierarchical, and rule-governed; the individual is subordinate to the group. In its flawed version it becomes a rigid, hollow shell, and if a runaway develops, this shell may crack as individuals become rebellious or violent, sometimes toward others, sometimes turning feelings inward. The anarchistic or random family sets a high value on personal individuation. "Do your own thing" is the motto, and there are few rules and little attention to boundaries. In the flawed version this family becomes totally chaotic; turbulence, caprice, and contradiction take over. Still, struggles of individual members to reestablish some kind of control may end in a shift to an authoritarian, closed system, or alternatively, fragmentation and dispersal will occur, or outside authorities will move in to take over. The democratic or open system, which seems a golden mean between the two other styles, balances order with flexibility and the rights of the individual with those of the group. In its flawed version this family type tends toward schism and divorce. Its most characteristic stress comes from the bind that results from taking features from both closed and random systems which, if not compatible, can lead to strain and impasse. Kantor and Lehr do not claim that these types exist in a pure form, but they do believe that families tend to cluster around these three different categories.

What is developing more and more is a process typology that, because it emphasizes movement and change, does not depend on fixed categories and does not assign negative characteristics to families as functional/dysfunctional typologies and typologies attached to symptoms of individual family members do.

Of particular interest in this respect is Reiss's later thinking about family paradigms, which is reflected in "The Working Family: A Researcher's View of Health in the Household."[10] First, Reiss is continuing to examine family worlds in a truly systemic sense. In his research he is continuing to use such variables as the shared ability of family members to perceive complex configurations when faced with strange data; the ability to coordinate responses when trying to make sense of the material presented; and the ability to delay closure until enough information has been received and passed around to guarantee the best possible response. Of course his experiments test family reactions to an unfamiliar environment, so it could be argued that this does not meet the family paradigm on its own home ground, when it might look very different. But Reiss obviously assumes that the strength of such a paradigm is precisely to help family members cope with the different and the strange.

Second, he is moving away from categorizing families on a scale from functional to dysfunctional, preferring to see dysfunction in relation to each family's idiosyncratic paradigm rather than to judge it in the light of preconceived ideas of health and illness.

Third, and perhaps most important, is Reiss's scrutiny of what happens when a paradigm breaks down. He does not believe that this is *ipso facto* a bad thing, although he is alert to destructive consequences. A central issue for him is how family disorder and breakdown may create the opportunity for its own self-healing potential. As he says,

> More speculatively I propose (recognizing both theology and Pollyanna in this proposal) that family crisis fills a positive function in the life of every family. Though filled with risk, it ultimately opens the family to new experience, altering their sense of themselves and the outside world and thereby transforming a paradigm which may have guided them for years or even generations.[11]

This amounts to taking an evolutionary position on paradigm change.

My own evolutionary position suggests a somewhat fantastic model that I call Spiral Platters of Family Organization. I owe the idea for this to a discussion with Paul Dell in Atlanta in 1978. It was he who first explained to me the thinking leading to an evolutionary rather than a homeostatic model, thereby seriously influencing the evolution of my own thinking.

Spiral Platters of Family Organization

For a long time the idea of a typology of families ranging from too richly joined to too poorly joined, in Ashby's sense, has been an intriguing one. We may speculate that a family could not exist at either extreme of such a range. If it were too tightly interlocked, it would not allow for change; if it were too fragmented, it would be in danger of dispersal. Most families are found toward the middle of the range, and few are pure examples of either category. All families must have some structure, no matter how primitive, and all families must be able to experiment with change.

The best measure of a family that seems to be working well, whatever its basic category, is whether it can go toward either pole, depending on what is useful. The "enmeshed" structure that is mandatory during Thanksgiving dinner may be totally inappropriate the day after, when the teenage son asks if he can eat supper at a friend's house. Life stages are important considerations, as are stages of the career of an individual. Family therapist Carl Whitaker has spoken of the "rotating scapegoat" in describing how each child in a family, on reaching adolescence, will take turns being the family problem. He suggests that as long as people take turns and one person doesn't get stuck in this role, it is not necessarily a bad thing but merely indicates that the only way this family can let go of its children is for the children to become temporarily impossible. An example related to individual careers would be for a wife whose husband is taking his law exams or medical internship to cope with her loneliness and depression by having migraines, rather than openly express her frustrations in a manner that could endanger the young marriage.

But the main problem with continuums or grids is that they give no clue to why a family or person undergoes a sudden change. It often happens that a family or group at the very fragmented end of our supposed continuum produces individuals who will suddenly snap into an extremely "enmeshed" format, characterized by shared fantasies, paranoid reactions, and delusions of grandeur. One has only to think of the strange leap taken by the German nation (or a subgroup within it) after the economic and social collapse of the Weimar Republic into the world's largest "folie à société," the Third Reich. One is reminded, too, of the present-day children from apparently permissive homes who become reborn as "children of the cults." Another example, perhaps somewhat different, is the tendency of boys from extremely fragmented poor families to form highly authoritarian and structured street gangs.

Cases such as these show clearly that what most typologies lacked was any portrayal of movement. Beavers's process model at least implied a passage toward more (or less) evolved structures, and made a place for the possibility of change. Dell had been arguing for some time for an evolutionary model in describing family systems, and Reiss's recent paper forcefully backed this concept.

These different ideas suggested a series of platters in a spiraling cascade. Families could be seen in terms of groups with contrasting or mixed characteristics, each group clustering at a different level of being "evolved" (see Figure 5.2). It could be argued that the enmeshed/disengaged (or centripetal/centrifugal) group would be at the low end of a set of levels ranged according to adaptiveness. Families representing an extreme of either category would fall off and become extinct, or the individuals would tend to fail or die. Alternatively, as we have noted, a person from a centrifugal family might flip suddenly to the authoritarian side of the next level up. Going in the opposite direction, a family on the bohemian side might produce individuals whose families showed up in the level just below, as fused or enmeshed. In addition, on each level, there is a possibility of moving from one style to another; some families oscillate between centripetal and centrifugal according to circumstance and need, and some portray a mix, with one grouping in the family very rigid, the other very loose. The variations are endless.

The reader will see that an intriguing concept is embedded in this model, the idea of discontinuous change. Development can, of course, consist of a move from one side to another on the same level. But to go from one platter to another involves a reorganization so total as to represent a discontinuity.

Another important concept is implied by the spiral. Movement is never really circular, since even the most static cycles or dances in families never come back to line one. The word "spiral" suggests movement that is open-ended. Even if a family is caught in a very narrow range on the centripetal edge, there may be either movement toward a mixed state on the same platter, or a leap to a radically new and different type of organization on another platter, in a sort of double helix.

Unfortunately, this figure has an intrinsic drawback. It suggests a set of stairs to Heaven, paralleling the many other attempts to show that nature follows an ineluctable path toward ever-higher forms. In psychotherapy, one finds the same idea in theories that emphasize journeys of the soul toward final goals such as autonomy or self-actualization. It would be too bad to create a typology of families based on this same model of infinite progress.

Rather, I would like to see my platters linked together in a cosmic

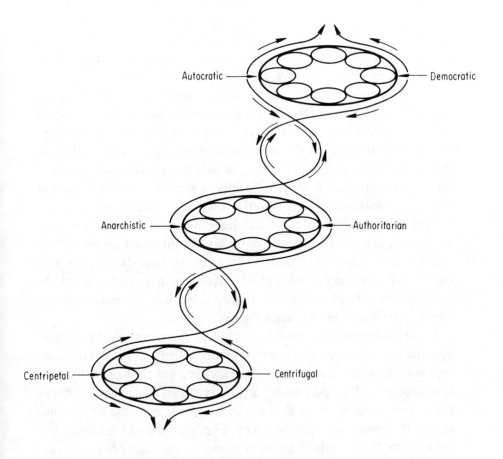

Figure 5.2
Spiral Platters of Family Organization

ring, with families or persons located on the "highest" platters able to skip to positions on the "lowest" platters—even temporarily—on the supposition that too much perfection stultifies and that one must sometimes go back to the original chaos that the Greeks believed existed before the world began. There is something hopeful about the pessimistic ideas of the Swiss physicist Roland Fivaz, who agrees with recent theories suggesting that living systems—at the price of using up energy and producing wastes—tend to reorganize at ever more sophisticated levels of complexity, toward more and more negentropy, in fact.[12] But he offers the happy thought that the higher the level of complexity achieved, the larger the amount of entropy (noise, disorder, pollution) it will give off. Past a certain point, the evolution of a living system (or eco-system) may be limited, because it will be swallowed up in its own garbage. Then the whole process will have a chance to start afresh.

A final proviso is that when making any sort of typology we violate the richness of combinations offered in nature. These designs are artifacts like Plato's Ideal Forms, which are more useful in imagination than in reality. It is impossible to prove that a family falls into this or that category, even if we agree that these categories exist, and the chances are that any given family will be fluctuating from one category to another, or have found its own unique combination.

This disclaimer offered, we will lean the other way and say that, at the very least, these designs build on and integrate a queer lurching research, conducted mostly by nonscientists during the past quarter of a century. One sighs wistfully at the crudeness of the constructions, hoping that the hypotheses they are based on will one day be subjected to more rigorous tests.

In particular we must guard against making categories to describe optimal organization. The "environment-sensitive" family is a concept which, since it assumes normalcy, implies that once a family is so designated it "possesses" a quality called normality. This is a grave error, and we have Bateson to thank for continually reminding us to beware of such mistakes. The attributes of a family will differ according to which point in time (on the family life cycle, for instance) or space (the particular arena or situation) one views it. Whether there are visible problems or no visible problems in a family may merely reflect where the family *currently* is on the combinatory axis of our grid or in the leaping spirals of our dance.

Having satisfied the need for some scheme of placing families, we can now begin to examine the ideas of researchers interested in one type of family: the family which we have called "consensus-sensitive," "centripetal," or "enmeshed." The great amount of research on this category reflects not just interest but availability of such families for study, since they are a clinically captive population. The next chapters will emphasize close analysis of the structures and sequences in these families, and will try to link formal aspects of family organization to symptoms and distress.

Chapter 6

The Pathological Triad

From Communication to Structure

In 1960 John Weakland, one of the original Bateson group researchers, proposed a formal version of the double bind hypothesis involving three-party interaction. This was a major shift and heralded a growing interest in family structure rather than communication as a matrix for symptomatology. In his article "The Double Bind Hypothesis of Schizophrenia and Three-Party Interaction," Weakland observed that according to the original double bind theory, the recipient of the double bind was said to be getting obscurely conflicting messages on different levels of communication on which he was not allowed to comment, nor could he leave the field.[1] Weakland then pointed out that this person might be getting obscurely conflicting messages from at least *two* people, on which he was not allowed to comment, nor could he leave the field. This would be the case with a young schizophrenic and his parents. Weakland says:

Clearly, parents can, on a given matter, give conflicting messages to a child. Clearly, it is important for the child, who is in an overall or collective sense *more* dependent on both parents than on one, to deal with the conflicting behavioral influences resulting by dealing with the inconsistency of these messages. But, equally clearly, one or both parents may also be giving messages that conceal, deny, or inhibit exploration of the inconsistency. . . .[2]

This track allowed Weakland to link the double bind theory with other branches of research on schizophrenic communication, mainly that of Wynne and Singer, which focused on the denial, ambiguity, disqualification, and inconsistency of messages given out by all members of a family with a schizophrenic.[3] He also cites Lidz's description of "marital skew," in which two parents put out the myth of total harmony and agreement, in spite of masked indications to the contrary.[4] Weakland also advanced the thesis that the three-party version of the double bind can be generalized to social groups other than the family. As evidence, Weakland mentions an important study, to be examined in detail later: *The Mental Hospital,* published in 1954 by the psychiatrist Alfred Stanton and the sociologist Morris Schwartz.[5] In this book, the authors found that agitation in a patient on a ward was associated with conflicting attitudes and directives about his or her behavior from two authorities who at the same time denied their disagreement and defined their overall position as one of benevolence. Weakland quotes the authors in describing the position of the patient: "The two most immediately important persons in his life were, so to speak, pulling him in opposite directions." This, of course, could apply equally well to a child whose parents were in covert disagreement about him.

Haley, too, was pulling out of the intense focus on the dyad which was such a cornerstone of the double bind hypothesis. He began to look closely at triads, or, as he began to call them (following current research on decision making in small groups), "coalitions." Haley observed that in families with a symptomatic member, the triad that surfaced most frequently was a coalition between two people, usually of different generations, at the expense of a third. Simple alliances not involving a third party were rare or did not persist. Haley noted that one might find a mother speaking for a child in a way that discredited the father, or the parents might fight with each other and then turn on the child and accuse him of causing their difficulties. Worse yet, if such a coalition were to be labeled or made overt, it would be denied or disqualified.[6]

In a later essay that describes the evolution of researchers' ideas during the life of Bateson's communication project, Haley states that in the beginning, schizophrenia was described as a reaction to a learning context in which levels of communication were habitually confused.[7] The type of message or repetitive interchange that embodied this confusion was called a double bind. As a result of exposure to such a context, a person would tend to qualify his messages with an indication that he was saying or doing something else, and then add a further qualification which contradicted that one. Thus, as Haley notes, schizophrenic behavior could be seen as a disorder of levels of communication.

After Haley began to study coalition behavior in families with schizophrenics, he changed his position and began to suggest that problems arose not only from a confusion of levels of communication, but from a confusion between levels *of a relationship system.* In an important 1967 paper, "Toward a Theory of Pathological Systems," Haley takes the position that when warring factions exist in a family or kin network, a family member may find himself in the predicament of being punished for choosing sides (since whomever he did not side with might exact a penalty) and at the same time being punished for not choosing sides.[8] Thus in such a case it might be necessary for a person to disqualify *all* his communications.

This idea, like Weakland's, made the irrational behavior of individuals the consequence of the social structures they inhabited, not simply a consequence of confused or contradictory messages. This shift brought family therapy to a new place. Family theory could no longer be dismissed as some kind of linguistic metapsychology but could be fairly placed with other contemporary behavioral research. In this and other chapters we will link up some of this other research as it seems relevant. Here we will look specifically at research on triangles in social groups: the work of Theodore Caplow on coalitions, James Davis's "cross-pressure hypothesis," Kenneth Boulding's "avoidance-avoidance conflict," and the like. In addition we will take up studies of triads in kinship networks and variants of conflictual triads in other cultures. But let us begin by examining

Haley's description of pathogenic triangles and the part they play in maintaining family balance.

The Perverse Triangle

In "Toward a Theory of Pathological Systems," Haley comments on a triadic structure that he believes will always cause distress in a social system.[9] He calls this the "perverse triangle," or cross-generation coalition, and observes that it seems to coincide with undesirable manifestations such as violence, symptomatic behavior, or dissolution of the system. The characteristics of this triangle are:

1. It must contain two persons from the same level in a status hierarchy and one person from a different level. In the family, this would mean two members from the same generation and one from another generation.

2. It must involve a coalition of two who are on different levels against the left-out one. A distinction must be made between an alliance, which can be based on common interests and not involve a third party, and a coalition, in which two people join together against or to the exclusion of a third.

3. The coalition against the third person must be kept hidden. That is, the behavior that indicates that such a coalition exists will be denied at the metacommunicative level. In sum, Haley says that the perverse triangle is one in which the separation between the generations is breached in a covert way.

Generalizing from the family to other social systems, Haley observes that in organizations, too, there is likely to be trouble when a superior secretly joins with a subordinate against a peer. The manager of a company may not play favorites with his subordinates and expect to be an effective manager. Similarly, a parent-child coalition not only undermines the authority of the other parent but makes the authority of the favoring parent dependent on support from the child. The inability of parents of an emotionally disturbed child to act together to enforce discipline is a reflection of their inability to maintain the generation line.

Theodore Caplow, in his book on coalition research, *Two Against One,* discusses a similar type of triad which occurs in hierarchical organizations.[10] The "improper coalition," as he calls it, is defined as any three-person coalition that increases the power of one superior while undermining the legitimate authority of another. An example is a triad in which A is as strong as B and C combined, and B and C are of equal strength. The organization containing such a triad will find it hard to function because of a built-in instability. As it is set up, A cannot form a coalition with either B or C that cannot be undermined by the other, yet B and C together cannot dominate A.

Caplow describes another organizational triad that is closer to Haley's perverse triangle. In it A is stronger than B, and B is stronger than C, but B and C together are stronger than A. The only way A could forestall a coalition between B and C that would outweigh him would be to form a coalition with B. Such a coalition would be appropriate and would uphold the status order. But since B could always threaten to make a coalition with C, and C could always provide the temptation, A could never be sure of his authority. B too would be stronger than C within that dyad, but not within the triad, where he would be as much at the mercy of C as A would be. Neither A nor B nor C would exercise power with any confidence, and the triad might find it difficult to function at all.

One could argue that this is not formally the same as Haley's perverse triangle because Haley is talking about two same-level superiors and one lower-level subordinate. But we very often find that two authorities will join in representing the interests of an organization, even though one of them is higher in status, has the final say, or culturally carries more weight. Thus A and B in Caplow's second triad might be represented by two parents when one parent's authority is slightly greater than that of the other; or by a manager and a foreman in a factory, where the two levels are distinct but both represent the authority structure.

What is strange is that Caplow does not arrive at the idea of a perverse triangle in his chapters on family triads. He seems almost to get at it in his description of the improper coalition, but then, in considering coalitions in family life, never links this form with family disturbance or individual distress. He discusses a normative progression of coalition choices in a typical nuclear family, but does not seem to realize that cross-generation coalitions can at times create difficulties. Thus he gives an example of a four-person family in which the father (A) carries most weight; then comes mother (B), somewhat less dominant; then son (C), who is the older sibling; and daughter (D), who is the youngest and weakest of the family. Using a game-playing analogy, with each person out to "win," he assumes that the player with the crucial decision to make is mother. If she joins father, the parental dyad will dominate the two children. This he calls an example of a conservative coalition pattern, because the appropriate authority structure is upheld. If she chooses to align herself with son, creating a "revolutionary" coalition pattern, this will upset the appropriate authority structure. In eithe case, it is mother who has the strongest hand.

This line of reasoning is persuasive but carries some assumptions that should be examined. The implication that family members, like the players in the experimental coalition games Caplow discusses elsewhere, have different "weights" and will make alignments to improve their positions relative to each other is questionable. The experimental games are done with strangers, not with persons living in ongoing groups. Caplow talks as though families act like subjects in experimental games. Thus he can assume that in the "revolution-ary" family the father has "no reason to join an AD coalition; it would not enable him to dominate the BC coalition of mother and son together, and he can already dominate them separately."

This statement further assumes that what drives each individual is a desire for power or domination. One could argue that in a family this may be one element but hardly the entire story. The idea that the self-interest of the individual might at times be subordinated to the survival of the group, and that his coalition choices might be influenced accordingly, is never examined. In fact, a father-daughter coalition in Caplow's family would be a strong probability—even though it might not outweigh the mother-son coalition—with the presumed result of helping to balance the parental axis. The family with "a boy for you and a girl for me" is not just a song writer's fancy but is common and, pushed to an extreme, indicates difficul-ties. Similarly, a son who is drawn into closeness with a neglected mother may not be acting out of a wish to "win" against father, but out of a desire (not necessarily conscious) to comfort mother, to protect father from demands that father may not be able to fulfill, and to act as a buffer in marital strife. All this may enter into his behavior quite as much as any presumed personal power he may derive from his attachment to the authority figure.

Caplow himself seems uncomfortable with his focus on the "need to win" as a major factor in individual decision making. In his treatment of the family he often takes a leap to the system-wide level. One rule of triadic relationships, as he observes early in the book, is that a person cannot be both a coalition partner and an opponent in the same network. When he begins to apply this rule to family groups, a whole new framework appears. If daughter sides with mother against father, she will not be likely to side with grandmother, who is on father's side against mother, because this would subject her to the pressures of divided loyalties. According to this line of reasoning, alliances are not necessarily based on motives originating inside the individual but on what Caplow calls the "strain toward compatibility" across a social network.

Haley is ahead of Caplow in deliberately trying to formulate a systemic rather than an individually oriented explanation for coalition behavior. He refuses to accept the traditional decision-making model with its assumptions about interior motivation. He suggests instead that a conflictual situation arising within different orders of coalitions will interfere with the proper functioning of a social system and that of persons in it. And in describing this, Haley uses a quite different metaphor from the game-playing metaphor: the analogy of the Russellian Logical Paradox, with its apparent conflict between different levels of meaning. Both Haley and Bateson, whose ideas were at one point intertwined, use this analogy, but Haley extends it to explain how membership in coalitions within an organization can under special circumstances put great stress on certain individuals.

Haley describes this situation as follows: Normally, peers in an organization are in coalition with each other, a fact expressed by the presence of administrative levels or, in a family, generation lines. If an employer joins with one employee to form a coalition against another, the latter is faced with conflicting definitions of his position. Within the larger framework of the organization, his fellow employee is aligned with him. But at the same time that employee is siding with a superior against him. As Haley says, "Being forced to respond when there is a conflict between these two different orders of coalitions creates distress."[11] There is a clear similarity between this formulation and Caplow's insistence on the importance of compatibility between coalition partners in a group, but with the difference that Haley links conflictual coalition membership with individual distress. He is beginning to assign more and more weight to a conflict between loyalties at different levels of social organizations as a factor in the etiology and maintenance of disturbed behaviors.

To restate the problem in other terms: Assume that A offers behavior which fits the operating needs of System One (which might be the person or might be a subsystem like the parental dyad), and that conflicting behavior is simultaneously demanded that fits the needs of System Two (which might be the extended kin group). If one system is a subset of the other, and the two arenas are not clearly differentiated or kept apart, confusion will arise. It is the same kind of confusion that Bateson saw as the heart of the Russellian paradox: the difficulty of discerning the difference between class and subclass. There will always be a two-level dilemma, never clearly spelled out, regarding which system's rules are to be obeyed.

For instance, a child, who at home is not required to behave in any special way at the table, is required to sit still and display "manners" during a long Sunday dinner at the home of his mother's parents. He gets confused signals from the overangry scolding of his mother (much of whose anger is really at her own parents) and contradicting suggestions from his father (who hates social etiquette) that he be allowed to leave the table. The situation escalates until the child has such a bad tantrum that the parents decide to leave early and go home. Here the demands of conflicting behavior from different people and subgroups in the family are clear, as are the different levels on which these demands are made (for instance, the mother tells him to sit still, but by overreacting implies that she really does not agree with what she is telling him).

Haley's leap from a fascination with communication to a fascination with structure was a crucial one. It allowed him to begin to consider the possibility that schizophrenia may be, as he put it, the result of a conflict of groups.[12] That is, a person exhibiting schizo-phrenic behavior may be trying to please conflicting groups in which he has simultaneous membership. This led Haley to study the formal characteristics of alliances in the schizophrenic's family.

At the Nexus of Warring Triangles

Counting the number of triangles in an average-size extended family, where there are two parents and two children and each parent has two parents, Haley noted that any one person in this group is involved in twenty-one triangles simultaneously. If every-body is living together harmoniously, there is no problem. But if a child is at the nexus of two triangles or groups that are in conflict, he will be in a difficult position. If his mother and maternal grand-mother are in conflict with his father and his father's mother, he will have to behave carefully, because if he pleases one group he will displease the other. If all twenty-one of the triangles the child inhabits are in divided states, he will have to exhibit conflictual behavior in order to survive. Such behavior is often considered crazy or strange.

The dilemma of a person caught between two positions is echoed by James Davis's "cross-pressure hypothesis."[13] Davis asks us to consider a person (P) aligned positively with two others (O_1, O_2) but undecided about a fourth person (X). Suppose X is a candidate for office who is supported by O_1 but not by O_2. This puts P in a quandary. If P votes for X, he will please O_1 but displease O_2. If he does not vote for X, the reverse will be true. One can diagram this situation in triadic form (see Figure 6.1). If one assumes that O_1 and O_2 represent political blocs as well as themselves as individuals, one can say that P is under cross-pressure from simultaneous member-ship in loyalty groups. Clearly much of Davis's thinking comes out of structural balance theory, which is very close conceptually to coalition theory and will be discussed in the next chapter.

Boulding, in his book *Conflict and Defense,* makes a similar analysis of what he calls an "avoidance-avoidance conflict."[14] Using the analogy of an ass between two skunks, he describes the situation as a "trough equilibrium," with the ass being pushed toward one of his negative goals every time he moves away from the other. The ass is in what Boulding terms a stable psychological conflict, or "quandary." In Boulding's opinion, if the ass (representing a human being) cannot jump over one of the skunks or otherwise escape, his behavior may become disjointed and random, and he risks a nervous breakdown. An alternative route is to retreat into the realm of daydream, fantasy, art, or, in a more pathological manifestation, schizophrenia or paranoia.

These contributions from different sources show that a remarkably similar group of ideas has been explored by different researchers. The core of these ideas is that symptomatic or bizarre behavior can be associated with a situation in which a person is forced to choose between two paths, each of which carries a penalty. It must be said, however, that not all of these writers are speaking from the same premises. There is a fundamental argument over whether the conflict is between choices on the same level, usually defined as "ambivalence," or choices on different levels, and herein lies a distinction of considerable philosophical import.

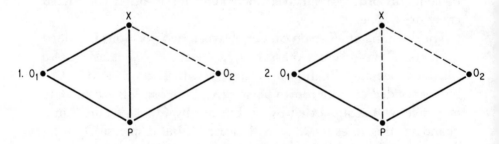

1. P votes for X; triangle $P-O_1-X$ is congruent but $P-O_2-X$ is not.
2. P votes against X; triangle $P-O_2-X$ is congruent but $P-O_1-X$ is not.

Figure 6.1
Davis's "Cross-Pressure Hypothesis"

Ambivalence versus a Conflict of Levels

Caplow defines ambivalence as "an emotional strain which arises from interaction with someone who is both an opponent and a coalition partner."[15] This is essentially a restatement of Davis's cross-pressure theory in a three-person rather than a four-person form. The double bind is also popularly equated with ambivalence, but both Bateson and Haley declare that the contradictory situation described by the double bind is something quite different. Haley says that ambivalence as a psychological term refers to the state of mind of an individual when faced with choices of equal or near value about which he has mixed feelings.[16] By contrast, he states, the double bind has to do with a conflictual context within which it is difficult to function. Haley, following the ideas of the Bateson group, gives a paradox as an example: someone who is asked to do something spontaneously. If he does something, it is not happening spontaneously, and if it is truly spontaneous, how can he be obeying the request?

Bateson, the originator of these ideas, puts the matter somewhat differently. He describes two types of internal contradiction which are commonly found in human communication.[17] One, defined as "ambivalence," will occur when two same-level Gestalten, A and B, are negatively and positively perceived, respectively. However, they overlap in such a way that the overlapping section may be viewed positively when perceived as part of A, and negatively when perceived as part of B. The viewer cannot perceive the same section positively and negatively at the same time, but there is nothing to prevent him from peacefully experiencing whichever Gestalt he happens to be settled in at the time.

Bateson's second type of internal contradiction involves two different levels, one of which is inclusive of the other. Bateson cites as an example the paradox of formal logic (for example, the sign on which is written, "This statement is untrue") and adds that these forms are "systems of contradiction in which temporary preference for one pole promotes preference for the other and vice versa."[18] As a more concrete analogy, Bateson takes the electric bell buzzer. He describes the way the electromagnet in the buzzer acts upon an armature so as to cause an oscillation between two positions which, for the purposes of his illustration, he labels "yes" and "no." The armature goes from side to side because the implications of the "yes" side send the armature back to "no," and vice versa. But Bateson emphasizes that the "yes" and "no" belong to two different levels of abstraction: "Yes" refers to position of the armature, and "no" refers to direction of change. This oscillating motion may be equitably endured by a bell buzzer, but Bateson points out that it is hard on humans who are in an analogous position.

One final point Bateson makes about paradoxes has to do with time. In thinking about a paradox, a person will at first accept the "yes," but further pondering will drive him to "no," and so on. Thus from the psychological point of view, the time aspect is important; we are not dealing with a problem of static indecision, Bateson says, but one of alternating durations. This time element will bear further thinking about; for now, it is sufficient to consider that the length of time a person is allowed to rest at either end of two incompatible poles could have something to do with the degree of stress he would experience. One can imagine a situation where this time period became shorter and shorter, following a progressively faster sequence, until incompatible demands are being made on the individual almost simultaneously. At this point one might expect some kind of sudden shift, cutoff, or breakdown.

In a covert cross-generation coalition there may be an effect similar to the bell buzzer. The implication of a child siding with either parent may be harmful to the system at a level other than the one where the person is being asked to take sides. What is missed in the analogy of the ass between two skunks, or in any other model for a same-level dilemma, is that in family alignments there is a whole vast web of systems and subsystems which will often be disarranged, whichever side is taken. It is also possible that it will be disarranged if no side is taken.

The child in a pathological triad, in accepting a coalition with one parent, may counteract the too-great power of the other parent, but in doing so he not only undermines the authority of the governing dyad but may upset the balance of power between the two extended kin groups. If, on the other hand, he tries to remain close to each parent, and both are negatively involved with each other, he is caught in a conflict of loyalties. Add the time factor, which suggests that there may be a point at which judicious alternate siding may achieve a fatal momentum, and you have a situation where extreme reactions might occur.

The question that follows is what sort of behavior can be expected when a person is in the position described above. The answer brings us back to the communicational model but within the context of levels of organization.

Schizophrenic Communication as a Way of Not Defining Relationships

Haley describes schizophrenic behavior as an effort to avoid defining one's relationships with other people.[19] Usually, Haley says, people qualify the statements they make to one another with metamessages which indicate the following:

1. I
2. am saying something
3. to you
4. in this situation.

Analyzing a transcribed conversation between two hospitalized schizophrenics, Haley illustrates the many ways in which two determined people can deny any or all of these types of metamessages. Each of the comments by the two participants is of the variety: This is not a hospital, it is an air base; I am not a patient, I am a man from outer space. In addition, by non sequitur responses to the other's comments, the validity of these comments is denied. Thus do these speakers avoid defining their relationship to each other. They deny that they are speaking, deny that anything is said, deny that it is said to the other person, and deny that the interchange took place in this place at this time.

Haley offers an example of a similar response in a family context, citing the case of a schizophrenic girl who had just been released from the hospital.[20] On her return, her parents quarreled, and the mother took the daughter with her to her own mother's house. The daughter called her father as soon as they arrived to tell him where she was. When her mother complained that she was siding with her father, the daughter explained that she had to call him because before they left she had given him an "odd look" (one of her symptoms). The father, finding out where his daughter and wife had gone, came and persuaded the mother to go back with him. Before leaving to go home, the mother asked the daughter to go on an errand; the girl refused and the grandmother went instead. While her parents were in the next room discussing her refusal, she began to scream and was subsequently rehospitalized.

In looking at the larger family picture, Haley notes a number of cross-generation coalitions. The girl's two grandmothers competed for her loyalty; the father's mother sided with him against his wife; and the girl sided with her mother's mother against her own mother. The parents each sought the girl's favor, and each accused her of siding with the other. Haley points out that if one takes these circumstances into account, *any* response on the girl's part could be seen to carry a penalty. Allowing for this peculiar context, then, the girl's communications could be seen as eminently adaptive. As Haley puts it:

At the nexus of warring family functions, what should be an "appropriate and normal" response to this situation? It would seem to be one in which the girl would behave in one way to satisfy one faction and in another way to satisfy another and then disqualify both ways by indicating that she was not responsible in any case. Such conflicting communication would be diagnosed as schizophrenic behavior.[21]

Haley is not alone in his observation of the way alignments are denied in this type of family, not just by the patient but by all members. Similar examples have been cited in research on "thought disorders" in schizophrenics and their families, although this term can be seen as a misnaming. Haley's "The Art of Being Schizophrenic" is a tribute to the skill with which schizophrenics caricature the need for concealment in their families.[22] When the family is busily denying some obvious fact, the schizophrenic member will offer crazy-sounding statements which teeter perilously close to the truth. At the same time, if someone comes too close to the truth, the schizophrenic will say or do something crazy.

For example, in the case described by Wynne in Chapter 1 (the case of the catatonic girl), the daughter parried her father's inappropriate advances to her by saying, "Petting between teenagers sometimes gets out of hand." The father replied, in equally evasive fashion, "A father's love is a father's love, a wife's love is a wife's love, and a daughter's love is a daughter's love."[23]

Wynne also remarks ruefully on the tactics of the family whenever a therapist would try to comment on the splits and alignments that were being so studiously denied. The daughter would answer such a comment with something like, "If you try to do *right,* you don't have to worry," and then add, "I think someone may have done something to my body." The father would immediately jump in to ask whether she meant the boy she met at church the summer before, and the mother would cut across to correct the name of the boy mentioned by the father. The exchange between the therapist and the daughter would be effectively disrupted by this kind of interaction. The therapist might well have begun to wonder whether this was a pattern of thought disorder or a system of sabotage.

Clearly, then, denials, ambiguities, covert messages must all be seen within a context where they have a peculiar logic. Such a context is exemplified by a family in which no relationship with any family member may be defined or acknowledged without disruption, stress, or other penalties. This will happen most often when the organization of the family cannot allow open alliances across the generation lines because these alliances would threaten important same-level relationships like (in our society) the marriage. Assuming that this sufficiently answers the question of why these alliances —which are actually coalitions against others—go underground, let us move on to a consideration of covert cross-generation coalitions in the extended family. This will take us back to our initial emphasis on family structure.

Regularities in Larger Networks

In discussing covert cross-generation coalitions Haley notes that they never occur alone but always in pairs.[24] In disturbed families a coalition of a parent with a child will often be matched by a coalition of another parent with a grandparent. This could be called a "countervailing coalition." Haley even states that a parent-child coalition occurs so often in conjunction with a parent-grandparent coalition that this hypothesis could be offered: "a breaching of the generations with a child will coincide with a breaching at the next generational level." If this is true, says Haley, we can assume that there are regularities in family networks, that the patterns in one part of the kin group are formally the same as those in some other part.

This formulation carries with it an entirely different assumption about the "cause" of many behaviors which have in the past been thought to be motivated by an individual's unhappiness or anger. Haley observes that to examine the question of cause in terms of somebody's dissatisfaction is to focus once more on the individual. If one shifts to the larger context, more circular explanations of "cause" appear. Wife may join child against husband not only because she is unhappy with husband but because a good relationship with her husband would have a disruptive effect on her relationship with her own parents. In this sense, Haley writes, "cause" is a statement about regularities in larger networks.

In these paragraphs Haley begins to expand on his idea that stress derives from a conflict between membership in coalitions in social groups. Caplow's basic premise in describing coalitions is that a coalition partner may not be an opponent in the same set of relationships. The argument follows that relationship sets will exhibit a tendency toward compatibility. If this is true, one would expect to find a premium placed on strategies which protect a person against the penalties of responding to incompatible demands. This may be why formally instituted separations between levels within social systems are so widespread. In families, as in business organizations, there are many customs and sanctions which enforce a status difference or a generation line. Caplow cites as examples the ritualized avoidance behavior between persons in delicate kinship relationships in various societies, and the exaggerated distance between officers and enlisted men in the army. In some societies joking behavior is often prescribed between men and their sisters-in-law, their grandmothers, and their female cross-cousins. This seems to be a friendly type of avoidance behavior. According to Caplow, joking seems to deny a dangerous coalition in circumstances where one might be expected to develop.

A more serious ritual schism is the almost universal "mother-in-law avoidance" practiced between a man and his wife's mother. From a coalition standpoint, Caplow says this operates to prevent an unworkable triad, that is, a coalition in which one or more members will be forced to assume incompatible positions. In the husband/wife/mother-in-law triad, the wife is apt to be in a situation where she must be close to each party at the expense of her allegiance to the other. There are other considerations too. Caplow makes the point that

In addition to the hint of inadmissible sexual rivalries, a coalition between a man and his mother-in-law becomes unthinkable as soon as we identify it, as we must in linked triads, as a coalition against the father-in-law, the wife's brother, the husband's mother, and sundry other persons in the kinship network.[25]

The incest tabu is perhaps the most ubiquitous of all the sanctions against dangerous coalitions. Both Haley and Caplow describe Freud as an early explorer of family alignments that violate these sanctions. Of course Freud formulated the problem in a manner consonant with the individual orientation toward nervous disorders of his day. Caplow defends Freud's concept of the oedipal conflict as an instance of a culturally determined coalition found mainly in modern Western families. Haley reinterprets it as the most generic example of a secret coalition across generation lines. He further states that

It could be argued that this pattern is portrayed symbolically as a reflection of the incest tabu, but one could also argue that the incest tabu is a product of the recognition that cross-generation coalitions result in distress for all participants in the family network.[26]

From this standpoint, the incest tabu has more to do with making family structures workable than it has to do with preventing improper sex.

The Perverse Triangle in Different Cultures

We have examined here the idea that when a person in the parent generation makes a secret bond with someone in the child generation against the other parent, there will be trouble. The implication is that no authority structure may have two adjoining generations in it. This is patently not true. Many women in female-headed households in our society have workable relationships with their own mothers and depend on them for help in bringing up their children. Or they may enlist the help of an older child without causing pathology.

A look at other cultures is even more enlightening. Caplow mentions the important contribution of the sociologist Francis Hsu in tracing out a typology for kinship and culture that depends on what he calls the "emphasized relationship" characteristic of that culture.[27] This relationship would correspond to what I would call the governing dyad, even though it may not always be formally thought of as such. Hsu divides cultures into four types, depending on what this "dominant axis" might be: In Type A, found in many Asian societies, the dominant axis is the father-son dyad. In Type B, characteristic of many Western societies, it is the husband-wife dyad. Type C emphasizes the mother-son dyad, and is exemplified by traditional Hindu families. Type D consists of a brother-brother dyad, which is found in many African societies.

One could assume that whatever governing dyad exists in a given family, it will be workable so long as it is not suborned by coalition arrangements between one of its members and other family members. The term "cross-generation coalition" may be culture-bound in the sense that strains may arise from same-generation coalitions in societies where the dominant family type is organized differently from our own.

In other words, the strain lines emanating from perverse triangles will differ depending on the culture. In a study of Hindu family relationships, Aileen Ross shows that the strain line in this group lies on the tie between son's wife and son's mother, a relationship which is highly charged with potential conflict. In this society (or in it as it used to be), the wife is in a particularly difficult position. She leaves her family of origin to live with her husband's family after marriage, and then is under the absolute power of her mother-in-law. What justice there is operates over time, since the daughter-in-law can expect redress of her grievances only by living long enough to be a despot in turn over her own son's wife.

What is illuminating about this example is that in traditional Hindu society, husband-wife closeness is discouraged as a possible source of distress to the family system. Aileen Ross describes the problems faced by a young wife in her new family:

If she was attractive enough to elicit her husband's support, her position became even more difficult. If he sided with her, the delicate balance of family relationships was upset, and tensions created which might react back on her. Her supervision was not given over to her husband for this might have developed a warm personal relationship between them, which again might have caused strain in the joint family system.[28]

This is one more piece of evidence that the secret breach of generation or status lines, analyzed as an intrapsychic artifact by Freud and redefined behaviorally by Haley, is really a theme consisting of many variations. Western society seeks to weld the married pair closely, to avoid the dangerous possibility that a child may enter a subversive coalition with either parent. Traditionally, Hindu society has sought to place distance between man and wife to avoid subversion of the all-important mother-son tie.

For other variants one can turn to African society, which the Hsu typology tells us is generally based on a brother-brother axis. Robert LeVine, in a study of typical African family tensions, shows that in many societies the strain line is apt to be between father and son, who have a culturally prescribed avoidance pattern. LeVine notes that intergenerational male homicides are the most common form of murder in many African groups.[29] Part of the reason may derive from the custom that forces a firstborn male to wait until his father is dead before he can share any of his father's accumulated wealth. As there are not too many other opportunities to acquire possessions, this can become a focus for considerable conflict. Bateson noted that in the Iatmul, fathers and sons were culturally forbidden to become intimate, and also guessed that this might come from the mutually opposed interests of the older and younger men. This opposition is reinforced by the close ties of sons to their mother's brother's clans. We have already investigated the connection between the threat of cleavage between fraternal clans in Iatmul society and the social devices that apparently evolved to prevent this.

But we could go further and observe that the problem of social fission is one that affects all governing structures, and that forms countering fission in a given culture may have their own potential for distress, depending on the makeup of the governing structure and what forms are used. Some ways to counter fission will be benign—an integrative custom like the *naven,* for instance. Less benign ways will entail the involvement of a third party, as when a child's symptom has the apparent result of keeping a pair of parents from separating or when one of the spouses develops a symptom, seemingly forestalling such an eventuality in a different way. If such counteracting behaviors are insufficient, one possibility is that the "dominant axis" may split along the line of cleavage. In our society this often means divorce; in African societies it may mean the splitting off of a fraternal group.

It is important to keep in mind the cultural variants of the "perverse triangle." If we do not realize that this triad will differ depending on the way families are organized in a society, we will begin to think that the family structures associated with symptoms in our society are the only ones. We must also guard against seeing symptoms in a linear causal sense, having the "purpose" of saving a marriage, for example. All we can say is that they are sensitive responses which are usually associated with relationship dilemmas in hierarchical groups, and which join with many other interlocking factors to favor family balance.

Stepping back now to the behavior of triads in social networks, we go on to deal with an important mini-industry in the field of social psychology: the theory of structural balance. Much of Caplow's thinking in *Two Against One* is heavily influenced by balance theory, although he only mentions it in a footnote. Haley, too, seems to be struggling with the idea that there are laws governing the compatibility of relationships across social networks; and Davis is purely in the tradition of balance theory. The effort of the next chapter will be to select useful pieces of this intricate and fascinating set of ideas, without getting too seduced by its elegant logic.

Chapter 7

The Rules of Congruence for Triads

Balance Theory and Family Theory

The major difficulty with applying structural balance theory to an understanding of families is that this theory was originally devised within a framework of individual psychology. The laws of relatedness described by balance theory were used to promote a widely shared premise: that a state of "cognitive dissonance" or perceptual inconsistency creates discomfort which a person will attempt to correct. The main emphasis was on the focal person's attitudes, sentiments, and cognitions. As a result, explanations having to do with his social context—his family or other groups—became invisible. However, the theory contains core ideas that offer clues to some of the rules governing relationships in families and kin groups, and is particularly applicable to triadic behavior patterns in families with psychotic members. The patterns that balance theory predicts widen the possibilities of clinical intervention.

The tenets of balance theory, derived by Dorwin Cartwright and Frank Harary from research by Fritz Heider, rest on the premise that linked sets of relationships abhor interior contradictions.[1] Heider's interest was in cognitive fields, and he hypothesized that such fields would tend toward a consistency of attitudes or sentiments. He intended to formulate rules of congruence that might govern the way an individual perceived persons and other entities, whether material or abstract. Cartwright and Harary stress the difference between this emphasis and that of researchers like T. M. Newcomb, who have extended the theory to explain social as well as cognitive fields. For instance, if Person P liked Person O and Person X, but Persons O and X were enemies, there would presumably be pressure on one of the parties to shift his attitude until a situation where there were no conflicting loyalties prevailed. But this would not necessarily mean that Persons O and X would have to become friends. "Balance" is not synonymous with harmony. The rules for the interpersonal interpretation of balance theory are often put this way (see Figure 7.1):

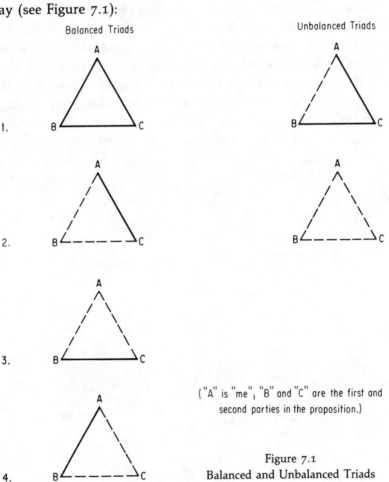

("A" is "me"; "B" and "C" are the first and second parties in the proposition.)

Figure 7.1
Balanced and Unbalanced Triads

1. The friend of my friend is my friend.
2. The enemy of my friend is my enemy.
3. The friend of my enemy is my enemy.
4. The enemy of my enemy is my friend.

This is essentially a theory of coalitions. Under these rules, triads are *balanced,* or, as it might be more descriptive to say, *congruent,* in two cases: (1) when all relationships between the three possible pairs are positive (a word defined by balance theorists in terms of liking, similarity, affinity); (2) in the classic "two against one" situation, where two of the parties are friends but have a negative attitude toward the third ("negative" being defined in terms of hostility, opposition, distance). Triads are *unbalanced* in only two cases: (1) if there are two positive relationships and one negative one; (2) if all three relationships are negative. Some reservations about these terms "positive" and "negative" will be explored later; for now, the balance theory definitions indicate adequately what is meant. If we apply this formula to the P-O-X triad described above, it is clear that three routes can be taken to make this triad congruent. O might become friendly to X, or the relationship between *either* P and O, *or* P and X, could become unfriendly (see Figure 7.2).

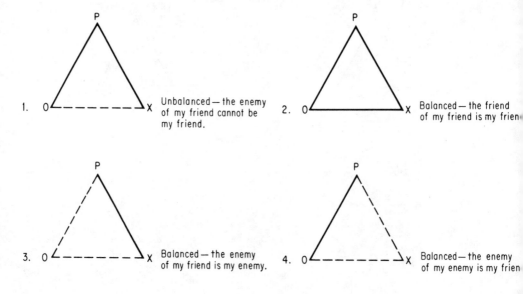

1. Unbalanced — the enemy of my friend cannot be my friend.

2. Balanced — the friend of my friend is my frien

3. Balanced — the enemy of my friend is my enemy.

4. Balanced — the enemy of my enemy is my frien

Figure 7.2
Balanced Solutions to Unstable P-O-X

To make these propositions more concrete, if Betty and John and Bill are all getting along, fine. But if John and Betty have a falling-out, there will be pressure on Bill to take sides, especially if they are all members of an ongoing group. If Bill cannot play mediator and reestablish harmony, or if Bill finds the stresses of a divided loyalty too hard to take, he will probably end up on one side or the other. This is a balanced form, the classic two-against-one. Of course, Bill may not like his position. If so, it would be good if he could leave the field and say, "A plague on both your houses."

But not everyone in this situation has these options. If Bill is a child and Betty and John are his parents and drag him into their quarrel, all his choices will be dismal. He might side with Betty and lose John, or vice versa. Or he might seesaw between them, always careful not to alienate either by seeming too close to the other. I have called this option (the triangle with two positive sides) the "inadmissible triangle" because of its potential for stress. Alternatively, Bill could create a closeness between the warring pair if he could worry them by getting ill or behaving strangely. He might also unite them if he acted troublesome and bad. But none of these courses is a very comfortable one, even though, technically, each of them is "balanced."

Balance theory applies not only to single triangles. Cartwright and Harary take Heider's formulation and extend it in an important way. They are trying to describe rules that will cover not only a unit of three but larger configurations as well. Thus they take Heider's original statement that a balanced state exists among a set of three entities if relationships between all three are positive, or if two are negative and one is positive, and expand it to include units of n number of elements.

For our purposes Cartwright and Harary's original theorems and proofs can be restated very simply in terms of triangles. Let us start with a triangle that is balanced by having one side positive and two sides negative, and then decide to add any number of points, linking them together in a grid and still following the rules for congruence. The result is that two, and only two, coalitions will appear. Two clusters of points joined by positive lines will be separated by negative lines, and this will be true no matter how many points are added (see Figure 7.3). The reader who doubts this may want to play

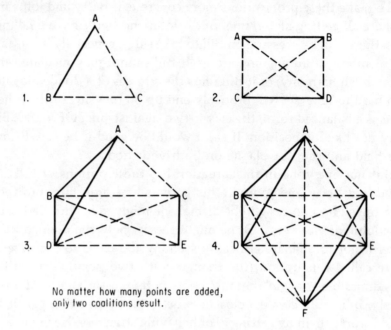

No matter how many points are added,
only two coalitions result.

Figure 7.3
Two Coalitions

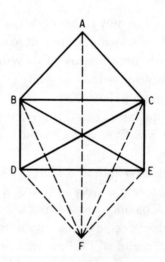

Figure 7.4
Single-Deviant Arrangement

around with triangles, adding new points and labeling arcs between them "positive" or "negative" according to the rules outlined above. The result will be two opposing groups no matter how large the structure becomes. The apparent exception is when one of the two subsets consists of only one point and all the other points are in the other subset (see Figure 7.4).

The interest for social psychologists and clinicians is that these two forms occur naturally in families and other small groups. One often finds forces polarizing a social field so that everybody is on one side or another. As an alternative form which seemingly counteracts the first, everybody will join together against one member. This will solidify previously warring factions into a single bloc. William Taylor comments on these patterns in an article that relates balance theory to interaction sequences in families in which one member is symptomatic. He suggests that balance theory may offer some key to understanding the process whereby a group makes use of what he calls the "single deviant arrangement" as a way to prevent a split or civil war.[2]

One proviso that critics of balance theory make is that all the elements of the structure must be connected, otherwise there will be no pressure for relationships to be compatible. This point coincides with Caplow's assertion that in any set of triads the prohibition against the same person being an opponent and a partner at the same time is not true if the people in question meet in different systems of action.[3] Balance theory seems mainly to apply to extremely close-knit relationship systems, not to loose ones, collections of strangers and the like. In addressing himself to this question James Davis has come up with a formulation which suggests that "balanced" forms are special cases under an overall rule for what he calls "clustering."[4]

Clustering Theory

Balance theorists have noted that the tendency of balanced structures to divide down the middle is one explanation for the peculiar phenomenon of polarization. Simmel commented on this facet of social behavior many years ago: "Periods of excitement generally place the whole of public life under the slogan, 'Who is not with me is against me.' The consequence of this is a division of elements into two parties."[5] But there was no set of laws explaining this activity until the advent of balance theory.

The trouble with applying these laws arises when one asks how a society can manage to cohere at all if there is a tendency for polarization to occur whenever a negative relationship appears in any part. Coser's work on the importance of multiple group affiliations provides a partial answer.[6] Coser's point is that an extremely closed group risks polarization because it does not allow the existence of differentiated subgroups. If, he says, one conflict cuts through a society, this will put into question its basic consensual agreement, thus endangering its existence. On the other hand, if attachments to many groups are allowed, thus creating a multitude of competing loyalties, these will act as a balancing force, preventing a deep cleavage along one axis. Coser notes that in a closed society, where all loyalties are focused on one or two ideas, objects, or persons, there is greater danger of polarization (or, one might add, the alternative of scapegoating) than in an open society, where many loyalties are allowed.

Davis extends this line of thinking in his article on clustering theory when he notes that polarization is only one way that a group can be divided. It is common to find in a society many cliques or islands of close-knit persons with mild hostility or distance between them. Davis modifies the basic propositions of balance theory to include this possibility. Specifically, he changes the rules for congruence to include the negative triad. He states that the first three conditions cited by balance theorists still hold: a friend of a friend will be a friend; an enemy of a friend will be an enemy; a friend of an enemy will be an enemy. The fourth proposal, that an enemy of an enemy will be a friend, he excludes. An enemy of an enemy may be an enemy. This last rule may result in a structure that is "clustered"—containing many isolated groups—rather than "balanced."[7]

To take an example from a kin network, we might diagram two types of family structure, one clustered and one balanced (see Figure 7.5).

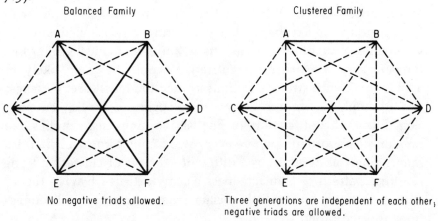

Figure 7.5
Graphs for Balanced and Clustered Families

In the balanced group, the "negative" arcs usually occur between parents and children. Between grandparents and grandchildren, however, the lines are usually positive, meaning that these are relationships of particular warmth. This is a common situation for three-generation families in our culture. Apple has made cross-cultural studies which indicate that if the parents have primary responsibility for disciplining the children, there will be an attitude of respectful distance between these generations, while the grandparent-child relationship will be one of friendly equality.[8] If, as in a few cases, the grandparents wield authority, the "negative" status line will exist between them and the children while the child-parent relationships will be more companionable. Kinship terminology often enshrines these differences in terms like "cool" and "warm." As in balance theory, relationships across such a network will tend to be compatible: the warm relatives of my warm relatives will be warm to me, etc.

On the other hand, a "clustered" kin group of three generations would be depicted by a structure in which same-generation persons were positively aligned with each other and there would be "negative" arcs between cross-generation persons. The difference would be that the arcs skipping a generation would also be "negative." Thus you would have a set of three generations, none of which is closely tied to any other. These are both normal ways for a family to be organized—that is, one would not expect pathological behaviors to arise in them. But the latter form is not likely to occur in family groups, given the tendency of intimate relationships to develop mild compatibility. In less tight-knit, hierarchical groups like bureaucracies, the rules for clustering would be more likely to apply, albeit with strong sanctions against too much peer closeness and an emphasis on vertical loyalty to superiors. Davis also mentions Elizabeth Bott's study of English working-class families in a London neighborhood (where every two families known by a third family knew each other) as a different example of clustering.[9] The resulting pattern of connectedness exactly satisfied Davis's theory in that there were many little social islands with no special connections to each other.

The concept of clustering gives some backing for the suspicion that balance theory, which predicts that all relationships in a given set must be compatible, applies only in some cases. When we see families in which the rules for balance theory strictly apply, this is a signal to look more closely, for it is exactly in families with severe pathology that these rules seem to be most strongly enforced.

Balance Theory and Family Pathology

Caplow and Haley agree that there is a tendency for relationships to be compatible across any family network. If so, what is the difference between a relationship structure that induces distress and one that does not? One could explain this by saying, as Haley does, that in the distressed family all or most relationships seem to turn into coalition relationships. Mother-child are close at father's expense. Parents can get together only in opposition to a child. The nuclear family can achieve solidarity only by scapegoating a grandparent. Conversely, a conflict between two parties will be interfered with by a third party who will side with one or the other of the combatants or will deflect attention to himself or herself. Closeness and apartness are both important aspects of family relationships, but it seems that these processes in a distressed family are always triadic, because no closeness, or any apartness either, is ever comfortable between two people.

Another factor is intensity. In families that produce symptomatic members, there will be some triads in which the relationships are experienced as if the family were a highly charged electromagnetic field—and the terms "positive" and "negative" are metaphorically apt in this connection. Relationship values may shift abruptly, but, whichever value appears, it will have the character of an invisible force. By contrast, in a family that functions normally the alignments are much milder and far less binding. As a result, people seem free to make alliances appropriate to necessary operations of the moment, or stages in time. This is perhaps why clinicians so often use the term "flexible" to identify a well-functioning family and "rigid" to identify a dysfunctional one.

It should be pointed out, however, that inflexibility may not always be attached to particular alignments but rather to the order in which they appear. There may be a dominant coalition pattern for one or more family triads, but these triads would take different forms so that they would look different at different stages of the total sequence. Because of this shifting quality, a family exhibiting extreme pathology may seem chaotic and confused, and the rigidity will be noticeable only in the redundancy of sequences across time.

A fourth factor is degree of connectedness of the family relationship field. Sometimes a pressure for compatibility will spread to all corners of the network and not be limited to just one or two adjacent triads. When Bowen noted this phenomenon he found it happening most often in times of crisis, with more and more persons brought into the triangulation process by a sort of contagion. Kalman Flomenhaft and David Kaplan, describing families in which a member has been brought to a psychiatric facility for hospitalization, comment on the tendency for relatives to appear from nowhere and to involve themselves in ways highly influential to the outcome of the case.[10]

The pressure toward compatibility cannot be understood without reference to the importance of hierarchy or levels in family structure. If there is a tendency toward rigid cross-level joinings in a family, this will mean that there will be a pressure for "negative" same-level ties. But this will create a conflict between family subsystems. If mother is ignored by father and turns to son for closeness, this may be useful for her, but it will create an improper coalition which will weaken the executive dyad. This coalition may not be useful for the child either, especially when he begins to move away from home. Families have a special mandate to keep generation lines distinct, because each new generation has the task of eventually disengaging itself from its predecessor.

However, intense cross-generation alignments are not the only source of difficulty. Many kinds of family trouble arise from the reverse situation, where there is extreme peer closeness and a huge generation gap, one might almost say gulf. This can occur in family structures where parents are extremely disconnected from their children and the siblings form an overclose subgroup or gang, as in Minuchin's "disengaged" families.

The point is that no type of structure is itself bad or good. What is good is a reasonable degree of independence (in Ashby's sense) between parts. A family that works well seems to have built-in separating devices that interfere with a tendency for relationships to follow rigid coalition rules. The generation line, like other status schisms, puts a distance between parts that might become too close. So does the demarcation around a subgroup such as the spouses. When parts can temporarily split off, so that mother can be close to baby at feeding time without making father jealous, or husband can visit his mother without wife feeling threatened, this means that a certain separation of relationship areas is occurring. We then have Caplow's optimal situation, where players can be opponents or partners without disloyalty because they are meeting in different activity systems.

To summarize, a family that produces members with psychotic or psychoneurotic symptoms is also likely to provide us with the following clues: (1) a high degree of family connectedness; (2) covert coalitions which cross generation lines; (3) closeness and distance between family members determined by rules for congruence of coalitions; (4) third parties interfering with or deflecting conflict or closeness between pairs; and (5) relationships with a high intensity factor.

It is becoming clear, however, that many of the axioms of balance theory are better dealt with by coalition theory. This leads to the questions: why has there not been an explicit joining of the two areas of research, especially in Caplow's *Two Against One*. A close reading indicates that at times Caplow does follow a line of reasoning based on balance theory, but, much of the research on coalitions he describes comes from game theory. Hence there is an implicit war of metaphors in his book. The "causation" implied by a person's desire to win a game is not in the same universe as the "causation" implied by the strain toward compatibility characteristic of "balanced" family networks.

Scholars in the field are still struggling with many other questions raised by balance theory. Howard Taylor's exhaustive study, *Balance in Small Groups,* surveys these questions and attempts some answers.[11] For our discussion we need to keep in mind primarily the premise that close-knit relationships will tend toward compatibility. Clinical observation indicates that when this state of affairs is carried to an extreme, so that no person in a social group can shift his allegiances without affecting everybody else, the group is in trouble. In family systems, in particular, there will be trouble if there are intense, invariant cross-generation involvements.

Trade-offs for Balanced Forms

One observation that seems to be borne out by clinical studies is that a polarizing process in a group tends to change to a scapegoating process, with obvious advantages for the larger unit. Family literature is replete with notions of the child as scapegoat or family healer who "rescues" the family from the threat of parental splitting or worse, but these formulations place the motivation, albeit unconscious, within the individual. A more systemic view would see the matter in terms of two formal patterns.

Here it would be well to go back and reconsider Bateson's ideas on the matter. In discussing symmetrical versus complementary patterns, he suggested that each pattern might operate to check the exponential tendencies of the other, and even proposed that the two types of schismogenesis might be psychologically incompatible. Putting this concept into an evolutionary framework, one could speculate that those groups who survived were able to substitute one schismogenic pattern for another, rather than accept the consequences of either schismatic pattern getting out of hand.

The result, which seems sometimes like a sacrifice of the individual for the group or for some other person, is not always made explicit. And yet it is this trade-off that family therapists often find themselves confronting. Clinical examples abound of the process whereby parental conflict seems to be averted by the symptomatic behavior of a child, or sometimes a spouse. If the symptom carries a benevolent label of "sick," this will create a concerned, united group in place of a conflicted one. If it carries a label of "bad," this also unites the family, but in opposition to the problematic member. There is always an element of "bad" in the "sick" label and vice versa, but one definition usually prevails as the dominant one. At the risk of suggesting a functional use for a symptom in a family, there does seem to be a link between symptoms and family balance.

In some cases there seems to be an oscillation between family conflict and a symptomatic display. One process takes over when the other threatens to get out of hand, in a kind of alternating mechanism that prevents the worse consequences of either state. Again we see the applicability of Bateson's self-corrective circuits. Haley's case of the schizophrenic girl, discussed in Chapter 6, is a vivid example of parental conflict that was resolved when the daughter returned to the hospital. The family had polarized, only to become reunited with the girl once more in the position of odd man out. Cycles of hospitalization can be seen as an alternation between threats of splitting to single deviant arrangements that temporarily heal the split, back to splitting *ad infinitum.* This oscillation from symmetrical to complementary movements seems to depend on a substratum of fixed coalition sequences. One goal of therapy would be to attack the rigidity of coalition sequences, not merely to interfere with specific behaviors like scapegoating. A value of seeing the formal structure that surrounds a symptom is that this structure has to be seen in a circular rather than a linear fashion, and thus may be interfered with in more than one way to produce symptomatic relief.

In any case, it is clear that rigid coalition sequences such as we have described in this chapter have positive as well as negative value for the family or other entity; otherwise, with the dangers they entail, they would not be tolerated. Haley suggests an answer, saying that in most cases the subordinate party in a cross-generation coalition seems to be involved in a split or conflict which is dividing two superior parties. This split is not always between the two superior members of the triangle but can occur between two larger groups with which each of these persons is identified. The triadic mechanisms in mediating conflicts in social fields will be the focus of the next chapter.

Chapter 8

Triads and the Management of Conflict

The Natural Triad

Up to now we have been looking at triads that relate to distress in a social system with the implication that these forms are themselves the source of some malignant tension. The position taken here is that they are neither good nor bad. They are natural regulatory mechanisms which may or may not—depending on the point of view—exact too high a price. They take a benign shape when a group is functioning well, and what we have come to think of as a pathological shape when it is not.

Let us start with the "natural triad" of Morris Freilich, which Caplow mentions in *Two Against One,* as a good example of a benign triangle. Freilich, an anthropologist with an interest in triads, noticed a peculiar three-person arrangement that occurred over and over again in kinship groups in many countries. What is interesting about this triangle is that it has many of the same basic characteristics as Haley's "perverse triangle" and Caplow's "improper coalition." There is a close tie between a superior and a subordinate;

there is a hostility or distance between the other superior and the subordinate; and there is a clear difference of attitude between the two superiors.

Freilich formally describes the cast of characters of his triangle as follows:

1. a High Status Authority (HSA)
2. a High Status Friend (HSF)
3. a Low Status Subordinate (LSS)[1]

Freilich posits a positive or friendly relationship between HSF and LSS and a negative or distant one between LSS and HSA. Regardless of the kinship structure of a society, the person who wields authority over a child, whether his father, his uncle, or his grandfather, is the HSA, while another relative without that responsibility would play the part of the HSF—perhaps mother's brother or sister, or a grandmother, or some such. Freilich observes that similar sets of relationships are represented in societies like our own by triads within occupations or institutions. In a prison it might be "warden-chaplain-prisoner"; in a hospital, "psychiatrist-social worker-patient"; in the army, "officer-chaplain-G.I."; in a university, "authoritarian professor-friendly professor-student."

Freilich discusses the many-sided uses of this triadic form. For one thing, he says, it is a kind of buffer, upholding the hierarchical nature of a society that contains some who lead and some who follow, while mitigating the strains between the levels. The HSF, he says, is a power balancer within the group, mediating between the severity of the demands of the group and the needs of the individual. In our society, a grandparent, not usually being the disciplinarian of the child, can act as the HSF. But if the grandfather, for cultural or other reasons, is the main authority, the father or mother can be a chum or pal.

In addition, the HSF is a tension-reducer. If the HSA creates tension in the group, the HSF ameliorates it. Freilich turns to the concept of "expressive" and "instrumental" leaders originated by Talcott Parsons and Robert Bales, who wrote that in every group there will be one person who is the "task specialist" and one who is the "social-emotional specialist." Both Caplow and Freilich equate these roles with two necessary but conflicting polarities. There is the program of the individual and his own interest, and there is the program of the organization and its survival. Caplow argues that, at times, it is healthy for a "revolutionary" coalition of subordinates to override the sanctioned program of the organization. At other times, especially when the group is in danger from without, the authority structure of the organization takes precedence.

We could say that these polarities represent Ashby's adaptive mechanisms for the survival of any organism. The administrative side of the continuum falls into Ashby's category of "constraint," the rules and regulations necessary for the maintenance of the system. The individual side falls into the category of "variety," the pool of idiosyncratic elements from which new solutions can be drawn when the system is facing previously unknown circumstances. These polarities are the systole and diastole of the tension between stability and change.

Parsons, applying his version of these polarities to the American family, gives the mother the expressive role and the father the instrumental one. Empirical research has found this not always to be true, and latterly, of course, changes in parenting styles and sex roles make the linking of any position with any gender a doubtful enterprise.

Freilich points out that Bott's studies of family networks may clarify at least some of these issues. In families embedded in close-knit kin networks (usually working-class or ethnic groups) there is a fairly rigid differentiation of labor with instrumental and expressive roles clearly parceled out to father and mother respectively. Nuclear families with sparse or loose networks have a less rigid division of labor, and the parents' roles are more interchangeable. But whatever the arrangement, the possibility of an alternation between relatively "authoritarian" and "permissive" positions acts as a system of checks and balances which may be integral to the survival of any group.

Freilich tries to incorporate the principles of balance theory in explaining how his "natural triad" works—but this poses some problems. If Heider and other balance theorists are correct, the HSA, HSF, LSS triangle will have built-in difficulties. As soon as we posit a positive relationship between HSF and LSS, this means that the relationship between the two authorities will have to be negative, or else the triad will have to change, either with all sides becoming positive or with the HSA becoming friendlier with the LSS, and the HSF becoming more distant.

To guard against the pressure for change in such directions, Freilich suggests that "formality systems" equivalent to Caplow's status schisms between levels in a hierarchy, or Haley's generation line, will act as role protectors. As an example of my own, a student in trouble with the principal of his school might be befriended by the guidance counselor. Balance theory predicts that the friendlier the student and the counselor become, the more likely it is that the counselor will side with the student and that relations between counselor and principal will become tense, thus subverting the authority structure of the school. Usually the pressure for solidarity among school personnel will keep that tendency in check, so that principal and counselor do not become divided over handling the case, with possible worsening of the student's problems. This is an illustration of how a "formality system" or status line operates.

As this example suggests, Freilich's formulation applies mainly to a normal situation. It is appropriate for the leaders of a social system to represent two contrasting positions, either of which may be needed, depending on circumstances. The HSA (the principal in this example) is important at times when the survival of the group is at stake. The HSF (the counselor) is important when exceptions must be made on behalf of the individual, or when outside forces or interior stresses point to the need for change. If the "formality systems" are working right, they will counteract the strain toward compatibility predicted by balance theory, even when the leaders disagree.

But the "formality systems" do not always have sufficient weight when conflicts between leaders or in-groups become too great, or when there are pressures to form, or to intensify, cross-level or cross-generation coalitions. Here we will see an economical twist by which the natural triad, as described by Freilich, becomes the "perverse triangle" of Haley, and a third party is employed which diverts the threat of splitting or a war. It is at this point that we must return to the extraordinary insights of Alfred Stanton and Morris Schwartz, mentioned in Chapter 6, in their description of what they called "the special case": a configuration which seemed to act to encapsulate a conflict and prevent the social fabric from being torn apart.

The Problem of the Special Case

In *The Mental Hospital* Stanton and Schwartz explore the influence of triadic forms in mitigating conflict.[2] Published in 1954, the book was intended as a "social structural" study of a large institution. The authors were, by and large, committed to an organization theory framework that put the focus on elements such as chains of command, formal versus informal structures, flow charts for decision making, lines of communication, arrangements for handling conflicts, questions of morale, and all the other problems that interest the student of administration.

However, for family researchers, the study turned out to be an unexpected corroboration of some of their hypotheses. Clinicians working with families had long suspected that a hidden conflict between parents might have something to do with the symptomatic behavior of a child. Stanton and Schwartz's findings, which linked outbreaks of pathological behavior on a hospital ward to unaired disagreements among members of the staff, seemed to provide a suggestive confirmation for these hunches.

Oddly enough, few if any other organization theorists picked this idea up—which is why Stanton and Schwartz's work is so unusual. No study in small group or organization theory literature has explored in such detail the workings of the three-person form that Haley calls the "perverse triangle," Caplow calls the "improper coalition," and Stanton and Schwartz call the "problem of the special case."

What is so special about their "special case"? The phrase itself seems to lack color. It is almost as if the authors did not know that what they had stumbled on deserved a more glorious signature. Their book would have been, in fact, merely another organization theory study had not they allowed themselves to be sidetracked when an unidentifiable object swam into view.

This object first appeared during what began as an inquiry into breakdowns in staff morale. It seemed always to be around "the problem of a special case" that both patient outbursts on the wards and crises in the administrative life of the hospital clustered. This led the authors to put a circle around these events and start documenting their circumstances. They noticed that the problem invariably occurred when a patient was treated in such a way as to be marked off as a favorite or pet of some authority. It was not the same thing as "unique treatment." Sometimes a person had an objective reason for being treated differentially, as when he needed a special diet for a physical condition. To be a true "special case," the following features had to be present:

1. "special person" treatment
2. one who administers that treatment
3. one who protests it
4. an audience group whose norms are violated

Often the irritation around special treatment would be expressed most loudly when an item in short supply was specially given, so that others got less, or when the regimen ordered involved extra work for staff. When it was seen as connected with a patient's demand for particular recognition, or when it involved waiving of a hospital rule that others had to follow, this would also cause resentment.

The problem of the special case was also curious in that it seemed to appear only under certain circumstances. For instance, if matters on a ward were unusually disorganized or weren't going well, a staff member might start to favor one patient at such a time. Others would then begin to criticize the staff member, and feelings against the patient would run high. A division would make itself felt along a line of cleavage implicit in most organizations. In this hospital as in other institutions, persons in authority tended to cluster around two poles: some represented the official program, with all its rules and regulations, and others took a more permissive attitude, arguing that each case must be judged individually. Stanton and Schwartz noted that at the center of each "special case" disturbance, there would be two persons on the staff who represented those two poles.

The authors also noted that these persons were unable to deal directly with each other over the issues that divided them—and there was usually at least one issue which was not directly related to patient care—but that they chose to do battle through a third party, so to speak. Thus the one whose style came closest to the permissive pole would side with the patient against the unfeeling bureaucracy and would engineer all kinds of favors for him. The other, believing in an across-the-board enforcement of rules, would insist that the patient be treated like everybody else. The "protective" party might be a therapist and the "punitive" party a nurse, since these two opponents often represented the two opposing groups within the institution. After a while the staff closest to the main participants would begin to take sides and a polarization would appear along authoritarian versus permissive lines. The patient would usually respond by becoming extremely agitated. Although he might be seen as a successful manipulator, playing both ends to his own advantage, his position was actually not enviable. He was forced to respond to contradictory definitions of his situation by two superiors who each had power over his fate. This often resulted in the patient becoming extremely disruptive and upsetting his entire ward.

The authors go on to observe that the disruption might not only spread downward among the patient population, but upward, invading each echelon of the administration. As the controversy between the two staff members mounted, each of them would talk to (or, as Bowen would say, "triangle in") more and more personnel. If the major figures were influential in the hospital structure, the entire staff might end up divided into two warring camps, with the patient as the *cause célèbre.* Subsidiary disagreements would cluster about the main one, differentiated from it primarily by the fact that their resolution would leave the core situation relatively unchanged.

The resolution of the main problem could happen in several ways. One of the two combatants could go over the head of his opponent to protest to a superior, usually by threatening to hand in his resignation. Sometimes one of the two parties would begin to attract more and more opprobrium to himself until he ended up a "minority of one." In this case, if his resignation was accepted, it was tantamount to an extrusion, an example of Taylor's single deviant arrangement. This would in essence free the patient, who had until then been the major recipient of stress.

But a more effective way to resolve the crisis, according to the authors, was for the opposing pair to settle their differences directly, face to face. The striking fact about the "special case" situation was that the real disagreement, whatever it might be, was something the principals were not always aware of. The authors began to believe that this matter of covert disagreement was central to the special case, if not actually its cause. They go so far as to state that:

All patients who were the center of attention for the ward for several days or longer during the period of study were the subjects of such a covert disagreement. The most striking finding was that pathologically excited patients were quite regularly the subjects of secret, affectively important staff disagreement; and, equally regularly, their excitement terminated, usually abruptly, when the staff members were brought to discuss seriously their points of disagreement with each other.[3]

The authors present a detailed, day-by-day account of one such difficulty between a staff administrator and the patient's therapist, which documents the above assertion. The state of the patient fluctuated according to the intensity of the unexpressed disagreement between these two staff members until they finally talked matters out, whereupon the patient's excitability immediately subsided.

Stanton and Schwartz also discuss a related phenomenon: the collective disturbance, which in one case involved a change that was imposed by administration in the name of economy but that was seen as detrimental to patient welfare by many of the staff. Personnel took sides for and against this change, and after it was finally instituted a crisis in morale occurred, not only among staff but among the patient population. It was during this period that the agitation of one patient on a ward spread contagiously, until the whole ward was in a turmoil. A therapist who was an outspoken critic of administration policy had disputed the treatment of this patient with a member of the administration. The authors make the point that in this case the background of the patient's agitation was not only the conflict between the therapist and the administrator but the crisis involving a collective polarization of the entire institution. It did not matter that the disputed policies had been dictated by sources quite outside the hospital itself.

The Mirror-Image Disagreement

In Chapter 2 we paid attention to one very important aspect of social groups: the appearance of self-reinforcing repeating sequences. Haley, Caplow, and Freilich, in the works cited, tended to describe their triangles in static terms, like pieces of architecture or bits of Euclidian geometry. Yet, on a closer look, these triangles are not static but embody the type of mutual-causal processes referred to above. Stanton and Schwartz were the first researchers to link the rigid triadic forms characteristic of social contexts where symptoms appear to these peculiar redundancies. They became fascinated with the dynamics of their "special case" and invented a phrase to describe the polarization that invariably took place around it: the "mirror-image disagreement." If, during the management of a "special case," the two authorities took opposing views along authoritarian versus permissive lines, a deviation-amplifying process would ensue that would increase their differences exponentially. The more the protector protected a patient, the more the punisher would punish him. But a central rule seemed to be that the parties must remain polarized. If one party changed position, the other would, apparently unconsciously, make a simultaneous about-face, so that the structure of contraries in which the patient was locked remained the same. By this process, an originally small conflict between two authorities could become enormous. This could happen even in benign circumstances, with ludicrous results.

One could say that the patient, caught in such a vicious cycle, is the unwitting agent who exponentially transforms a difference or conflict between two staff members into a full-blown mirror-image disagreement. But if one is to remain circular, one should not forget the part the patient plays in maintaining and intensifying this disagreement. In some strange way the intensity of the conflict gets disssipated by going through the patient, almost as if he were a lightning rod, and with the unconscious connivance of the apparent "victim."

This amelioration of the conflict does not happen without a price, however. In a brilliant insight, Stanton and Schwartz surmise that this type of polarization becomes internalized and surfaces in the patient in the form of a pathological condition known as "dissociation." This simply means that a person begins to perceive events and persons around him in purely black and white terms. One person will seem all bad, another all good. The patient will see himself, too, as alternately "bad" or "good."

The authors observe, however, that the patient may not be perceiving the facts as unrealistically as supposed. As they observe, two important persons in the patient's life are in fact pulling him in opposite directions. If these two persons are authorities with fateful power over him, and one of them sees him in need of strict controls and punishment and the other as deserving of favors and kindness, a social context emerges in which the patient's "dissociated" fantasies may be justified. This is not only true in regard to the perception of the favoring person as good and the nonfavoring person as bad, but may also pertain to conflicting notions about treatment or about the self. The authors conclude by saying:

If our hypothesis is correct that the patient's dissociation is a reflection of, and a mode of participation in, a social field which itself is seriously split, it accounts for the sudden cessation of excitement following any resolution of this split in the social field.[4]

Stanton and Schwartz thus share with Haley the idea that certain behaviors associated with schizophrenia are an appropriate reaction to a real split between real others with whom the patient is intimately engaged, if not deeply dependent on. This is very different from assuming that there is a split in his personality, or a dissociative process taking place in his brain. In particular, the idea is presented that the person at the nexus of a pathological triad is somehow deflecting splits in the wider social field—between kin groups in the case of the family, or between professional groups in the case of an institution. It is of interest that the line of fission on which the split takes place is simply an intensification of the polarities inherent in the dual executive structure which seems to be most functional for any group. The dynamic model of Stanton and Schwartz, which deals with an escalation of intensities along this line of social cleavage, also explains the severity of the symptom displayed by the person who is mediating the split, which may psychically, if not literally, tear him apart. It also offers the thought that this person may indeed be an unwitting sacrifice, so that he, rather than the body politic, absorbs the split.

Stanton and Schwartz concerned themselves with pathological escalations in the context of a hospital ward. The logical next step is to examine such escalations within a family that has a member with a psychiatric symptom to see if the family acts in the same way as a matrix for symptomatic behavior. Of all clinician-researchers, Salvador Minuchin has done the most interesting work in this area.

Conflict-Detouring Triads

A recent contribution to the literature connecting triads to the management of conflict is Minuchin's *Psychosomatic Families*, a ground-breaking study of children with psychosomatic disorders: asthma, diabetes, and anorexia nervosa.[5] Minuchin and his coworkers started from the hypothesis that children could be used to obscure or deflect parental conflict. In analyzing relationship configurations which coincided with symptoms in a child, Minuchin formulated a typology of what he called "rigid triads."

These "rigid triads" are: "Triangulation," "Parent-Child Coalition," "Detouring-Attacking," and "Detouring-Supportive" (see Figure 8.1). "Triangulation" describes a situation where two parents, in overt or covert conflict, are each attempting to enlist the child's sympathy or support against the other. This form would correspond to what I have called the "inadmissible triangle" of balance theory, the triangle with two positive sides, connoting intense conflict of loyalty. "Parent-Child" is a more open expression of parental conflict, even though the family may come for treatment with a child problem. One parent will side with the child against the other parent, and at times it is difficult to determine whether the child or the outsider spouse is in more difficulty. The intense closeness of the child to the preferred parent can result in symptomatology, however, especially when the natural process of growing up begins to put stress on the parent-child stasis.

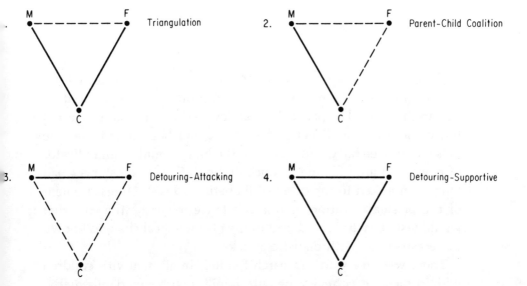

Figure 8.1
Minuchin: "Rigid" Triads

There are two types of "Detouring" triads. In a "Detouring-Attacking" triad the parents are most often perceived by the clinician as scapegoating the child. The behavior the child shows is disruptive or "bad," and the parents band together to control him, even though one parent is often apt to disagree with the other parent over how to handle him and both may handle him inconsistently. Most behavior disorders in children fall into this category. In a "Detouring-Supportive" triad the parents are able to mask their differences by focusing on a child who is defined as "sick," and for whom the parents show an enormous, overprotective concern. This brings them close together and is a frequent feature of families in which tension is expressed through psychosomatic disorders. All these triads, or permutations of them, can be found in families with psychosomatic children, but they are prevalent in families where children have other problems as well.

The Transfer of Stress

Using this triadic framework, Minuchin's team came up with a research idea that ties parent-child interactions to symptom production in the child. The particular test devised was originally directed toward a group of diabetic children. It had been noted that the presence of free fatty acids (FFA) in the blood could be an indicator of emotional arousal, and a concentration of these substances had long been linked to the onset of diabetic acidosis. A measurement of the plasma elevation of this substance might be the clue that would test out what could lead to the physiological changes known to be associated with diabetic attacks.

There were forty-five research families in all: ten with children with intractable asthma; nine with families with superlabile diabetes; and eleven with children with severe anorexia. The control group consisted of seven families with diabetic children whose illness was well controlled, and eight families with behavior-problem diabetics whose condition was not life-threatening. The purpose of the experiment was to provide evidence for Minuchin's hypothesis that the symptom of the child is intimately connected with the presence or absence of stresses between his parents. The larger research purpose of the study was to prove that a therapy that concentrated on changing the structure of relationships which constrained the child would also alleviate the symptom.

The question that especially interests us here, however, is the smaller one dramatized by the structured interview. This interview was designed so that blood samples of parents and symptomatic child could be taken at regular intervals. After a baseline FFA level was established for each family member, the child was placed behind a one-way screen to watch while an interviewer induced an argument between the parents. After half an hour the child was asked to come into the room, and parents and child were asked to work together on a solution of the argument.

The researchers found that the symptomatic children in the experimental group showed a far higher rise in elevations of plasma

FFA than children in the control group. In addition, their FFA level went higher and took longer to return to baseline after the interview was over than anyone else in the family, while the FFA level of the "higher parent" began to go down shortly and sharply after the symptomatic child entered the room. Examination of family interaction data (all sessions were videotaped) confirmed the hypothesis that in some way the parents "passed on" their emotional arousal to the child, as one would transfer a heavy weight. In the experimental families almost all conversation involved the child, while in the control families much more interaction took place between the parents.

Although there is no known direct link between levels of free fatty acids in the blood and the symptoms connected with asthma and anorexia, the children with these disorders behaved much the same in the interview as the diabetics. For instance, the FFA profiles of all the anorectic children, averaged out, rose in a high, steep curve as the parents argued; the level of the "normal" diabetics stayed below baseline level; while that of the "behavioral" diabetics rose slightly above it. This experiment, limited though it may be in population, is the first to my knowledge that has ever established a direct tie between an interactional sequence involving a symptomatic child and chemical changes associated with his illness.

Therapeutic interventions based on Minuchin's hypothesis that a child's symptom can be linked with parental conflict proved unusually successful. The goal of therapy was a structural one: to disengage the child from his position between the parents and to help the parents deal with their problems more directly. Follow-up studies of the group of fifty families of anorectic children over an eight-year period showed that 86 percent of these children had recovered. In addition, they were doing well on other indices of normal functioning. Most of the group reached normal weight within less than a year of treatment, some in the first weeks after therapy started. To date, there have been no deaths, which contrasts with the standard fatality rate for anorectics of 12 percent. In addition, the return to social and personal functioning contrasts with the average 40–60 percent success rate of individual therapy treatment programs, in which the anorectic may regain normal weight but continues to show symptoms and to function poorly.

At this point it is useful to reconnect with the idea, suggested by Stanton and Schwartz, that a child's symptom may be associated with a mirror-image disagreement between the parents (overt or covert) which can be enormously stressful if it involves the child. In the four cases illustrating therapy with anorectics in Minuchin's book, this form repeats itself over and over in the beginning interviews. It is almost as if there were a hidden program in some famlies, no matter what social group they come from. Otherwise, how do all these families, from such diverse backgrounds, come up with such a similar reaction to threats to family stability? Over and over in the initial lunch session (a standard feature of Minuchin's treatment program for anorectics) there is one authoritative parent who tries to force the child to eat and another who pulls back, gives way, attempts to calm the child and soften the other parent. The child is caught in the classic "ballot box" situation: If he eats, he will be voting for one parent, and if he does not, he will be voting for the other. In addition, the action escalates so that he is being pulled harder and harder in two directions.

Nevertheless, it is important to realize that we are not dealing here with a simple triangle or cycle, but a complex force field with surprisingly similar characteristics from family to family. It is almost as if there were sets of instructions in families—perhaps in all social groups—having to do with the ordering of behaviors in the face of change.

We have seen that the most obvious single characteristic of families with "disturbed" members is their apparent lawlessness, most strikingly conveyed by the lack of boundaries or appropriate status lines. The family is governed—if that is the word—by a powerful politics of secret coalitions across the generations. What is so intriguing about the families in which this subterranean structure prevails is that one also finds processes equivalent to Bateson's corrective circuits, with symmetrical escalations tending to polarize the family, blocked by complementary sequences of a counteracting nature; threats of civil war or reciprocal violence, blocked by symptomatic displays or, alternatively, the emergence of the kind of solidarity which only a common enemy or an outside catastrophe can create. Of all these forms, the most common check to violence or splitting is, as we have noted, the "single deviant arrangement," in which the group attains unity at the expense of a symptomatic member. At the same time, the family fails to evolve toward an organization more appropriate to its stage. How to intervene in these schismogenic operations, and in the fateful spirals that characterize them, will be the material for the next few chapters.

Chapter 9

The Simple Bind and Discontinuous Change

Evolutionary Feedback

At this mid-point in our discussion we shall shift from a structural taxonomy to a process taxonomy, in line with Bateson's model for mapping phenomena at increasing levels of complexity: the "zigzag ladder of dialectic between form and process."[1] It has been useful to note the early impressionistic descriptions of the flow of interaction in families that produce disturbed persons, and then to try to codify structures from the information provided by this flow. In families with psychotic members, in particular, generalizations about deviant and normative structures are ways of imposing an external order upon flow. One can snatch out of the booming, buzzing confusion of family interaction certain clear redundancies and say, "There it is, and there, and there again!"

The emphasis on structure, however, does not reflect the power of living systems to reorganize in sudden and transcendent ways. A recent paper by Paul Dell and Harold Goolishian examines the concept of "evolutionary feedback," a term developed by the physicist Prigogine to describe a "basic, nonequilibrium ordering principle that governs the forming and unfolding of systems at all levels."[2] One can turn to Bateson's *Mind and Nature* and find a similar description in his comparison between epigenesis and evolution:

In contrast with epigenesis and tautology, which constitute the worlds of replication, there is the whole realm of creativity, art, learning and evolution, in which the ongoing processes of change *feed on the random*. The essence of epigenesis is predictable repetition; the essence of learning and evolution is exploration and change.[3]

Prigogine's concept of "order through fluctuation," as Dell describes it, emphasizes not stability and homeostatis but the idea of discontinuous change:

. . . at any point in time, the system functions in a particular way with fluctuations around that point. This particular way of functioning has a range of stability within which fluctuations are damped down and the system remains more or less unchanged. Should a fluctuation become amplified, however, it may exceed the existing range of stability and lead the entire system into a new dynamic range of functioning. An autocatalytic step or surge into positive feedback is needed to obtain such instability.[4]

Dell's point is that the cybernetic analogy based on a mechanical model of closed-system feedback is limited and inaccurate. There is a different cybernetics of living systems which was incompletely explained by the negative feedback view. This point is dramatized by the sudden, step-wise leaps to new integrations characteristic of such systems, which are not only unpredictable but irreversible. The conceptual emphasis is not on processes that tend toward equilibrium, but rather on self-organizing processes that reach toward new evolutionary stages.

What makes this argument so crucial is that families that come for treatment with distress in one or more members seem to be having difficulty with evolving—they are or seem nonevolved, stuck in an outmoded stage. Perhaps it is this being stuck that made the early version of the homeostatic model so convincing to therapists working with troubled families. The emphasis in those families is on maintaining equilibrium, too much so. For those families that become more and more like a homeostatically controlled piece of machinery, the task of therapy should be to make available the power inherent in all living systems to transcend the stuckness and move to a different stage.

To recast our cybernetic analogy within an evolutionary framework is certainly in itself an evolutionary step forward in family theory and theory of change. For one thing, it fits the process we are trying to describe far better than the static model of error-activated feedback mechanisms does. For another, it affords a far more satisfying rationale for the success of some of the so-called paradoxical approaches to therapy that produce rapid shifts in families or individuals. These shifts can take place with incredible suddenness, and indeed seem to be self-generated. To go further into this subject, let us turn to the ideas of another physicist who has written about discontinuous change, John Platt.

Hierarchical Growth

One property that families share with other complex systems is that they do not change in a smooth, unbroken line but in discontinuous leaps. Platt, in an imaginative paper, speaks of a process physics in which the emphasis is not on static structure but on what he calls a "flow hierarchy": forms that maintain a steady state while matter, energy, and information continually flow through them.[5] A bit of thought will convince the reader that families, too, are like waterfalls or cascades, with the many-tiered pattern of the generations persisting as an overall structure, even though individuals pass through it as they are born, grow old, and die.

Platt argues that many natural systems are of this type, and that change in such systems occurs in a startling and sudden way. He cites falling in love, acts of creation, conversions, evolutionary leaps, reformations, and revolutions as examples, and says that when a system is conflicted or dysfunctional this may not necessarily portend disaster but may indicate that pressure toward a new and more complex integration is mounting.

Platt makes a useful distinction between three kinds of change, each of which depends on the way the entity in question is organized. If the entity is externally designed (a watch, for example), then any change will have to be imposed by an outside agent, the watchmaker, who may take apart and reassemble the watch. If it is internally designed (a plant that contains a genetic blueprint), then only mutations of the gene pattern can produce a change.

A third model for change is found in living systems that, unlike plants, have the capacity to evolve to new and unpredictable levels of organization. In such systems, change is not prefixed but takes the form of a transformation, a sudden appearance of more functionally organized patterns that did not exist before. Platt calls this type of change "time emergence." One might think of a kaleidoscope, which keeps the same geometric pattern as the tube is turned until all at once a small particle shifts in response to gravity and the whole pattern changes to an entirely new one. The most interesting feature of a kaleidoscope is that one can never return to an earlier pattern, and this is consonant with the way systems that have what Ashby calls "bimodal feedback mechanisms" operate.[6] Such systems will remain stable as long as the environment around them does not change, or as long as internal elements within do not change; but if either of these events occurs, the system will break down or else respond by shifting to a new "setting" that will meet the demands of the new field. The change in the setting creates a discontinuity because the range of behaviors, the "grammar" for allowable activities, has changed. Thus a set of completely different patterns, options, and possibilities emerges. The new organization is usually more complex than the previous one, but it too is rule-governed and will not change again until new pressures from the field enforce a new leap. Not to sound too purposive, it must be emphasized that the source of newness most often comes from some random element. As Bateson says: "The ongoing processes of change *feed on* the random."[7]

The natural history of a leap or transformation is usually this: First, the patterns that have kept the system in a steady state relative to its environment begin to work badly. New conditions arise for which these patterns were not designed. Ad hoc solutions are tried and sometimes work, but usually have to be abandoned. Irritation grows over small but persisting difficulties. The accumulation of dissonance eventually forces the entire system over an edge, into a state of crisis, as the stabilizing tendency brings on ever-intensifying corrective sweeps that get out of control. The end point of what cybernetic engineers call a runaway is that the system breaks down, or creates a new way to monitor the same homeostasis, or spontaneously leaps to an integration that will deal better with the changed field.

Families are notable examples of entities that change through leaps. The individuals making up a family are growing (at least partly) according to an internal biological design, but the larger groupings within the family, the subsystems and the generations, must endure major shifts in relation to each other. The task of the family is to produce and train new sets of humans to be independent, form new families, and repeat the process, as the old set loses power, declines, and dies. Family life is a multigenerational changing of the guard. And although this process is at times a smooth one, like the transitions of political parties in a democracy, it is more often fraught with danger and disruption. Most families do not leap to new integrations with ease, and the "transformations" Platt refers to are by no means self-assured. This brings us to the research of sociologists and clinicians studying the family life cycle.

Expectable Life Stage Crises

The family life cycle was discovered by a circuitous route. Of major importance was the work of Erik Erikson during the 1940s and 1950s, whose depiction of individual life stages, and of the interplay between these stages and the shaping processes of social institutions, challenged the narrow focus of intrapsychic theories of development.[8] After World War II, clinicians studying individuals' responses to stress began to question the notion that some people had better coping patterns or better "ego strengths" than others. One of the first pioneers in this area, Erich Lindemann, noticed that the difference between a normal and an abnormal grief reaction had to do with the overall makeup of the family network of the bereaved one, not with his coping mechanisms as shown by previous attempts to handle stress. In his classic study of survivors and relatives of victims of the Cocoanut Grove fire, Lindemann notes that

Not infrequently the person who died represented a key person in a social system; his death was followed by disintegration of this social system and by a profound alteration of the living and social conditions for the bereaved.[9]

The intensity of a grief reaction did not have to be tied in with a previous neurotic history, but was linked to the type of loss for the person involved.

Researchers who came after Erikson and Lindemann began to see that in terms of the family life cycle, one man's adolescence might coincide with his mother's change of life, and possibly his grandmother's demise. Rhona Rapaport has singled out as stress events "the critical transition points in the *normal, expectable* development of the family life cycle: getting married, birth of the first child, children going to school, death of a spouse, or children leaving home."[10]

Reuben Hill, at the University of Minnesota, has found differences in the way families respond to these stages. He speculates about the factors that predispose a family to treat a normal life stage stress as a crisis.[11] For instance, a child going to kindergarten might in some families produce a crisis, as the retirement of the head of the household would in others. A growing number of researchers, such as Michael Solomon, have extended these observations to show that psychiatric and medical symptoms tend to cluster magnetically about those times.[12]

Building on these observations, Thomas Eliot contributes the idea that a crisis in a family often follows a revision of membership. He offers two unusual terms: crisis of dismemberment, meaning when a family loses someone; and crisis of accession, meaning an addition to the group.[13] Lindemann's work, as the passage just quoted makes clear, falls into the category of dismemberment, or, to use a less grisly word, separation. A crisis of accession is exemplified in studies like that of E. E. LeMasters on "Parenthood as Crisis."[14]

Not only a loss, it then appeared, but the acquisition of new family members could trigger an upset. In 1967, a now classic study by T. H. Holmes and R. H. Rahe, who compiled a "Social Readjustment Rating Scale," indicated that there was no correlation between the negative perception of an event and the degree of stress that was attached to it.[15] Out of a list of forty-three life stress events, rated by 394 subjects in terms of intensity and length of time necessary to accommodate to them, ten out of the top fourteen involved gaining or losing a family member. It is fascinating to realize that events with presumably positive meanings, like "marital reconciliation," ranked as more stressful on the scale than some with negative connotations, like "difficulties with sex."[16]

If it is true that crises tend to erupt at times when a family is faced with a normal revision of membership, then it is logical to assume that these crises would be most intense in families that have difficulty reorganizing—letting members go or taking in new ones. It is only one step more to the surmise of family researchers like Haley that symptomatic behaviors tend to surface at points in the family life cycle when the process of disengagement of one generation from another is prevented or held up.[17] For instance, members of a family in which a child is one of the possible factors that is mediating a parental conflict may resist or even block the child's departure. A symptom seems to be a compromise between staying and leaving; the child becomes incapacitated to a greater or lesser degree and never really leaves home, or may leave but find it hard to negotiate the transition to marriage and fall back, or else a child of the new marriage may have to serve as mediator in turn. One can often see the truth of the biblical statement: "The fathers have eaten a sour grape, and the children's teeth are set on edge." Sometimes one frail, psychotic child seems to be holding an entire kin network on his shoulders, like the key person in a family high-wire act, displaying incredible strength and impeccable sense of balance.

We may now justifiably ask what the arrangement is that somehow prevents people in a family from making the leap to a new integration? The answer is suggested by the concept of another kind of shift, which occurs when an entity is about to exceed its parameters or break. For this we shall have to turn to Ashby and his idea of step-mechanisms.

The Concept of Step-Mechanisms

In *Design for a Brain,* Ashby described four types of movement by which natural forms or substances pass from one state to another.[18] A "full-function" moves in a progressive fashion without a finite interval of constancy between states, like a barometer. A "step-function" has intervals of constancy separated by discontinuous jumps, like a set of stairs. A "part-function" is like a step-function except that from one state to another the line is progressive, rather than instantaneous. A "null-function" indicates simply an absence of movement or change.

Ashby comments that many step-functions occur in the natural world. His examples include the tendency of an elastic band to break when the proportion of pull versus length reaches a certain point, or of a fuse to blow when the circuit is loaded beyond a certain number of amperes. Looking at more complex entities, such as machines, Ashby notices that some of their variables may exhibit a sudden shift in character whenever they reach a certain value that he calls a "critical state." In fact, he says, it is common for systems to show step-function changes whenever their variables are driven too far from some usual value. He speculates that it would be useful for a system to have at least one such element. For instance, in the electrical wiring of a house, if there is no circuit breaker, the whole system will break down and have to be replaced. But if there is a circuit breaker, only a fuse will blow, and when that is replaced (assuming the overload has been corrected), the system will still be functioning. Ashby calls this type of arrangement a step-mechanism.

One difficulty with Ashby's ideas is that he was not really concerned with living systems at the group level and above but was trying to devise a cybernetic model that would account for the evolution and structure of the brain. Thus most of his examples are drawn from the worlds of biology, chemistry, and physics, and one has to pull his ideas out of context to make them apply to social systems. But without some notion similar to the step-mechanism, the sudden shifts in behavior one often sees in families with symptomatic members could never be explained.

163

In the family, one essential variable is the relationship between members of the executive dyad, who are usually the parents. This relationship probably has particular arrangements regarding the management of such dimensions as closeness/distance and balance of power, which limit the behaviors allowed in this dyad. Let us hypothesize that one of these sets of limits is constantly being overpassed. With an even-Stephen or symmetrical couple, a slight advantage accruing to one person may provoke an escalation that, if not blocked, could end in violence or divorce. With a one-up/one-down or complementary couple, too much inequality may produce depression in the "low" spouse and concomitant anxiety in the "high" one. Whatever the nature of the plateau (and it is usually not a pure example of either of these models), there will be a "critical state" that represents some value beyond which the couple as a system may not go and remain intact.

At this point different things can happen. A couple may have techniques for handling this threat, like a cooling-off period for an angry symmetrical couple or a "good fight" for a distant complementary one. Another technique would be for one of the spouses to develop a severe or chronic symptom, which will also prevent a split, though at a cost. However, it often happens that a third party, very likely a child, becomes drawn into the conflict. Once this happens, the child's discomfort grows while parental tensions lessen. Some minimal cue indicating parental conflict may incite anxiety in the child, who reacts with irritating behavior. At this point one of the parents may start to attack him or her, while the other moves to the child's defense. Caught in the tightening spiral, the child may respond with a physical or emotional symptom. This will cause the parents to stop their covert struggle and unite. A very real issue joins the couple, since the child's well-being is at stake. Their getting together, especially if it is accompanied by supportive behavior, allows the child's anxiety to diminish.

In this example one could say that warning signals are at work whenever a feedback chain reaches a critical state in a set of relationships. These signals forestall events that might endanger relationships important to the group. For instance, the child's symptom is a warning signal that diverts the parents from having a fight.

But what if the child's discomfort proceeds to a level that is unacceptable, and a positive feedback chain develops that cannot be countered by the usual family responses? Here we move up to the next level, where the interface is not between the child and his parents but between the family and the wider society. Ashby writes:

A common, though despised, property of every machine is that it may "break." . . . In general, when a machine "breaks," the representative point has met some critical state, and the corresponding step-function has changed value. . . . As is well known, almost any machine or physical system will break if its variables are driven far enough from their usual value.[19]

It is possible that what is generally called a nervous breakdown is similar in function to what Ashby is talking about. In a family, the individual's "breakdown" operates as a step-mechanism signaling the failure of the family's stabilizing arrangements and often activating interventions from the larger system, the community. Here is where helpers in various guises come in and an attempt is made to repair the broken element, the person.

But to go back to the image of the electric circuit, as long as it continues to be overloaded, it will not do any good to fix or replace the fuse. Sometimes the problem is temporary; the overload has been due to a sudden plugging in of an extra appliance (a mother-in-law visiting, for instance), and once that is taken away, the system will return to normal. But often the change is permanent. Somebody has died, or there is an irreversible shift in family circumstances, or a family member has reached a new maturation level. Then the family must make a shift in its overall organization to meet the new demands. Otherwise the person's symptomatic behavior may continue, or another problematic behavior may replace it. In a family with a troubled member, we may be dealing with a fear on the part of family members that the leap to the next stage may impair some important family member or subsystem, or threaten the survival of the family itself.

It follows that symptomatic displays can be thought of negatively as aborted transformations or positively as negotiations around the possibility of change. In his *Prison Notebooks,* the Marxist philosopher Antonio Gramsci writes: "The crisis consists precisely in the fact that the old is dying and the new cannot be born; in this interregnum a great variety of morbid symptoms appears."[20] A symptomatic redundancy is an arrangement that usually springs up to handle this interregnum between the old and the new. It represents a compromise between pressures for and against change. The symptom is only the most visible aspect of a connected flow of behaviors and acts as a primary irritant that both monitors the options for change, lest too rapid movement imperil someone in the family, and also keeps the necessity for change constantly alive. What results then is a turmoil of behaviors that spiral rather than cycle around the possibility of a leap. Sometimes the leap is taken simply because of some accidental shift brought about by the spiral, which is always moving forward in time. Even a very narrow, bunched-up spiral that chronically circles around some central point is still always shifting and is never without some potential for change. Reiss, in his paper on family paradigms, describes a nice example of this change-by-accident. A teenager in a family fell seriously ill while the family was on a camping trip. The father, who had been seen as nice but boyishly undependable, took over during the emergency, carving out a new and lastingly authoritative role for himself.[21]

The next question is how to help the family to make a leap up, rather than continue in the chronic spiral, and to achieve a transformation to a new stage that will obviate the presence of symptoms or distress.

Paradoxical Injunctions and the "Sweat Box"

Platt, as we saw, was stressing the positive—even extraordinary —capacity of living systems to achieve transformations that go beyond what could previously have been predicted or achieved, thus not only "saving the day" but pointing the way toward a new one. Ashby was looking at a different kind of shift, perhaps equally extraordinary: the ability of one element of a system to "break" if too much pressure for change has been introduced. In a family or other group, the shift to a symptomatic configuration saves the day, but it does not always point the way to a new one. It may be seen as a nonevolution, or failed leap, since it not only keeps the family from making a new integration but seems to happen at the expense of one family member, who has often sentimentally been thought of as the "scapegoat." On the other hand, it may be valued as the only persistent pressure toward change that is going on in the family.

The question for therapy then becomes: How does one disrupt an arrangement that in some ways promotes family stability (morphostasis) and instead help the family achieve a transformation that will represent a more complex integration (morphogenesis)? Here a discussion of what Richard Rabkin calls "saltology" (from the Latin *saltus*, "to leap"), and that might more prosaically be called "leap theory," is in order. Also important in this connection is some extremely good thinking Rabkin has done in relating transformations or leaps to the appearance of that communicational oddity the "paradoxical injunction."

In a paper called "A Critique of the Clinical Use of the Double Bind," Rabkin has presented a refreshing examination of the original double-bind concept.[22] This paper reclassifies most of the examples used by clinician-researchers to illustrate double binds into masked hostility, sarcasm, strategic deceit, and ordinary "damned-if-you-do, damned-if-you-don't" dilemmas.

A case can be made for equating at least one of these dilemmas, the paradoxical injunction, with the double bind. A paradoxical injunction is a statement that intrinsically contradicts itself unless teased apart into a "report" level and a "how this report is meant" level, with the second level inclusive of the first. An example, from Sluzki et al.'s article on transactional disqualification, is the following exchange:

SON (to mother): You treat me like a child.
MOTHER: But you are my child.[23]

The mother's answer on the "report" level is absolutely true, but in the context of the exchange the mother is doing some devious reframing: the son is wrong; the son is unfairly criticizing her; the son should furthermore accept these distortions of his original message *because he is her child.* This would be a fair example of what the researchers in Palo Alto would have thought of as a double bind, whether Sluzki does or not. And the double bind was, as we know, associated with manifestations of irrational behaviors such as schizophrenia.

Nevertheless, there is a terrible simplification here. Rabkin points out that the paradoxical injunction is a form of communication that all parents and all children (all superiors and all subordinates, for that matter) encounter at some time in their lives without going insane. Of course they may get upset—but ideally they shouldn't, Rabkin argues, because the paradoxical injunction is the best our poor language can do to suggest that a systems change is required.

Rabkin takes an example clinicians have used to equate a paradoxical injunction with a double bind. The parent says to the child, at a point when the child is about to pass into the gray area of adolescence: "I insist you go to school because you enjoy the beauties of learning." (The Bateson group in Palo Alto used a similar example, a *New Yorker* cartoon in which an employer is telling an uncomfortable-looking employee, "But, Jones, I don't want you to agree with me because I say so, but because you see it my way.") Rabkin then quotes Arthur Koestler on the process of creation. Before a creative leap can occur, says Koestler, all previous pathways must be blocked. It is only from the accumulated intensity of the stress that pressure to take the leap will occur.[24]

Seen in this light, the paradoxical injunction appears to be the communicational form most likely to create sufficient pressure for change. The paradoxical injunction of parent to adolescent child says, in effect, "I want you to be independent, but I want you to want that independently of my wanting that." What might be called, for want of a better term, a "simple bind" is set up. The receiver is directed to remain simultaneously in a symmetrical and a complementary relationship with the communicant. This being impossible, a leap must be taken to what Rabkin calls an "achievement," his word for Platt's transformation or new integration.

The impossible situations that the Zen Master sets up for the student are understandable in this light. The Master says to the student: "Here is a stick. If you say it is real, I will hit you with it. If you say it is not real, I will hit you with it. If you say nothing, I will hit you with it." One response is for the student simply to take away the stick. The whole point is for the student to become "equal" to the Master, but this cannot be done by an order from the Master, or from within the Master-student relationship at all. The student must somehow get the idea "on his own" that this is the course he must take. In line with this thinking, one should reserve the term "paradoxical injunction" or "simple bind" for the confusing directive that often appears as a harbinger of a leap to a new stage, and the term "double bind" for communication sequences that block this leap, or imply unthinkable consequences should it occur.

The introduction of this concept of the simple bind solves many issues that have perplexed researchers and clinicians for years. For one thing, there is no longer the vexing question: If paradoxical communication is operating in art, fantasy, play, and most creative activity, how do we distinguish between forms of paradoxical communication that are associated with schizophrenic communication and forms that are associated with the achievements of the artist or the prophet? For another, we have a way to explain the idea of the therapeutic double bind or counterparadox, which has been likened to homeopathic medicine: The cure resembles the disease. A therapeutic double bind might be rephrased as a reinstatement of the conditions of a simple bind, although this time within a different context: the relationship between the therapist and the client or family. The bind is reimposed, the period of confusion is gone through, the family or client takes the requisite leap, and the new integration is then rewarded, rather than invalidated or dismissed, or is its own reward.

An example of this process is described by Bateson in an essay on "learning to learn."[25] Bateson had become interested in porpoises who were trained to show "operant conditioning" to the public by exhibiting special behaviors, hearing a whistle, and then receiving a fish. The porpoises possessed a considerable repertoire of these behaviors. Bateson realized that these animals, since they did not produce the same behavior every time, must have "learned to learn" how to produce a piece of conspicuous behavior. He asked to watch the process by which a porpoise was taught to do this, and in fact created an experimental situation in which to conduct his observations.

First the trainer was to reward the porpoise for a piece of conspicuous behavior. The animal quickly learned that raising her head would produce a fish, and several repetitions reinforced this impression. However, the next time the porpoise came in and repeated the behavior, no fish. The trainer would wait for the animal to produce a new piece of conspicuous behavior—perhaps an annoyed tail flap—and then would reward that. The behavior was reinforced three times in the session in which it occurred but not in the next. Rewards occurred only when the porpoise again produced a piece of unusual behavior.

This process was evidently so disturbing to both man and beast that the trainer kept breaking the rules to reinforce the creature at times that were not appropriate. The porpoise, in turn, began to act more and more agitated as attempts to gain a previously reinforced reward would prove futile, exhibiting behaviors that, in a human, might be called psychotic.

Before the fifteenth session, however, a remarkable event took place. The porpoise rushed about the tank, appearing intensely excited. When she came on for her performance, she put on an elaborate display of eight behaviors, three of which had never been noticed in this species before. Bateson makes the point that the disruption of habitual patterns of stimuli and response can be intensely upsetting if this disruption constantly puts the creature in the wrong in the context of an important relationship. But he adds that if the disruption and pain do not cause the animal to break down, the experience may produce a creative leap, a fact noted also by Wynne in his essay "On the Anguish and Creative Passions of Not Escaping the Double Bind."[26]

This example reinforces the notion that a prerequisite for creative leaps in complex systems is a period of confusion accompanied by self-contradictory messages, inconsistencies, and, above all, paradoxical injunctions: I command you to be independent; I want you to spontaneously love me; I order you to be the dominant one. These messages, with their threatening implications that the relationship between the communicants may be endangered if the change does not take place, can be called the "sweat box." The "sweat box," in mild or severe form, often seems to be necessary before morphogenetic or basic structural changes can take place in a person, in a family, or in larger systems like tribes or nations.

It is important to note that if and when a move in an appropriate direction is taken, there must be immediate confirmation and reward. The essence of the double bind is to disconfirm a leap once taken, to indicate that change is not desired, or to disqualify the whole event. Thus the double bind could be described as a simple bind that is continually imposed and then continually lifted; pressure to change followed by injunctions not to change; a yes-do, no-don't kind of thing that produces the disruption and pain that Bateson argued were untenable for humans and other creatures. Rabkin, carrying this idea further, states that a paradoxical injunction that brings about a systems change followed by a paradoxical injunction to undo that systems change might well result in intense disorganization in the recipient of such messages.

Take the example of a mother caught in a struggle with an adolescent son. She wishes him to display more adult ("symmetrical") behavior. But if she enjoins him to do so, she is defining him as a child (a "complementary" relationship). There is no way out of this difficulty, as every exasperated parent and resentful teenager knows, except through some shift whereby both find that they are relating more pleasantly and more as peers than as parent and child, at least in the area the struggle was about. This shift can take place suddenly, or a long back-and-forth battle may be required. But the necessary condition is that the shift in the rule governing their relationship should happen "spontaneously," since for the mother to enforce it, or for the child to seize it, would merely reaffirm their previous situation.

If the parent giving the original paradoxical messages responds positively to an integration of the relationship at a more equal level, then this is a successful resolution of the dilemma. There has been no double bind, or at least no harmful one. But if at the moment the child and mother do reach that desired state, one of them, or someone else in the family, signals that this is bad or might be dangerous, then you have the preconditions for a double bind. And then you have the appearance of symptoms embedded in cycles in which the pressure for change builds up, followed by injunctions against change, in endless sequence like a stuck record: the famous "game without end."

The way a simple bind might either become resolved or else turn into a symptom can be illustrated by this hypothetical case. Thirteen-year-old Peter begins to sleep late in the morning and be late for school. His mother becomes tired of pushing him to get up and finally says, "Why do I always have to kick you out of bed to go to school? Act like a grownup. You ought to want to go to school for the sake of your own future. Your father used to get up at six and run a paper route before he even got to school—in zero degree weather," and so on.

This is a bind (simple variety), because if Peter "acts like a grownup" he is demonstrating a symmetrical relationship, but at the same time, if he does go to school, it is in response to his mother's demand, and his relationship to her is thereby defined as complementary. What he does do is become even more reluctant to go to school. His mother oscillates between washing her hands of him and going after him, a process that only escalates the tension between them. The school staff telephones to say that Peter is beginning to cut whole days, thus putting on even more pressure. Father, who can usually sleep later than Peter and hates to get up early, is constantly awakened by the morning fusses. Although he prefers to stay out of his wife's dealings with his son, he begins to protest. "Lay off the boy," he says to his wife, "You're only making things worse." He compares her to his father, who made his own adolescence miserable by insisting that he get up and take the paper route. He says that he can sympathize with the boy. This statement brings out the latent split within most parenting dyads, the split between a permissive stance and an authoritarian stance. The mother, intensifying her position, says, "It's about time you stopped babying the boy." Father says, "It's about time you stopped nagging him." They end up shouting and get into a state of unresolved anger with each other. Peter draws the covers up over his head and succeeds again in not going to school.

This is the normal type of confusion a family faces when children become adolescent. It is usually resolved if the parents can overcome their differences and establish a united front. Perhaps adolescent rebellion not only serves to establish beginning independence for a child, but offers an issue that the parents, who by a natural process will one day be child-free again, can use to test out the nature and strength of the bond between them. It seems not to matter which way the parents go; the situation is solved if the parents can say, "It's your own life, mess it up and take the consequences," or "Get to school and no more nonsense." Somehow, from this microtest of whether the parents (or others in the family who will be affected) will survive their son's eventual departure, he gets sufficient confirmation to really begin to leave, and the school issue drops away. The boy may find that an attractive female schoolmate waits at the same bus stop. Suddenly it is no longer, "Why don't you get up and go to school?" but "Why aren't you ever at home any more?"

Here is the alternative scenario that might establish a symptom. The boy does get up and go to school. He finds the female schoolmate and also regains his interest in studying (an unlikely story, but this remains a hypothetical case). However, the father begins to feel more and more depressed. His work is not going well, and his ulcer begins to act up. It seems that this is the last child at home and the one the father was especially close to, all the more in that he has a rather domineering wife and chooses to remain distant from her rather than fight anything out openly. The father experienced a small feeling of elation when the boy defied his mother over not going to school in a way that was never possible for him when he was growing up. The boy is very important to him. The mother, too, is strangely caught up in the fight she has with her son. It is as though he is able to stand up to her in a way that her husband never can, and although she is angry, she gains a kind of satisfaction from his assertiveness. With her husband, there is only shadow boxing; with her son, someone is really there.

At the same time, perhaps both are unconsciously aware that the boy's growing up means the emergence of many difficult issues between them, and the father's ulcer seems to signal that he will probably turn his feelings about these issues inward, rather than hazard an open conflict with his wife. A sense of ominous possibilities fills the air. The father eats little at night and complains about his ulcer. When he does, the mother seems annoyed rather than sympathetic and says, "I'm sick of your always going on about your ulcer and never going to the doctor about it. I always have to push you to make an appointment. Why can't you take responsibility for your own problems instead of making the whole family miserable?" The father becomes moody and quiet, and the son feels his own stomach tighten. He says, "I don't want any more supper," and starts to leave the table. Mother says, "You sit there till we're all finished." Father says, "Let him go, for God's sake, do you have to run everybody's life like you run mine?" The evening ends with the boy in his room, depressed, the father watching TV in silence, and the mother furiously washing the dishes.

The next day the boy complains that he has an attack of nausea and cannot go to school; in fact, he throws up. The parents fight about whether or not he should be made to go school. In the end, he stays home. This is the beginning of a school phobia. Two months later, having tried everything and on the advice of the school, the parents start looking for a psychotherapist. What the psychotherapist decides falls outside the lines of this story, but a contextual reading of the situation would be to perceive that the boy's appropriate behavior in going to school was not rewarded. Instead, intimations of catastrophe (parental discord, father's illness) erupted. The polarization of views, permissiveness versus punitive action, increased, with the boy's symptom now at the center, maintaining these parental behaviors and being maintained by them in a self-perpetuating loop. The bind quite evidently cannot be resolved by a creative leap, such as the boy's falling in love (an involuntary act that could be seen as an appropriate response to a simple bind: "He" did not decide to go back to school; "falling in love" is what decided it). Indeed, the hints of catastrophe increase when he mentions that he has met a wonderful girl. The leap that should be made is invalidated not by any one villain, but by the *context,* which covertly frames his eventual departure as a betrayal, a harmful thing.

This, then, is an example of the way a quite ordinary problem of growing up could become a symptom. Now let us take a closer look at the larger configurations that seem to accompany most symptomatic displays: the patterns of behavior that reinforce a problem while at the same time attacking it, and that exemplify in systems terms the double-binding sequences said to "drive men mad."

Chapter 10

The Thing in the Bushes

What-to-Change

Up to now the family therapy movement has done better in the area of how-to-change-it than of what-to-change. Descriptions of the creature that family therapists are out to get have been notoriously unsatisfactory. Clinicians know that there is something rustling about in the bushes, but nobody has done a good job of finding it and explaining what it is. It has eluded efforts to put it in terms of communication patterns (the double bind, for instance), as well as attempts to be more global and tie it to a type of family structure (Minuchin's "enmeshed" family; Bowen's "undifferentiated family ego mass"). Qualities or traits indicating a family guaranteed to produce dysfunction, such as Wynne's "pseudomutuality" and Bowen's "fusion," are suggestive but poorly attached to any particular symptomatic configuration.

As the search continued, the triadic concepts of coalition theory seemed to point to a more useful unit, one larger than the interchange but smaller than the family. Constructions like Haley's cross-generation coalition, or Minuchin's depiction of "rigid triads," seemed to be going in the right direction but were static. On the other hand, the emphasis of Watzlawick, Weakland, and Fisch in Palo Alto on tracking the behaviors around the problem, although process oriented, were not tied sufficiently to the larger context.

The Palo Alto group, in adopting a cybernetic analogy, seemed to be going in the right direction. A symptom or problem looked "as if" it were controlling or monitoring behaviors in a face-to-face relationship, so that they do not pass beyond certain limits. Conversely, it looked "as if" the problem were being supported and controlled by the context in which it appeared. But the context is in actuality an ecological field made up of more than one level of system, and the problem acts as a contrary presence, urging the very changes it apparently prevents, and ambiguous regarding the level on which change, if it does take place, may occur. Bateson puts it very well:

"Stability" may be achieved either by rigidity or by continual repetition of some cycle of smaller changes, which will return to a *status quo ante* after every disturbance. Nature avoids (temporarily) what looks like irreversible change by accepting ephemeral change. "The bamboo bends before the wind," in Japanese metaphor; and death itself is avoided by a quick change from individual subject to class. Nature, to personify the system, allows old man Death (also personified) to have his individual victims while she substitutes that more abstract entity, the class of taxon, to kill which Death must work faster than the reproductive systems of the creatures. Finally, if Death should have his victory over the species, Nature will say, "Just what I needed for my ecosystem."[1]

This argument allows us to get out of a linear trap. At each level of structure stability and change have different implications; if we choose to emphasize one implication over another, we are "chopping up the ecology," to use Batesonian terms again. Nevertheless, to see more clearly, one must at times put a little circle around a phenomenon, as one would single out an area of the abdomen to sterilize and prepare before doing surgery, temporarily forgetting that the organ we are going to tamper with or take out is linked with a living human being, in a family, in a world. So this chapter will be an exercise in "chopping up the ecology." We shall be looking at a problem in a triadic context even though this does injustice to the richness of concentric rings and levels within which each behavior is embedded.

The Mystery of the Essential Variable

There is no one value or factor in the family that a symptom can be said to be associated with. The closest concrete proof that there are any such variables at all has been offered by Minuchin in his experiment linking stress reduction in parents to a successful attempt to pull the symptomatic child into their argument. One variable here would be "conflict between the parents," and the assumption is that it must be kept from surfacing, for whatever mysterious reasons. Minuchin's families were a psychosomatic sample, though, and there is a strong link between somatization of stress and conflict avoidance. This variable would apply only to families in which open conflict is toxic.

There are other families with constant arguments between the parents or other family members and extreme symptomatology in the child. In many such cases the arguments occur *only* around the symptomatic behavior. Alternatively, incipient battles between the parents seem to be averted or diverted by the symptomatic behavior. Whether the conflict is open or hidden, the symptom still appears to be part of a recursive cycle or set of many such cycles, which seem to hover around the possibility of change.

The strains in the family which seem to trigger a child's symptom are not always (or only) between a pair of parents. They may involve a mother and a grandmother, or a mother and a parental child, or a wife and her mother-in-law. The opposing parties may be two competing clans, as in *Romeo and Juliet,* or may be outside the family, as when two therapists disagree about the handling of a case. There seems to be one common feature in all these cases: The symptom arises in a more expendable party when the relationship between at least two other parties—who often constitute an executive unit or are otherwise extremely important to the group—is threatened. The nature of the threat can be answered if one knows what the possible consequences of the disappearance of the symptom might be, but this is not anything that can be predicted. One must guess. In the case of the Capulets and Montagues, one could argue that had not the lovers died, the two clans might have engaged in a destructive war; instead they peacefully united. If the husband whose ulcer seems to unite his wife and mother recovered, the marriage might be threatened, as the conflict between wife and mother (or, potentially, between any other pair) might surface. It does not matter if the danger seems real or not.

In the case of a single parent, one finds that abdication or depression in the parent is one variable that seems to need to be kept within bounds. Sometimes much of the child rearing is left to a parental child. In such cases, a "bad" child (one who causes acute disruptions, creating trouble at school, starting fires, and so on) probably behaves this way whenever the mother abdicates her responsibilities or becomes too depressed. The disruptive behavior not only seems to bring mother back into the picture but unites mother and parental child against the culprit. The cycle is clear, since this coalition inspires the "bad" child to make fresh trouble as soon as the mother once more starts to abdicate, leaving the parental child once more in a vulnerable position.

The Interfering Grandmother, a common feature of single-parent families in which the young mother is very dependent on her own mother, offers a variant. Here one variable is the maintenance of the relationship between the two women. Often a child who is "spoiled" by the grandmother becomes the stabilizing factor. His difficult behavior helps to keep the young mother dependent on her own mother, while the favoritism shown by the grandmother toward the child forces a wedge between them. Closeness *and* distance are monitored by this particular arrangement. If mother acts too independent, the child defies her, forcing her to rely on grandmother to help keep the child in line; this in turn works to make the mother feel even more like "leaving" and the cycle continues.

The Homeostatic Seesaw

Let us, for the sake of simplicity, confine ourselves to one type example: the case of the child whose symptoms or problems seem to be monitoring a mother-father relationship. In a large proportion of these cases the parents present what looks like a very uneven marriage. One partner seems to be the "strong one" while the other is more dependent. Family researchers like Robert Ravich have observed that the "complementary" or one-up/one-down pair makes up one of the largest groups in their clinical population.[2] Attributes of this structure seem to be: (1) an intense clinging; the pair can be deeply unhappy, but will put up with utmost misery rather than separate; (2) in many cases an equally intense avoidance of conflict or behavior that might call the relationship into question; and (3) an inordinately high proportion of children who are disturbed. The marriage can seem very happy, with both partners apparently content, and yet they may have a psychotic child. However, their apparent contentment sometimes disappears if the child stops being a problem. In such cases one might almost say that the more severe the child's problem, the more severe the "trade-off" will be in terms of somatic or psychological illness in a spouse or other relative, or the emergence of marital difficulties.

Looking at the supposed happy pair with the disturbed child, we may well ask, "How can this be? How can there be a conflict that does not appear and that the participants do not experience?" The answer is provided by a fascinating study by Cynthia Wild and her coworkers that focuses on communication disorders in families with a symptomatic member.[3] In a research project comparing the communication styles of families of hospitalized schizophrenic males with those of a control group of hospitalized males with character disorders, the authors found, among other things, that the behavior of an unusual number of the fathers with schizophrenic sons could be described as "overcontrolling," while the communications of the mothers were classified as "amorphous." This combination allowed one spouse, the father, to seem dominant, but a close reading of conversations showed that mothers, by the use of non sequiturs, scattered thinking, topic changes, and the like, were able to nullify any decisions the fathers might try to make. The authors point out that these behaviors have a mutual causal effect: "Mothers' vagueness increases the likelihood that fathers will take over and control situations, and fathers' arbitrary and often irrational style of control increases mothers' vagueness." One can see how these linked behaviors would minimize any appearance of disagreement between the parents, while still fostering an intense struggle. Wild speculates that this arrangement might also account for some of the confused thinking of their sons.

As we observed earlier, this kind of uneven marital arrangement seems to produce a disproportionate share of disturbed children. We might think of a child caught in the situation Wild describes not so much as a victim of a confused environment but as part of a family balancing act. If we stick to our cybernetic analogy, and consider the relationship between the parents to be governed by set limits, like a seesaw that can go only so high or so low, we see how a child can influence the tilt. If he sides with one parent against another, or makes trouble for one of them with the covert support of the other, this behavior influences the balance of power between them.

Suppose the mother, in the marital subsystem, takes the one-down position. Add the child as the secret ally of the one-down parent, and add also a behavior that seems guaranteed to provoke the one-up parent. Rage and bluster though he or she will, the one-up parent cannot do anything with the child, and his authority is reduced to nothing. The seesaw tilts upward. But by and by it will get too high, whereupon the authoritative spouse probably will begin to push the partner down again, only to have the child come in before the seesaw gets too low. The cycle is no longer dyadic, as in Wild's study, but involves a triangle. At the same time, we must guard against the linear assumption that the child's behavior stabilizes the marriage. We are dealing with circular chains in which no one element controls or serves another.

When a couple's struggle is open, the symptomatic display of the child seems to block the fighting. Such a couple may only start to bicker and the child will come in with his usual number, an asthma attack, an obnoxious behavior, or whatever. If the problem is a somatic one, the parents are more apt to unite in anxious concern.

If it is a disruptive behavior, they may unite to scold the child. But scratch the surface and the mirror-image disagreement about the problem, or at least about the management of the problem, will come out. Beneath the appearance of unity, one parent can be seen to be less upset or more protective; the other is more upset or more punitive. However, it is important to note that the parents' fight does not call their own issues into question, since they are merely disagreeing over the problem of the child.

This "homeostatic seesaw" can be seen as a mutually sustained imbalance that holds the parents together. Symmetrical couples seem to have little trouble fighting—in fact, that is what usually brings them into treatment, rather than a somatic symptom or problems with a child—and they also have less trouble deciding to divorce. Complementary or one-up/one-down couples are far more locked together, with the supposedly more powerful partner in reality just as fragile and as dependent as the other. Seen only in a linear dimension, the child's behavior keeps this seesaw within safe confines. If it were to become too uneven, the one-down parent might become depressed or develop a symptom. If, on the other hand, it became too even, the couple would be more symmetrical and there would be the danger of splitting, or (in the case of abusive spouses) violence might erupt, which would endanger one partner. Oddly enough, if the child's symptom disappears, it is the one-up parent who is at most risk for a symptom, as though it were his job in the absence of the child to prevent the seesaw from going into reverse tilt and endangering the other spouse.

A proviso must be made here. Families in which severe blowups occur periodically between the parents do not necessarily present "symmetrical" spouse relationships. In particular, the presence of a severely symptomatic child predicts the opposite. If one looks closely, one finds that the "pseudohostility" of these families is part of the sequence that enshrines a symptom. There is probably a hidden seesaw operating, and the child "knows" the cue that indicates when it is time for him to come in and break up the quarrel between his parents' or other family members.

Lidz's classic article, "Marital Schism and Marital Skew," describes the spouse relationships in eight families with hospitalized schizophrenic children.[4] In some the conflict went underground, with one parent deferring to the other; in others the parents fought openly. But even in the "schism" cases, one spouse was described as more controlling and the other as more compliant. If our model is correct, one outcome of the child's symptom was that the realistic possibility of splitting never arose.

A simplified example of such a cycle might be something like this. Six-year-old Tommy has tantrums and is difficult to control. Close inquiry into the context of the tantrums reveals that they tend to get worse at suppertime. Father, who is an old-fashioned pater-familias, works long hours and comes home fairly late. Mother, a nonassertive, domestic person, sets great store by a family dinner, and so she makes Tommy wait for his meal till the family is ready. She also puts much care into making a good supper. The preceding Friday, we learn, she made a dish which her husband specially likes. That night, when it is time to eat, she calls the family to table. As usual, Father is so deep in the newspaper that he has to be called more than once (we learn later that this is a frequent reaction of Father to any request made to him by his wife). Tommy sits down with Mother, and she begins serving. She is annoyed because Father has still not come to the table, so she reacts with irritation when Tommy whines, "I don't like that stuff." "I'm sorry, Tommy," she says, "it's all we have for supper." Tommy still refuses to eat. Father puts the paper down, comes to the table, and says, "Tommy, eat your food!" Tommy looks at Father and pushes food off the plate. Father says, "Okay, no dessert."

Now Tommy throws himself on the floor and begins to kick and scream. Father grabs Tommy's arm and drags him upstairs. He puts him in his room and slams the door, coming down to take his place at the table. Instead of serving him, his wife is standing with a pained look on her face. "What is it, for God's sake?" asks Father. She responds by asking, "Why are you always so hard on the boy?" Father, in a rage, leaves the house and spends the evening at the corner bar. Mother fixes a plate of ice cream and goes upstairs to Tommy to calm him down. When Father comes home, late at night, she is in bed asleep, and for two days she is very cool to him. Father affects not to notice but starts to go out of his way to be nice to both wife and son, and so calm is restored, until the next tantrum.

If one looks at this episode as a recurring dramatic event, one is likely to ask, "What is the meaning of Tommy's behavior for different people in this family?" Some guesses could be made. The mother seems to feel that she has very few rights regarding her husband, and one assumes that she takes a one-down position in the marriage. However, as tensions build up, one assumes that there will be a greater tendency for the cues to arise that set off a tantrum. Mother, in siding with the boy, makes her husband feel not only ineffective but criticized and excluded. One might say that the seesaw becomes rebalanced by the addition of the child and his problem. In the parental subsystem, the mother temporarily "wins." At the same time Tommy's misbehavior is reinforced, both by Mother's extra comforting and by a very obvious reduction of tension all around. If one goes outside of this very artificial depiction of a parent/child triangle and includes other family members or important persons such as Father's mother or an older sister, one gets a far more complicated set of interlocking feedback chains, but the general principle remains the same. An unusual closeness between Father and his mother, or the beginning of a struggle between Mother and the daughter who was always her best helper, may be aspects of a family dilemma of which the boy's symptom is only the most visible sign.

Couple Cycles

Since a piece of the total symptomatic sequence is often a regulatory arrangement between spouses, some attention should be given to research in this area. One could, and probably should, make an argument for not treating couples as a separate universe. It is entirely possible that no purely dyadic cycle exists independent of third parties. These paragraphs, therefore, are a separate section only because couples have so often been studied (and worked with in therapy) as independent entities, rather than as pieces of more complex balancing acts. And we must remember here that some of the Bateson group's most interesting studies of complementary and symmetrical sequences were based on observations of spouse interactions.

Jackson in particular had a genius for describing couple interaction as it related to workable, unworkable, or difficult marriages. Since the profile of the couple can determine the design of therapeutic interventions, it is worth expanding here on his couple typology. In *Mirages of Marriage,* Jackson arranges couple types from best to worst. The Stable-Satisfactory marriage is on top, with its two subgroups: the "Heavenly Twins" and the "Collaborative Geniuses." The Stable-Unsatisfactory marriage contains the "Spare-Time Battlers" and the "Pawnbrokers." The Unstable-Unsatisfactory marriage is characterized by two miserable pairs: the "Weary Wranglers" and the "Psychosomatic Avoiders." At the bottom of the heap are two love-matches made in hell, the "Gruesome Twosome" and the "Paranoid Predators."[5]

The interest of this rather dashing set of categories is that they do not assume a rigid set of attributes, but assign what we have come to see as a "world view" or "paradigm" to these couples. Jackson made it clear that no one couple is ever a pure representative of any of these forms. In fact he had an uncanny ability to spot positive elements even in unhappy marriages. For instance, he concedes that the "Spare-Time Battlers" usually do not seek professional help; they may fight, but they get enough out of the family aspects of the marriage to keep them going, and they are less apt to have problems with sex. The "Pawnbrokers" are the covert marriages of convenience which people will put up with as the lesser evil to remaining alone. The "Weary Wranglers" are far more pathogenic, and probably would show up in Lidz's category of "marital schism" which Lidz associated with psychosis in a child. Jackson agrees that these couples may have a child suffering from severe pathology. The "Psychosomatic Avoiders" are an underground version of the Wranglers; they are unable to express anger openly, and often one of the spouses or both has a stress-related psychosomatic complaint. Sexual difficulties and drinking problems are another way in which these couples express their discontents. The Avoiders often present themselves in a "sick/well" formation, or take the familiar one-up/one-down position of apparent victim and apparent victimizer. I would add that these couples may have highly disturbed children if a spouse does not take on the symptomatic role.

But the couples who are the most disturbed, in Jackson's eyes, do not seem disturbed to themselves. The most mystifying category is the "Gruesome Twosome," who are perfect turtle doves, have never had a cross word in twenty years, and only present themselves in therapy because of a symptomatic child, most often a psychotic one. The last group, the "Paranoid Predators," maintain their closeness in opposition to a supposedly hostile world, and again their relationship, though they perceive it as happy, may be extremely toxic to their children.

Jackson makes one further important point about these categories: Couples can move up or down this ladder as they go through life. The Stable/Unsatisfactory Couple, for instance, may drop into the category of Unstable/Unsatisfactory if one of the spouses finds a new partner and realizes that there is more to life than he or she had assumed. And in therapy, even though some categories seem to promise less hope for relief than others, there is always the chance that a couple may be helped to get to a less stressful place on the ladder of discontent. Of course there is one proviso. The apparently contented marriages in the last two categories, if they come into therapy with a disturbed child, may become *less* contented if therapy works. The trade-off for a nonsymptomatic child may be that one of the spouses will become emotionally disturbed or medically ill, or that the couple will break up. But this is still, perhaps, a better human solution than the previous one.

A more recent attempt to link therapy with a typology of married couples comes out of Robert Ravich's Interpersonal Behavior Game-Test, or Train Game.[6] The game is set up so that the two partners each have toy trains going in opposite directions, with one section of track passable by only one train at a time. There is an alternate route that takes longer, but neither person can see the other's side of the board; and each partner can lower a gate to the other person's access to the direct route. Collisions occur frequently as a result. The payoff is based on the amount of time it takes both partners to get their trains to the end point. Obviously this is a game in which cooperation and communication are more essential than competition.

Ravich isolates three major patterns. The "Competitive" pattern resembles a price war, as each partner tries to inflict the most harm on the other to gain the most for himself. Of course in this case the couple's joint score will be extremely low. The second pattern is "Dominant-Submissive," with one spouse habitually letting the other take the direct route, either taking the alternate one himself or waiting till the direct route is free. The third pattern is a "Cooperative" one, in which the couple takes turns using the direct route in a polite manner. Couples who use the two latter patterns often score highly.

Ravich interviews these couples after they take the test, and has found that their behavior with the trains reflects the way they handle issues in other areas of their lives. However, none of these patterns seems to predict for or against married bliss. The competitive pattern, which seems like the most destructive, may not be so, for these partners are at least in contact with each other and there is a certain balance in their respective strengths. The uneven pair may do better in arriving at decisions, but the submissive spouse often pays dearly in the form of depression or other symptoms. The evenly cooperating couple should present the ideal state, but even there a hitch may arise. Ravich has found that such couples are often using this pattern for mutual avoidance, and that one of the spouses is apt to be having an affair on the side. In a study of a small group of couples that took turns by using the direct route–alternate route pattern, insuring minimum contact, he found that every one ended in divorce. Ravich's therapeutic stance is that whatever pattern a couple is using, the therapist should help them to add others to their repertoire, variety and flexibility being the goal rather than any particular form of decision making.

Ravich's research did not lead him to a model built on cyclical lines, even though he often noted sequence regularities. For instance, there was one version of the Dominant-Submissive pattern which he called the Flipflop Phenomenon. One spouse would habitually take the direct route with the other dutifully following after, but after a certain number of trials the roles would be exchanged, with the submissive partner taking the direct route. This flipflop would usually occur in a cyclical pattern, as predictable, Ravich comments, as the variation of the tides. He feels that this is an antistress mechanism that mitigates the uneven balance of these one-up/one-down marriages and may account for the longevity of these unions even though they constitute the most clinically unhappy group. Interestingly, he finds that couples with problems related to drug or alcohol abuse usually fall into the Dominant-Submissive category, and they also, one assumes, use this flipflop pattern for relief.

This brings us to another observation. Most work on couple and marital problems has stressed the problems of one or both of the pair, and not the sequence of behaviors in which these problems are embedded. It is perhaps because this sequence is such an obvious one with alcoholic couples that the literature on this problem has been the first, outside of the family field, to focus on the interaction context. There has been a notable shift in ideas on how to treat alcoholism from working with the individual, to working with the dry spouse, to working with the whole context of maintenance people, including the would-be rescuers who only spur the alcoholic on to more heroic boozing.

One recent study of alcoholic couples by Steinglass et al. indicates that their cycle has a wet period and a dry period, as a tropical climate has wet and dry seasons.[7] Both are essential to the ecology of the couple. Certain behaviors can take place only during the "wet" season (like sex or fighting) and are prohibited during the "dry" season. One can also notice that the shift includes a monitoring of relative power positions, much like the child-parent seesaw described previously. The apparently one-up position of the responsible dry spouse is effectively challenged during the "wet" season, even though it is reinstated with a vengeance the morning after. And like any other symptom, the drinking glues both spouses together, since the drinker is automatically defined as weak and needing care.

There is growing evidence that spouse abuse is also a cyclic phenomenon. Berman, Pittman, and Ratliffe suggest that here again is an "overadequate" spouse (the abused one) and an "underadequate" one (the abuser).[8] The abuser is often a man who feels or is socially, culturally, and financially inferior to his wife. But the wife also feels very insecure, and apparently needs a man who is extremely dependent on her. Triggering behavior seems to occur when the one-down spouse feels too low (when the wife has gotten a raise, has been out seeing friends too much, or simply starts acting too independent). An episode of physical abuse follows, which reequilibrates the relationship and is in some way accepted by the abused one. The aftermath of the beating can be remorse, forgiveness, renewed tenderness, at best; at worst, the "superior" spouse will have a sense of intimidation and powerlessness which may nevertheless act as a security bond for the relationship. Evidence for this curious premise is the extraordinary attachment these partners have for each other. If the wife leaves, the husband will scour the world for her, and she, even when safely ensconced in a shelter, will often manage to leave some clue that allows him to find her. If the woman does escape, there is evidence that such a man will simply find another woman to fit the vacant niche.

What we may be seeing there is a skewed relationship in extremis; a complementary schismogenesis which is always tilting two ways: either toward annihilation of the abused by the abuser or abandonment of the abuser by the abused, in an endless oscillation. Unlike the alcoholic couple cycle, this one has not yet been "discovered," and so the usual treatment plan calls for an assumption that the woman is a victim and will cooperate in efforts to leave this unsatisfactory relationship. This assumption ignores the profound significance the arrangement may have for both partners and the potentially devastating consequences of change. A natural history of this cycle, which will lead to more intelligent strategies to break it, has yet to be done.

Another fascinating class of couple cycles falls in the purview of doctors who treat somatic problems: ulcers, headaches, arthritis, cardiac problems, and a host of other far-from-minor ills. The number of marriages held together by a somatic illness is legion. Stranger yet are cases where both spouses are in a suffering contest and are competing over who is the sicker one. Here the competition is to be the one-down partner, yet the competition itself is symmetrical. Some grim pairs will literally compete with each other to the death, if need be.

Last, not least, are the couples whose bond seems to rest upon psychiatric symptoms—depressions, periodic psychotic episodes, obsessions, phobias, anxiety attacks—the price many people will pay for the assurance that they will never be alone. Insufficient attention has been given to the cyclical nature of these problems in the life of a couple, and to the interlocking behaviors of the presumably "well" spouse; what are his or her benefits from the arrangement, and what is the price? One of the few serious studies of couples in which the wife was periodically hospitalized for psychotic episodes is that of H. Sampson, S. L. Messinger, and R. D. Towne.[9] Their documentation of the cyclical nature of these episodes and the part they played in the family relationship picture deserves attention. Of most interest is their classic account of a group of wives whose periodic departure into the hospital allowed the entry of the husband's mother into the home. The husband-mother tie seemed to be monitored by the hospitalizations and recoveries of the wife, just as the husband-wife tie was monitored by the availability of the older woman, in a fine example of a two-generation adult relationship cycle. Couple problems, in any case, often involve other family members or third parties in roles that are crucial in maintaining the problem, and this is true to an extent which has not been sufficiently realized.

Some other books and articles on couple therapy that should not be missed include Carlos Sluzki's highly original piece "Couples Therapy: Prescription for a Systems Experience," which expresses a strategic conceptual framework through the use of clinical vignettes; Peggy Papp's inventive "The Use of Fantasy in a Couples Group"; Norman and Betty Paul's *A Marital Puzzle,* which focuses upon unresolved mourning; and Clifford Sager's *Marriage Contracts and Couple Therapy,* a highly regarded text in the field.[10]

Power as a Family Issue

A discussion of what brings about distress in a family system leads directly to a critique of the basic assumptions some researchers have made about family interaction. Much of the work we have discussed in this book seems to posit power issues as the basis for family difficulties—whether expressed as open discord or hidden by disqualifications. But power is never an absolute item; it always has to be "power for what?" In an absolute monarchy the answer is simple: "Power to make my subjects do as I say." In a war between countries it is "power to subdue, if not crush, my adversary." In a game it is "power to win."

But in a family, even an authoritarian patriarchy of the old school, the issues are not so simple, because the *objectives* of a family, even allowing for cultural difference, are not like those of parties who have no stake in each other's well-being. One also has to assume that the family does have a particular "good" which everybody wants a part of, or a "product" which no other institution can replace. But what are these goods or products? What can a family do that the state or some other group cannot do? A family can exist without being an economic unit; a family can exist without being a child-rearing unit; these and many other functions can be taken over by other parties or organizations.

There is only one invisible but important task which few other institutions can perform as well. This has to do with an orderly access to intimacy. It may also be related to an invisible systole and diastole of connecting and withdrawing shared by all the social animals. This unconscious but orderly arrangement can be a function of the nuclear family, but it can also extend to the borders of the face-to-face community in which the family lives, or include connections with extended kin.

It is possible that this "social envelope," to quote Kai T. Erikson, is as important for individual survival as amniotic fluid is to an unborn child.[11] In a masterful and poignant study of the aftereffects of a communal disaster, the Buffalo Creek flood that devastated an entire mining community in West Virginia, Erikson makes the point that the survivors were unable to get over the impact of this event not only because houses and people were destroyed, but because the fabric of the community, rooted in history, proximity, and time, was ruined beyond repair. This is the first time, to my knowledge, that a social scientist has made such a strong statement, backed by such ineluctable evidence, that individuals need a network of people, obligations, customs, houses, furnishings, objects of reference, space-works, time-works, all of which go to make up each person's "social envelope." Without the surroundings to which he is accustomed, the individual may go on living but his will to live may not. To a man and woman the survivors of this flood continued to experience life as disjointed, without meaning and without hope long after the event. They seemed to have a mass neurosis.

But Erikson points out that this looks like a neurosis only if one examines each individual complaint. Taken as an aggregate, the findings point toward a reality, not a neurosis. The people who survived the flood were relocated, but in flimsy trailer camps without reference to old neighbors or old neighborhoods. Those linkages that might have remained to build on were ignored. And Erikson doubts that enough linkages did remain to have allowed this particular group of people, which had been grounded in a special communal arrangement, to survive in any functional way at all.

Moving from the particular to the general, it seems probable that a "social envelope," like the family, is distinguished from all other kinds of social organizations in at least one respect: the regularity of the rhythm that pulls individuals together and pushes them apart. The person who has written most cogently on the makeup of this interactional ebb and flow is Eliot D. Chapple. In a book called *Culture and Biological Man,* Chapple describes interaction rhythms in ongoing relationships as analogous to and connected with circadian rhythms in physiological processes.[12] If the two are, in fact, connected, an upset in biological rhythms may coincide with an upset in social rhythms and vice versa. Both types of rhythms require a high degree of internal calibration, and there are optimum frequencies and intensities involved.

Chapple has hypothesized that in social interaction there may even be a daily "interaction quota" for each individual. If a person does not get some as yet undefined degree of this requirement, it may bring about untold deleterious effects on the physiological rhythms of his body—affecting blood sugar, sleep patterns, and the like, which may in turn get out of kilter with each other.

At any rate, it is reasonable to hypothesize that any kind of satisfactory interaction between people in a family would involve a balance of giving and getting, and of being touched and being left alone. Chapple goes so far as to say:

Each individual needs to interact for so much time, with so many people, as well as to experience intervals when he is by himself and *not* interacting. ... Even if each person gets the quota of interaction which his daily rhythm requires, he also is seeking interaction with his complements. Any old interaction will not do; he needs to utilize his endogenous rhythms of action and inaction, at a *tempo* within the natural limits of his repertoire, and thus experience a maximum degree of synchronization by the other person.[13]

It would be hard to prove that there is a quota of interaction on an individual basis, but it is easy to see that there is a highly stereotyped sequence and frequency of contact for each dyad or cluster in a family. Once the clockwork of interaction frequencies within a family has evolved, there would necessarily be a premium on keeping that particular regularity going. The need for people to get together on necessary tasks and to accomplish important daily business itself creates a need for scheduled contact. Simply because "primitive" peoples do not use clocks and watches to calibrate their touchings does not mean that they do not use other mechanisms. Rather, these mechanisms operate below the level of consciousness, and are built into the periodic routines of everyday life.

And even as physiological processes seem to build their rhythms on geophysical cues like diurnal and lunar cycles, or the turn of the seasons, so social interactions also seem to follow periodicities external to themselves. Intimacy between couples often follows peaks and lows according to the woman's menstrual cycle; women in the same family tend to synchronize their periods; and the seeming superstition of workers on mental hospital wards that patients will become most agitated at the full moon may have a similar explanation in an ebb and flow of social tension following a lunar monthly clock. The adaptive usefulness of some type of calibration makes it unnecessary to posit a "need" for rhythm in a person or an individual "quota" for interaction.

Thus the ability to control access routes to other people—to both get enough interaction and block it off when necessary—may be of far greater importance than has been realized. If there were no question about the equitable distribution of supplies, then the supply routes would not be in question. But if the supplies are in question, anxiety about the means for getting them may become intense.

Consider the following scenario. A mother who is overinvolved with her baby son, perhaps because his father pays her very little attention, might show behaviors like picking him up when he wants to sleep, talking to him when he wants to be alone, waving things at him, poking him, dressing and undressing him unnecessarily, and so forth. Depending on the type of temperament this child was born with, he might develop behaviors for blocking her out: avoiding eye contact, stiffening on being picked up, resisting being dressed. Later on, he might refine these behaviors into ways of walling himself off (and walling off others), become a stubborn, inward kind of person, perhaps a "workaholic" or an "absent-minded professor," or enter a career in which contact with people is slight. He might, however, look like a "strong, silent type" to some unwary female who had, contrastingly, been ignored by the adults in her early life, and who had learned to cling to every little shred of attachment as if it were a prize. How well this pair would complement each other at first—and how inevitably the struggle for "access control" would overshadow their later life. It seems to me that most of the so-called power struggles that researchers have noticed in disturbed families are of this type and over this kind of issue. And it also seems clear that because of the interdependent nature of the "goods" competed for, there is no way to win unilaterally.

An experiment with newlyweds devised by Harold Rausch and a group of colleagues supports this thesis.[14] The research was designed to study the behaviors of husbands and wives as they coped with interpersonal conflict. To this end, some quasinaturalistic scenes were set up which the couples in the experiment were asked to role-play. Two scenes dramatized a conflict of plans or interests involving very specific issues (whether to go out to dinner or to eat at home, for instance). But the third and fourth scenes involved exactly this area of access routes we have been talking about. Scene Three was called Husband Distant. The instructor would tell the husband to imagine that he wanted to be alone that evening and would do anything to accomplish that goal, while the wife was told that she was to try to engage her husband in any possible way. In Scene Four, Wife Distant, the reverse was to take place. In addition to the outcome of these scenes, the tactics spouses used during them were recorded: avoidance, coercion, reconciliation, backing down, and so on.

One small group of these newly married couples were called "discordant," because they reported a high degree of conflict and marital dissatisfaction. In the issue-oriented scenes, the wives were quite domineering and used coercive tactics to a much greater degree than wives in the other groups. The husbands, by contrast, behaved very meekly and readily gave in to the wives. But during the distance-maintaining scenes, the husbands turned from lambs to tigers. They not only clung to their instructions to remain distant at all costs, using coercion and other aggressive tactics which they had not previously displayed, but continued to use these tactics when it was the wives' turn to be distant. The wives, in contrast, behaved far less coercively in response to their newly assertive husbands than their female counterparts in the other groups. And when it was their turn to maintain distance, the strength of their husbands' attacks on their fortresses led to escalating battles and mutual recriminations.

This little piece of the experiment illustrates the difference between getting one's own way (power in decision making) and being in control of access routes (power in seeking or blocking intimacy). It also shows that the one who looks like the dominant one can keep his or her own fortress intact but may have a struggle to conquer the other person's. Ravich's Train Game shows this feature clearly. Even though a spouse might let the other partner go first on the direct route, he or she could always lower a gate so that the train could not get to its destination. In Rausch's experiment one could see that the wives in the "discordant" group were only apparently dominant. In the matter of the crucial issue, access to intimacy, they were powerless except for the option of playing tit-for-tat.

This is only one small example of how struggles around issues of intimacy could affect a young family right from the start. It is possible that all major struggles in families with psychiatric disturbances have to do with this issue, which lies at the heart of the ecology of family life.

Having reached this point, we may consider the present chapter a kind of watershed or Continental Divide. It is time to call a halt to this abstract exploration of issues of change and targets of change, and move to consideration of models of intervention. From here on, we will be concentrating on issues of therapy—in fact, how to catch "The Thing in the Bushes."

Chapter 11

Breaking the Symptomatic Cycle

First and Second Order Change

In describing symptomatic sequences we are dealing with arrangements that influence the schismogenic tendencies of relationship processes, as Bateson first surmised. If this is true, then any ideas about how to change these processes must deal with the nature of recursive, cybernetic systems.

We have already cited Ashby in describing the change processes involved in entities that have what he called "bimodal feedback mechanisms." As he said, these mechanisms entail two types of corrective action. First order changes are the minor fluctuations from state to state within the limits for behavior that are already set. Second order changes have to do with resetting the rules for those limits and usually require a transformation, the discontinuous change described in Chapter 10.

An example of first order fluctuations in a family would be a mother who knows she can serve any main dish for dinner as long as it is not fish. Or a child may know that he can come in any time after school as long as it is not later than six o'clock.

Second order change applies to any situation in which the usual range of behaviors is no longer applicable because of developments in the outer field or inside the system itself. In their book *Change,* Watzlawick, Weakland, and Fisch furnish an apt metaphor for the two kinds of change by citing the difference between pressing the gas pedal and changing gears when driving an automobile.[1] In a family, a second order change might be set off by any major shift in the rules governing one or more relationships in the family. These can be associated with unlooked for repercussions, as when a fifty-year-old woman for the first time in her life defied her ninety-year-old mother-in-law by insisting on her right to invite a group of friends for lunch. The older woman entered the hospital with a serious illness four days later. Or in a couple relationship, a man who regularly comes home immediately after work to please his wife suddenly starts coming home at unpredictable times, or a child starts to disobey his curfew and stay out all night. In both cases the change is from a complementary to a more symmetrical relationship on the part of the person whose behavior has changed. But basically what is at stake is a possible reorganization of the structure of the family.

Second order changes may also be part of the natural evolution of a family through time. To take the example of the mother and food, she may find that lately nothing she serves pleases her thirteen-year-old son, who prefers a snack when he comes home from school and is never hungry for supper. It is a good guess that the problem is not really food; the problem is that the rules which govern their relationship are being challenged. The boy is getting to be more independent, more defiant. But his mother still expects him to accept her choice of what he is to eat. It is a familiar struggle that erupts when children reach adolescence. The mother reacts to the defiance by mixed resentment at his behavior and anxiety that he will not get proper nourishment. She intensifies her efforts to make him eat, and he escalates his refusal to comply.

This is a good example of a problem which develops into what Watzlawick, Weakland, and Fisch call the "game without end." In their language, *the solution has become the problem,* because attempts at first order change are being applied when second order change is needed. The setting for the mother-son relationship has been by the nature of things complementary, or unequal; now it is, also by the nature of things, moving toward a more symmetrical or equal one.

Some families, after a period of confusion, arguments, attempts at compromise, will take the leap by themselves. Mother will decide to let the child eat what he wants, or he will go on doing so and she will stop fighting him. Or they may reach some other compromise that gives him more autonomy.

In other cases, the relationship setting may be hard to shift, perhaps because the father never speaks up to the mother, and in a way depends on the boy to put her in her place. Or the mother may feel she is losing her baby, the child she turns to when the father is absent or works late or otherwise distances himself. The escalation of first order solutions produces a problem that makes the family suffer more and more, and they finally take the son to a therapist on the grounds that they can't control him. The therapist's business is to find out whether, indeed, this is a problem that calls for a second order change or total reorganization. As the authors of *Change* tell us, he will do well to check out the family's previous solutions, to be sure there is not some obvious piece of advice that would set everything right. Perhaps the mother has suddenly gone on a gourmet cooking binge and the son hates spicy foods. If this is worked out, and peace descends, one can assume that no major structural change was indicated.

But if the issue really has to do with the range of allowable behaviors between mother and son, the food is only a symbol of a larger battle. A second order change has to be negotiated. The therapist might make a direct attempt to make this change by asking the mother if she would allow the boy to choose his own diet, at least for two days out of the week. Again, if this solution is accepted no more therapy is indicated; the family is amenable to an outside push to solve the problem. But this is not always true. The mother may resist any suggestion of this kind because it will mean that the boy will "win," and she is angry at his attitude of disrespect. This kind of reaction usually indicates that the therapist has a self-reinforcing cycle on his hands: a behavior (the mother's reaction) that feeds the problem (the son's defiance).

The therapist must now look closely to see evidence of this type of recursive cycle. He notices that the father feels less upset than the mother about the boy's eating problem. It turns out that the father has a long-standing struggle with his wife over his crude table manners. He is not willing to take a stand on his own issue, and neither is he willing to take sides with the boy against his wife, except when the battle between them gets to extreme proportions; then he has to go to her defense. One could stake out the cycle this way: The more the father feels one-down to the mother, the more the boy acts defiant; the more the boy acts defiant, the more the mother tries to control him; the more she tries to control him, the more one-down she feels; the more one-down she feels, the more the father will come in to help her; the more the father comes in to help her, the less defiant the boy is; the less defiant the boy is, the more the mother resumes her domination of the father—and the whole sequence starts again.

One simple move would be to arrange that the father take his wife to a fancy restaurant one night a week, rewarding her for all she has to put up with on other nights and leaving the ungrateful son to forage for himself. If this suggestion is adopted, the boy will be taken out of his place in the sequence, at least for that night, and the couple will have to deal directly with each other. This may force the problem between them to the surface—or it may be the small shove that pushes the whole family toward a leap, and they may return to the next therapy session with the boy no longer a problem and the couple beginning to rediscover the possibilities of their own relationship.

Sometimes, of course, neither direct advice nor a structural move is sufficient to combat the rigidity of the cycle. Here is where moves that prescribe the symptom or situation come in. These usually consist of suggestions that fly in the face of common sense. Instead of trying to eradicate the problem as the family wants him to do, the therapist begins to point out aspects which might make them less anxious to have that happen. If the problems were to vanish overnight, what would the consequences be? Could Father deal with Mother's energies if they were released from the combat she is in with the son? Who would bring spirit into the home, which is otherwise rather lifeless?

In our example, the therapist might reframe the mother's preoccupation with her son's diet as a normal maternal concern that usually intensifies just at the time a boy is ready to grow up. The son's defiance is defined as his unconscious wish to attract her concern to him, because in reality this new independence is very threatening to him. The therapist might prescribe a ritual that will symbolize the closeness both of them are about to give up. Mother during the next week is to twice make the kinds of meals she used to give him when he was small, sitting by him while he eats, maybe even cutting up his food. She might get out his silver baby cup, just to give the proper ceremonial touch. Father would have to eat the same meal, and she would have the right to dictate father's table manners. After all, he will want to be a good role model for his growing son. Even humorously suggested, this task usually hits at both sides of the dilemma—the very real difficulty all three are having in saying goodbye to their old positions, even though on the surface they wish to be rid of them.

Ideally, the reaction will be recoil on the part of all, not only against the therapist's slightly absurd assignment, but against the prescription of maternal control over both father and son, which is pushed far beyond the limits the family, including Mother, is willing to tolerate. This should effectively disrupt the cycle. The aftermath is, of course, unpredictable. What one hopes is that at least one stabilizing link in the "game without end" will break, and force the family into the "sweat box." They may then take the desired leap toward a new integration. Alternatively, some other stumbling block to achieving this goal will come into view, such as the parents' difficulties with facing a life together alone. This new problem may need to be dealt with in a move to a new therapeutic stage. Alternatively, it may simply resolve itself, once the boy is out of the way.

Of course family therapy includes many more maneuvers than breaking the chain of behaviors in a self-sustaining loop, but therapists who address themselves to relieving specific complaints do seem to be looking for that cycle. If the problem behavior is a disruptive one, it usually stands out clearly and the cycle it is embedded in is not hard to find. This makes the question of how and where to intervene much easier than when the problem behavior is a chronically pervasive condition, like many psychosomatic illnesses or communicational disorders associated with psychosis. Here the clinician may have to work to find the cycle, and it appears most readily if he focuses on management of the condition rather than the condition itself. This will usually cause what Stanton and

Schwartz called the "mirror-image disagreement" between the parents to emerge, and the problem can be redefined as one of helping them to get together so that they can make the child behave responsibly in spite of his "illness."

Breaking a Cycle in the Room

Bateson, as we have seen, used a cybernetic framework to describe the recursive, cyclical patterns he considered characteristic of many relationship sequences, especially those dealt with by psychotherapy. His most down-to-earth analogy, described in Chapter 2, was the steam engine with the governor and two weighted arms. It is important, however, not to take this analogy of a servomechanism literally; one cannot equate human mutual-causal processes with mechanical ones. Dell, in his previously mentioned article on evolutionary feedback, points out that in most living systems, behaviors may occur in recursive or self-reinforcing sequences, but they never come back to exactly the same spot. They are not like self-stabilizing mechanisms such as a house thermostat or biological mechanisms such as the body's arrangement for calibrating its own temperature. A spiral rather than a cycle is a more useful image, as this allows for constant fluctuations and change no matter how stuck such a sequence may be.[2]

Thus, when we say "symptomatic cycle," we must take care not to think that this is anything more than an imprecise analogy for what goes on in families and other human groups. Although we have for simplicity's sake picked out only one cycle associated with a symptom, we are always in these cases dealing with many interacting cycles and loops. We must also allow for the possibility of change, because as long as the sequence is moving forward in time, it may seem constricted and unchanging, but there is always the possibility that one small fluctuation will lead to a larger amplification which will set off a leap to a new place.

Keeping these ideas in mind, let us take the case of an asthmatic child whose asthma seems patently due to emotional stresses originating within the family. Assuming for the sake of argument that (among other things) the child's symptom is part of a closeness-distance dance between the parents, a self-stabilizing chain can be described: The more the parents distance, the more the child wheezes: the more the child wheezes, the more the parents unite; the more the parents unite, the less the child wheezes; the less the child wheezes, the more the parents distance; ad infinitum, or until some factor intervenes to break the cycle.

Watzlawick, Weakland, and Fisch have eloquently described this type of feedback loop in *Change.* They define a whole class of psychotherapy problems as deriving from incorrect solutions. This is a simplified way of describing the self-reinforcing sequence shown above. In almost any problem, when the common-sense effort to eradicate it fails, it is probably because the solution itself is part of what keeps the problem in business. *Change* uses the example of a wife who complains that her husband is not open enough and never tells her anything; the husband reacts to her by clamming up even more, which leads her to even greater suspicion and more questioning, which leads to even more reticence on his part; until the outcome is a case of pathological jealousy on the part of the wife.

What the authors do not do is to put in the element of "less" that would keep this cycle from turning into a runaway. Perhaps, periodically, the situation reaches such a pitch that the husband or wife "blows up," frightening both of them, but at least creating some willingness to achieve more effective communication. The "less" here might be that the husband would stop, temporarily, his taciturn behavior. One would assume that the wife's suspiciousness would in turn descend to a more acceptable level.

Perhaps the clearest and most dramatic example of a sequence that contains a symptom, and of a therapist's successful effort to derail it, is in a transcript of a family session reported in Minuchin's *Psychosomatic Families.* [3] As usual in his first interviews with families of anorectics, Minuchin arranges for lunch to be served and observes the Kaplan family's interaction around eating. In this case he finds that the family will not be moved easily from their rigid patterns; hence, he assumes that the anorectic daughter's symptom will not be moved easily either. We will go through this session carefully, because it not only illuminates a "family dance" but demonstrates how the therapist can use his influence to provoke a runaway, or positive feedback loop, which destabilizes the family and forces it to change.

This is the first time Minuchin has met with the family. A brother, seventeen, is present along with the parents. An older daughter and son are out of the house and live far away. The youngest girl, fifteen, has wasted away to about seventy-eight pounds. She is losing one or two ounces a day in the hospital, where she is staying at the time of the interview, despite a behavior modification program that usually results in weight gain for such children. The family seems very well motivated, eager to please the therapist, and the girl is apparently quite docile, hardly uttering a word, although she merely toys with the food on her plate. When the rest of the group have finished the meal, the therapist decides to ask the parents to make the daughter finish her meal. He then leaves the room to watch from behind a screen.

The dialogue that ensues can be summarized as follows: Mother, who also appears mild and unassertive, asks the girl if she wants to eat the rest of the mother's sandwich. The girl, given her choice, naturally answers, "No." The rather overbearing father comes in with a demand that the girl eat. The girl objects, saying that the dietician has said she can eat what she likes.

As if to join her daughter against the too strong position of the father, the mother tells the girl that she ought to be able to understand why she has to eat. Mother consistently "reasons" with daughter, placing responsibility for choice with the girl, rather than saying as the father does, "Eat because I say so." One feels in this behavior a hint that the mother's coalition with her daughter is so important that she will not jeopardize it by forcing the girl to do anything against her will. It also seems to add strength to the girl's ability to stand up to her father. Perhaps he now feels threatened; at any rate, he abruptly interrupts his wife, saying to the girl, "Just eat!" This seems to annoy the mother, who turns directly to him for the first time and blocks him, saying, "Let her finish eating."

Now the scene begins to escalate. The mother repeats her argument that the girl ought to realize how important it is for her to eat, and the daughter continues to protest, saying she does not like the food. Father comes in again, bent on forcing the issue. The girl states that she won't eat the food even if it is shoved down her throat. Her voice is now pitched very high. Mother asks, in a soft reasonable voice, why she hasn't ordered something she likes. The girl calms down. The parents now take turns, with Father insisting, "Eat!" and Mother asking questions like, "Why are you losing weight?" The father's stance defines the relationship as unequal, complementary; the mother's defines it as equal, symmetrical. Father is forceful and threatening, Mother gentle and comforting. At the same time, however, the parents are escalating symmetrically *vis-à-vis* each other, and the girl is beginning to scream more and more hysterically in response to this tightening spiral.

At this point the mother increases her pressuring tone, saying to the girl, "You won't have another chance" and beginning to sound hysterical herself. The girl shrieks back. As if to balance off the mother's shift to a more insistent position, the father suddenly turns gentle and reasonable, saying that he cannot understand why the girl is making so little effort to put on weight. The girl again calms down, but the calm is short-lived, as the father quickly resumes his domineering tone and the girl once again starts to cry. Now Mother comes in, quietly rebuking her husband by saying, "Wait a minute," and then remarking to the girl, "You don't have to eat much." Seeing the redundancy of this pattern, the therapist enters the room to stop it.

This is a classic example of pathogenic interaction. Studied carefully, it can be shown to be a recursive cycle or self-sustaining feedback loop: The more the father threatens, the more the girl cries; the more the girl cries, the more the mother protects; the more the mother protects, the less the girl cries; the less the girl cries, the more the father threatens; ad infinitum, or until something intervenes to stop the sequence—quite possibly the girl's death, in this very serious case.

Looking closely at this configuration, we see many features we can place in the context of our triadic concepts. Smoked out by the therapist's insistence that the parents push the girl to eat, we see a familiar triangle: the high-status authority, the high-status friend, and the low-status subordinate. Father takes the disciplinary position, Mother the permissive one; and the girl, caught between the two sets of directives, oscillates from one to the other.

These directives amount to a splitting of the field. Our old friend the mirror-image disagreement is clearly displayed as the parents start to fight, using the child as the battleground. We can even see the phenomenon of the temporary switch-about. When one parent goes momentarily to the other side, the other takes the vacated position. Here, when Mother begins to intensify her demands on the girl, Father calms her down by making his voice low and tender and taking the mother's "reasonable" approach—at least for a while.

One can see the beauty of this triangle and its cyclic dance only if one forgets the seriousness of the problem it generates. As Minuchin explains, each person gives the cues for the behaviors of the others. Daughter knows exactly when to come in, how pitiful the tone of her voice has to be to activate Mother; Mother knows when to back off and leave the field to Father; Father knows when to start his harangue. Of course this all happens on a covert level, not consciously. And we can see that this sequence is the result of an aborted transformation, in the sense that it keeps the family from taking a leap to the adolescent-departure stage of the family life cycle, this girl being the youngest child.

The paradoxical injunctions, which Rabkin says usually accompany the "time of a leap," are striking in the statements of each parent. Mother says, in effect, "Eat because you want to eat, not because I tell you to." But when the girl responds to this paradoxical directive by asserting a clear symmetrical position: "I will eat what I want," Father comes in and places her in a complementary position by saying, "Eat what I tell you to," while at the same time paradoxically criticizing her for acting "like a two-year-old child."

Not only does each parent give a paradoxical injunction, but the two types of injunctions are incompatible with each other: if the girl controls her own eating, she is disloyal to Father: if she follows Father's orders, she is disloyal to Mother. In a normal situation, at some point the parents would join together and give some clear and consistent message, whether to honor the girl's right to choose for herself (a symmetrical definition of the relationship) or tell her to obey orders and eat (a complementary definition). In either case, the girl would probably eat, and this behavior would then presumably be rewarded. But the diabolical beauty of this cycle is that any time one position in regard to the symptom is taken, it is invalidated or contradicted by somebody taking the opposing position. If by chance the girl did start to gain weight, her mother or father would find some way to remind her not to eat or she would find some way to remind them to remind her.

At the same time, this push–pull, eat–don't eat, yes–no increases the girl's agitation. One can see that she is held within a very narrow band, with upper and lower limits that keep her perpetually under stress. Just as Father pushes daughter to the breaking point, Mother stops the action by blocking Father and calming the girl. As soon as she is calm, Father reinstates the battle all over again. The girl can never rest. She is caught in an ever-intensifying upward spiral.

From the parents' point of view, of course, their reactions are logical. Each feels that the other's way will not work and is intent on checking the destructive excesses of the other. Father thinks: "If I insisted, my daughter would eat, but my wife keeps leaving it up to her, so she will starve." Mother thinks: "My daughter would eat if left to herself, but my husband is making her angry and rebellious, so she will starve." The fight between them is not on any conscious level. It is another example of the "game without end" that keeps a symptom alive. Relationship patterns—especially the mother's covert coalition with the daughter against the father—are too strong in this family for the parents to take any other positions. And there is another important relationship pattern: We learn during the interview that the father's mother, to whom he is very close, is dying of cancer. How, then, can the daughter choose the mother over him under such circumstances? It may not be coincidental that the grandmother's illness and the daugther's anorexia occurred at the same time.

Hence the endless cycle that now presents itself, sharpened by the therapist's insistence that the parents make the girl eat. In some of Minuchin's anorectic cases the parents manage to get together enough so that this move is sufficient to break the back of the symptom. But in this family the parents are too conflictual.

The therapist now decides to embark on a new strategy that will unbalance the cycle and place the family under considerable stress.

To this end he removes one party at a time from the triangle. In describing this particular technique Minuchin uses cybernetic language rather than his usual spatial-structural terms:

The only way to separate the daughter from the parents is to break the sequences that maintain the homeostasis. One way the therapist can do so is to position himself in the system in such a way that the cycle cannot repeat itself.[4]

Thus, in directing the parents to continue to try to get their daughter to eat (in this sense moving with the symptom-related behavior), Minuchin introduces one crucial change. First Mother, then Father, must take on the job alone. By eliminating the constraints each parent uses to counteract the excesses of the other, the therapist makes the behaviors in the sequence overpass their usual limits.

We now see the critical limits of the relationships in this triangle. Mother, when allowed to go to the far edge of her position, becomes more and more feeble, while her daughter fights her more and more strongly. At one point Mother cries in despair, "In a mental hospital, that's where you'll put me!" At the edge of this limit lies breakdown and death. Father, when allowed to the far edge of his position, abandons all restraint and tries to use force, grabbing his daughter by the hair and attempting to cram a hot dog down her throat. At the far edge of this limit we see the potential for violence.

At this moment Minuchin comes in and calmly stops the father, in effect taking on himself the function of the limits which had been prevented from operating. He places the distraught parents together and reframes their problem as having a daughter who is in a struggle with them and is "stronger than you are." He next turns to the girl and asks her to drop on the floor the hot dog she has clenched in her hand because "it is not a very good victory." She does so. He asks her quietly why she has such a need to defeat her parents. Is it because she wants autonomy and they will not give it to her? She sits very still, almost in a trance, while Minuchin speaks for her. For the first time, it seems, the family allows Minuchin to take charge.

During this session a shift occurs. The parents have begun to blame the daughter for misfortunes she could not possibly be responsible for, instead of treating her like a fragile doll. And the daughter, formerly so obedient and docile, has not only defied her parents openly but has succeeded in humiliating them in front of a group of professionals.

Minuchin's explanation is that he has tried, by his intervention, to move the parents from a "detouring-benevolent" triangle in which the daughter is perceived as "sick" to a "detouring-attacking" triangle in which she is perceived as "bad." It is certain that the parents' perception of her, as well as her behavior justifying that perception, is radically changed by the end of the session. The father says, "We always spoiled her, but I think maybe we've been too good to her." Meantime, the girl goes back with the nurse to the ward. The session ends with Minuchin talking to the parents solely about their own problems—the father's business, the grandmother's illness—and the need for both of them to pull together during this difficult time.

For whatever reason, the daughter immediately begins to eat, and by the next session has gained almost enough weight to leave the hospital. When she does go home, however, she becomes a "behavior problem," refusing to eat meals with the family, which causes a feud between mother and daughter. There is another, apparently less dramatic shift when the father comes in some weeks later asking, "Doctor, is it always true that when the patient improves, the rest of the family gets sick?" It turns out that he and his wife are having the first problems they have experienced together in the twenty years of their marriage. There are some marital sessions as well as family sessions.

Eventually the girl becomes a fairly normal teenager, with some relapses along the way, not into anorexia but involving other symptoms, including a suicide attempt. No claim is made that the girl is permanently "cured," even though these other crises were handled with relatively little difficulty. The point is that the therapy broke a deadly pattern of constraint that had involved the girl in a problem which absorbed other family strains at a crucial point in the life cycle. The example illustrates the suddenness of the shift that can occur when a therapist disrupts such a sequence and throws the system into disequilibrium.

Breaking the Cycle Through an Interpretive Approach

Another repetitive, cyclical sequence between father, mother, and child is reported in the interview "No Man's Land," in Haley and Hoffman's *Techniques of Family Therapy*.[5] Charles Fulweiler is the therapist. The triangle consists of an ineffectively domineering father, a mildly rebellious adolescent son of thirteen, and a mother who sides with the son. Father keeps getting into an argument with son over smoking, which both parents say they disapprove of. However, Mother will break into these escalating arguments to protest, after which Father will back down. Eventually Father does not even wait for her to come in; he backs down anyway. This sequence occurs several times, with variations, during the interview. To give some idea of the flavor, here is one of the shorter versions; the mother has just said she is not in favor of taking away the boy's allowance:

MR. K: (to Mike) Would it please you, I presume it would, it would please you if I said that it was all right with me for you to smoke: Would that make you feel better?

MIKE: Yes, I guess it would.

MR. K: Well, for your sake, Mike, I wish I could, but I honestly and truly can't. I still don't think it is the right thing to do. I really don't.

MIKE: Well, by taking my allowance away, you're, you're both, not being, I'm not able to buy cigarettes, or I'm not being, I'm not able to do anything. I can't go to the show, I can't . . .

MR. K: Now, Mike, whenever you have come to me in the last two or three weeks and asked me for money for some specific thing, I have given it to you.

MIKE: Those things I had to do.

MR. K: You're right. You're right.[6]

As in Minuchin's family, this cycle is an example of a sequence that seems to direct attention away from more threatening issues in the family. Here at least one such issue involves the marriage. If the parents began to struggle with each other directly, their own relationship might be imperiled. One can see that the stakes are high in favor of some arrangement that will allow the parents to express their disagreement but will limit the disagreement to the topic of the boy's behavior.

As usual, this arrangement means that one parent will take a positive or neutral attitude and the other a more negative attitude toward the behavior. The disagreement may be hidden beneath the parents' concern for the symptomatic child, as in the case of the anorectic girl, or it may appear as a united antagonism toward the child, but a persistent effort to get each parent to describe his behavior toward the symptom will usually cause the disagreement to surface. Most family therapy with a child includes an attempt to uncover this disagreement and to refocus it as an issue between the parents. In this family, the disagreement is not so secret as in Minuchin's family, but what marital issues are involved is not clear. A surface reading of the case gives the impression that the marital dyad is mildly one-up/one-down, with the husband trying to take an authoritarian stance toward his not-too-compliant wife. We find out that he maintains considerable emotional distance from her, a situation she reinforces by investing herself in other relationships, like a girl friend of whom the husband is jealous, and, of course, the son. The wife's weaker position in the marital subsystem is counterbalanced by her strong position in the parental subsystem, where she has the son as an ally. The son's involvement is able to affect both the power difference in the marriage and the closeness-distance axis, so that neither variable is driven too far from its usual limit.

What has apparently happened to upset the family balance is the advent of a major transition point: the adolescence of the son. He is entering a period where he can realistically challenge his father. On the other hand, the normal pulls of growing up tend to detach him from his mother and female ways. It is logical that the behavior that brought the family to therapy was breaking into a tobacco store and stealing cigarettes and some change. The action also relates to the major issue between the father and son: smoking. In the repetitive argument over smoking, the problem the boy faces is the mirror-image disagreement between his parents. If he does not smoke (is not rebellious), he supports his father against his mother; if he does smoke (is rebellious), he supports his mother against his father.

The therapist knew it was important to disrupt this sequence. The methods Fulweiler used were mostly blocking maneuvers, supported by interpretations. A special feature of his style is to enter and leave the room without warning. Fulweiser took advantage of his entrances to inhibit the sequence we have described at strategic points and turn it step by step into a different direction. He used his first entrance to cue the mother to be more explicit in her defense of the son; the second entrance to pick at the disagreement between Mother and Father; the third entrance to back up the father's authority in the face of the mother-son combine; and the next two or three to stop the father from playing the role of pathetic victim, while at the same time clarifying the mother's part in rendering the father ineffective. The interview ended with Fulweiler pointing out that nobody was to blame, since all these events had their roots in the past. After about nine sessions with the threesome and twenty-odd with the couple, the father came in announcing a major change for the better, but pinned the cause to an experience they had in going to hear Billy Graham. Fulweiler said he was pleased when the family gave credit to an outside source because they then could own their own change rather than owing it to the therapist.

Haley identifies standard roles for this type of triangle: the "overinvolved parent," who seems extremely concerned with the child's problem and is fighting it actively, and the "peripheral parent," who seems more neutral and stands apart.[7] Often, of course, the overinvolved parent is in a submerged struggle with the peripheral parent, but the peripheral parent is often peripheral in regard to marital issues too, and will not hazard an open fight. The child seems to act as his secret agent in successfully defying the other parent. Once clue that indicates that the child has been fronting for the peripheral parent occurs when marital issues come to the fore and the overinvolved parent criticizes the spouse in the same terms he or she used to describe the defects of the child.

Assuming that this kind of triangle is operating in the above example, one sees the son offering his disruptive behavior like sticky bait to the overinvolved parent, the father. The resulting argument escalates to the point that the peripheral parent, the mother, is triggered to step in. The overinvolved parent is at times the outsider in the triangle, and in this instance much of the father's inappropriate anger and sense of helplessness may stem from this fact. In the closeness-distance area, the wife maintains the upper hand by having an affair to go to, so to speak, as she moves closer to her son to make up for her relative weakness in the marital relationship. In the same way, the husband, by periodically parading his own helplessness, uses the magic power of complementarity to glue his wife back to him. Obviously, if a therapist breaks this sequence, he then has to help the couple with both the closeness-distance problem and the one-up/one-down problem, so that a third party no longer gets drawn in as a monitor.

A Parsimonious Technique

If a clinician is successful in identifying the sequence of which the symptom is a vital part, a very small change can presumably be pinpointed accurately enough to have a wide-reaching effect. Watzlawick, Weakland, and Fisch represent an extremely parsimonious school of family therapy in this respect. This economy of technique was clearly shown at a demonstration by Dr. Richard Fisch, who interviewed a couple at the Center for Family Learning in New Rochelle, New York, in 1976. The problem the family reported on was embedded in much the same type of sequence we have been talking about, but the therapist's intervention strategies were completely different.

In this instance the family consisted of the father and mother, both in their thirties, a girl of nine, and a boy of six. The children were not present. Dr. Fisch asked what the problem was, and the parents told him they were having difficulty controlling the girl, who was willful, self-centered, obstinate, and disobedient. She was so unpleasant that she had only one friend, and even that friend she treated badly. Mother would get into daily battles with this child over issues like drinking her orange juice at breakfast. Mother might win, but these were Pyrrhic victories, as Mother's nerves would then be shattered. When the father was home in the evening, the struggle would get to such a pitch that he would come out of his study and browbeat the girl into obedience. The parents described their own relationship as close and loving, and stated that they knew the fault could not be in their parenting, since their younger boy was as delightful as his sister was difficult. Fisch offered one small suggestion. He remarked that one reason the parents were unable to combat the child's behavior might be because they had become too predictable. If they were to confuse her by doing something odd and unexpected, they might have more success. He then told the father that the next time he came out of his study to scold his daughter, he should simply give her a penny. If she asked him why, he was to say, "Because I felt like it," and go back to his room.

This intervention may seem clever but inconsequential until we examine the nature of the sequence it is designed to interrupt. The pattern Haley describes is apparent: one parent who is overinvolved with the symptom of the child, and the other parent less involved but often secretly allied with the child. In the Fulweiler example, the less involved parent could acknowledge the coalition. But here, perhaps because of the need to keep up the appearance of a united front despite a hint of covert disagreements, the father never challenged his wife in favor of his daughter. He could go no further than to say he did not have as negative a view of her as his wife, since he and the child both liked music and he enjoyed taking her to the opera. Thus the task given to the father altered the sequence in an important way: It undermined the myth of the child-monster that seemed to keep the spouses tightly joined.

At the same time the therapist anticipated with the couple some of the consequences of altering this sequence. There might be some side-effects, he said, if their daughter, despite the hopelessness of the case, did improve. First, the "good" child might begin to seem less than perfect once the "bad" child no longer offered such a total contrast. The father agreed that the boy was indeed somewhat immature for his age, signaling another matter on which he differed with his wife. Second, the therapist said, the mother might miss the intensity of her feelings for her daughter, which were a product of her motherly concern and a proof that she really did love her. The mother accepted both the positive relabeling of her hostility and the idea that she might find the change a hard one. Third, the therapist warned, the mother might at some point have to restrain her husband—who was in fact rather mild and rational—from losing his temper at his daughter and perhaps being too harsh. If one thinks about it, these consequences alter or reverse the value of nearly every relationship reported on in that family.

But the most interesting event of the session came after the therapist agreed with the mother that the most that could be hoped for was that she would react less strongly to her impossible daughter. The father then stated that he was not about to give up hope that easily; he, for one, had higher expectations of his little girl. The mirror-image disagreement, out of sight till that moment, had come to the fore.

The results of this interview are not known, but they are not crucial to an examination of the sequence we are studying and the methods used to break it up. As we shall see later, the Palo Alto group specializes in small changes, and even in their tasks they stick to "small change." The contrast between the limited nature of the intervention and the many points of interaction it touched make this a good illustration of therapeutic economy.

When the Cycle Includes Larger Systems

Haley redefines the problem of working with hospitalized adolescent schizophrenics as one of helping them leave home. The process which takes these young adults from home to hospital and back again is merely another version of a homeostatic cycle that monitors the parents' relationship. Nevertheless, breaking a sequence that includes not only the family but other social systems is an unusually complex operation and requires a series of maneuvers which may take time.

Haley documents this process in a training tape based on a case in which he was the supervisor and Sam Scott the therapist, while both were working at the Philadelphia Child Guidance Clinic. The tape is entitled "Leaving Home," and involves a twenty-four-year-old deaf man who had been shuttled between home and hospital for eight years. The sequence was predictable: After he came back home, he would become threatening and abusive; he would then be moved out to an apartment; after that, he would get on drugs and go out and cause trouble in the community. The police would find him, the parents would hospitalize him, and the whole cycle would start again.

Haley conceptualizes the therapeutic task as one of breaking up this cycle. If one part is blocked, the whole will have to change. The therapist who was working on this case could use sign language, and therefore could communicate both with the young man and with his parents, who did not use sign language. The first intervention he made was to change the type of institution the son would go to the next time he was picked up by the police. He had the parents sign a paper, in the presence of the son, saying that the next time he got in trouble they would have the police put him in jail. This changed the consequences not only for the son but for the parents. They could still maintain some control over him if he were in a hospital —visiting him frequently, for instance. In jail this would no longer be possible. In addition, his actions were reframed from behavior that could not be controlled to behavior he was held accountable for.

Another change was to interrupt the cycle at the point when the tension between the parents increased. When their son maintained good behavior for a while, irritation between the parents would begin to surface, and he would get into fights with his mother. Mother and son were in a kind of sticky bond. She would protect him from his father, who would beat him up if he misbehaved; on the other hand, she would push him away from her, insisting that he go out of the house and not make so many demands on her. To some extent the mother could ignite an outburst from her son just by this way of treating him.

The therapist, during a period when the deaf son was living at home, prolonged the time of good behavior beyond its usual limits by betting him a sum of money that he would not get into trouble with the police during the next two weeks. The son stayed out of trouble and won the bet. As a result of this period of calm, the father went on a trip he had long been planning. During his absence the mother angered her son by trying to make him spend time out of the house. He became violent, threatening her with a knife and his

216

sister with a baseball bat. At the next family therapy session the therapist showed up with a knife and a bat and laid them on the floor. Although the patient acted as if he were not responsible for what he had done to his mother and sister, the therapist questioned him so intensely that he grabbed the bat and threatened the therapist. The father took the bat away from him. The therapist then insisted, and had the parents insist, that their son was not allowed to use violent threats and weapons to intimidate people. He could argue or criticize, but he could not use knives or bats. This move blocked the patient's part in the sequence, labeling it as intolerable behavior and making the other parties in the sequence join to resist it.

The next shift was to have the son move into an apartment and continue to live there. In the past, he had usually moved away only when he and his parents were angry with each other, and no matter where he lived, the parents treated him as a handicapped person who could not be expected to take care of himself alone. The therapist laid some groundwork by insisting that the son do his own laundry while he was still at home, and contribute housekeeping money from his welfare check. He was also expected to repay debts. Thus the self-fulfilling prophecy that labeled him incompetent was cut into in an active way. After the scene with the bat, the young man moved out once more. He got into trouble with the police again and was briefly hospitalized, but this time his parents stayed out of it and he handled the situation on his own. According to the therapist, this was the last time he got into trouble, and, more important, the last time he was hospitalized.

In this chapter we have addressed ourselves to some of the ways therapists of quite different persuasions block or alter a rigid pattern or cycle that accompanies a problem and that seems to monitor the possibilities of change. The next question we must deal with is a tricky one. The fact that most experienced therapists seem to recognize and deal with the same type of configuration does not mean that they base their therapeutic ideology or techniques on the same premise, or that they would even agree with this analysis of their work. Accordingly, we shall devote the next chapters to a more detailed analysis of the work of the family therapy pioneers and to the emerging schools of therapy that have begun to dominate the family field. We shall try to describe more fully the confusingly different approaches of various therapists and schools, and to relate their theories to their techniques.

In addition—and this is an even more serious concern—our model has become small, constricted, and mechanistic. To speak of a triangle of two parents and a child, or the recursive cycle that may be played out in the sequence of behaviors between these persons, is too reductive. We must go back to the booming, buzzing confusion again, to shake up this position and bring in richness, depth, and breadth. An examination of the work of clinicians who pioneered the family field, and of those who built on the work of these early figures, will move us toward variety and the possibility of envisioning new and more complex models in our examination of systems and systems change.

Chapter 12

Family Therapy and the Great Originals

The Family Movement Comes of Age

The family movement in therapy resembles the Protestant movement in religion. It follows on the heels of a highly organized body of ideas and practice which has a well-recognized founding father, Sigmund Freud. Despite multiple heresies and schisms, psychoanalysis has formed the basis for a mental health establishment. Some pioneers in the family therapy field have mounted a revisionistic assault, almost amounting to revolution, against the ideas of the Freudian establishment, and this revolution has produced a host of rival messiahs, gurus, and sects, all claiming primacy but none finding legitimacy.

How, then, to comment on the differences and similarities among the major approaches to family therapy which have developed in the United States? Since Madanes and Haley have covered the large territory of transpersonal therapies,[1] our next chapters will focus on five major approaches within the field of family therapy: the historical, the ecological, the structural, the strategic, and the systemic (leaving out the approaches to family therapy which have been claimed in the name of previously existing models such as behavior therapy, Gestalt therapy, and other schools that arose independently of the family therapy movement but might technically be seen as interpersonal).

Before dealing with the established schools, however, we must focus on a few pioneering figures whose contributions are of great value and yet who fall into no schools. They can fairly be called the Great Originals. Virginia Satir, the late Nathan Ackerman, the late Don Jackson, the late Milton Erickson, and Carl Whitaker are among those who cannot be categorized. In this chapter, we will attempt to describe the approaches to therapy and the therapeutic ideas of these inimitable souls.

Satir and the Family of Angels

Satir's place in the family movement is extraordinary and unique, even though she has transcended the confines of family therapy to join the wider scope of the Human Education Movement. In 1963, Satir was conducting a family therapy demonstration project at the Mental Research Institute in Palo Alto. I had been asked to help edit her first book, *Conjoint Family Therapy,* and was amazed and enchanted by the power of her presence with families.[2] Even more impressive was the accuracy with which she seemed to discern the features of that elusive creature she called a "dysfunctional family system." When she would say, "I always judge therapy by the pronouns," she was referring to the tendency in such families for everybody to say "we" rather than "I," a common attribute of "consensus-sensitive" or "enmeshed" families. This explains her interest in exposing "discrepancies" in communication; her emphasis on helping people accept the "differentnesses" between them; her formulas for blocking repetitive sequences that end with one person taking some standard role like victim, martyr, scapegoat, rescuer. She had pungent phrases for such situations: "Did you ever see the cause of death on a death certificate that you said 'no' to somebody?" Or she might ask, of a family that resolutely refused to acknowledge that anybody disapproved of anybody else, "Well, I go on the principle that no humans are angels." Finally, she had an uncanny ability to pull the label off an "identified patient."

There is a related tactic—more a stance, actually—for which Satir has become justly famous: her ability to take the most negative problem or situation and turn it into something positive. An example is a first interview with the family of an adolescent boy, the son of a local minister, who had impregnated two of his female classmates. The seating of the family vividly expressed their sense of shame. The parents and siblings sat at one side of the room and the boy, head down, sat in the opposite corner. He was a handsome blond young man, and he had on the whitest and tightest pair of jeans imaginable; if his manner seemed repentant, his dress and body did not. Watching the interview, I felt that there was no way for the youngster to get out of his extremely difficult spot, and no way for the therapist to dislodge him. I underestimated Satir, who, after introducing herself to the family, said to the boy, "Well, your father has told me a lot about the situation on the phone, and I just want to say before we begin that we know one thing for sure: we know you have good seed." The boy's head shot up, his back straightened, and he looked with amazement at Satir as she turned to the mother and asked in a bright, crisp voice, "Could you start by telling us your perception?" Her strength seems to lie in her ability to join with people not in terms of anger, blaming, hostility, but in terms of disappointment, pain, and hope.

However, if one were to classify her in terms of her work as a family therapist, one would have to place her as a master of the art of disentangling people from the mystifying communicational traps that are a particular hallmark of families with a psychotic member. The best demonstration of this aspect of her work that I know of, outside of a live interview, is "A Family of Angels," a first session with the family of a psychotic boy, to be found in Haley and Hoffman's *Techniques of Family Therapy*.[3] The patient, seventeen, has just had a psychotic break. Early in the interview, Satir asks family members how they show disapproval of each other. She is told that in their family nobody ever disagrees with anybody else. However, the parents admit that in spite of what the mother terms "an amazing relationship," she and her husband occasionally have cross feelings toward each other. When asked how she shows such feelings to her husband, the mother says that she would hurt him with her silence. The father explains that he never gets angry but lets time heal things over. Both agree that it is merely a temporary lack of communication when this happens.

Satir comfortingly supports this idea and goes on to remark that the patient, too, seems to feel that he cannot communicate with his parents. By indirection, Satir implies that there may also be disguised anger between the parents and their son. It turns out that the boy's breakdown took place while the family was staying in a hotel abroad and his parents had confined him to his room. Satir turns to the parents and asks sharply, "Now why did you lock him up?" The parents quickly reply that the door was not actually locked, but it becomes clear that they had prevented the boy from leaving the room.

The boy then explains that the reason he wanted to run away was because he was afraid that his parents would lock him up in a hospital. Satir asks the parents if they wanted to punish the boy. They deny this vehemently, saying that their action was merely protective. Satir remarks, "So this was a way you wanted to protect him," and then, "But Gary [the son] didn't feel that way about it." In this way, Satir validates the boy's experience of concealed anger and punishment which is always going on between people in his family, and now between his parents and himself.

Before the family can react to this sudden confrontation, Satir switches to the past, finding out that the parents were first cousins who had married against the protests of the father's mother. Nevertheless, this mother has lived nearby for twenty years and is a constant visitor. The family portrays her as extremely domineering and the mother says she can never say "no" to her. Satir asks the mother what would happen if she told her mother-in-law "no." It turns out that the mother has always been afraid to do anything to push the mother-in-law away because her husband was so close to his mother, even though the two women have carried on an underground battle for years.

Here Gary is able to say, "And I have had a dilemma, which side to pick. Should I take my mother's side or my grandmother's side?

And I've been waiting and waiting." By this time, the fact that there are open wars, and sides to take, has been established. In the relationships between Gary and his parents, and the parents and the mother-in-law, unmentionable subjects are at last coming to light. In Satir's view, this clarification of communication is part of what will free the psychotic from his position of understanding the buried messages and having to respond to them, yet having to deny that he understands or responds to them or that they even exist.

Satir's major concern has always been with the individual and it is probably this concern that stimulated her interest in the human potential movement. In the past decade, she has shifted more and more from her initial focus on families to working with huge groups in a spellbinding, almost religious way. She has become a prophet of love and joy in what is now billed as the "Satir Experience." But before she entered that world fully, she left as a legacy to family therapy not only her writing but many therapists whom she trained and who have continued to extend her insights into families, and her unique approach to working with them.

The Irreverent Artistry of Nathan Ackerman

The late Nathan Ackerman is the most important family figure to come out of the psychiatric establishment of the Northeast. While using psychodynamic formulations to describe his work, he nevertheless created an art of psychotherapy that crashed through every known tradition. On the East Coast his name was synonymous with family therapy for many years. Starting in the late 1930s with an article on the family as a bio-social-emotional unit, he pioneered seeing families clinically during the 1950s.[4] But he did not merely sit and talk with people in a family, transferring psychodynamic techniques to individuals in the family setting. He worked with families as a bullfighter works with a bull. His demonstrations were famous for their theatrical ebullience, wit, and an almost shocking intrusiveness into private areas of personal and family life.

Most of the work he did for public display was consultative, with other therapists carrying the case. Even the film *In and Out of Psychosis,* which presents a long-term treatment case, consists of excerpts from the only two sessions he had with the family, an initial interview and an interview later in the course of treatment. Even so, an analysis of any one of his interviews shows that he had an uncanny nose for "the thing in the bushes"—the thing the family therapist is out to change—and an extraordinary ability to use his own presence to induce change.

Perhaps his best single analysis of a treatment case was contained in his and Paul Franklin's article "Family Dynamics and the Reversibility of Delusional Formation."[5] This paper includes part of the filmed material that was the basis for "In and Out of Psychosis." It is the story of a girl who believed she lived on a planet called "Queendom," peopled by creatures who were like females but reproduced by fission; no men were allowed. Ackerman shows, both in his description of family dynamics and by the treatment strategy, how this delusion was actually an allegory for the skewed structure of the family. The father appeared remote and fond of intellectualizing; the mother was bland and self-righteous. Both were dominated by the rigid tyranny of the mother's mother, who lived with them. Father was in effect divided from any real contact from Mother by the powerful inhibitory effect of the grandmother's presence. This Queen Mother, too, seemed to say: No Men Allowed.

The parents nevertheless presented themselves as united and harmonious, especially in their concern for their psychotic daughter, whom they felt was a victim of a too vivid imagination. Only when Ackerman began to challenge the rule of the grandmother, help the father to assert his right to a real relationship with his wife, and lessen the mother's dependency on the grandmother, was the daughter's delusion broken. At the same time, the conflicts between the parents came to the fore, and the grandmother was sent to live with other relatives. These changes were the price of the daughter's recovery, which took about a year of regular family therapy sessions.

Ackerman had the foresight to film many of his interviews, and he published some of them in book form. Examining these records we have the opportunity to look closely at his actual performances.

Despite the psychodynamic phrasings, an analysis of the transactions in even one session convinces one that Ackerman was struggling toward what was later to be known as the "structural" approach to family therapy, an approach that links symptoms to dysfunctional family structures. It is no accident that the inventor of that school, Salvador Minuchin, was first introduced to family therapy through Ackerman in the early 1960s, when Minuchin was invited to join Ackerman in his work with adolescent boys. One imagines that the imprint of the older man's work stayed with Minuchin, who restlessly searched until he found a language, grammar, and conceptual framework that would explain his own modifications and extensions of this radical therapeutic form.

In defense of the thesis that Ackerman worked in an essentially structural way, let us examine one of his most irreverent interviews, an excerpt that opens *Treating the Troubled Family*.[6] In this session Ackerman plunges into the here-and-now, ignoring the family's ostensible reason for coming to therapy in favor of tracking the relationship sequences connected with the presenting symptom. Tactics consist of blocking behaviors and sequences by a quip, a quick movement of hand or posture, or an interpretation of nonverbal cues. These are not only diagnostic but fall into the category of what Minuchin would call "restructuring moves," pushing the configuration of the body politic toward a more normal state. Ackerman tends to take the stance of a benevolent if wary pugilist, and is not afraid to lock horns with family members, although at other times he will turn into a most seductive *agent provocateur*.

This segment is the first part of the second interview with a family that came for treatment because of serious fighting between the eleven-year-old daughter and the sixteen-year-old son. The girl had recently threatened to stab her brother with a kitchen knife. The son had a long history of temper outbursts and was doing poorly at school. The father, in his forties, was a businessman, the mother a teacher.

The father sighs as he sits down and Ackerman immediately asks him why he is sighing, refusing to be put off by the father's insistence that he is tired and suggesting that maybe he has some reason to sigh. An attempt to get the son to comment on why Father is sighing is interrupted by Mother, who breaks in to announce that she has been keeping a notebook of all family transgressions during the week. She shows the notebook, explaining that she keeps anecdotal records of the children in the school where she teaches, and decided to do the same with her family. She is a sharply assertive woman in her forties, in contrast to the father, who seems mild and complacent. The therapist reacts with an ironically amused comment: "You come armed with a notebook," and extends the metaphor by saying, "Fire away!"

Now follows a maneuver that undercuts the mother's authority while never directly challenging it. In spite of his invitation to Mother to proceed, Ackerman picks up on the nonverbal behaviors of other family members as they react to Mother's threatened exposé. He turns to the father and says, "You're picking your fingers." This diverts Mother, who cannot resist commenting on Father's many nervous habits. The son comes in to defend his father and challenges her about her own habits. All family members start to talk at once, but the therapist clears the way for the son, who tells the true story about Mother: She belches! Mother calmly confirms this habit, and admits that the person in whose face she belches most is Father's. Now when she tries to go back to the notebook, the therapist continues to ask about the belching. The mother giggles; it's a habit she doesn't think should be taken seriously. She suggests that her notebook contains items about the marital relationship that will show her husband in an unfavorable light. The therapist is deaf to her effort to unloose these damaging facts and keeps focused on the belching, which the mother says mostly occurs when she is lying down. Father says that her habit of belching in his face upsets him a great deal.

At this moment, when it looks as if there may be some tense issues coming out between the parents, the children start a rescue operation. The daughter taunts her brother about a lipstick mark on his neck, indicating that he has been intimate with his girl friend. The son gets furious. The therapist comments that this interruption has occurred just when the parents were going to talk about their love life. Father, who sounds as if he is beginning to enjoy this session, describes how it feels when you want to kiss a woman and she belches in your face; you need a gas mask. The daughter again tries to intrude, only to have the therapist ask her to move her seat so that Mom and Dad can talk together. He points out that the children really do know about their parents' marital situation, even though the son states his unqualified disgust at the topic. He wants to leave. The therapist draws a generation line by remarking that the boy may be afraid that if he intrudes on his parents' love life, his parents and the therapist may invade his. He tells the boy that he would like him to stay, but that he can leave if things get too intolerable. The daughter, in a coy, teasing voice, says she is scared her brother will want to kill her after they go home for telling about his girl friend. Ackerman responds to this third rescue attempt by labeling the girl's preoccupation with the girl friend as jealousy, putting a little circle around the siblings. The son gets angry and leaves. The daughter soon follows. The children are clearly mirroring their parents' quarrels, while at the same time acting in a diversionary manner.

All this is an adroit way of restructuring the family to induce change. Ackerman has quickly disarmed the mother, who came in ready to blast her husband on the subject of his sexual inadequacies, and has exposed an area where the father could be the accuser. Very quickly Father is up, Mother is down. We note that even though Ackerman is not always decorous or polite, the mother does not get angry; it is the children who get upset and try to fight Ackerman off by inserting the symptom (their fights). Ackerman reframes this intrusion as an example of a lovers' quarrel—exactly as he will later do with a quarrel between husband and wife. The children are pushed out of their parents' bed, as Ackerman puts it, and placed on their own side of the generation line. Their reaction is to leave, which they presumably would not do if their anxiety about their parents were not somewhat relieved.

Once they have gone, the therapist gets into the marriage bed himself, listening to all the lurid details of the wife's disappointed sex life. The wife complains that her husband is not romantic and attentive; in particular, she resents having to be the one who attends to contraception by using a diaphragm. Throughout, Ackerman uses a style of blunt, playful vulgarity, which detoxifies issues by pushing them to the edge of absurdity. The belching is blown up to such heroic proportions that the wife starts to laugh. Her husband's rather nervous attempt to respect her is brushed aside by the therapist, and he is encouraged to be bold and breezy himself. Ackerman teases the wife away from her imperious, commanding position by going back to her early married days when she was "green and innocent" and her husband was a sexy man of the world. In recent years, as Ackerman finds out, the husband has lost interest in sex. Is that because his wife is not a good "piece"? Is she a "dog"? The wife is enjoying the exchange, in spite of (or perhaps because of) the impolite language.

Ackerman then starts a flirtation with the wife, asking her, "How can you cooperate with me so beautifully, so juicy-like . . . and with [your husband] you don't cooperate?" He tells her what a pleasing woman she is to him. At the same time he has been challenging the husband to make demands on her, get her off her "fat ass." Unbelievably, this grim couple is beginning to laugh, to appreciate each other, and the positions they came in with are far more balanced. The wife seems softer, the husband firmer. In fact, they have achieved something like parity in a remarkably short time. The notebook has long since been forgotten. The children return and arrangements are made for the next meeting.

This analysis gives an idea of Ackerman's provocative style, but also indicates an approach to family therapy that can be thought of as essentially political and organizational. Although Ackerman is not as explicit on this point as Minuchin, he is clearly revising the configuration of relationships in the room and pushing them toward a more "normative" state.

Whitaker and the Therapy of the Absurd

An equally provocative therapist is Carl Whitaker, whose work seems calculated to shock, amaze, enchant, and confuse. Whitaker, who calls himself a therapist of the absurd, specializes in pushing the unthinkable to the edge of the unimaginable. He will suddenly suggest to a young "psychotic" woman that she sit on her father-in-law's lap, announcing, "Incest is better than love." If asked about his reasons for such statements, he is likely to answer, "To please myself. If I don't get something out of therapy for myself, I know it's not going anywhere."

Whitaker uses many techniques that, as he puts it, push over the leaning tower of Pisa. In one interview Whitaker turned to an expressionless young man who had recently made a serious suicide attempt and said, in the presence of his family and his slightly upset therapist: "Next time you try that you should go first class—take someone with you, like your therapist." For the first time during the interview, the boy's eyes snap awake. He continues to watch Whitaker, who casually begins to describe a new invention he has been working on which will take the messiness out of suicide—a human Dispos-all, "like that thing in the sink only bigger." By the end of the session he has not only reached the boy but activated the boy's father, the other one in the family who has given up on life and is in despair. Whitaker says, "My tactic has become a kind of tongue-in-cheek put-on, an induced chaos now called a positive feedback —that is, we augment the pathology until the symptoms self-destruct."

One of Whitaker's techniques is to spread the problem around:

We started with Mother's alcoholism. She gets one point for that. Now we've uncovered Dad's gruesome collecting disease, so he gets two points, John's revealed his school phobia and bared Henry's delinquency. Mary, do you plan to destroy yourself by being the family heroine and the nurse to every patient in the entire hospital? . . .

Jim, if Mary tried to kill herself because she sensed you'd like her dead, do you suspect that if the gang of you would help her, she might convert to killing you?[7]

If all else fails, Whitaker will prescribe an impasse in such a way that the family will be very reluctant to let him win. In one case he came into an interview as a consultant and finally said,

Well, it's been a dismal hour. Your therapist has worked hard to help you to change but to no avail. He even asked for this consultation, to see if he was too blind or too feeble and failed you in that way. I'm convinced that I can't help either. It looks hopeless. I guess it'll just stay this way for ten more years. Maybe this is the best you can do and that's all right even though it is discouraging. I doubt if it will get worse and that's some consolation.[8]

In writing about therapy, Whitaker focuses a great deal on the area that comes under the heading of taking control. Whitaker counts on achieving some of his most powerful effects from what he calls the backlash of the encounter. He very effectively uses indifference, gentle ridicule, boredom, even urging a family not to come into treatment, as a "negative come-on." Whitaker feels that he must win at establishing the rules of the game that will be played in therapy, and he will not even admit that therapy has begun until this stage is reached.

He is justly famous for his colorful tactics in achieving these victories. When one couple called for an appointment, each was having an affair, but they wished to discuss the future of their marriage. They objected to seeing Whitaker with a cotherapist because of the double price. Whitaker gave the couple a choice: he and his cotherapist would consent to see the couple: (1) under a contract specifying no sexual relationships during therapy, "to potentiate the affective relationships with the two therapists"; or else (2) the two therapists would see the couple together with their respective lovers and the spouses of the lovers, in a group of six. The couple declined both offers, but called six months later to say that they had gone back to being a pair.[9]

The delicacy of Whitaker's dance through an interview has to be seen to be appreciated. In a videotaped consultation Whitaker did for a Philadelphia Child Guidance Clinic family, the symptomatic child was a boy with a soiling problem who came in with his mother and father and a baby brother. Whitaker pushed his way into the good graces of the family by sitting down on the floor with the baby and playing with him. In one of the nicest recorded examples of nonverbal reframing of symptomatic behavior, Whitaker noticed that the baby was straining and grunting while having a bowel movement, and he strained and grunted along with him.

Whitaker's manner with the family was equally casual. This turned out to be a family in which the men sat on their anger. Neither the father nor the boy found it easy to stand up to the mother, who was something of a drill sergeant, chunky and brisk, and quite annoyed with her problem son. She launched into a loud diatribe about him at one point, and Whitaker, who was sitting at the other side of the room, got up and sat next to the boy. Addressing the mother, he began to compliment her on the "fire in her eyes." As a result of this move, her manner immediately softened. The father was sitting next to her like a large, plump Buddha. He held the baby part of the time and fed him his bottle. He was as placid as she was sharp. Whitaker reframed the marital skew by saying that it was lucky a fireball like Mother hadn't married another fireball, otherwise there would be continual explosions. He declared that he and his own wife shared the same lucky situation, since she was also a fireball and he was sort of a blob. He added that two blobs shouldn't marry either.

Operations of this sort were constructed so deftly that most of them did not reach the family's awareness. By the end of the interview, however, the boy seemed noticeably less depressed than when he came in, and the mother had responded to Whitaker by becoming milder and the husband by livening up. The family's reaction to the interview was very positive, although they remembered very little about it afterward except "that nice doctor." One could assume that this reaction was a natural response not only to Whitaker's appeal but to a more normative structuring of family relationships.

The interview was notable in that Whitaker did not call up his big guns; the family was easily persuaded to move with him and "therapy of the absurd" was not needed—unless one takes the position that a professional man of mature years sitting on the floor and grunting along with a defecating baby is absurd.

A more intensive, session-by-session account of ongoing cotherapy with Whitaker is given in Napier's *The Family Crucible,* one of the best introductions to the inside experience of being a family therapist.[10] Whitaker has said that he must be "captured" by the patient for therapy to work. To this end he plays hard to get, setting up hurdles and obstacles to the therapeutic relationship like a spoiled and haughty courtesan. Implied in Whitaker's therapy is a Zen-like theory of change. As he says, "Psychotherapy of the absurd can be a deliberate effort to break the old patterns of thought and behavior. At one point, we called this tactic the creation of 'process koans.'"[11] It would be hard to think of a better term.

The Uncommon Therapy of Milton Erickson

Although Erickson is known primarily as an experimental hypnotist, it is due in part to Haley's great interest in his work that he has been included as one of the grandfathers of family therapy. Readers will find Haley's account of Erickson's therapeutic miracles in *Uncommon Therapy* both fascinating and mystifying.[12]

Perhaps the most outstanding feature of his art is in the broad category of "encouraging the resistance." This common hypnotic technique has become the basis for the development of the paradoxical directive, a hallmark of the strategic school. Historically, then, it makes sense to emphasize this aspect of Erickson's work, even though it is by no means representative of the whole of it.

A vivid example of Erickson's way of encouraging a symptom while subtly introducing change occurs in the case of a young man about to enter military service.[13] His problem was that he could urinate only through an eight- or ten-inch metal or wooden tube. Erickson induced a trance and suggested that he get a twelve-inch tube of bamboo and substitute it for his other equipment. He was to hold the bamboo with his thumb and forefinger and his other three fingers flexed around his penis, alternating his right hand with his left. At the same time, he was to try to feel the passing of the urine through the tube. He was also told to mark the tube off in quarter inches, and the suggestion was made that he might begin to consider shortening the tube but that he must not feel compelled to do so but let the decision happen of itself; he was to concentrate instead on what day of the week he might choose to shorten it. Finally, he was told that his army physical examination would be postponed but that he would be called up for a second examination in about three weeks and would probably be accepted.

The young man did get a bamboo tube and used it as instructed. After a week, he decided to saw an inch off, then (for some reason on a Thursday) two inches, and so on, until he had a ring of bamboo only a quarter of an inch wide. Soon afterward he realized that his three fingers around his penis constituted a tube, and he discarded the bamboo ring. Erickson writes, "He [held the tube] with both the right hand and left hand and even experimented by extending the little finger and then realized that he could urinate freely without resorting to any special measure."[14] The tube had become the penis itself.

This is as nice an intervention as one can find, even in Ericksonian annals. The patient was not asked to change, instead he was directed to continue to urinate through a tube. But the idea of change was most certainly introduced: the tube could be longer, but it could then also be shorter, and it could also be of a different material. The wording of the suggestions given during the trance insured that the young man would "of himself" gradually abandon the artificial tube. And the idea of a successful outcome was contained in the message that his next examination would probably be successful. The patient reported with some bewilderment at what he found himself doing (he had been told to have amnesia for the trance, although he remembered some of the suggestions), but began to have a sense of hope that he would begin to break the habit he had been carrying for so long. Although the habit seemed to have originated from a humiliating experience when, as a small boy, he was caught urinating through a knothole in a fence, there was no attempt to "work through" this initial incident or to use it as part of the treatment. The charm of the story, of course, is that Erickson did not cure the young man of urinating through a tube at all; he simply helped him to substitute a natural tube for the artificial one he had been using.

Reading accounts of Erickson's work, one is struck by how little attention he pays not only to the past but to the relationship context of the problem. In the cure of an enuretic young man also about to go into the army, the anxiety about having a wet bed was transferred, using hypnotic suggestion, to "pseudoanxieties."[15] For instance, Erickson directed him to stay three days in a hotel in a strange city and, while remembering how distressed he would be when his mother found a wet bed, to suddenly think that it would be an amazing joke on him if, after all his agonizing, the maid in the hotel should discover a *dry* bed. What shame and embarrassment he would feel when the maid found the dry bed. In addition, he was told that on checking out of the hotel he would find himself in a conflict as to which set of grandparents to visit first, since he was making good-bye visits. One consequence of his enuresis had been that he could never visit relatives. Although one might guess that the enuresis protected him from any conflict of loyalty regarding sides of the family, Erickson never mentions this possible aspect of his symptom. He dealt with it indirectly by suggesting that the young man would resolve his obsession with the problem of which relatives to visit first by making the visit to the first set shorter than the visit to the second, and that, once he got there, his visits would be pleasant and comfortable. The young man experienced all the obsessional thoughts suggested, and found himself shamed by having a dry bed in the hotel. He also reported feeling "crazy" and confused about which relatives to visit, but that the visits had gone well.

Erickson describes his goal as trying to substitute other anxieties for the enuresis while still addressing the central anxiety: the young man's shame at his mother's finding a wet bed. The tie with the mother was not explored in any way; Erickson gives it a minor place in the story by saying that when he was accepted by his draft board, his only worry was his concern about his mother's adjustment to his going into the army.

Unfortunately, the immense interest in Erickson has focused mostly on his inimitable talent. One can read through Haley's book on Erickson, or peruse Erickson's own articles, and appreciate the amazing ideas and the incredible outcomes but be no wiser as to how one might replicate such work. Richard Bandler and John Grinder's more recent microanalysis of Erickson's sessions with clients (speech patterns, use of tonality, pauses, metaphors, and so on) is no more helpful.[16] Here, too, one studies the ingenious subtleties laid out for the neophyte and feels that these things are simply not replicable. The art of therapy is still the art of the shaman, the high priest, the medicine man. For all the fascination with Erickson's work, and for all the brilliant studies that have been made of it, it remains something that only an extraordinary individual can achieve if initiated into the mysteries by an extraordinary teacher.

Another unfortunate by-product is that none of these analyses of Erickson's work lead to a further understanding of "what is to be changed," but only to a refinement of the art of persuasion. The unit of treatment is narrowly defined as "therapist plus problem." Thus schools of therapy associated with what eventually emerged as the strategic approach deal with theories of persuasion or behavior change, but do not bother overmuch with the shape or pattern of that which is to be changed. With an Ericksonian therapist there is no such thing as a problem, only something defined by somebody as a problem. Change the definition, the perception that "creates" the problem to a different one, and the problem will no longer exist. So we are back to dazzling sleight of hand, elegant magicianship, and the triumph of the arcane.

Jackson and the Therapeutic Double Bind

Don Jackson, like his colleagues at the Mental Research Institute, was interested in a hitherto undescribable phenomenon: the recursively shifting, yet interlocking, sequences of behavior in families which correlated somehow with a symptom. He sensed that altering one element in the pattern might alter others and, he hoped, the symptom as well. Thus he was moving in a holistic, or what we might call now a systemic, direction. There are few examples of Jackson's work during an entire family interview, but the chapter "The Eternal Triangle" in Haley and Hoffman's *Techniques of Family Therapy* shows him at his best and is critiqued by Jackson himself.[17] In addition, Jackson shared the Bateson group's fascination with the double bind and wondered whether there might be such a thing as a homeopathic use of the double bind or a "therapeutic double bind."

An example of what Jackson thought of as a double bind is described in a study by Jackson and Weakland of the case of an adolescent boy whose parents were afraid he might be homosexual.[18] The young man tried to assert his manliness by staying out late one evening with a group of friends and was greeted on his return with a marked display of worry by his mother. As a result, he began to come home early. His mother then threw out a new worry: that he was not popular enough. Although uncertain which way to go, the boy decided the next night to come home early, only to find that the mother had left him a note telling him that she was out and would be home late. The authors say, "Here was an opportunity to break the bind they were in, but it is in the nature of these reverberating cyclic sequences that he could not pull out." So he started dinner for his errant mother, and when she came home he covertly agreed to hide from his father the fact that he had cooked the meal, with its homosexual implications. As the authors note: "And so the cycle was perpetuated." In other words the solution to the original "simple bind" was punished, not rewarded.

Jackson's accounts of working with families with schizophrenics emphasize constructing a therapeutic double bind as a major strategy for change. The term "prescribing the symptom" had first been used by the Bateson group, and Jackson was particularly ingenious in experimenting with this format. In this, he was probably influenced by one of his teachers, the psychoanalyst Frieda Fromm-Reichman. In "Toward a Theory of Schizophrenia" an anecdote is told about Dr. Fromm-Reichman's treatment of a young woman who was in contact with powerful gods.[19] The girl told Fromm-Reichman that God R would not let her talk to her doctor. Fromm-Reichman replied that she herself did not believe in this god, but that since the patient did, the patient must ask his permission to talk to her doctor. After all, the patient had lived in the god's kingdom for nine years and that had not helped her. So now the patient must ask the god to let Fromm-Reichman try. This could be explained as a therapeutic double bind, because if the patient became doubtful about her belief in this god, she would be giving power to her doctor. But if she went to her god with the request that since he had failed, Fromm-Reichman must be given a chance, she again gave power to her doctor.

In *Pragmatics of Human Communication,* Watzlawick, Beavin, and Jackson discuss this type of therapeutic double bind in fuller detail.[20] Most of their examples are directed toward individuals or couples and not toward larger or more complex family contexts. In an example similar to the one described above, Jackson is shown teaching a paranoid patient to be more suspicious. The patient was refusing to respond to Jackson at all. Jackson said that the patient must think he was God, and might really be God, and if he really wanted to be treated like God, the therapist would comply. Jackson then got down on his knees and presented the patient with a large hospital key, saying that since he was God he would have no need of a key, but if he were indeed God, he deserved to have the key more than the therapist. The patient dropped his stony demeanor, came over to Jackson, and said, "Man, one of us is certainly crazy."

In another example, a woman with intractable headaches was told that since her headaches were obviously not amenable to cure, the therapist could only help her to live with her condition. The woman, possibly to prove the therapist wrong, came back reporting her headaches had abated. In another case, a young woman was unable to get up in the morning to attend her college classes and was in danger of flunking out. She was told she must set her alarm for the proper time for getting up, but then must rest in bed until eleven. After several days of this regime, which she found unbearably boring, she began to get up on time, and then was able to discuss more openly some of the reasons why she was so afraid of going to class.

Two examples in *Pragmatics* extend therapeutic bind interventions to problems with couples rather than individuals. In one example the couple consists of a compassionate caretaker wife and an alcoholic husband. The wife is instructed to drink along with her husband but keep one drink ahead of him. This reverses her usual role of caretaker because she will become drunker than he and he will probably end up being the caretaker. To avoid this outcome, he will either have to drink much less or not at all. In any case, the pattern is disrupted.

The second example is the case of a couple who argued constantly. They are told that their arguing is a sign of emotional involvement and that this apparent discord only proves how much they love each other. As the authors say,

No matter how ridiculous the couple may consider this interpretation—or precisely *because* it is so ridiculous to them—they will set about to prove to the therapist how wrong he is. This can best be done by stopping their arguing, just to show that they are *not* in love. But the moment they stop arguing, they find that they are getting along much better.[21]

The authors of *Pragmatics* describe how therapeutic double binds work by pointing out that in a pathogenic double bind the patient is "damned if he does and damned if he doesn't." In a therapeutic double bind, since he is told not to change in a context where he has come expecting to be helped to change, he is in a similar trap. If he resists the injunction, he changes; if he does not change, he is "choosing" not to change. Since a symptom is something which, by definition, one "can't help," he is then no longer behaving symptomatically. Thus he is "changed if he does and changed if he doesn't."

It turns out that nearly all of these illustrations refer to simple moves with one problem and the unit is in only one case larger than two. But in a few of Jackson's clinically oriented articles, one finds far more attention paid to the matrix of the problem, as if it were a hub with spokes that touched many points of a larger circumference. One also finds a sense of therapy moving in stages, so that the complexity pertains to time as well as to the immediate configuration.

The question, posed by the therapist to the family, "What would be the negative consequence of change?" first emerges in the MRI literature in an article by Jackson and Yalom.[22] This question challenges the family to prove that they can, despite the therapist's doubts, live happily ever after without the presenting complaint. However, it sometimes also happens that the predicted "negative consequences" appear as soon as the presenting complaint clears up, and this not only can upset the family but may unnerve the therapist. Problems vanish, only to be replaced by others. As Jackson says ruefully of one such family he treated, "I felt like a paper hanger with bad glue, running around, never organized the way I would have liked to be."[23]

The article mentioned above not only illustrates the idea of the negative consequences of change but gives some idea of the multiple dimensions that characterized Jackson's clinical thought and work. Dave, twenty-four years old, had been diagnosed schizophrenic about five years before. Since that time he had been in and out of hospitals, returning to live at home and take jobs, only to collapse and be hospitalized again. The family sought therapy mainly because individual and group approaches had not worked, and when the family therapist came on the scene, they resisted family treatment as well. At that time Dave had been continuously hospitalized for one and a half years. His family consisted of his mother, father, and a "well" brother, who was a very polite, controlled young man of eighteen. Eighteen sessions in family therapy had not cracked the façade the family presented of three very caring people whose only problem in life was Dave, their crazy son. The parents, it was noted, seemed to behave like a single person, so tight was the bond between them. Attempts to gain a portrait of the family only elicited assertions of "happiness, cooperation, love, and inexorable financial success." At one point, the authors note, Dave pounded on the table and shouted, "My God, I come from a perfect family." Mother asked, "Dear, have we said anything that wasn't true?" Dave, perceptive even in defeat, replied, "No, but now I see what a goof-ball I really must be."

Jackson decided to counter the family's position by placing the question to them: What problems might arise for this family if Dave improved? This is a therapeutic double bind, or, as the Bateson group also called it, a therapuetic paradox:

It is a paradox in which the family as presently organized "can't win." The question encourages problems in a framework of help . . . the consultant takes advantage of the family members' view of themselves as helpful individuals and implies they would be uncooperative if they did not provide some difficulties to discuss with him. Backed as it is by an expert, the question is heavily weighted to evoke at least token answers. Yet any indication of family difficulties which might be caused by Dave's remission can be amplified as barriers to his recovery and, hopefully, force the family to consider, at some level, that they must change before recovery is possible.[24]

The family—like most families placed in this position—reacted with incredulity to the question. The father, however, finally admitted that if his son got well enough to come home, he would be embarrassed by some of his son's public behaviors. The mother was openly upset by the father's failure of support, and the first sign of a rift in the marriage appeared. In the ensuing conversation Dave helpfully suggested that he might fall in love and want to get married. It would be a problem for him to introduce the girl of his choice to his parents. His mother countered by saying she would be delighted, but then qualified her statement by saying, "Of course, I would always hope it would be the right one." Mainly, the parents said, they agreed with Dave's many doctors that he ought to become independent, in which case all their problems would be gone.

Dave then came in with another helpful remark: He might become so independent that he wouldn't even want to see them, and as he began to leave home, "I see associations with my family more or less going down the drain." To which Mother could not resist a little rejoinder: "Well, other people's don't." Then Dave brought up still another "problem": If he got more successful than his father, how would his father feel about it? Although the father said, "I'd be thrilled," the nervous laughter that erupted spontaneously indicated some discomfort.

At this point the consultant asked the brother how he felt about the patient's weekends with the family, after which Dave usually became quite agitated and upset. The brother admitted to being nervous because he never knew what mood Dave would be in or how to handle him. The consultant pointed out that it was as if Dave were being asked to bear the whole burden of the family's solicitousness. Dave thereupon burst out with a quite amazing analysis of his position in the family, and reframed his own symptom positively within the total family context: "Well, it's just the story that I'm the sick one in the family and so this gives everybody else a . . . a chance to be a good Joe and pick up Dave's spirits whether Dave's spirits are down or not."[25]

Here the consultant decided to use a second tactic to shift the family system, this time an injunction to another member to change. He asked Charles, the "good" son, if he could help his brother by becoming more of a problem during the time Dave was away from home. Charles asked, "You mean rebel against my parents?" and the therapist said, "I mean you would be more of a problem in the sense that you would get a little more honest about some of the things that trouble you, or some of the uncertainties you may have, or whatever you don't share with your parents now because you don't want to bug them." Charles, being a good son, agreed.

This apparently innocuous intervention caused havoc. Father began the next meeting with the announcement that he would like to be the problem for a change. When asked how he might go about doing this, he replied that he might come home late from work some night without telling his wife. It turned out that a covert rule in the family was that everyone had to "sign out" with mother, who would become worried and upset unless she knew exactly where everybody was at all times. In the following session the mother came in very depressed and astonished the family with an account of her own history: her mother, now dead, had been a severe asthmatic who became addicted to narcotics; the daughter had feared that her father would remarry and bring in a stepmother who would not love her; later, the mother had known that her first husband was unfaithful to her; and so on and so on. Father continued to bring up things that worried him: his lack of confidence in himself and feelings of failure as a parent. He told Dave, "If you think I'm superhuman, that I don't have feelings or hurts or problems, that nothing inside bothers me, then I've got news for you."

This news apparently made an impression on Dave, for after this session he went out and got the first job he had found for himself in years. Although he lost it because he lacked the appropriate skills, his family was supportive and he got another at which he did well. Gradually he moved to disengage himself from the family, and with their encouragement he got an apartment for himself, continued to get better jobs and support himself, and a year and a half later was completely on his own. Although therapy did not stop then, an important step had been made, and in subsequent sessions Dave found better and different means of handling the many ways in which his family and he were continually binding and rebinding each other.

After Jackson's death in 1968, his colleagues at the Mental Research Institute (mainly John Weakland, Paul Watzlawick and Richard Fisch) continued to work with and expand these ideas, both in terms of theory and clinical practice. In the next chapters we will move on to discuss the establishment of schools, starting with the approaches that seem most congruent with the major positions of psychodynamic theory, though by no means identical. I have called these approaches "historical," because of their emphasis on the past and their multigenerational view of family pathology and theory of change.

Chapter 13

Historically Oriented Approaches to Family Therapy

The Lingering Influence of Psychodynamic Thought

Although the family therapists we will discuss in this section are not, in any formal or literal sense, associated with psychoanalytic theory or practice, there is one group of therapeutic approaches that seems to be more acceptable to the psychodynamic establishment than others. Even when the unit worked with is different, the theory of change (abreaction of repressed material) may be very similar; or the goals (to achieve an individuated self) may be similar; or the techniques (exploring feelings, gaining insight, "working through" past events) may be similar. We might say that the central strand linking these approaches is that they aim at disentangling the individual from the family web (or disentangling all family members), and therefore the individual patient is still the major focus of concern.

The other approaches, which we have called ecological, structural, strategic, and systemic, do not take the final blossoming of the individual as their objective, but move to change the context of whatever problem is presented (in most cases the family, or the family plus other systems), in the expectation that once this is achieved, individuals will blossom on their own. Let us start with the practitioner who, in many respects, has focused most clearly on the individual within the multigenerational family context: Murray Bowen.

Bowen and the Differentiated Self

The more psychodynamically oriented family therapists believe that one must get at historical or causal factors to relieve a symptom or achieve change. Family therapy versions of the psychoanalytic concepts of insight, catharsis, and abreaction seem to be the major avenues of change, and a mature objectivity is, as with most Freudian therapies, the desired end result.

Bowen's approach is the most influential of these more historical therapies.[1] Since by his own say-so he does not emphasize symptoms or problems, he may fairly be placed in the larger movement that includes individual-oriented "growth therapies." His method of coaching family members to go back to their families of origin offers a path for achieving personal individuation and autonomy, albeit via a family route. Many followers have found that his approach does relieve symptoms and problems, and his theory of the multigenerational transmission of emotional illness has laid the conceptual groundwork for an important school of family therapy.

In explaining the emergence of emotional illness in a family member, Bowen suggests that it has its origin in the difficulty previous family members have had in separating from the core family. This difficulty is mitigated, if not solved, by involving (or as he calls it, "triangling in") a person from the next generation. As this process unfolds from generation to generation, family members' inability to individuate intensifies until one or more children exhibit the extreme case of undifferentiation known as "symbiosis," which keeps them stuck forever in the family, and the family stuck forever around them. It is a kind of repetition compulsion applied to the generations, except that each generation pushes more of its trouble onto the next.

Bowenian family therapy is designed to identify the patterns originating in the past that have such a hold on people in the present, and to help people unlock themselves. Thus he emphasizes searching out clues from living members of the extended family, especially from older generations, to trace a pattern, and if possible alter it. To do this, he uses the genogram, a visual diagram of the family tree going back in time and extending collaterally, with an individual or a couple as the focal point.

Bowen's theory of change resembles Freud's dictum: Where id was, there ego shall be—if one substitutes the darkly primitive condition of "fusion" (which Bowen equates with being ruled by one's emotions) for "id," and the objective condition of "differentiation" (defined as an ability to remain detached yet connected within one's own family) for "ego."

Critics say that this makes therapy too intellectual a process. But people who have been coached to revisit or reconnect themselves with family members, to change some aspect of their interaction with those persons, often report an enormous impact, both on their own lives and on the lives of other members in the family. If the family is, as Bowen feels, a huge interconnected web, the repercussions in one corner may be felt in another corner far away, if not across the entire web. Even remembrances of relationships with parents or relatives now dead can be influenced or changed, at least in the mind of the searcher, with helpful results.

The model for this procedure was first presented in a paper Bowen read during a symposium in 1967; it was later revised and published in a book based on that symposium.[2] In this paper Bowen describes his own family of origin, a large extended kin group going back many generations which dominated a small southern town. Bowen tells of deliberately intruding into most of the dominant triangles in the immediate family by means of an astonishing strategy. He sent off letters that told various relatives of the unpleasant gossip that others were circulating about them. These letters ended with endearing salutations such as "Your Meddlesome Brother" or

"Your Strategic Son," and announced an impending visit. Bowen then showed up as heralded, to deal with the predictably indignant reactions of his kin.

The effect on the family was dramatic. It loosened up many closed-off relationships and—once the original fury against Bowen himself had died down—it created a climate of better feelings all round. The effect on the symposium was equally dramatic. Bowen had prepared a theoretical talk, scrapped it at the last moment, and instead gave a blow-by-blow account of his incredible journey—the first time, in the experience of most of his audience, that a practitioner had ever attempted to change and influence his own family *or* described such a literally "convention-shattering" procedure to an august body of colleagues.

This experiment of Bowen's set the stage for the development of an entirely new therapy process. The commonest form of Bowenian therapy is the quest for the differentiation of self. A trainee is not considered fully developed until he has been "coached" in differentiating himself from his own family of origin—a process that Bowen says can take twelve years. There is a resemblance here to the mandatory training analysis that a neophyte psychoanalyst has to undergo before being given full responsibility for patients. And the goal—to produce a person who is free of crippling entanglements with family relationships, past and present, and can therefore get on in a more unfettered way with his own life—is certainly close to the goals of psychoanalysis.

A side benefit of Bowen's training process is that it allows a family therapy induction to take place in a facility where no clinical families are available. The trainee can use his or her own family to practice on, or else the group of trainees role-plays one trainee's family, taking the various parts of family members and being directed by either the trainee or the teacher. A weakness may be that the trainee learns only how to coach similar individuals in achieving a "differentiated self," rather than to do family therapy per se. This is also an advantage, however. The coaching process can be used as a therapy format when the client is a young single person pursuing a career (like social work) in a city far from home.

Many essays have appeared in family therapy journals describing trips back to families of origin that resulted in extraordinary shifts, intended and unintended, affecting an entire kinship group. These stories have the flavor of testimonials, and emphasize the appearance of more positive and meaningful relationships and a general opening up of lines of communication. The approach is especially appealing to individuals from families in which strains in kinship ties are handled by emotional distancing, use of secrecy, and pseudocommunication, as with the powerful extended clans one finds in the South and Midwest, and families from ethnic groups, such as the Irish.

Bowenian therapy with families is an adaptation of Bowen's preference for coaching individuals. Even when Bowen is dealing with a couple, he insists on communications being channeled through him, to lower the anxiety and irrationality that he believes foster the reactivity of pathological family relationships. This technique increases the power and leverage of the therapist. It also has the effect of setting up a therapy of two dyads simultaneously, since each person interacts only with the therapist. It is a curiously one-to-one model, in spite of its obvious impact on a couple system, and may betray Bowen's fidelity to a more individual-oriented stance. It is for reasons such as this, and for his emphasis on the importance of objectivity and the supremacy of the rational, that he has been placed in the psychodynamic group. Although the content of his work is different, many formal aspects are similar, including the training implications, the longevity of the process, and the final goal of an autonomous self.

As for dealing with whole families with children, Bowen clearly excludes this from the center of his repertoire but his disciples do not. Such practitioners as Philip Guerin, Elizabeth Carter, and Monica Orfanides have translated Bowen's theory and practice into an intriguing multigenerational family therapy. They take Bowen's cool Euclidean model and map out the key triangles attached to the problem or presenting complaint. These triangles may go back several generations, even when the identified patient is a child in the present one. Here the use of the genogram is a standard tool. With its help the therapist identifies for the family the reactive processes which link key triangles in self-repeating chains. Typical interventions are designed to block "triangulation," to cool off escalations, to restate heated matters more objectively, to detoxify dangerous issues, or to expose and nullify the effects of buried secrets. In general, Bowen therapists try to lessen the extreme emotionality which they feel is the amniotic fluid that nourishes symptomatic behaviors.

These goals are often achieved by straightforward interpretations. For instance, in a family therapy case described by Guerin and Guerin, the wife is complaining that her husband makes hypercritical remarks to her when they are in public.[3] The wife says this upsets her and she starts to escalate emotionally, unlike her husband, who stays calm and collected. The therapist may reframe the wife's emotionality as no less a choice than her husband's self-control. This is the side of Bowenian therapy which works through making people aware of their own steps in the reactive dance, and in this sense is a training in objectivity about the self.

Bowen's concept of "reversals," however, comes closer to one of the hallmarks of what has come to be known as strategic therapy. To get one person in a self-reinforcing relationship process to reverse his usual reaction to the predictable response of the other is to inhibit or break the mutual-causal cycle. In the Guerins' example, the therapist also asked the husband if he could agree not to try to rescue his wife when she behaved foolishly in public, instead of feeling so responsible for her. The husband responded by backing off. This intervention is a nice example of positive reframing—the husband's behavior was not condemned but described with adjectives of praise. This makes the intervention a nonconfronting one and is apt to get a cooperative response.

Reversals sometimes work better if only one of the parties in such a pattern knows about the plan. Coaching one spouse or family member in a reversal has the added power of placing the therapist and that family member in a secret pact and reinforces compliance with the directive. Carter and Orfanides describe how a Catholic woman, who had angered her extremely religious mother when she married a Protestant, was helped to regain closeness with this offended mother.[4] Instead of getting into the usual quarrel over religious issues, the woman was instructed to write her mother and tell her how much she appreciated her strong faith and envied the inner peace it brought her, and furthermore that she felt lonely and cut off from the family because of her marriage. The mother responded with unexpected warmth, confessing how much she missed her daughter and voicing her doubts about her own faith. As a result the tie between them was reestablished.

Finally, although Bowenian therapists do not speak about using paradoxical techniques—Bowen's framework having no place for this concept—they do not hesitate to use them when resistance in a family makes them necessary. In the Guerins' family case the presenting complaint was around the inappropriate social behavior of the daughter. The father criticized the daughter, and also criticized the mother for bringing the girl up badly, while the mother seemed ashamed and paralyzed, not happy with the child's behavior but feeling somehow responsible. Guerin started by asking the father to increase his efforts to make his wife improve the behavior of the daughter. Predictably, this task failed, as everybody backed off from intensifying the pattern. The therapist was then able to give a straightforward instruction: the mother was told to get more involved outside the family while the father was asked to step into the mother's place. The girl began to behave more appropriately and stopped being a problem. But the husband became anxious about what his wife was doing outside the home, now that he didn't have her under his surveillance, and therapy shifted to a marital issue. This double maneuver is not only paradoxical but also a common way of "rocking the system": pushing a stuck pattern so hard that the participants react against the push and then are quite amenable to a direct suggestion for change, in this case a simple structural one.

A major difference between Bowen's approach and structural and strategic approaches is that therapy does not stop when problems go away. The girl in the case above improved and the couple began to get along better, but at this point the job of the Bowen therapist has just begun. Now it becomes time for each of the spouses to fix on their dysfunctional ties to their respective families of origin. This is the final stage of reaching the elusive "differentiated self." As Guerin writes, "The therapist must provide individual family members a degree of emotional freedom from their reactive triggers. That way they won't continually be in a responsive position, caught up in the reactive flow of the family process and behaving like predictable robots."[5]

This is clearly where Bowenian therapy comes closest to the

psychodynamic model, in that the desired result is a mature, autonomous self for every adult family member. Therapists who take a problem-oriented, shorter-term approach feel that this elongation of therapy can be exploitive, resembling Freud's "therapy interminable." In this case, however, the wife had never been able to respond sexually to her husband and was able to do so only after revisiting her family of origin, discovering that her aunt had really been a surrogate mother to her, and reestablishing intimacy with the aunt. The sexual improvement seemed to happen "of itself," since it was not being focused on, but Guerin cites this kind of change as the side benefit of a shift in the bonds that hold individuals in the grip of a powerful relationship system of which they are not aware. Certainly it is true that a problem may remain frozen until patterns connected with the original laying down of the problem are changed. But let it be understood that one is still dealing with an addiction in the *present.* Bowen's use of history suggests strongly that it is not the revisiting of the past but the redoing of the present that counts.

The Theory of Repression and Family Therapy

Other family therapists who have emphasized the past, like Norman Paul, seem to have picked up echoes of Freud's theory of repression, applying it to the family unit instead of the individual. The idea is that if one goes back to some event in the past which has been closed off and relives it, uncovers it, "abreacts" it, the symptom presumably attached to it will disappear. This is much the same as saying that if an individual goes back to the repressed traumatic incident underlying a symptom and works it through, all will be well. In Paul's concept of "unresolved mourning process," a death or loss in the family that was not properly mourned at the time is exhumed, so to speak, and the whole family goes through the ritual in a symbolic way.[6] Paul is usually able to find some important loss or death to work with in any family where there is a symptom.

Other historically oriented therapists emphasize uncovering family secrets and hidden skeletons—the fact that a child was adopted, or a great-aunt went insane. The presumption is that once the dreaded item is made public, it will lose its fearfulness, and the symptom which served as a cover will wither away.

A related group of family therapists believes that getting out feelings, whether of anger or grief, is a way of "abreacting" family or individual issues which are embedded in affect that is buried or covert. This is, of course, very close to the psychoanalytic theory of repression as an explanation for symptoms. Critics who take a systems view complain that this is an oversimple approach. Simply airing a feeling does not always extinguish the symptom that presumably arose to hide or mask it. Family therapists in particular quickly found that helping a family member "let it all hang out" in the bosom of the family either subjected the person to later reprisals or, by transferring blame or inducing guilt, reinforced the sequence that perpetuated the original problem.

Yet another school of therapy that emphasizes the past-in-the-present is represented by the work of James Framo. Framo has adapted Fairbairn's theory of objects relations, and insists that Fairbairn's "introjects" (memories or imprints of parents and other significant figures still deeply influencing the patient) be asked to come in person to the patient's or family's therapy sessions. For this reason Framo insists on including as much of the extended family as possible, and will sometimes create a large tribal event, finding this a way to break up old, repetitious relationship patterns.[7]

Family sculpting—pioneered and developed by such therapists as David Kantor, Fred and Bunny Duhl, Virginia Satir, and Peggy Papp —is still another way of influencing family structures. Sculpting is something like a form of psychodrama in which people re-create the family, usually to elicit major coalition formations and homeostatic sequences, so that old patterns can be perceived and played out differently. It is useful in training, because the training group can take the parts of a trainee's family members, who are of course not present. It can also be used by members of a family in therapy as a geospatial metaphor for various aspects of a relationship system: closeness/distance; splits and alignments; the experience of being one up or one down in reference to another—all aspects not usually elicited by verbal reports and often powerful in their effects on family members' appreciation of situations that had been hidden from view. Papp's article on sculpting in family therapy—or, as she prefers to call it, "choreography"—explains the uses of this technique.[8]

Ivan Nagy and the Family Ledger

There is a difference between transposing elements of a psychodynamic point of view to the family setting and using information from past generations strategically to add power to an intervention. Like Bowen, Ivan Boszormenyi-Nagy does both. Much of the time he operates from a framework that has a strongly psychoanalytic flavor, but at other times, seemingly inadvertently, he uses data from the past to construct multigenerational paradoxical interventions. His most interesting contribution, however, is a rich and poetic metaphor of families as a multigenerational account book.

Nagy, in the book *Invisible Loyalties,* speaks of a "family ledger," which consists of a multigenerational system of obligations incurred and debts being repaid over time.[9] No matter when an injustice occurred, there would be a retributive move at some future point, although not necessarily by the original debtor. Problems, in Nagy's view, arise when this justice comes too slowly or is insufficient, and then what he calls "the chain of displaced retributions" occurs. A symptom might be the signal that there has been too great an accumulation of injustices. To deal only with the symptom, without looking at the history of the problem in terms of the family account books, would be a grave error.

One example he and his coauthor, Geraldine Sparks, cite is the case of a tense, irritable nine-year-old girl brought in for therapy. It seems that she has been raised by her mother's parents, because her mother became psychotic and is now living in a hospital. In the course of family therapy it turns out that the grandmother, at the age of fourteen, was sent to live with her own mother's parents after her step-father tried to rape her. Her mother, siding with the stepfather, refused to believe her and sent her away. Later the grand-mother made a marriage fraught with tension and unhappiness. Nagy remarks:

It is easy to see how an unsettled account between herself, her mother and her step-father will have to be "taken out" on her marriage. The resulting helplessly hostile and frightening atmosphere of the home must have been reflected in the child's desperate call for attention at school.[10]

Thus the injustice done to the grandmother emerges as a symptom in a child two generations later (and, one might add, a disabling psychosis one generation later).

Another example would be the common pattern in which a mother who was angry at being rejected by her own mother would compensate by offering total devotion to a daughter of her own. The daughter, in the language of balance of payments, is asked to rees-tablish family justice by giving the mother all that her own mother did not give her. If this child grows up with an unexplained negative feeling toward the "loving" mother, she can then be made to see how her mother has used her to make up for her own deprivation, and can perhaps forgive her mother. Or, alternatively, the mother can be made aware of how she has unwittingly asked her daughter to make up for the grandmother's deficiencies, and perhaps change her expectations of the child.

Nagy does not perceive these patterns negatively but points out that they may have a profound function in sustaining the family. He pictures the family as a group of people caught in an ever-unfolding web of obligations that acts to keep the family or individ-ual members from harm. Family members impose their own primi-tive obligation ties through what Nagy calls, comparing his concept to Wynne's "pseudomutuality," a "counterautonomous superego." Individual interests are thus sacrificed to the survival of the group. Confused bickering between parents may be keeping a mediating daughter close to home, and she, in turn, may be keeping the mar-riage together. The sacrifice of a child who is symbiotically attached to a mother who was herself emotionally deprived is a way of redressing that old wrong. It may also be a way of keeping the impaired mother from collapse. Or a child of harsh parents may push his unspoken bitterness to them onto his wife, thus loyally preserving his relationship to them at the expense of his marriage. Nagy does not condemn this complex accounting system as long as it ultimately balances out, and above all if role obligations are not so frozen that they do not allow a more just order to be periodically established.

Elegant as this logic is, it selects only what Elizabeth Carter has called the "vertical stressors"—the linear chain of events cascading down the generations. The assumption is that A causes B causes C till at last we end up with Z. Something happened in the past that set off compensatory behaviors and eventuated in a symptom in the present. The horizontal picture in the here and now is virtually ignored, and this limits the richness of contextual clues, which tell the therapist what, in the present, is recursively maintaining the problem and vice versa.

Thus the therapeutic approach that grows out of this linear, causal explanation of pathology is close to a psychodynamic approach. First, Nagy says, the chain of injustices that led to the particular symptom in the present must be explored. The therapist is seen as a benevolent moralist, creating an atmosphere in which it is possible for people to face their own emotional debts or injustices, and, once they have this insight, correct them. This is made easier if they can see that they themselves were victims, and that the way they are acting is dictated by wrongs previously done to them, as when it turns out that a tyrannical father was himself treated harshly as a child. This father can then more easily obtain forgiveness from the people he in turn has been so harsh to. Or two spouses who bitterly attack each other may redirect their anger toward their families of origin, once it is pointed out that their anger at each other is their way of loyally refraining from criticizing their own parents. At the same time, the newly designated "victims" are not thereby allowed to seek revenge. Forgiveness is the key to this therapy, which works only when the reactive blaming and hurting process—"the chain of displaced injustices"—is halted.

One cannot help noticing the usefulness of this approach as a therapeutic rationale very close to what we will later describe as strategic or systemic approaches, with their emphasis on positive reframing as a tool for change. If one can make a patient believe that his hatred of his wife is only displaced hatred toward his mother, he is likely to end up behaving more pleasantly to his wife. She, in turn, may reciprocate in a benevolent fashion. Thus their cycle of recriminations can be broken. Similarly, if spouses redirect their enmities toward a mother-in-law, this can create a bond; with further therapy it may grow into one that does not need a mother-in-law to cement it. And the face-saving implications of this displacement are wonderful; if a mother can point to her own unhappy childhood as the reason she has been unable to show more love to her offspring, she can say to herself, "Oh, it was not because I am a bad person, but because I had an unfortunate history; now I can behave better without having to thereby acknowledge that I have been in the wrong."

There are obvious limitations to taking the somewhat straightforward and moralistic stance Nagy seems to prefer. The therapist may be tempted to act like a wise rabbi or priest, and there are many patients and families who know how to use this against him. Some resistant families are experts at games of pseudo-atonement, having used them as weapons for years. Another possibility is that this approach may enforce negative self-awareness and perpetuate guilt, blame, and other unwanted behaviors.

Nevertheless, Nagy seems to be one of the few clinician-writers (with the exception of Helm Stierlin, who has been much influenced by him) who have redefined symptomatic behavior as evidence of family loyalty and indicative of a sacrifice of individual growth to the interests of the group. How different this is from using a negative language that defines symptoms as dysfunctional or indicating a dysfunctional family. In spite of his use of words like "scapegoat," "victim," "injustice"—all part of the vocabulary of therapists who have simply substituted "bad or sick family" for "bad or sick patient"—Nagy is edging out of this linear position and coming close to a more circular epistemology.

In his descriptions of one or two cases Nagy seems almost to be using a system-wide therapeutic double bind. In one of these cases a teenage boy was on drugs and was getting into minor but potentially serious trouble. It turned out that the parents had separated, then the older children had gone, and this boy was the last child left at home with the depressed, obese mother. Nagy says:

While on the overt level this boy was conducting an irresponsible pleasure-determined life, on the family loyalty level he performed a valuable sacrifice for the whole family. . . . In fact, the self-destructive pattern of his living served as an assurance that as the last member he is not capable of leaving mother.[11]

After the therapist had made the loyalty aspects of the boy's behavior visible to the boy and his family, a major shift apparently took place. The boy got off drugs and got a job. The mother temporarily lost hers, and for a period really did depend on the son, but then moved ahead in her profession.

The hint of a move toward a concept of circular causality rather than the historical linear approach also appears in a discussion of the futility of siding with a presumed scapegoat. Nagy notes that the therapist will often be rejected in such an effort by the scapegoat as well as the rest of the family, since the scapegoat is, as Nagy puts it, just as addicted to the game as everybody else. A better way to handle such a situation, Nagy says, is to congratulate the scapegoat on his position as the "winner," in that he is able to make everyone else feel guilty, and to sympathize with the rest of the family for their uneviable position as underdogs.

These interventions, with their paradoxical flavor, are described out of context. They do not reflect the main thrust of Nagy's work and seem to arise as an almost accidental consequence of his emphasis on seeing symptomatology in terms of loyalty to the family. Nagy's theory of change is a basically historical one of cause and effect proceeding down the generations. To get to a less linear position, we must move on to those pioneers who made a sharper break with the therapeutic establishment: the ecological, structural, strategic, and systemic schools.

Chapter 14

Ecological, Structural, and Strategic Approaches

The Ecological Model

In this chapter, we shall start by examining the group of systems therapists who flourished during the period of the late 1960s, when there was money for community programs and for treating the psychosocial problems of the poor. In 1962, Salvador Minuchin, together with E. H. Auerswald and Charles King, got a research project funded to study and work with families of delinquent boys at Wiltwyck School. Minuchin's project, reported on in *Families of the Slums,* was more than just another research study.[1] One might say that if the Bateson research project became a magnetic center for talent and ideas on the West Coast in the 1950s, the Wiltwyck project provided a similar climate on the East Coast in the 1960s. Even though Minuchin led the project, the people he recruited represented a diverse and brilliant array of talent. Gathered together were researchers and clinicians like E. H. Auerswald, Richard Rabkin, and Braulio Montalvo, to mention only a few. Most of these people continued to contribute original ideas and to seed new projects long after the Wiltwyck project ended in 1965.

Rabkin and Montalvo should first be singled out for the intense and poetic vision each contributed to the field of community psychotherapy. Rabkin left Wiltwyck and eventually went into private practice in New York, but wrote in 1970 a brilliant treatise on what he called "social psychiatry": *Inner and Outer Space.* [2] To date, there is not a better metapsychology for the family systems movement. Montalvo went with Minuchin to the Philadelphia Child Guidance Clinic in the late 1960s. There he created a series of exquisitely crafted training tapes, analyzing the contextual meanings of behaviors in family interviews, many of them with minority families. Some of these can still be seen at the Philadelphia Child Guidance Clinic.

Of all Minuchin's collaborators, E. H. Auerswald took perhaps the most interest in using a systems approach to transform the structure of community psychiatry programs in public settings. He left Wiltwyck to create a unique "Applied Behavioral Sciences Program" at Gouverneur Health Services on New York's Lower East Side. His aim was to construct a new kind of health service which would respect the total context of the problems experienced by the poor population served by Gouverneur. Here he had some support, since the head of Gouverneur was an innovative public health official, the late Howard Brown, who had just turned Gouverneur from a municipal hospital with a record so bad that it was locally referred to as The Morgue to an attractive and well-planned ambulatory care clinic.

Auerswald's "ecological systems" approach, as he called it, was directed at the total field of a problem, including other professionals, extended family, community figures, institutions like welfare, and all the overlapping influences and forces that a therapist working with poor families would have to contend with. His essay "Interdisciplinary versus Ecological Approach"[3] best summarizes his position. This paper attacks the idea that to create a fully rounded health care system it is enough to put together a team of professionals each grounded in a different discipline. What is needed, said Auerswald, is a new kind of health professional who takes a holistic, "systems" view of the problem. The Batesonian aversion to "chopping up the ecology" is well illustrated by this article and its central thesis. Two companion articles—Lynn Hoffman and Lorence Long's

"A Systems Dilemma" and Emery Hetrick and Lynn Hoffman's "The Broome Street Network"—show the application of the multi-vectored ecological model to the treatment of crisis situations combining biological, psychological, social, and environmental factors.[4]

In creating health care formats that would carry out his ideas, Auerwald proposed such unheard-of activities as convening conferences in which every member of a multiproblem family, plus attached professionals, would all gather in one room to work out a plan for coordinating all services relating to that particular family. His Family Health Unit, set up to serve the immediate neighborhood of Gouverneur, was made up of professionals from the entire health spectrum and a representative from the local Department of Social Services as well.

Auerswald was also one of the first to advocate what I call "outdoor," as opposed to "indoor," therapy; he insisted that a community psychiatry unit should not only be responsive on a temporal basis (twenty-four hours a day) but on a spatial basis as well. If the contextual integrity of a problem was to be heeded, the limitations imposed by the time and space requirements of health professionals had to be done away with. To this end Auerswald created a Mobile Crisis Unit, a team of mental health professionals who operated out of a van, and who would go from home to school to hospital to court, as needed, wherever trouble arose.

Auerswald left New York in the early 1970s to head a small mental health center on the island of Maui, but his ideas are now incorporated into many health services in the form of crisis units and quick-response teams. In addition, the need for mapping out the dimensions of mental health problems in their total ecological context has begun to be accepted in major institutions, schools, and training programs.

A piece of research that particularly influenced the course of community psychiatry in the late 1960s was Donald Langsley and David Kaplan's project to study brief family crisis therapy at the Colorado Psychiatric Hospital in 1964.[5] This research was a crucial piece of evidence backing the trend toward crisis intervention in working with poor populations. It not only compared the effects of brief family treatment with routine hospitalization in the case of acute psychiatric problems, but it had a well-constructed research design. Family or "systems" therapy had made many claims and had a growing number of advocates, but outcome studies providing hard data were scarce. In this sense, the Denver project was a milestone piece of work.

The design of the project was simple. Selected at random, one of every five persons who appeared at the emergency room of the Colorado Psychiatric Hospital and was judged by the resident psychiatrist to need hospitalization was sent to the Family Treatment Unit. This Unit consisted of Frank Pittman, a psychiatrist; Kalman Flomenhaft, a social worker; and Carol de Young, a public health nurse. The Unit treated each patient with his or her family on a brief, outpatient basis. The other patients who were hospitalized according to the usual procedures constituted a natural control group. In all, the experiment included 36 pilot cases, 150 experimental cases, and 150 control cases. The groups were found to be well-matched, and the only requirement for admission to the experimental group was that the patient be between the ages of sixteen and sixty and be living with at least one relative in the Denver Metropolitan area.

The approach was essentially pragmatic. The aim of the team was to get the patient back to his or her previous level of functioning and the family past the immediate crisis that brought them in. The whole family was convened, along with any other persons or helpers involved, for the first meeting. Occasionally an over-night stay at the hospital was recommended, but in general the patient went home with the family that first day. An attempt was made to understand the reasons for the crisis and to mobilize resources within the family, or block pressures that seemed to have intensified the crisis. Medication might be prescribed, but it might be given out to the whole family, not just the patient. Considerable direct pressure might be used to get a patient back on his or her feet. A woman who was unable to function might find the public health nurse on the team out at her home, standing over her while she mopped the kitchen floor. A home visit was routinely scheduled within the first thirty-six hours. Surprisingly few office visits were needed in most cases, and two and a half weeks was the average length of time the Family Crisis Unit was intensively involved in a case. It should be added that external resources from the community were routinely brought in (visiting nurse services, vocational rehabilitation, and so forth) to continue the work of the Crisis Unit in whatever area was most essential. At the earliest possible point the unit would back out, always with the proviso that they were available to the family if the crisis flared up again. Usually, subsequent crises were handled with a minimum of involvement, often only a phone call or two.

The most important finding of the project was that acute cases could be treated equally well, if not better, with a brief crisis approach. Patients did not waste time being "sick" in the hospital but started to function almost immediately. Patients who did go into the hospital not only took that much longer to get back to normal, but became addicted to hospitalization. Thus their rate of recidivism was much higher than with the experimental group, most of whom did not use the hospital at all for future crises. Other natural benefits, of course, were the obvious savings in time, money, and personnel. This finding may have contributed to the fact that soon after the book describing the success of brief family treatment appeared, the unit was disbanded and the Colorado Psychiatric Hospital resumed hospitalizing all acute cases.

An illustration of the rather unconventional methods used by the Family Crisis Unit has been described anecdotally by Frank Pittman, the psychiatrist of the team. Pittman recounts a time when the team went out to the house of a woman who had discovered her husband was having an affair. The team found her lying in an apparently catatonic state on the kitchen floor. All efforts to get her to get up were to no avail. Pittman looked out the screen door to the back yard and saw a wet cocker spaniel whining to get in. He had also noticed that the woman was wearing a very pretty housecoat. Pittman opened the screen door, whereupon the muddy dog rushed to its owner and began to lick her face and climb all over her. The woman immediately got up and offered to make the team coffee. It is for this reason that Pittman sometimes characterized their approach as "wet cocker spaniel therapy." A very nice presentation of their work on a case can be found in Haley and Hoffman's interview with the Denver team, "Cleaning House."[6]

Another center that pioneered in developing the crisis intervention model was Bronx State Hospital in New York. Family therapy had been introduced as part of the training program at Bronx State by Israel Zwerling during the 1950s, but its Golden Age came during the 1960s. During this time, the Family Study Section was started at Bronx State by Andrew Ferber, with the collaboration of clinician-researchers like Chris Beels, Marilyn Mendelsohn, Norman Ackerman, Thomas Fogarty, Philip Guerin, and many others, making up a distinguished, if peripatetic, faculty. As well as doing research and offering training in family therapy, this group extended the use of crisis techniques to the turbulent psychiatric problems of families of the South Bronx.

A profound influence and presence at Bronx State during this time was the late behavioral scientist Albert Scheflen. Working with anthropologist Ray Birdwhistle in Philadelphia in the 1950s, Scheflen had helped to invent the field of "kinesics": the microstudy of human communication patterns in social settings. During his stay at Bronx State, Scheflen inspired many of the family therapists who learned from him to analyze family sessions as well as other behavioral events, producing some striking documentation of the hidden patterns that shape communication. Scheflen's own focus at the time was on collecting data by videotape which would allow him to compare the use of space and territory in the homes of families from different ethnic groups in the community. Indirectly, he helped train a generation of clinicians dealing with poor, minority families to think and work like anthropologists, broadening the family field to include a growing concern with issues of ethnicity.

At the time when researchers like the above were developing new methods for working with poor communities, other practitioners were experimenting with natural systems—tribal networks or neighborhood configurations—which seemed more logical arrangements for helping the poor and the isolated than artificial groups. Ross Speck and Carolyn Attneave are the pioneers of this branch of therapy, which goes outward from the nuclear family into the larger groupings around it. Speck and Attneave became known for forming huge community or kinship networks that met ceremonially on a regular basis to deal with problems such as a symbiotically attached mother and child, and that often continued to meet after therapy stopped.[7]

Minuchin worked with the ecological model for a brief time but abandoned it to concentrate more narrowly on child problems within the nuclear family and to work out the "structural" approach for which he is now widely known. Harry Aponte, who had joined Minuchin in the early years of his directorship of the Philadelphia Child Guidance Clinic, stuck to the families of the very poor as his main concern. He found the combination of an ecological framework with a structural model peculiarly effective with these families. His essay describing an eco-structural approach to a school-family problem and his article on "underorganization" in the poor family are unique descriptions of a way of applying structural therapy to fields that include systems other than the family.[8] The concept of "context replication," in which dynamics in the home are repeated in the child's situation at school, is dramatically illustrated in the school-family article.

Aponte is especially good at conceptualizing the layering of contexts and is sensitive to dilemmas that include systems other than the family. The "ecological" therapist must be prepared to deal with the larger professional scene: doctors giving medication, the use of hospitalization by families, and the role played by other systems such as schools. It would be a mistake to assume that any therapy can safely be "indoor therapy" and to abandon the field-oriented ecosystems model, whatever the presenting problem may be. At the very least, the therapist himself brings a wider ecology to the family as soon as he steps into the case.

The Structural Approach

Minuchin's approach is best represented in *Families and Family Therapy*, a book that has become a classic.[9] Minuchin has a clear method and a theory consistent with that method. He also has striking proof that his methods work with severe problems of childhood, as demonstrated by his research with families of psychosomatic children.[10]

Minuchin's normative model for a family that is functioning well is especially useful. According to him, an appropriately organized family will have clearly marked boundaries. The marital subsystem will have closed boundaries to protect the privacy of the spouses. The parental subsystem will have clear boundaries between it and the children, but not so impenetrable as to limit the access necessary for good parenting. The sibling subsystem will have its own boundaries and will be organized hierarchically, so that children are given tasks and privileges consonant with sex and age as determined by the family's culture. Finally, the boundary around the nuclear family will also be respected, although this is dependent on cultural, social, and economic factors. The extent to which kin or agents of larger social institutions are allowed in varies greatly.

With this model in mind, the therapist then has the task of noting the angle of deviance between it and the family that comes in the door. Therapy, from a structural point of view, consists of redesigning family organization so that it will approximate this normative model more closely. For instance, a functional family will have a clear generation line. This means that if mother and daughter are acting like siblings, the therapist may put the mother in charge of the daughter's activities for a week. Similarly, one finds a fair degree of individuation in a family that is working well. If the boundary that delineates an individual is not being respected, the structural therapist may ask each person to think and speak only for himself. Or, since in a functional family the marital subsystem and the parental subsystem have distinct boundaries, the therapist who finds that a couple spend all their time parenting may ask them to go away together without the children.

The process seems very logical and very simple. It is as though one began by saying, "What are the organizational characteristics of a family in which things go well and family members do not have problems?" and, when somebody does have a problem, noting which of these characteristics are absent and changing the family accordingly. The assumption is, of course, that a symptom is a product of a dysfunctional family system, and that if the family organization becomes more "normal," the symptom will automatically disappear. If this were one's central theory, one would not have to worry overmuch about the particularities of the symptom, its history, its present effect on other people, or any other specific detail. One would merely scrutinize the way the family was organized (Does everybody go through mother? Is father treated like a child? Is oldest daughter acting like mother?) and shift it from a less normative to a more normative state.

In practice, this approach works. There are detractors who say that Minuchin's idea of what is normal is biased and does not account for families of other classes and cultures. On the contrary, his model is flexible enough to include the alternative ways in which poor or ethnically different family structures can be organized, and respects these ways insofar as they work for the well-being of the individuals in those families.

One further point should be made about Minuchin's conceptual framework. It owes much to systems theory, yet it leans very little on the cybernetic paradigm that has been stressed so much in these pages, and that in my view is one of the identifying facets of the family therapy movement. Only occasionally, as in the case of the anorectic girl described in Chapter 11, does Minuchin speak of "cycles" or creating a "runaway." For the most part his language seems to derive from organization theory and role theory, drawing heavily on spatial metaphors like boundary, mapping, territory, structure, role.

Of major importance therapeutically is Minuchin's inclusion of the therapist as an active intruder, changing the family field by his very presence. Schools of therapy that emphasize getting information or delving into history miss the fact that the focus on content can obscure for the therapist extremely important matters: To whom does he speak? Who is allowed to speak? Whom does he elevate? Whom does he challenge? Which persons does he bring together? Which does he push apart? With whom does he make a coalition? With whom does he not? It is by such moves that the therapist begins to restructure the relationship system in the family, and to alter the context that supposedly nourishes the symptom.

Minuchin's method of "mapping" the psychopolitical terrain of a family saves a therapist much time since the nature of the family's organization gives a structural therapist the clues he needs to determine which directions to go in revising patterns of relationship in the family. In Chapter 5 of *Families and Family Therapy*, Minuchin shows his own method of mapping family groups, indicating important factors such as membership in coalitions, the nature of boundaries, and how the subsystems are structured.[11] By delineating the form these aspects take in a family that comes in for treatment, and by revising the map as treatment progresses, Minuchin gives us a graphic method for documenting the stages of therapy.

To demystify Minuchin's expertise, it may be useful to summarize a commentary on one of Minuchin's most elegant interviews which was published as "The Open Door: An Interview with the Family of an Anorectic Child."[12] The article is a step-by-step analysis of the therapist-family interaction throughout the interview. This is the first time Minuchin has met the family and also the last, because he is a consultant here and will be handing the case to another therapist. Minuchin has spent some time getting to know the family: a mother and father in their forties; the thirteen-year-old anorectic girl, Laura; the twelve-year-old sister, Jill; and the eight-year-old brother, Steven. He has found out that the girl started dieting while away at camp that summer, and has been losing weight ever since. However, she has not yet had to be hospitalized.

In a move to assess family interaction around the symptom, Minuchin challenges the father's statement that family members never disagree by asking how the parents deal with Laura when she does not want to eat. The mirror-image disagreement starts to surface. Father, the more domineering parent, pushes food on the girl and gives up only reluctantly. Mother says she tries to push and then stops, because she sees it upsets Laura. In this pattern the "one-down" parent covertly supports the symptom that so successfully eludes the authority of the "one-up" parent. Minuchin's request that family members enact behaviors elicited by the symptom is a typically structural move. The therapist is not satisfied with a report of what goes on at home; he wants to see the sequence with his own eyes.

Next Minuchin goes to the twelve-year-old sister, Jill, and asks what happens when she disagrees with her father. She replies that her father gets angry when he asks her to comb his hair and she refuses. For some reason she is able to be more open and forthright than her sister. Minuchin thinks she means that her father objects to her not combing her hair. He goes over and musses her hair and asks her to play out the scene. The father tells Minuchin he has misunderstood, and describes a nightly ritual that consists of himself and the children lying together on the parents' bed while the children comb the father's hair or massage his legs or rub his back. Father says that he sometimes does these things for them, but that he and the older daughter "have not done so much for each other" during the past year. Minuchin finds out that Mother is usually busy at these times, folding laundry or washing the dishes. When asked if she rubs Father's back too, she says yes in a doubtful way, but when further asked if she ever shuts the bedroom door and sends the children out, she responds, "Never!" In fact, she says, the doors are hardly ever shut to anyone's room.

With this piece of information, the contextual circumstances of the girl's symptom seem clear enough. Laura has been close to her father; she has in a way been a present from Mother to Father, the wife having felt it necessary to remain somewhat distant from her husband. However, as the girl nears adolescence, the dictates of nature and society enforce a movement toward more autonomy. At the same time the implications of this move are threatening because it will disrupt the parents' relationship. By becoming anorectic the girl remains close to home and very close to her mother. At the same time she is still available to Father but not sexually available, since many of her sexual characteristics are inhibited or disappear. Finally, by refusing to eat, she asserts herself in a desperate caricature of adolescent rebellion. This symptom, like all others, is a perfect artifact of nature, with something in it for everyone.

Minuchin's response to the father-children closeness described by Father is to disrupt it. He does not point it out or challenge it, but interferes with it by the way he directs personal exchanges with and among all family members. The father is clearly the dominant figure in the family and Minuchin never confronts him directly. Instead he carefully reframes the sensual activities of hair brushing and back rubbing as "nurturance" between Dad and the kids, saying, "Dad is a cuddler, he likes people to be close to him."

Then, once he has joined with the father, who relaxes visibly, Minuchin moves to the all-important boundary issue, and begins to talk about the open-door policy Mother has described. He asks Laura whether she ever closes the door of her bedroom. When she says she does, he asks whether people knock before they come in. Does the sister knock? Yes. Does Mom knock? Yes. Does Dad knock? Laura says yes, but her tone is uncertain. Minuchin says, "You are doubting," and she agrees that sometimes he does and sometimes he doesn't. Minuchin asks if she would like him to knock at her door before entering. Very softly she says, "Yes." Minuchin now asks whether she ever tells her father that she would like him to knock. She says no. He asks her if it would bother her if she asked her father to knock at her door. She says she doesn't think so.

Here, in one of those shifts that make his work seem like delicate choreography, Minuchin challenges her statement, siding with the father: "I have the feeling that it would bother Dad because he is a very loving Dad that likes always to have people respond to him and he respond to people—to the children, certainly." Minuchin has moved to support the thing that is not normal, the kind of behavior that presumably reinforces the symptom. Why? Perhaps because he is going to ask the girl to do something she does not often do, which is to tell her father that she wants privacy. He knows that for this to be possible, he must back the father; otherwise the girl's loyalty to him will make it hard for her to take a position against him. He says to Laura, "Ask Dad if it will bother him if you asked him to knock at your door." Laura, in an almost inaudible voice, does so. The father says, "Probably so," and adds, "because I like to have all the doors open."

Jill, the forthright sister, now interrupts to say that he doesn't knock because he can't stand closed doors and will open them if they are. Minuchin asks the other children if they, too, sometimes want their doors closed and get answers in the affirmative. Even though the father has not given verbal consent for Laura to close her door, Minuchin does not push further. He has engineered a very gentle confrontation between Laura and her father on the issue of privacy, and has helped the other children, who can state the same position more strongly, to back her. That is all, yet that is much.

Moving from the Father-Laura dyad, Minuchin now takes on the Mother-Father dyad. The mother is equally involved in the behaviors helping to sustain the problem, although it is the father who plays the most visible role. The mother is compliant to her husband in one way, but by being unavailable to him for intimacy, she is not at all compliant. To help free Laura, Minuchin will have to give Mother as well as daughter some different ways to oppose Father. So far, the mother has mainly used the denial of intimacy and a covert mutinous coalition with the children, especially Laura. After much work, Minuchin finally gets the mother to stand up to the father on an issue of her own—she objects to his phone calls at dinner, especially as the phone wire goes right across her neck. The couple falls into an arguing sequence typical of an apparently one-up/one-down pair; the mother makes a feeble complaint, the husband interrupts, then begins a monologue that collapses into silence. Minuchin finally has to get out his big guns, and starts repositioning people and moving chairs about until he has finally placed himself between Father and Mother. Once he has blocked Father's access to Mother, he carries on a cheerful conversation with Mother about her loneliness. He goes back to the picture of the father and the children on the bed, saying, "Your children are not employing you and your husband is not employing you—what kind of corners are there where you are?" For the first time in the interview, the father (who has been desperately trying to break in on this flirtation) capitulates to Minuchin, saying, "You have a point." Minuchin goes on a while longer in his tête-à-tête with the wife, and then stands up and gives his chair to the father, saying, "I want you to come back to your wife." This is one of the clearest examples of a structural, in-the-room, rebalancing of a couple that I know of. It is an important move because it is clear that no conflicts will be allowed to arise, much less be resolved, between them, until the timid wife feels that she has gained some parity with her overbearing husband. And until that time, Laura will probably have to remain anorectic.

During the last act of this drama, food is brought in. Minuchin focuses solely on Laura and her eating, even though the subject of food is never brought up. Instead, Minuchin launches into a conversation with Laura about her age. One of his major contributions to family therapy has been to point out the confusion of the normal sibling hierarchy in a family that is not working well. Here he remarks to Laura that her younger sister seems more like a twin, or even older, and that the parents treat the two of them alike. He asks Laura if she likes being treated as if she were the same age as Jill. He says, "Maybe you are telling them that you are twelve, and maybe you are telling them that you are ten, and maybe we are just making a concession in treating you as if you are twelve. But something is wrong here."

Minuchin sits by Laura as the sandwiches are brought in and continues to direct a rapid stream of conversation at her while she eats—Does she buy her own clothes? Can she say when she can go to bed?—and finds out that she is allowed all these minor freedoms. Minuchin presents her with an interpretation—her not eating is the only way she has to rebel in this permissive household where by being given so much autonomy she actually has so little. But he is clearly concentrating on her sandwhich, which she keeps toying with. He times his bites with hers, at the same time, paradoxically, directing her not to eat:

At the point at which you are fourteen, Laura, you will eat without any problems. But I think it is good that you are not eating now because I think that this is the only area in your family in which you have a say-so. And at fourteen you'll need to have a say-so in another way. And you know, at this point, that's the only way in which you say, "No."

The parents are not allowed to intrude on Laura during this time. Minuchin suggests that maybe Daddy doesn't want his big girl to grow up. He asks what will happen if she grows up, and she says softly, "I don't know . . . get married?" Minuchin says, "You will then be interested in rubbing the back of someone else. Dad, what will happen then? Maybe you will need to have Connie [his wife] rubbing your back." At this moment, in an apparent accident, the father spills his drink onto his lap and the wife helps to clean him up.

The session ends with Laura finishing her food and Minuchin giving the family some "homework." He extends the metaphor of the open door, with its implications of intrusiveness, by telling Laura that she is to close her bedroom door for two hours a day, during which time her parents must knock if they wish to come in. Jill is to keep her door open, since she will not earn Laura's privilege until the following year. The little boy, who has been staying up late and sleeping with Jill, is told to obey his mother and go to bed when she tells him to. Turning to the parents, Minuchin tells them that they are to close the door of their bedroom every night from nine to ten and watch television together without the children. The session ends.

This was only a consultation interview. The rest of the case was handled by another therapist, who brought it to a good conclusion. The importance of the interview described is that it contained the blueprint for the eventual restructuring of family relationships, and gave every person the temporary experience of living in a normally organized group. When the family first came in, the children were overtly presented as father's bosom companions, but they were covertly allied with mother. This seesaw arrangement of child-adult alliances kept the parents in uneasy balance. By the end of the interview, however, the children were disengaged from the parental struggle; the marital dyad was cordoned off and evened out; and the sibling hierarchy had been revised, creating a set of stairs up which the oldest daughter would, one hoped, march on her way out.

A serious deficiency is that Minuchin's theory of change contains no provision for so-called paradoxical techniques. If asked, he often says that he does not use these methods, although, as in the interview just described, he comes very close to doing so. A more obvious example is reported in a profile on Minuchin written by Janet Malcolm for the *New Yorker*. She quotes Minuchin as telling the parents in a family with a girl who had been hospitalized for a psychotic break:

I am concerned that when you leave here today your daughter will go crazy again. And I think the reason she will do it is to save your marriage. . . . Yvonne, I suggest that you go quite crazy today, so that your parents can become concerned about you. Then things will be O.K. between them. . . . You're a good daughter, and if you see a danger, go crazy.[13]

Other gifted practitioners who have worked under Minuchin—Braulio Montalvo and Harry Aponte, for instance—use symptom prescription and paradoxical interventions in many inventive and subtle ways. It is a genuine limitation that although Minuchin's theory is most eloquent about family systems and family structure, it does not contain a comprehensive enough theory of change to cover the area misnamed "resistance," and the moves which deal most successfully with it, especially in cases of what Minuchin would call "enmeshed" families.

Another difficulty with Minuchin's approach is that it sounds simple but is hard to teach. Minuchin works with analogic behaviors so much that his trainees must see many families before they can begin to recognize the invisible patterns that an experienced structural therapist knows at a glance. It is not much help to rely on one's rational faculties when working structurally, any more than it is helpful to learn ballet by reading about it or watching it. Suffice it to say that to be a good structural therapist requires much experience, and extensive live supervision by a master.

The Strategic Approach

Haley first coined the term "strategic" to describe any therapy in which the clinician actively designs interventions to fit the problem. The term has become identified with the work of Weakland, Watzlawick, and Fisch as represented in the article, "Brief Therapy: Focused Problem Resolution," and the book, *Change: Principles of Problem Formation and Problem Resolution.* [14]

These therapists say that they are not interested in family structure or the family system. Unlike Minuchin, who starts at an abstract level and works in, they start at the most specific level and work out. Consequently they have a very clear procedure for the initial interview, much like the questioning a detective might do to solve a mystery. What is the problem? Who did what the last time it happened? When is it likely to occur? When did it first appear?

This extreme interest in the details of the symptom is misleading if one assumes that the symptom is the only thing the therapist is interested in. Using the model of the self-reinforcing sequence, this group assumes the symptom is being maintained by the very behaviors that seek to suppress it—by the "solution." As we have seen, a careful analysis of these behaviors will indeed show that at the same time the problem is being attacked by behaviors opposing it, it is being supported covertly by eliciting behaviors. The therapist is looking for this cycle or sequence. With the wife whose constant jealous questioning of her husband only reinforces his reticence, which only reinforces her jealousy, *ad infinitum,* the strategic therapist will seek to find a way to interrupt or block this vicious circle. It may be enough simply to point out to the wife how her behavior is achieving the opposite of what she wishes to happen. But the therapist assumes that if the problem were that easy to solve, it would probably not appear in his or her office. Therefore the therapist looks for a more tactful way to change or disrupt the sequence.

It is in this light that one must understand the strategic therapist's emphasis on reframing, the technique by which the therapist restates a situation so that it is perceived in a new way. The strategic therapist might persuade the wife that if she suddenly stopped her constant questioning, or if she even became mute for a week, this might make her more mysterious in the eyes of her husband. With some women this idea alone might make enough impact to cause them to change.

On the other hand, the behaviors may be so entrenched that the wife literally cannot stop herself. Getting the husband to be more open may not succeed either. The next move will probably be in the direction of encouraging rather than trying to stop the jealous behavior. The therapist might tell the wife that her husband seems strong and self-sufficient but that he is really a shy, dependent person who is unable to ask openly for her attention and concern. Since he cannot ask for a more direct confirmation, her jealousy is for him a proof of love. Therefore she should redouble her jealousy. This directive may well produce a recoil. Not only will the wife feel somewhat reluctant to continue her supervisory behaviors, especially if the therapist asks her to intensify them, but her husband may not like the implication that he is a shy, dependent person. Both parties may collude against the task, and announce the following week that they did not follow it, but that their relationship has nevertheless improved.

At this point, if the couple does not come in with a new problem, the strategic therapist feels that his work is finished. He has not tried to look at the context of the problem any more than was needed to resolve it. He has not inquired into the history of the marriage, or the extended family, or their children, or the background and early childhood of each spouse; nor has he made a guess about the meaning this jealousy may have in the larger context of the family. It may be that when the husband's father died, he found himself faced with a lonely, demanding mother, but that it would be unthinkable for him or his wife to push away this suffering person. The jealousy may be the only way the wife is able to communicate to her husband that she wishes she had the time and attention from him that she used to have, at the same time that it insures a distance between them that protects the husband's loyalty to his mother. But this is not a piece of information, or a surmise, that will necessarily interest the strategic therapist.

Nor will he concern himself with other dysfunctional behaviors in the family if they are not presented as problems. The couple may be taking their six-year-old daughter into bed with them when she has nightmares, but if they do not complain about this, the strategic therapist does not investigate this habit or suggest a change. And he does not assume that he must work with a marriage when a child who seems to be mediating the relationship between the spouses, and consequently becomes a problem, gets better. The partners may choose to bring their marriage in, and make a new contract over it, but the strategic therapist does not push himself in where he is not asked. In the world of therapy, this person is a minimalist.

As a more extensive example of the brief, strategic approach, we might review highlights from a case that the Palo Alto group presents during seminars and workshops. The therapist in this instance is Paul Watzlawick. The family consists of Mother, Father, a sexually acting-out fifteen-year-old girl and three younger siblings, two girls and a boy. The girl has run away from home and seems headed for a career as a juvenile delinquent. Therapy consists of five sessions, mostly with the parents. The therapist does not include the younger children in therapy.

In the first session the therapist meets first with the parents. They describe their daughter as boy-crazy, argumentative, flighty, angry, and impossible to control. They present themselves as ground down by the constant fights and arguments. The therapist, taking advantage of their frustration, asks if there is any way they could give her a taste of her own medicine—"grate on her nerves the way she grates on theirs." They say they would love that. This is an important response for the therapist to note, as they might also have said, "Oh, no, poor child. We couldn't do that." But these parents are willing to go along with the therapist's suggestion. He insinuates that they think of a way to be unreasonable instead of reasonable. He suggests, for example, that when she asks to go out in the evening they say, "No." When she protests, instead of trying to justify their position, they are to say something absurd like, "Because it's Friday." The parents like this idea, but the therapist restrains them, saying, "Don't try anything like this yet, just think about it."

He then meets with the girl alone. As with the parents, he works upon the girl's self-interest, as she sees it. When he asks what she would like to see changed for her own advantage, she says she is tired of all the fighting. The therapist remarks that she has gotten herself into an extremely powerful position, and that her parents have become quite helpless to deal with her. The best way for her to maintain her position, he says, is simply to persist and go even further; if they deny her something, she is to ask them for their reasons, and keep hammering at them until they finally give up. He adds in a musing tone of voice that there is always a price; she may be in a chronic state of rage, because at first the fighting will get worse; she may even end up at times in Juvenile Hall, but she can get used to that; the most important thing is to pursue her advantage because then she will win. He then says that he will continue to see her parents, because his task will be to teach them how to live with this situation.

He never sees the girl again. The next four interviews are with the parents alone. When he sees them, he asks what they have been able to come up with. The father can easily think up frustrating answers to the girl's demands, but the mother turns out to be the more benevolent parent. She says she feels helpless. The therapist, far from challenging this position, goes with it. He argues that they should change from a position of strength to one of weakness, because if one is helpless, there are all kinds of things one can get away with. For instance, if the daughter is bolting down her dinner before going out on a date, the mother might do a stupid thing like spilling a glass of milk on her, and then apologize, saying, "Oh, I'm so upset, I've been so depressed lately; I do all kinds of stupid things." If the girl comes home later than she is supposed to, they can lock the doors and put the lights out; then, after having made her wait a long time, the mother can go out and say, "I'm sorry I left you out in the cold; I do the silliest things these days."

In this way the therapist captures the resistance of the mother, shown as reluctance to fight her daughter directly; the father does not have to be pushed. In general, the rule seems to be that when the child is perceived as "bad," the parents will be encouraged to seize power directly; if the child is perceived as "sick," the goal will be the same, but the tactic will be labeled as benevolent, and re-framed as "strong medicine." If the parents are scapegoating the child, the therapist may push their vengefulness to an extreme, suggesting not just temporary placement but permanent placement, and commenting perhaps on the terrible conditions in facilities of this kind, over which parents will have little control. With a surly youngster, the therapist might comment on how cooperative he is being in helping his parents prove he is a rotten kid. And so forth.

In the case we are describing, the parents came in for the second session saying that they were carrying out the therapist's sugges-tions with success. Instead of arguing with the daughter, the father was responding to every request with, "I'll think about it," which frustrated her terribly. Mother simply agreed with her and did not argue either. The daughter was more and more furious because they wouldn't fight with her. The therapist pushes on, suggesting that during the following week they take an even more powerful posi-tion of extreme helplessness, and telling the mother to say that something upsetting came out in the session that she cannot tell about but that has made her very depressed. Watzlawick, a master of reframing, says, "You should give her that creative doubt and insecurity that a youngster needs in order to grow up."

The mother then mentions that the girl's sixteenth birthday is coming up, and the daughter has asked for a pair of boots which cost about thirty-two dollars. It turns out that the mother is irritated over her daughter's old, worn-out bras. The girl refuses to buy new ones (she has a large cup size and her bras cost eight dollars apiece) and never washes out the few she has. The therapist suggests that the parents buy her four new bras for her birthday—they will cost exactly the same as the boots she is hoping for—and when she opens her present and expresses disappointment, the mother must act genuinely upset. The suggestion was acted upon and the parents reported with delight on their daughter's baffled reaction.

By the fourth session the parents are conniving together, plotting how to get the best of this infuriating daughter, and are mystifying her completely. The girl undergoes a miraculous personality change. The parents can hardly recognize her as the same person. She has become a pleasant, cooperative child, with a normal life and interests. She has taken up sewing (after the mother "stupidly" sewed the back of a dress to the front in response to the daughter's request that she mend it); she is eating dinner like one of the family; one day she even bought her mother a box of chocolates.

During the last session, the therapist (as is customary with this group) expresses concern about things going too well. He warns the parents that the outcome of their success with their daughter will almost certainly be that she will become a delightful child; then it may become difficult for them to let her grow up. So it might be a good idea for them to reinstate the old situation so that they will not be too unhappy when she does leave. He asks them to imagine how they might have their first relapse into their old pattern. This, predictably, only reinforces the change which has taken place, and after a three-month follow-up it turns out that the parents have begun to go out together (which they couldn't do when the girl was acting so badly); her grades have jumped from Ds to Cs and Bs, and she seems altogether a much happier person.

A structural therapist would say that the change came about because the therapist got the parents to unite and take control of the girl's behavior, where previously mother was covertly supporting her against father and subverting the generation line. The strategic therapist would agree but would ascribe the change to the therapist's ability to reframe the situation so that the parents would behave differently with the girl. It is not necessary to change all behaviors in a self-reinforcing cycle to remove the problem, and not essential to have all family members present to bring about change.

The strategic school focuses on the problem as the unit to be attacked, not the family. Thus, unlike the structural school, strategic therapists do not worry about seeing all members of a household together. They even prefer to see individuals or family subgroups separately, maximizing change by setting one group or person secretly against the other. One might also say that where the structural therapists actively repattern relationships in the room, the strategic therapists are strangely inactive in the room. For them the key to change is the art with which they can reframe the client's perception of the context of his behavior. They use the analogy of salesmanship in teaching their method, and actually send students out to watch how car salesmen persuade customers to buy a product. The point is to change the perceived "reality" of the client so that different behaviors become possible.

An example cited by the authors of *Change* is the case of a man with a stammer who was taking a job as a salesman. His understandable belief that his speech problem would interfere with his ability to become a good salesman was challenged by the idea that, far from being a liability, his defect would be an asset. People always pay more attention to someone who has trouble talking, in contrast to the way they often turn off in response to a fast-talking huckster. Therefore this man was encouraged to increase his stammering as a way of becoming a better salesman. This is an example of the use of positive reframing in connection with prescribing the symptom. Clearly, in their clinical work the strategic therapists use a variety of therapeutic double binds and a variety of benevolent rationales for making them seem palatable.

For strategic therapists, the Art of Therapy becomes the Art of Rhetoric, and strategic therapists indeed have the bad reputation that the Sophists had in ancient Greece. It does not matter, our Palo Alto friends say, whether we believe the ingenious rationale we give the client to make him change his ways; as long as he changes them, our job is done. This position has been objected to by more traditional therapists, who feel that the use of such currency debases the profession. Charges of "manipulation" and "social engineering" are heard in the land, and are cheerfully accepted by the strategic people. They claim only to be simple craftsmen, solving people's problems in the most expedient (and least expensive) way.

And in truth, this is the strength of their position. They have a narrower focus than other types of therapists. Thus, like the strict behavior therapists, they have a good chance of achieving what they set out to do. Oddly enough, because of this they also have a better chance of accomplishing more. Although they disclaim interest in the family as a "system," they work systemically, and quietly hope, if not expect, that a small change in an important family relationship will have a domino effect on other relationships: a marriage may "of itself" get better after a child improves, simply because for the first time in years, the parents will stop thinking about the child all the time, rediscover each other, and start having a good time.

The contribution of the strategic school has been to create an elegant and parsimonious model for change. The group's procedure for tracking the behaviors around the problem is an invaluable clinical tool, all the more so because it is based on such a clear understanding of the self-perpetuating sequence of behaviors around a symptom. Their use of paradoxical techniques to counter this kind of problem has been another invaluable tool. They take a strong therapeutic position in constantly challenging the family's wish to change, and insisting on their minimal powers to help. This not only maintains the therapist's control but draws on the oppositional qualities of most families with psychiatric symptoms, almost obliging them to change by resisting the injunction not to.

The strategic approach offers its own hazards for beginners, providing a deceptively simple formula for identifying what to change and how to change it. It is really not enough to ask about the problem, find out what solution is being tried, and then interrupt or reverse that solution. These are the shortcuts of master therapists who have an understanding of the complexity of the processes they are dealing with, and who have evolved an intuitive methodology for redirecting these processes. They can well say that they do not have to bother with the structure of the family—they know it by heart. In the same way, the structural therapist can elect to ignore the particularities of the symptom or the behaviors sustaining it; he knows very well how to recognize a symptomatic cycle and to break it.

We might conclude by saying that if the structuralists need to admit to their knowledge of process, the strategists need to admit to their knowledge of form.

Haley's Problem-Solving Approach

Although in some respects Haley should be placed with the strategic school, he is really a bridging figure between the strategic and structural positions. Haley presents his strategic side most clearly in his writings on the clinical work of Milton Erickson. In *Uncommon Therapy*, Haley not only coined the term "strategic therapy" but attempted to create a model for therapy based on hypnotic techniques.[15] Many of these techniques are unobtrusive ways of managing resistance. For instance, there is the technique of "providing an illusion of alternatives": Would you like to go into a trance now or later? The question of whether or not to go into a trance, which is what the subject is really resisting, is bypassed, and the subject has an illusion of choice. A therapist might thus say to a resistant family: Would you like us to make a home visit on Thursday or Friday? The question of whether or not to visit is bypassed. An elaboration of this tactic is called "providing a worse alternative," and it consists of setting up two choices, one of which is so dreadful or difficult that the client either thinks up a different but equally effective solution on his own, or else goes along with the less bad idea. In one case that a friend being supervised by Haley described to me, the problem was a school-phobic child, but a home visit showed that a psychotic sister was living in the home, as well as a senile grandmother. The family had resisted efforts by other agencies to get the child back to school. Haley adopted the tactic known as the "Devil's Pact," in which the therapist tells the family that he has a sure solution to the problem, but the family must agree to do it before it is disclosed. The family fought the bargain but finally agreed. The therapist then told them that as long as the child remained home from school, the parents must disconnect every TV set in the house. As not only the child but the psychotic sister and the grandmother constantly watched TV, the family rejected this idea. They left, angry with the therapist and threatening not to come back. However, some weeks later they called and told the therapist that they had in fact disconnected the child's TV set, and had also enrolled him in a school to which they planned to drag him bodily.

In writing about strategic therapy, Haley stays mainly with process language. After he decided to join Minuchin in Philadelphia and started to develop his own clinical work, he also moved to a different conceptual universe. He began to downplay the use of hypnotic techniques and paradoxical directives (although by no means abandoning his sense of their importance) and concentrated on a more organizational model for therapy. Using his knowledge of hierarchy and coalitions, he evolved his own method for disrupting or changing abnormal family structures, as well as attending to the triadic configurations that accompany them.

What is peculiar is that the two worlds depicted in Haley's *Uncommon Therapy* (1973) and his *Problem-Solving Therapy* (1977)—the book that came out of the Philadelphia years—are so far apart. It is as though Haley makes a strange leap, from one side of Bateson's zigzag to the other, from process to form. Most of Haley's career, in fact, can be seen as an oscillation from one side of this zigzag to the other, from the early microstudies of schizophrenic communication to the research on coalitions in families, to the development of a strategic model for therapy, to an interest in a more structural model, and so forth.

In *Problem-Solving Therapy*, Haley makes the point very strongly that one must identify sequences of behavior that circle around a problem, not just concentrate on the problem alone.[16] Here, of course, he is joined by the strategic therapists Watzlawick, Weakland, and Fisch. But where they point out that most "problems" consist of self-reinforcing cycles, Haley describes these cycles in terms of family organization, laying out "problem sequences" which may involve a mother, father, and child; or a grandmother, mother, and child; or the therapist, parent, and child; or parental child, mother, and child. Unlike the Palo Alto group, Haley thinks of therapy in terms of a step-by-step change in the way the family is organized, so that it goes from one type of abnormal organization to another type before a more normal organization is finally achieved. By then, presumably, the symptom is no longer necessary.

These two ideas, of tracking organizational sequences in assessing the problem, and going through stages in the process of changing it, are perhaps Haley's most distinctive contributions to theory of therapy. His emphasis on appropriate hierarchical lines, although not his particular invention, should also be mentioned. This emphasis extends to an awareness that therapists and other professionals may be contributing to organizational abnormality by crossing these lines in their efforts to help.

A nice example of a way of dealing with the latter problem comes from Peggy Penn, who studied with Haley and his wife, Cloé Madanes, in 1978 at the Family Therapy Institute in Washington. A mother came into therapy because of her retarded daughter's rocking behavior at school. This behavior made the teacher angry with the child and her family, and the mother felt especially helpless with this teacher. Madanes, the supervisor, had the teacher come into the session and helped the mother show the teacher how to "supervise" the child's rocking at school. This put the mother hierarchically above not only the child but also the teacher, just as the therapist was above the mother, and the supervisor above her. All status levels were thus respected.

Haley has included in *Problem-Solving Therapy* the transcript of one of the minidocumentaries he made with Braulio Montalvo while both were at the Philadelphia Child Guidance Clinic. This videotape, called "A Modern Little Hans," contains a clear expression of the idea of therapeutic stages; it is also an outstanding example of therapeutic art. In this case of a six-year-old boy with a phobia about dogs, previous attempts to treat the problem with individual psychotherapy had been unsuccessful. The strategy devised by the supervisor (Haley) for the therapist (Mariano Barragan) to carry out was a charming one: to ask the boy to find a puppy that was afraid of humans and to "cure" it. The treatment was a metaphor exactly approximating the problem, but placing the boy in a reverse position, so that by following the therapist's instructions, he would have to stop being afraid of dogs. And indeed, in teaching the puppy not to fear a boy, the boy conquered his own fear.

The strategy was also designed to accomplish a structural shift in the organization of the family. Haley, as we remember, had observed that when a child in a family had a problem, one parent would seem very upset and would be alternately exasperated and forgiving while the other parent would seem far less concerned.

"Haley's Triad" is as common a constellation in families with problem children as the Big Dipper is in northern skies.

Haley considers it important to interrupt this formation or to shift it, and describes several ways of doing so. One is to disrupt the more intense parent-child dyad by encouraging the overinvolved parent to redouble the involvement in the hope that this will bring about a recoil. A second way is to focus on the parental dyad and tease out the parents' differences about the child's behavior. In so doing the therapist inserts himself into the triangle with the parents, replacing the child, who is often serving as a covert battleground for marital issues anyway. The third way is to enter through the peripheral parent's relationship with the child. This can be done either by making this parent the disciplinarian, thus disturbing the covert alignment with the child, or by giving the child and parent a task to do together, making the alignment overt. This last tactic can, however, have the effect of distancing the overinvolved parent and unbalancing the marriage.

A simple step-stage model for therapy with two parents (or any executive dyad) and a child became a cornerstone for Haley's thinking about therapy. It has resurfaced in *Leaving Home,* a book that contains Haley's more recent ideas for dealing with what he calls "crazy young people"—adolescents undergoing a first psychotic break.[17] Here Haley recommends that the parents be encouraged to set limits on the adolescent's behavior: the approach is one version of "going through the parental dyad." If the parents do set limits, the child will usually improve. If they cannot, the therapist engages them with himself in a struggle to resolve their differences over the adolescent child's behavior. During this process, Haley observes, they are often metaphorically dealing with marital differences. In this case too, once the child is disengaged from the struggle, he or she will improve.

Haley is an artist at making the complex seem simple. His recipes for creating shifts in triads in easy, geometric sequence have helped many clinicians extricate themselves from mounds of useless data and therapeutic sprawl. His cookbook-style outlines for therapy display a sound respect for principles of good organization and introduce the idea that persuasiveness alone is not the whole story in bringing about change. It would be interesting, though, if Haley's concern with structure and organization were to double back to include his original fascination with strategic maneuvers, especially those that have been subsumed under the rubric of paradoxical interventions. One hopes, in fact, that he will take another "strange leap."

Chapter 15

The Systemic Model

The Quiet Revolution in Milan

In 1968, the year Jackson died, the ideas of the Bateson group leaped across an ocean and took root in Italian soil. Mara Selvini Palazzoli, a child analyst, had been working for many years with anorectic children. Discouraged by her results, and impressed by the family therapy literature that was coming out of Palo Alto, she decided to discard all elements of psychoanalytic thought and adopt a purely systems orientation.

In that key year, she organized the Institute for Family Studies in Milan. After an initial process of winnowing, the group narrowed down to four psychiatrists: Luigi Boscolo, Giuliana Prata, Gianfranco Cecchin, and Selvini herself. This group, working together over some ten years, developed a family systems approach that they used not only with families of anorectics, but with families of children who had serious emotional disorders.

Selvini's first book, *Self-Starvation*, published in 1974 in the United States, documents her therapeutic trajectory. It is only the last part that describes her shift from the analytic model to the circular, cybernetic epistemology of the Bateson group and to working with families.[1] A second book, *Paradox and Counterparadox,* published here in 1978, was written by the Milan Associates (as they now call themselves), and is currently the most comprehensive description of their work and methods.[2]

The Milan Associates, although influenced by the Palo Alto group, evolved in quite a different direction, creating a form unique and distinct enough to be considered a school of its own. In Europe, where the approach has stirred up much interest, the term "systemic" is used to describe it. From the beginning, the group used an unusual format. They work (or did, when *Paradox and Counterparadox* was published) as a foursome, with a man and a woman therapist in the room with the family and a man and a woman behind a one-way screen.* Periodically the observers may summon one of the therapists out of the room to offer a suggestion or ask for more information. Toward the end of the session, the therapists break for a consultation with the observers, during which time all four share opinions and come up with an intervention or a recommendation. This may be a ritual, a task, or a prescription. It comes from the whole team and is shared with every member of the family. If it is in letter form, each person in the family is given or sent a copy. Sometimes, if an important family member has failed to come to a session, he or she will be sent a copy of a letter that may address his absence.

From the beginning this group has attempted to prevent their approach from being based on factors of personality or charisma. For this reason, they change partners from family to family. Therapy begins with the first phone call, and much attention is paid to details like who made the call, tone of voice, and attempts to control the conditions of treatment. The entire household is required to be present in a first session. In later sessions, the team may decide to see different units. Information sought during the initial phone call is minimal: who called; who is in the immediate family or household; who referred the family; what is the problem; and of course

---

*More recently, only one therapist conducts the interview, and one to three may be behind the screen.

items like address and date of call. Information must also be gotten from the referring professional.

Before each session the team meets to discuss the previous session or, in the case of a first interview, to examine the family intake. The sessions last about an hour, and during that time the team not only asks for information but carefully notes nonverbal communications. The team discussion is conducted in a special room; and at the end, the two therapists rejoin the family to present the recommendations of the team.

Treatment usually consists of about ten sessions at monthly intervals or longer. This practice first began in order to accommodate families who lived far away, but it was then decided that this relatively long time lapse between sessions was favorable for therapy with families with psychotic members. In an important article, "Why a Long Interval Between Sessions," Selvini connects this practice to the nature of families with schizophrenics, and to their resemblance to the too richly cross-joined systems of Ashby, already described in these pages.[3] Each family has its own time span for processing a complex set of information: and the more richly joined the system, the longer the time it will take for this process to come to rest.

Calls and attempts to schedule earlier sessions are handled by the team as responses trying to undo the effects of a given intervention. They are treated with care and respect in the sense that if a family goes into crisis after a session, the team will be especially careful to avoid any move that might stabilize the system and negate potential for change. Thus they will tend not to give in to requests for extra sessions and will respond calmly to reports of dire emergencies, in the belief that this is the best possible indication that change is taking place.

Obviously this stance requires nerves of steel and good team support. On one occasion a wife called to say that her husband was so depressed that he was threatening to cut off his penis, and she asked for an earlier session. The team, sensing that the wife was making a bid to control the treatment and that the husband was not in any imminent danger, told her that this extreme anxiety on her part was a predictable reaction, foreseen by the team, but that the session would be held as scheduled.

The Milan Associates call this treatment a "long, brief therapy," because the number of hours with the family is small but the length of time needed for family reorganization can be very long. Each session is videotaped, and notes are made of each session. Follow-up studies have not been routine in the past but are planned for the future.

The Counterparadox

A question that was raised in Palo Alto in the 1950s, and has been haunting the family field ever since, was how to use the discovery of the part played by double-level communications in the family of the schizophrenic. The Bateson group, experimenting with "therapeutic double binds," reasoned that it would have to use the same type of paradoxical communication with the family that the family itself was using. The Milan Associates, taking the same position, elaborated on the idea of the therapeutic double bind, called by them a "counterparadox," and used it as the cornerstone for an intricate, elegant, and logical methodology for change. In *Paradox and Counterparadox* the Milan group states:

As far as paradoxes are concerned, we can say that our research has shown how the family in schizophrenic transaction sustains its game through an intricacy of paradoxes which can only be undone by counterparadoxes in the context of therapy.[4]

A good portion of this book is devoted to a discussion of the ideas of Bateson, Haley, Watzlawick, Weakland, and other contributors to what is rightly described as not just a movement in the field of mental health but a much larger epistemological shift necessitating a new approach to human behavior and a new language for describing it. Perhaps more than any other clinician-researchers, the Milan Associates have used this epistemological shift as a base for their approach.

Central to their thinking is the Batesonian concept of circular causality that has been discussed in previous chapters. Along with this goes a conscious distrust of being caught in the traps of "linear thinking"—the illusion, peculiar to our Aristotelian heritage, that there is a historical causality in which A causes B, which then causes C, and so on. These traps contribute to—are even part of—the dilemmas the clinician must deal with, and at the same time augment his most frequent clinical mistakes. A familiar example would be the position taken by the family therapist who prides himself on realizing that the child is the victim of a "dysfunctional" family system. The therapist sympathizes with the child as the scapegoat for the unexpressed hostility between the parents and immediately tries to pronounce the child blameless and moves to the dysfunctional marriage as the "real" cause of the child's problems. Not only is this an extremely linear view, but it often provokes resistance and reduces therapeutic effectiveness.

A systemic approach, the Milan Associates make clear, involves abandoning these notions and realizing that the enemy the clinician must attack is not any family member or even the malfunctioning family itself, but what they call the family "game." The way they describe this game recalls elements of Haley's control theory of communication in families of schizophrenics, whereby each person tries to win control of family rules while denying that he or she is really doing so. Unless all can agree on the rules of the family game, there can be no winning it, of course, and no finishing it; in an eternal cycle, the game about the game, or the metagame, goes on and on.

Since such games are not overt, one can only infer them from communications that go on in the family, but here is a good example, quoted by Selvini in *Self-Starvation* and related to the struggles about leadership that are disqualified even while they are going on:

MOTHER: I don't let her wear miniskirts because I know her father doesn't like them.
FATHER: I have always backed my wife up. I feel it would be wrong to contradict her.[5]

It has been the genius of the Milan team that they have devised a method for breaking such games-without-end. First, of course, one would have to expect that the therapist would not be exempt from the control moves of family members. Any attempt to get the family to do something different will automatically call forth counter-moves and disqualifications. Therefore, the first step in therapy would be to establish what game the family is playing with the therapist, and to agree with the game and encourage it. The game is usually: Here is our burdensome, sick, or bad person, fix him or her and relieve us, but do not make us change. The therapist knows that to fall into the trap of trying to do this will only lead to his own downfall.

The opposite move, then, would be to ask the symptomatic member to continue with the problem, rather than try to fix it. But this is nothing new. Clinicians doing individual therapy have been using "reverse psychology" or similar tactics for years, and the strategic school pioneered by Watzlawick, Weakland, and Fisch has elevated to a high art the technique of prescribing the symptom. What is different about the Milan Associates is their insistence on prescribing not just the problem behavior or set of behaviors but the larger configuration of relationships surrounding the problem. To understand this, we must examine their concept of the "positive connotation," linked closely both to the development of a systemic hypothesis and to their interventions.

The Positive Connotation

The positive connotation is a therapeutic device that may be one of the Milan group's most original inventions. Initially they wished to give a rationale that would be consistent with encouraging a symptomatic behavior. Since, by taking the family into therapy, they had implicitly agreed to help the family get rid of the problem, it would be inconsistent simply to prescribe it without giving a good reason. In this, they are addressing the necessity, also recognized by the strategic group in Palo Alto, of "reframing" a situation so that this type of intervention seems logical.

One possibility would be to say that the symptom of the patient was in some way required by the family; that the family "needed" a sick person. But to do this would go against the prohibition against linear causality. It is no more correct to blame the rest of the family and praise the sick one than vice versa. The solution to this puzzle would be to connote positively *all* the behaviors in the family that pertain to the symptom:

It thus became clear that access to the systemic model was possible only if we were to make a positive connotation of *both* the symptom of the identified patient and the symptomatic behaviors of the others, saying, for example, that all the observable behaviors of the group as a whole appeared to be inspired by the common goal of preserving the cohesion of the family group.[6]

In effect, one cannot disentangle the positive connotation from the intervention, usually a paradoxical prescription, in which it is embedded. The positive reframing of the symptom as it is linked to other behaviors in the family is the core of a paradoxical prescription. Therefore, to explain one, we have to explain both. This is not easy to do. It is probably best simply to describe a particular example.

This case was a consultation (first interview, really) with a family the Milan Associates saw during a demonstration workshop. Peter, seventeen, had been briefly hospitalized with an acute nervous collapse, partly brought on, it was felt, by the use of LSD. He had been diagnosed schizophrenic at the hospital, although he seemed quite lucid in the session and kept weeping, which is not a classical sign of schizophrenia. The therapists found out that each parent had previously been married to an abusive and irresponsible spouse; the mother, in fact, had been driven to thoughts of suicide before she decided to divorce. The children came from these previous marriages. Mother had an eighteen-year-old son, Anthony; the patient, Peter; and a daughter, Sarah, fifteen. Anthony was about to leave for college, and Peter had apparently been very close to him. The father's two children were Linda, twelve, and Debbie, fourteen. According to the parents, not only Peter but Debbie was a "worrier." Linda, like Anthony and Sarah, supposedly had no problems. Although the parents seemed to have a good marriage, the mother was clearly the less assertive partner, and signaled her fragility by breaking down and crying when she recounted the hideous brutalities of her former husband.

It was clear that the impending departure of the oldest son might be triggering some of Peter's upset. The mother had leaned considerably on Anthony, and it seemed that Sarah, the mother's third child, was now coparenting with the stepfather. A change in the balance between the parents was clearly in the offing.

The team's intervention was slanted to do several things: first, to normalize Peter's role; second, to push Sarah into the child group, drawing a proper generation line; and finally, to counteract the effect of Mother's tears, which amounted to a message to the children, or at least to Anthony: Don't leave. The following ritual was suggested by the therapists, Selvini and Cecchin, in their message to the family:

You, father, and you, mother, had a tragic and disastrous experience in your first marriages. Each of you married the other to give a good parent to your children. And you, children, are working very hard in the service of your parents' wish to be perceived as good parents, and are trying hard to help them maintain this conviction. Anthony and Sarah, also Linda, are showing how good their parents are by their perfect behavior. But Peter and Debbie wonder whether it would be better to be perfect or to be a problem. If they are problems, this helps the parents even more to show what good parents they are. Not knowing which is best, perhaps the children should meet in a week to discuss how they should continue this work of helping their parents, who have this understandable need because of their tragic life. Peter, it is you who must call the meeting. If you children feel you cannot succeed, you have to phone this clinic and ask for help.*

The reactions were immediate and revealing. Peter looked startled but pleased on being asked to convene the children's meeting. Linda and Debbie brightened up. Sarah seemed less happy. Mother looked upset, and father perplexed. But it was the self-controlled Anthony who surprised everybody by throwing his arms around Selvini and bursting into tears, as if to say, "You finally understood the spot we're in."

It is hard to make claims for interventions like these, especially if one hasn't had first-hand experience with them; and in this instance, there is no follow-up. It is possible that the family never

---

*This message was taken down verbatim by the author while watching the team interview the family during 1979.

came back. Perhaps it did not need to come back. But it is clear that such prescriptions can touch and stir a family. An intervention of this sort will—sometimes only temporarily but sometimes forever —break a fixed family pattern. At the very least it will break the united front, or united story, a family presents to the therapist. One member will seem angry, another puzzled, another worried, while another may say, "I understand perfectly." In this case, reversals of what the family presented in the interview were noticeable. The two most worried children seemed happy, while the apparently "strong" oldest son broke into tears. In particular, the supposed fragility of the parents, especially the mother, was called into question by the message.

The effect of this prescription would certainly be to shake up or revise options for relative positions in the family. Linking Peter with the other children erased his special status as the sick one, and placed the "worrisome" children on the same level with the "responsible" children. Giving Peter the task of convening the meeting made him special again, but in a positive way.

Most important, the children were enjoined to continue their jobs of parenting their parents. It is true, as Madanes says in a recent article on paradoxical prescriptions, that the outcome is often to change the family structure.[7] The preceding example prescribes what Madanes refers to in her article as the "incongruous hierarchy" one almost always finds in families with symptomatic members. If there is a recoil, we may hope it will be in the direction of more appropriate boundaries and proper status lines.

Another tactic the Milan group used here is to put the therapists who may be working with the family in a one-down position to the children. This makes all the adults lower than all the children. It is another example of prescribing an incongruous hierarchy, but the professional context is included as well. In this case, it seemed likely that any therapist assigned to the family (which had been referred to the outpatient clinic by the hospital where Peter was treated) might unite with hospital and family to continue to see Peter as "crazy." The message would tend to challenge any hospital/parents/therapist agreement along that line. It would also alert a therapist not to form a coalition with the parents, but to claim an appropriate hierarchical position above parents and children both.

What is beginning to be clear, however, is the importance of "reading" the internal (and external) politics of the family. One must study the coalitions and apparent power balances or imbalances in relation to the symptomatic behavior. This is why the most important contribution of the Milan group may not be their most visible signature, the systemic paradox, but their detective work in devising a hypothesis that will explain the symptom in the family and how all the pieces fit.

The Systemic Hypothesis

In their article "Hypothesizing—Circularity—Neutrality," the Milan Associates state that a hypothesis must be circular and relational[8]—by which they mean that it will organize all the confusing data attached to a symptom so as to make sense in the relationship context of the family. They cite as an example an interview with a divorced mother and her adolescent son. The two came for therapy because of constant fights. At first the team entertained the notion that the boy's behavior might, in part, be a disguised effort to bring the natural father back into the picture. Questions along this line fell very flat, however, so present circumstances were investigated and a new hypothesis was devised. It turned out that the mother was seriously dating another man, for the first time since the twosome had begun their life together twelve years before, at the time of the divorce. The son was also at the age when he was seeing more friends. The mother-son couple were beginning to break up, with consequent distress.

This time the team's message was based on a simple hypothesis: that the two were undergoing a natural process of growing apart and making new ties, a process that brought with it unavoidable growing pains but was nevertheless "irreversible." The team therefore recommended that the couple come in, not for therapy, but for a "few meetings," to try to slow down this painful but irreversible process of separation.

The issue arises: Is there then one true hypothesis? Obviously some are more "true" than others, as this case shows. The Milan group handles this issue by citing the *Oxford English Dictionary*, which defines a hypothesis as "a supposition made as a basis for reasoning, without reference to its truth, as a starting point for an investigation." This immediately sets an intriguing framework around therapy—each case becomes an experiment of its own, a real-life mystery novel. But there is no one "solution" to this kind of mystery. One comes out of the dilemma with a Pirandellian notion of the "truth": There are as many possibilities of the truth as there are places to stand and look at it from.

Whether it is "workable," in the sense of a supposition on which to base an experiment, can be judged only in retrospect and even then inaccurately. By the time a hypothesis seems justified by the course of events, the family will present a different configuration, which means that the original hypothesis must be revised or even totally scrapped. One suspects, however, that a sufficiently complex hypothesis will stand the test of time and will at least form a core for the picture that begins to appear as family and team move through changes together.

A hypothesis does two important things. First, the hypothesis is useful in its "power of organization." It not only offers a rough scaffolding on which to hang the masses of information thrown out by a family, but can give the therapist a thread to follow in conducting an interview, thus blocking out the meaningless chatter that consumes so much of the usual session. Second, it suggests what meaning the symptomatic behavior has in this family at this time. In the case of the boy and the mother, it was clearly not a sarcasm to tell them that they needed help to slow down the process of growing apart. The problems they were having did seem to be intensified by their efforts at separation.

It is linear, however, to say that the hypothesis defines the "function" of the symptom. In *Self-Starvation* Selvini points out that the members of a family become "so many elements in which no one element can be in unilateral control over the rest. It would thus be epistemologically incorrect to say that the behavior of one person 'causes' that of another."[9] As a result, one cannot say that a symptom is caused by the family's reactions to it, any more than vice versa; rather, all these behaviors are circling around in a mutually supportive arrangement. One has to see a process in which activities dovetail with each other as rhythmically as the inhaling and exhaling of breath, or the systole and diastole of the heart.

What goes into an intervention or a prescription is never completely the same as a hypothesis. The hypothesis respects the circularity of family events as far as possible. When translated to a prescription, a linear epistemology is unavoidably adopted. This linear interpretation of the data presented by the family usually reverses the family's version, introducing a new "punctuation" into the family. The family may say: "So-and-so is to blame for our misery by his insensitive behavior." The team says, "We see things differently. We see your son not as insensitive but as extremely sensitive." What will follow is an explanation of his distressing or destructive behavior as crucial to the welfare of someone, or as confirming the unity of the family, or as a solution to a dilemma brought about by some shift in the family.

Is this linear? In a way, yes; in a way, no. I prefer to replace the concept of paradox with that of polarity. In the *I-Ching*, or *Book of Changes*, the meaning of each hexagram is modified by the inclusion of an opposing possibility. In the same way, by replacing the linear punctuation of the family with an opposite one that is equally linear, the Milan group creates a polarity. The essence of polarity is an interpretation that moves from one pole to another, neither true in itself but only in combination with the other, and always suggesting other, unforeseen possibilities which are never spelled out. When a family responds to a reverse punctuation with a rejection not only of the punctuation but of the behaviors it describes, and discovers a completely different way to organize relationships, one feels that this method of therapy could indeed be called a dialectic of polarities.

The Uses of Time

A crucial aspect of the way the Milan therapists develop a hypothesis is their attention to time. They are concerned with the way a family evolves new patterns in adapting to changing circumstances. A behavior, no matter how senseless or destructive, is always in some sense a solution. A dilemma arose at some point in the family trajectory when the natural processes of growth or an accidental shift required a change in family organization. A symptom can be a solution of sorts. A good hypothesis will often describe a symptom, or any irrational behavior, as an ingenious solution to the difficulties faced by the family on its evolutionary path.

An example is another North American family the team saw once for consultation; the family's problem was a beautiful, promiscuous daughter of twenty. The family consisted of the girl, her parents, and a thirty-year-old half-brother born of the mother's liaison before she met the father.

In the interview the team noted the constant twinning between mother and son, who both seemed very melancholy and even wept in tandem. By contrast, father and daughter were loud and lively; they fought constantly but in an amiable, affectionate manner. The father and mother were distant in the session, but the children reported that the father would often criticize the mother, who would then cry. The problem dated from the time of the son's return from the Vietnam War. Quarrels and fist fights between son and stepfather led to his banishment to an apartment below, where he lived like a hermit. Soon afterward the daughter, then in her early teens, began to go out with men, with the apparent knowledge of the mother, who deplored her behavior on the grounds of safety but insisted on knowing all details. If the father tried to scold or control the girl, the mother protected her.

The hypothesis of the team was that the girl's behavior kept dangerous couples apart at the same time that it prevented them from separating. The girl's behavior distanced the girl from her father because of the quarrels it set up; it distanced her mother from the half-brother because her mother was so preoccupied with her; it distanced the mother from the father because they kept fighting about how to manage her; and it distanced the two men because the mother's preoccupation with the girl kept the son out of a rivalry with his stepfather that would otherwise have surfaced. The behavior also kept the family stuck together in their attempts to deal with it.

The team's prescription addressed the evolution of the two coalitions, mother/son and father/daughter—defining the daughter's behavior as a solution to the father's original position *vis à vis* his stepson and wife. The prescription went as follows (this is a verbatim transcript of the message, taken from a videotape of the interview with the family):

DR. B[oscolo]:   [to father] This is our opinion . . . about the irresponsible behavior of D. . . . we feel instead that D.'s is a very responsible behavior —that what she has been doing for all these years that you might feel was irresponsible behavior was extremely responsible.

And why is she responsible? What she's been doing all these years, from the age of twelve, fifteen till now, she's been doing all this for you, L.— your daughter has been doing everything for you. And what is she doing for you? At the age of twelve, thirteen years old, when she would psychologically be getting out of the house, she felt that if she really would get psychologically, emotionally, out of the house, she would have left an intolerable situation at home for you, because she saw that mother and S. were the privileged couple. Mother and S. are very close together. And D. felt that if she got out of the house she would have left you alone. So, at a certain point, she herself decided, "I have to do something to help my father to be present in the house." And we have seen today that she succeeds in making you present in the house, in having rapport in the house, with your wife, with her—otherwise, you would have been completely cut off from the family, you would be completely out. So we feel that D. has been doing all this for you.

FATHER: And that includes her sexual behavior, and all that?

DR. B.:   Including everything.

FATHER: Think so? I don't know—I find it very difficult to believe.

DR. S[elvini]:   Because her affection is for you—she is separating the privileged, first couple, mother and S., and gives you the occasion of quarreling so warmly with her.

FATHER: Well, if she had done it to help, she certainly did not. If I had got my hands on her I certainly would have helped her.

MOTHER: D. said many times, "My father never embraces me, and never even gives me a kiss."

FATHER: [to D.] See that, you never give *me* a kiss!

MOTHER: She missed that.

FATHER: Because she's so fresh all the time.

DR. S.:   I understand. He is not grateful because he has not understood what she is doing for him. I understand she is very sad because Father has not understood what she has done for him.

DR. B.:   Certainly, what D. has done for her father, as we said before, is so that he can be present in the family and would not be cut off; she is a sacrifice; she gives up her adolescence to go out and lead a certain kind of life.

DR. S.:   She is doing like her brother—maybe forever. But we have seen in our experience in Milan many, many, many beautiful young girls in this situation do the same for the father. So . . . [rising to go].

FATHER: So you mean I'm the bad guy. [Laughs.]

DAUGHTER: Depends how you see yourself. [Gets up.]

FATHER: I don't see myself as anything.

DR. B.:   [standing] D., you have really been doing a lot for your father —the sacrifice that you make for him so he can be present in the family —and this can go on for all your life, as we see in many cases . . .

DR. S.:   [talking over] You insist on this—not to be excluded from the rapport between mother and S. . . .

DR. B.:   . . . is our conclusion. [Farewells all around.]

While Selvini is speaking of the sacrifice made by beautiful girls in Milan, the daughter is rising with great dignity, and sweeps out as if quite offended. The father seems upset too, although he laughs.

The thrust of the message may have been to bring down the current "privileged couple," father and daughter, and to create a split between them. This apparently succeeded, for the next session began with the daughter announcing that she had obtained a volunteer job at a local settlement house working with teenage girls. As she became more involved in her own life and career, the prediction implied by the message came true. After two more sessions, the father came in complaining that his wife and stepson were together all the time and that he had come to blows with his stepson. He felt so displaced and insulted that he had decided to leave home. The Milan team's message was revived by the family's ongoing therapist,* and the girl was advised to return to her previous behavior. Naturally, she did not do so; and as both she and the son began to become less involved with the parents, the couple began to complain about the inadequacies of their marriage. The therapist dealt with the situation with continued paradoxical prescriptions, and the case came to a good conclusion.

It is interesting that the original hypothesis remained valid during

*The family consultation was held at the Ackerman Institute for Family Therapy, which organized the Milan Associates' first visit to the United States in 1977, and the therapist was Gillian Walker.

the course of the case, even though it was added to and elaborated upon. The girl's behavior was tied to an evolutionary impasse, when she would normally have been leaving home. The mother's history furnished even more evidence for a difficulty arising at that time (at age thirteen the mother had been raped by her own stepfather and sent away from home). The message, in effect, said to the family, not that it was a dysfunctional family but that it had shown ingenuity in solving a dilemma created by its own history. The fact that it failed to evolve to a next-stage level is not criticized, except indirectly, by the overzealous way in which the team expresses admiration and praise for the ingenious solution. The hypothesis was justified by the fact that after the daughter improved, the family moved back to the place where the son, returning from the war, had fought the father for possession of the mother. What happened with the help of therapy was that the family arrived at a more "evolved" solution, one that allowed the crucial separations to take place. Son and daughter became more independent, while the couple took a memorable trip to Europe together, a thing they had never before allowed themselves to do.

The Referring Context

The Milan Associates see family and therapist as embedded in a larger context or field, and take the entire field as the unit of treatment. They pay strict attention to what could be called the "outer ring," the entourage of professionals and institutions that may be heavily influencing the family in its management of the patient. If therapy produces a crisis—which it often does before a change takes place in very rigid family systems—the patient may appear to deteriorate. The change may then be aborted by the family's move to rehospitalize the patient or find someone to dose him with massive medication. Gillian Walker's term for a professional who takes this role is "Dr. Homeostat," because this person acts to restabilize the field so that the symptom remains intact.

In their article "The Problem of the Referring Person," the Milan

Associates describe their efforts to counteract the influence of this kind of person, who is often the one who referred the family to therapy and who may have an emotional stake in the outcome of treatment.[10] Often the team will ask such a person to attend the session. They add: *"We no longer make the mistake of advising or prescribing the interruption of the relationship between the family and the referring person."*[11] Instead, they simply prescribe the situation. The family is told that it must not hazard any movement toward the change it desires because if the symptom were no longer present, the family (or some particular family member) would lose an important friend/ally/comforter. Alternatively, the team will prescribe the presence of the professional as essential to maintaining equilibrium and preventing a premature change.

The Milan Associates are clearer than any other group about giving priority to contextual issues of treatment, especially those pertaining to the professional field. If the family refuses to come to therapy at the time set, or if a member refuses to attend, this will take priority for the team, no matter how serious a problem the family may be presenting. They will either postpone therapy until the family agrees to their terms, or will address the issue in the intervention, which will usually prescribe that the family continue to behave in that particular way to prevent change. Sometimes, as we see, the question of the interfering professional may be the total focus of the intervention. This stance insures freedom of movement and is in part responsible for the extraordinary leverage the group maintains at all times.

Circular Questioning

For conducting the session, the Milan Associates have recently developed a format that is based on Bateson's statement that "information is a difference," and which they refer to as the technique of circular questioning. The team's article "Hypothesizing—Circularity—Neutrality" contains a good description of this technique and its rationale.[12] The method seems to augment powerfully the amount and quality of information that comes out in an interview. The basic tenet is always to ask questions that address a difference or define a relationship. Asking someone to comment on his parent's marriage, or to rank family members on the basis of who has suffered the most from someone's death, or to rate, on a scale from one to ten, his mother's and then his father's anger when his sister comes home late at night, are all "difference" questions. So are questions that deal with before and after: asking a child by what percentage the fights between the parents have diminished since the older brother was hospitalized, or posing "hypothetical" questions such as, "If you had not been born, what do you think your parents' marriage would be like by now?" or "If your parents were to divorce, which child would go to which parent?"

Using this method, one notices several things. First of all, such questions make people stop and think, rather than react in a stereotyped way. The people who are not talking also listen attentively. Second, these questions cut into escalations and fights, not only between family members but between a therapist and family members. And, third, they seem to trigger more of the same kind of "difference" thinking, which is essentially circular because it introduces the idea of links made up of shifting perspectives. The Milan Associates point out that in families in schizophrenic transaction people seldom define a relationship or notice a difference, and that this technique used alone may have a powerful effect on these families.

The questions may have a cumulative effect. One might ask a wife what kind of relationship the husband had with his mother, and then ask him the same question about her and her mother. This cross-referencing of information can be revealing and can lead to even more revelations. In addition, the therapist can use this technique to ask quite heavy questions without the usual constraints, since he is only getting the opinions of others. The Milan Associates will ask even young children what their opinion is of their parents' sex life. Since children always have an opinion, this does not in fact make them privy to information they should not have. And despite the horror of family therapists who have been drilled to make each family member talk only for him or herself, my sense is that in an indirect way these questions push people to differentiate quite as much as asking people directly to do so. For instance, the usual response of parents and children to the question about sex seems to reinforce the generation line, not blur it.

Another use for these questions is that they can be used to block behaviors by simply pointing to them. If a mother has a "death phobia," the team may ask the father: "What do you think would be the effect on the family if Mother died?" This puts the "worst case" on the table and takes away from the death phobia some of its old power to upset others. In the case of an attempted suicide, for instance, one might ask: "If X had managed to kill herself, who in the family would be the last to forget her?" And so on.

In general, it seems that the Milan Associates now have an elegant model for conducting the interview that is congruent with their Batesonian philosophy of treatment. Both the interviewing techniques and the systemic intervention at the end insert punctuations that emphasize difference and circularity. The questions reinforce and are reinforced by the prescriptions derived from them in a manner that makes the entire interview an example of circularity at a more complex level than if either technique were to be used alone.

The Importance of "Neutrality"

If one could say that there is any one stamp or signature that characterizes the Milan Associates' approach, I would not choose the ingenious interventions, the elegant interviewing style, or the meticulous care with which a hypothesis is made. I would say it is their entire stance, summed up in their concept of "neutrality." Again, the reader is referred to the article "Hypothesizing—Circularity—Neutrality." This short article is like concentrated space food: it contains in brief some of the group's best ideas.

"Neutrality," despite its hands-off implications, has more to do with effectiveness in therapy than with staying cool. The team maintains an impassive, if respectful, attitude during the interview, in contrast to the sociability adopted by many other schools and practitioners. However, the Milan Associates are only too aware of the power of families to render therapists impotent, and they place techniques for maintaining leverage above any other pragmatic achievement. To this end, they have adopted a number of devices that help the therapist or the team to stay in a position from which maximum change can be achieved.

In its simplest form, the Milan Associates describe "neutrality" as the ability to escape alliances with family members, to avoid moral judgments, to resist all linear traps and entanglements. If, for instance, no one member can say after a session that either therapist sided with him or her, "neutrality" has been achieved: "The therapist can be effective only to the extent that he is able to obtain and maintain a different level (metalevel) from that of the family."[13]

I would add to this many of the other devices and methods the team uses in its approach. For instance, what strikes an observer of the Milan Associates is their deliberate use of mystery and drama. The family knows that people are silently watching from behind a screen, not just as observers but as active participants. The therapists in the room come and go for mysterious reasons—sometimes on impulse, sometimes in response to a knock at the door.

In addition, team members—even those in the room—cannot be influenced, because they are controlled by invisible others. One is reminded of the old-fashioned analyst with his impassive position behind the couch. Messages and letters that emerge from behind the screen reinforce the notion of the one-way street. The attitude of the therapists toward family responses, always moving with them or remaining unmoved, rather than joining in outright battle, is also a way to remain "neutral."

This position fits with the basic tenets of strategic therapy. Unlike the therapist who pushes and pulls the family into shape, the "bullfighter" therapist, one could call these practitioners "henhouse" therapists: "Ain't nobody here but us chickens." These therapists take a low profile, speak softly, and carry a tiny stick. Like Judo experts, they use the momentum of the family's own resistance to effect change.

The surprising thing, for those who begin to work this way, is the power of the approach. I have sometimes called it the Therapy of the Weak, since the force seems to come from the very negation of using force. Shakespeare, in one of his most famous sonnets, describes a lover too cool even to notice his own influence on the heart of the Bard: "He that hath power to hurt and will do none/ That will not do that which he most doth show," is—to paraphrase the embittered and lovesick Shakespeare—a much tougher customer than your everyday activist. In fact, he has all the cards in his hand. "Neutrality" confers on the systemic therapist the power to be effective. But the ingredients are many: the quiet, nonreactive stance; the circular questioning, always placing the therapist at the metalevel; the devices that prevent the therapist from being endangered by family suction (the screen, the team, the messages, the unexplained and unexpected words and actions of the therapists); the concern with field and context issues in order of priority; and finally, the implacable attitude toward resistance. The team will sooner lose a family than insist on change.

In ending, let me cover myself by saying that by the time this book is out, this chapter may be obsolete. The Milan Associates' work is always in process, always changing. The group is now moving in very different directions than they did when *Paradox and Counterparadox* was published. The two men, Boscolo and Cecchin, are teaching in Milan and traveling extensively across Europe, Canada, and the United States, giving workshops. Selvini and Prata are also teaching, mainly now in Europe, as well as continuing with their research. The group is coming up with very different clinical instruments than before, and as they are now in many ways two teams, not one, it is to be expected that differences will develop between them, as well as between them and their ever more numerous followers.

Whatever happens, the Milan Associates have given us not only a pragmatic expression of a truly circular epistemology, but a new, more finely tuned apparatus for assessing and working with difficult families. In addition, as the next chapters will show, this method raises many novel and interesting clinical issues. And these issues in turn lead us back to a more rigorous look at our theoretical frameworks and the epistemologies that support them.

Chapter 16

Theories About Therapeutic Binds

The Puzzle of the Paradox

The work and theories of the Milan team have become the base for a new round of experimental thought about behavior and change. It would be helpful at this point to look at some of the theories about why counterparadoxes or therapeutic double binds work. We have seen that in *Pragmatics of Human Communication,* the term "paradoxical intervention" is used as a synonym for the therapeutic double bind.[1] In addition, "prescribing the symptom" was considered a form of paradoxical intervention and was first used by members of the Bateson group in various papers describing both the paradoxes people imposed on one another and those the therapist devised to combat them.*

In a therapeutic double bind, as we have seen, the client is told not to change in a context where he has come expecting to be helped to change. If he resists the injunction, he changes; if he does not

---

*The reader is urged to go to Richard Rabkin's *Strategic Psychotherapy* (New York: Basic Books, 1977) for a history of this idea, and an account of how therapists of various types at various periods stumbled on its effectiveness and invented terms for it like "negative practice," "reverse psychology," "paradoxical intention," and "prescribing the symptom."

change, he is doing what the therapist has asked him to do. In both cases, the therapist remains in charge. Usually, the client's "resistance" to the therapist gets the better of him and he chooses to change.

In a subtle variation on this view, Haley bases his thinking about therapeutic binds on analogies with game theory and an implicit assumption that people are playing power games with one another which they must at all costs "win." A person with a symptom derives immense power to control his environment—especially his relationships—by this behavior. Thus, if told to continue with the symptom by a therapist, he is in a bind, since the only way he can now control the therapist is by abandoning the symptom.

This argument for the success of paradoxical interventions has been a persuasive and pervasive one. Even the Milan Associates, in their earlier writing, seem to have adopted it. There is a central objection to it, though, which has to do with a continual tendency to use linear explanations positing special attributes in the individual. The rationale in question presupposes that certain kinds of clients have an "oppositional" trait or need to control others, due to some unknown personality component or to a family context which brings out this trait. Such a view comes close to assuming a motivational drive that, if cleverly harnessed by the therapist, will push the client in the direction the therapist wants him to go.

There is another universe of explanations based on an ecological or system-wide view. One such explanation has been developed by psychologists Duncan Stanton and Thomas Todd and associates in Philadelphia while working with addict families in the late 1970s. Their technique of "ascribing noble intention" to the symptomatic member, although it arose independently of the work of the Milan group, is similar to the positive connotation and equally systemic in that it places the symptom in the service of the family. Stanton gives credit to Nagy for the idea that symptoms are adaptive for the family across generations, but he differs from Nagy in using this formulation strategically. By way of explanation, Stanton proposes a novel theory of "compression," based on the notion that dysfunctional families continually oscillate from intense fusion with the nuclear family to intense fusion with families of origin. One is reminded of Bateson's bell buzzer analogy in that a preference for one state promotes a switch to the other, in a no-exit cycle. The therapeutic paradox, according to Stanton, intensifies this oscillation, or pushes it hard toward one pole, thus disrupting the cycle. The resultant crisis, and the therapist's response to it, forces the family to find new pathways.[2]

If one were to take as the major unit of investigation the configuration of relationships of which a problem is the most visible and central sign, one can hypothesize a somewhat different rationale for the success of so-called paradoxical moves. A good illustration is an interview that was part of a brief therapy project at the Ackerman Institute for Family Therapy.* The patient was a supposedly depressed three-year-old with a harassed young mother and a preoccupied, career-oriented father. The child improved quickly but then it seemed that the wife was depressed. She found the pressures of two young children and a purely domestic existence very difficult. However, the more the therapist suggested activities that would take this bright, well-educated woman out of the house, the more difficult she became. Accordingly, the therapy team, stationed behind a screen, called the therapist out and suggested that the therapist make an about-face, telling the wife that she has convinced him he has foolishly misjudged her nature. How could he have been so insensitive as not to see that she is probably one of those women who find their greatest happiness in serving others? Particularly now, when her husband needs to put all his energy into his career in order to help his family, it is essential that she protect him from the annoying distractions of domestic life. When he comes home in the evenings, burdened down by work from the office, she must under no circumstances let him do any chores or allow the children to bother him, but see that he remains in his study. Even if he should wish to come out and help her (and since he is a concerned and loving husband, he probably will), she should resist, even to the point of putting a lock on his study door. As the therapist transmitted this opinion to the couple, the young wife began to look more and more displeased, although she sat quietly and said nothing. The husband, by contrast, seemed very nervous and attempted to con-

*Led by Olga Silverstein and Peggy Papp, this team also included Joel Bergman, John Clarkin, Richard Evans, Betty Lundquist, Gillian Walker, Anita Morawetz, and myself. The intervention described was primarily the creation of Olga Silverstein.

tradict the therapist, who politely refused to listen to his arguments and ended the interview.

In the next session, the wife came in looking not at all depressed, and gave the psychiatrist a piece of her mind for having misread her character. She mentioned the projects that had taken her out of the house that week, and her intention to begin taking courses at a community college. The husband said that he had washed the dishes every night and had even cooked the supper while his wife went out to a concert. In fact he had discovered that he could get enough work done at the office so as not to have to bring it home any more. The therapist professed to find it hard to believe that he had been so far off in his judgment and stated that he doubted that things would continue in this way. However, he wished the couple well and terminated therapy. A one-year follow-up found the wife taking a graduate degree and the couple extremely happy with each other.

To explain what was going on in this transaction, one could simply say that these were two oppositional people who were struggling for control of the relationship, and that the wife's tactics were to play Cinderella in the ashes, making her husband feel guilty, while the husband retaliated by distancing himself in work. However, one could equally well ignore individual motivations and consider the relationship system alone. According to this view, the change in the couple derives its momentum from the forces already residing in the triangle.

First, this is a somewhat complementary couple, with the wife in the one-down position. When the therapist pushes the wife too far down, he overpasses one of the system's limits for relative power. The wife may in other contexts be quite assertive, but her systemic position vis-à-vis her husband requires compliant behavior. So she will "resist" any effort to make her more assertive. The husband at the same time must maintain a slightly higher position on the seesaw, but not too high. This explains why the husband becomes so agitated when the therapist defines him as needed to be served like a pasha. One can almost read his mind: "There will be sheer mutiny in the house if this happens; my wife will make me pay a thousand times." Monitoring behaviors to keep the seesaw from too great a slant immediately take over, with the wife refusing to play a menial role and the husband desperately anxious to see that she does not. But in their overreaction, the couple change their status to that of a much more symmetrical couple, a change that presumably will relieve both the wife's depression and the husband's less obvious malaise.

Another factor that must be considered is the outrageous position the therapist takes. Not only are both spouses eager to prevent any attempt by the other to assume the suggested new role, but both are irritated at the therapist who is giving them such absurd advice. Previously they have been covertly conflictual and unhappy with each other; now they come in united and speaking loudly in one voice. Never mind that the voice is saying, in essence, what an unmentionable so-and-so this therapist is. The therapist's rejected advice has brought them closer and has also evened out the balance between them.

The point is that the forces that accomplished these changes were the potentials for recoil built into the relative balance of the relationship. When the therapist tried to even out the seesaw, the couple, answering to interior laws, could not do so. But when he pushed the seesaw too far, it rebalanced itself, so to speak, empowered by a recoil from within five relationship arcs: husband/wife; wife/husband; wife/therapist; husband/therapist; and (finally) couple/therapist. Since a team was also involved in this situation, one must also add the relationship: therapy system/family system.

This activation of what could be called balancing responses in each person and subgroup in a complicated relationship network seems to be a more inclusive way to explain the success of this paradoxical directive than an imputed "need not to be controlled" within each spouse. The program the couple was caught in, and the rules of the overarching mechanism of this program, seemed to govern the type of relationship this couple had worked out for itself. Presumably the relationship, whatever its penalties, was adaptive for this couple's particular situation.

Once the therapist has figured out the rules of the relationship, or the behavioral redundancies which express them, he does not need to rely on advice, persuasion, or attempts to repattern the relationship or reeducate the couple; nor does he need to be especially charismatic or have the power of a prestigious setting or

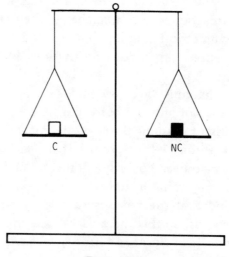

Figure 16.1
Family Balance Scale

status. Those who do not have huge reputations, important positions, or personal magnetism may yet by their wit and ingenuity prevail if they let the energy of the relationship system, and the energy of their relationship to that system, do the work for them.

The Metaparadox: Family-Team

Moving to a higher context level, there is still another way to describe how paradoxical directives work. Here we may ignore individual factors, or even recoil factors from within a given set of relationships, and look at the matter from the point of view of a family system worked upon by a therapy system. In thinking about symptoms in families, we have talked about a recursive cycle whereby the system is opposed, then encouraged, opposed, then encouraged, endlessly. Thus it remains, a wanted yet unwanted guest, neither sitting nor standing, staying nor going, but hovering in an endless and tantalizing stasis.

Imagine this recursive cycle in terms of a balance or scale in which one side has an "NC" (for "No Change") upon it, and the other side

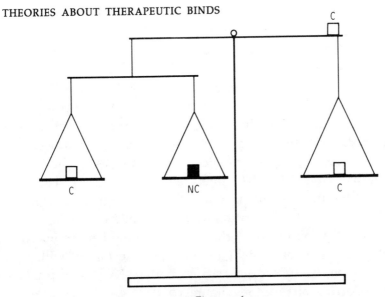

Figure 16.2
Family Plus Therapist or Team: Version One

has a "C" (for "Change") upon it, and imagine further that the C and NC are assigned roughly the same weights (see Figure 16.1). One could invent a rule or constraint for the family that keeps these two weights in equal balance at all times. If the NC becomes less important or slacks off, the C will have to compensate by becoming weaker too, or else a new element of NC will have to be added. One finds, interestingly enough, that if a person who usually supports a problem does not do so, or is absent, another family member will fulfill that task. Alternatively, a covert expression of symptom support will become overt, as when a mother of an anorectic who is eating well begins to worry that her daughter is eating too fast and follows her about, keeping watch over her food intake. Furthermore, let us keep in mind that this balancing act is vital to the family, for some reason that is not spelled out. A rigid family system faces the most danger when forced to reorganize, and the symptom, as we have said, may be one answer to this dilemma.

Now imagine what will happen if such a family, with its interior scale or balance, is joined to a larger scale or balance, represented by a therapy team or a powerful single therapist. The whole can be represented by a new double balance, with the family scale on one side, and the therapist scale on the other. (See Figure 16.2). The fact that the family has entered therapy, or just their presence in the room, must also be assigned a weight in favor of change; hence the "C" at the top of the therapy side of the scale.

If, as in the model portrayed above, the weight of the therapist is placed on the C side, in addition to the family's presence in therapy, one can see that the family "rule" that forces for change must be balanced equally by forces against change has been violated. Therefore one could predict that both sides of the family scale will have to shift to NC, interpreted usually as "resistance." What must the therapist do, if that is the case? Logically, his move would be to reverse his C position with a large NC, especially as any NC of his is still countered by the C of the family being connected to treatment. Then one might predict that the family will, if it follows its own rule for balance, change both its NCs to Cs, producing the following picture (See Figure 16.3).

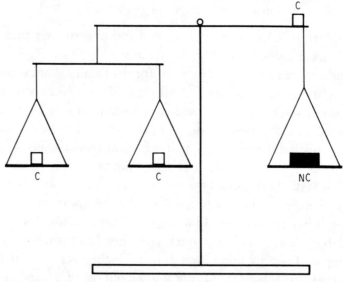

Figure 16.3
Family Plus Therapist or Team: Version Two

The Counterparadox and Levels of Logical Type

A serious problem with the balance scale analogy for change processes in therapy is that it does not offer a way to include the contradictions between overt and covert messages. The Bateson group originally based their ideas about double binds and therapeutic double binds on the confusion of levels of classification they found in families of schizophrenics and used when making interventions with such families. Here, then, is a double-level way to schematize our model, illustrated by another of the Milan Associates' cases.

A paper read by Selvini during a workshop in New York in 1977, entitled "First Session of a Systemic Family Therapy," describes the team's work with the family of a seventeen-year-old anorectic girl, Antonella. Her family consisted of mother, father, and a fourteen-year-old brother, Fabrizio. During the initial interview the therapists were struck by the impassive way the mother described her daughter's condition, which was extremely serious. By contrast, when she spoke of how much pain Antonella was causing her maternal grandmother, Grandmother Theresa, the mother wept. Father acted uninvolved, and the brother seemed interested only in his outside pursuits. The family had no hypothesis about the onset of the illness; all they could say was that the girl had been working in a factory when suddenly she stopped eating. The therapists asked Antonella herself what was going on just before she became ill, and she answered that she had a boy friend but had been afraid to tell her family because she felt they would not approve of him. Sure enough, when the parents found out about him they put a stop to the alliance. The fiancé subsequently got drunk in a local bar and spent a few days in jail for disorderly conduct. When asked, Antonella said that she would never stop loving this young man, and if she were to become well she would start to see him again. The mother looked upset and said that Grandmother Theresa would be horrified to have her granddaughter going out with a "jail bird."

Some questioning about the early married life of Antonella's parents brought out useful information. The parental couple had first lived with Grandmother Theresa, and Antonella had always been a marked favorite of the older woman. This living arrangement came to an end when the father's mother, who lived not far away, said that she could no longer visit her son while he lived in the house of "strange people." So the husband insisted that they get their own apartment, much to the sorrow of his wife, who was most unhappy about leaving her own mother.

Noting that the feelings and well-being of Grandmother Theresa were treated as if they were as serious as Antonella's illness, the team decided to attack the triangle of the three women first. Accordingly, this prescription was read and given to the family:

The specialists' team has decided that family therapy is very suitable, considering that Antonella's life is in danger and there are, in her case, high probabilities of recovery.

But we are faced with an extremely serious risk and worried about it. The risk is connected with Grandma Theresa. If Antonella should recover, she would probably start meeting Franco again. Grandmother would feel ashamed and suffer mortal pains because of this; in fact, she would suffer even more than she would if Antonella should die of her illness. During the next session . . . we shall discuss this danger threatening Grandmother.

This is a classic version of a therapeutic double bind. Look how neatly it reverses the contradictory messages of the family. Within a covert framing message of "Do not eat, because it will be too threatening if you get well" the family says, overtly, "Eat and get well." The team, by stating that they feel family therapy is indicated, imply covertly that the girl should get well; however, their overt message is that she should not get well, because Grandmother Theresa will suffer too much. It is a reverse of the contradictory messages the family gives the girl, and places the family in a metabind, a state of confusion and upset that hopefully will produce some change. (See Figure 16.4).

At the next session, two weeks later, Antonella looks much better; she has started to eat and has gained weight. But the mother complains that the girl eats at night and the mother has to get up to monitor her eating. It is a less covert version of the message "Don't eat." Interestingly enough, the girl had run to see her grandmother as soon as the family got home after the first session, to

1. Family "Paradox"

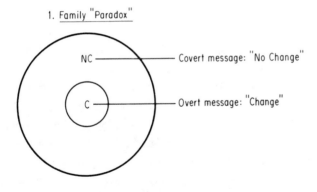

2. Team "Counterparadox"

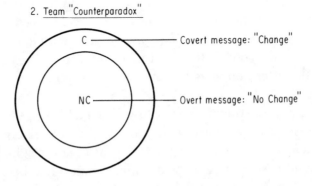

3. Family Countermove

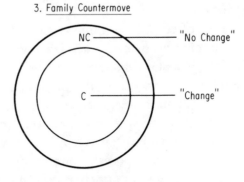

Result: Antonella eats.

Figure 16.4
Overt and Covert Elements of a Paradoxical Prescription

show her grandmother the letter. The old woman had said, "Nonsense, of course I want you to eat. Besides, there are many Francos in this world." As one would expect, the mother looked very depressed during the session, while the father and Fabrizio seemed the same as usual.

According to Selvini, who was asked about the progress of the case, Grandmother Theresa was invited to the next session. The team wished to block off the grandmother, but they did nothing more than treat her respectfully and thank her for coming; they did not communicate with her again. This time the message went by mail, to Antonella's household only, excluding the grandmother by design. The letter contained three different messages, which each family member in turn had to read to Antonella before supper each night. Father's message read something like: Thank you, Antonella, for refusing to eat because this will keep Mother at home and close to me. The mother was to say: Thank you, Antonella, for refusing to eat, because when Grandma Theresa scolds me for neglecting her, I can tell her I am taking care of you. And the brother was to say: Thank you, Antonella, for refusing to eat because in that way all the attention goes to you, and I can go out and play with my friends.

Only after the girl began to gain weight, to become more independent and less part of the family, did the underground quarrels between her parents begin to surface. The original fight around whose mother should have primacy had never been resolved, nor had other issues, and the struggle between husband and wife came to the fore.

It is, of course, an immense simplification to try to diagram such a complex process as placing a reverse fix on the moves people in a family make that simultaneously invite and discourage change. And yet, like a beckoning finger, the puzzle draws us on to assay more and more elaborate explanations. One clear idea emerges, however: Whatever configuration the family puts forward to the therapist must be seen as a punctuation peculiar to that context; the therapist then imposes a counterpunctuation that switches the first one about. Neither punctuation is more or less true, better or worse, than the other; both are equally drawn from the universe of linear causality. What seems to happen is that the confluence of the two opposing punctuations enforces a new punctuation, not heretofore suspected or present.

It is possible that the new punctuation comes from a vocabulary which was not available to people in the system as it used to be. The fascination of the phenomenon of binocular vision or the bicameral brain lies, as Bateson suggests, in the possibility of creating a transcendently different perspective—as with two eyes one moves from an experience of two-dimensional to three-dimensional space. Perhaps the juxtaposition of contraries is for living systems what metaphor is to poetry: a force that pulls, not pushes, for a leap.

Holding One Part Still

A growing discomfort made me start to rethink these models I had been playing with. They still separated therapist and family into two units, and they did not sufficiently attend to the characteristics of the entire field. Looking about me, as one might gaze idly at the ground, I began to see that what I had thought were pebbles were in some cases precious stones—they had been lying about my feet all this time. I am referring to a group of ideas that keeps reappearing in different forms, ideas that have been spelled out by different people, but which should be given the status of a concept. This concept would not only explain why therapeutic binds work, but include other kinds of therapeutic moves as well.

Let me start with Bateson's haunting phrase: "the infinite dance of shifting coalitions." There is a way in which a system stays structurally the same by virtue of a constant flutter of smaller movements that counteract any serious efforts to reorganize it. This observation, as we have said, accounts for the chaotic surface look of families with very disturbed members and the contradictory finding that on an underlying level these families are extremely rigid. This phenomenon is not unlike the experience of the canoeist who, seeing a particular configuration of wavelets on the surface of a stream, knows that there is a rock or log stuck firmly beneath.

In *Mind and Nature,* Bateson clarifies this general idea: Talking about stability, he argues that one must always keep in mind the entity whose stability is in question, for there are many types of mechanisms for maintaining equilibrium. When one comes to living systems, one finds that

the whole mass of interlocking processes called *life* may be involved in keeping our object in a *state of change* that can maintain some necessary constants, such as body temperature, blood circulation, blood sugar or even life itself.[3]

As a result, one must "follow the example of the entities about which we are talking." For the mammal, stability depends in part on the temperature of its body, with its variables that can change reactively with the environment. For the acrobat on the highwire, stability means balance. To describe that, one must take into account the smaller instabilities—the shifts of the pole or changes of posture—which keep the acrobat balanced. In these cases, instability (on one level) means stability (on another level), and Bateson argues that these different levels must always be held in mind.

In a family with a problem, one important stability is the way coalitions in the family are organized. In his early book, *Strategies of Psychotherapy*, Haley puzzles about how to describe a three-person system. He shows by an example how a relationship system is kept the same by compensatory shifts in the coalitions, as evidenced by family members' behaviors. For instance: son misbehaves, father reprimands son, mother chastises father, father defends his action, and mother looks exasperated with him. Change may be difficult to introduce in that system because minor shifts (small instabilities) will occur that counteract it. Haley notes a possible sequence:

If one merely persuades the child not to misbehave, the system does not change, for father is then likely to say to the child, "Why are you so quiet?" and mother will respond with, "He can be quiet if he wants, leave him alone," and father will say, "I was only wondering." That is, a change in an individual can lead to an adjustment . . . so that the system remains unchanged.[4]

There is a more abstract way to describe a system that is so constructed as to have trouble changing, and here we go back to Ashby's concept of the too-richly cross-joined system (see Chapter 5). Such a system, as we know, tends to erase inputs, since no change will persist unless all parts conjointly change. This is a highly unlikely possibility, given the fact that each time one part changes it sets off a change in another part, which sets off a change in another part—the result being that the first change can never become a state of equilibrium for the whole. The only help for this situation, Ashby says, is to introduce "interactive sequence constancies." These will temporarily interrupt the deviation-counteracting motions induced by a new input. Actual severing is not essential; it is enough to put in a "null function" by making one part quiescent.

In my 1975 article on this idea,[5] I was interested in the fact that clinical work with families with symptomatic members seemed to consist of putting in "interactive sequence constancies" all the time. Selvini then used my commentary on Ashby and Ashby's own ideas in an article, "Why a Long Interval Between Sessions."[6] Referring to Ashby's observations, she says that the therapeutic task is to avoid being caught in the organizational pattern of a too richly cross-joined family. From the beginning, the Milan Associates had regarded the family-therapist suprasystem as the unit to consider whenever making interventions, rather than thinking of the therapist or team as one independent unit acting upon another. Thus Selvini warns that the main danger would be for the therapists to be drawn by the family into a new system as richly cross-joined as its own. This would make it impossible for the therapists to keep outside the system enough to retain control, let alone introduce change.

The Milan team's answer to this dilemma, suggested to them by Ashby, is first to concentrate on interventions that would disrupt the connections between parts. They favor moves that will make reactive parts nonreactive or that mark off certain behaviors in such a way as to keep one part of the system still. This approach constitutes a pragmatic application of Ashby's remark, which struck me at the time I read it as both poetic and true: "Constancies can cut a system to pieces."[7]

Most of the Milan Associates' interventions are, like many other therapeutic interventions, designed to block, disrupt, or derail customary sequences. A ritual that places two persons together one day a week disrupts heaven knows how many redundancies, and that is one type of constancy. Reading a message every night is another constancy. Thus, Selvini notes, the therapeutic intervention itself disconnects the family members from their usual positions in the family system.

For tasks and rituals to succeed, however, the family must carry them out. Some families will comply, others will not. With families that will not or cannot comply, the best way to introduce a constancy is to seek out the most rigid and immoveable sequence or behavior that a family presents in therapy, and simply prescribe that. This may be the refusal of the family as a whole to attend therapy, or it may be a symmetrical struggle between the two groups of in-laws, or it may be the problem itself, linked to the position of every person in the family as a hub is linked by spokes to the rim of the wheel. Whatever that "most immoveable" item might be, that is the configuration to prescribe. Thus the therapists join the family in reinforcing a constancy that is already there.

To be sure, the so-called constancy probably is in Bateson's "state of change" and is not so constant. Whatever is activated by the therapeutic encounter is likely to be the family balancing pole, at least for that moment. To rigidify it further by prescribing it is to amplify it and put the family off balance, just as the acrobat is unbalanced when his pole is held still by an invisible force. If the pole is unusable, then other possible ways to maintain balance (body posture, slower movements) may be adopted. This may be why other "problems" so often follow the maneuver of freezing (amplifying) the presenting complaint or the configuration in which it is embedded. In any case, this is one possible explanation for the force of a systemic injunction targeted at the family's most palpable rigidity—the one facing the therapist or evoked by the therapeutic situation.

An additional therapeutic bind is placed on the family by the other method Selvini describes: the "long interval between sessions." At first accidentally, then by design, she and her associates scheduled sessions at least a month apart. This is not just because a richly joined system requires more time than less connected systems to process an input or intervention, but because it offers one more way to place what Ashby calls a null-function or "wall of constancies" between the family and the therapy team. They are still connected, but the family cannot reach the team. The usual feedbacks are not allowed to dissipate the force of the intervention by being bounced back on the team or otherwise disqualified. The block to reactivity is placed within the family, and then the therapist system withdraws and a block to reactivity is placed between family and team, allowing the first block to have greater effect. It is like a therapeutic bind plus a metabind.

The idea that a constancy can disrupt a system was always lying about in the back of my mind, and in my 1975 article I cited maneuvers from both structural and Bowenian schools that illustrated this principle. Now I would add maneuvers from the strategic and systemic schools, especially the techniques of prescribing the symptom or "system" (as a systemic prescription has been loosely called). In very richly joined systems, these moves may be stronger than direct attempts to introduce change. The Milan stance of prescribing elements from the entire field, including the referring context, is just a widening of the methodology. Perhaps the concept of "neutrality" is another way of describing the judo posture of that methodology.

One more pebble that fit my collection was a contribution from Paul Dell's paper "Beyond Homeostasis." Dell describes living systems as always evolving, always accommodating new inputs. He leans on Bateson in calling such systems "self-healing tautologies." What caught my eye was a sentence that included a reference to constancies: "An output or feedback that introduces a constancy into the system is a strong force that disrupts the preexisting organization of the system. When thusly disrupted or distorted, the systemic tautology will heal itself into a somewhat new tautology and a somewhat new steady state."[8]

Dell moves into line with Selvini's position on counteracting family suction by saying that the input or feedback introduced by a therapist will be "swallowed" by the family system. He observes that this process is a way the family cancels out attempts to change it. He defines therapeutic input on the basis of whether or not it really affects the problem or complaint. If it does not, then it can no longer be defined as input. It is just a piece of family life. Dell further notes, and many therapists will agree with him, that when this happens, the therapist himself has become a piece of family life. And if the family stays in therapy for any length of time, this is always true. "The only relevant question," Dell wryly remarks, "is whether the therapist is now part of a still dysfunctional family system or whether it has changed, and the therapist is now part of a non-symptomatic family."[9]

The genius of the Milan Associates' approach is that it addresses itself so precisely to Dell's point in the following ways: (1) by their concept of "neutrality" (always remaining nonreactive); (2) by the tactic of introducing blocks of time between sessions (reducing the chance that they or their input will be swallowed up by the family before it can be effective, and lengthening the amount of time before they become totally engulfed and useless); (3) by the use of tasks or rituals that introduce elements that remain invariant; (4) by their attention to those elements in the wider field which might nullify their input; (5) by their circular questioning, which not only introduces new information at the system level but makes them less vulnerable to the family's attempts to "swallow" them; and (6) by their systemic prescriptions which *hold one part still.* Using these techniques, they have achieved a remarkable methodology for "cutting the system to pieces" and forcing it to find alternatives. Like all therapists, they are always attempting to introduce what they call new punctuations, but more importantly they attend to the family's maneuvers to deamplify these punctuations or disqualify them, and have invented a brilliant set of devices for preventing the family from doing this.

This, then, would be another way to see the reason for the usefulness of so-called paradoxical prescriptions. I say "so-called" because the term is beginning to make many serious thinkers in the field uneasy. The Milan Associates are beginning to turn their backs on it. The term paradox in its conventional sense suggests that the maneuvers designated as paradoxical are illogical. They are only illogical, it seems to me, from the point of view of traditional norms of treatment. Seen from the perspective of intervening in too richly cross-joined systems, they seem to be extremely logical.

Obviously, this does not close the subject, which should continue to generate heated discussion for some time to come. I will now move on to a consideration of a few other issues that working in a systemic way brings to the fore.

Chapter 17

Issues on the Cutting Edge

The Turning Facets of Resistance

One of the first signals to early researchers that a psychiatric symptom might be a family phenomenon was the often noted fact that if the problem of the identified patient improved, other problems might arise. Clinicians called this tendency "symptom substitution" (a term used in individual psychotherapy), as if there were something about certain families that required a symptom, much the way a dragon needs a virgin for breakfast. This puzzling idea—why would a family "need" a symptom?—baffled therapists in the days before it was realized what a beautiful, serviceable, well-constructed artifact a symptom is, thoughtfully provided by nature to help families that were terrified (probably for good reasons) by the threat of change.

We have become more respectful of families since we have gained a better understanding of the intricate mechanisms that evolve to monitor such threats. Living systems usually have a number of ways to damp down fluctuations that might lead to change. The therapist may find himself feeling like those princes who keep going off and completing tasks against great odds to win the hand of the princess, only to be told that there is one more task, and yet one more. The therapist feels like the unhappy prince: Here I have solved one problem, only to be confronted by ten others. (Sotto voce: Is this princess really worth it?)

But for many families this is the normal course of therapy. They have a repertory of arrangements, usually seen as problems (at least by the therapist), that fall out of the defeat of the problem that brought the family into treatment. To foresee at least the probabilities of what these other stages might be is part of the art of therapy, even when it seems impossible to make specific predictions. A new problem may be a less life-threatening or serious problem than the first, *or* (a very big *or*) it may not. Will the "good" sibling become a "bad" sibling if the "bad" sibling reforms? Or will the marriage, which seemed to depend for its unity on the worry caused by sick child, go on the rocks? Or will the mother become seriously depressed if the psychotic son regains his sanity and moves toward independence? The negative consequences of not having a symptom can be (although they don't have to be) at least as serious as the seriousness of the symptom, and any therapist who works with an entire family begins literally to ask: Is it better or worse for this family not to have this problem? If I tamper with it, will I be able to handle the consequences?

The Milan model, with or without a team or a screen, is useful because it so clearly seeks to define and coopt whatever countermove the family presents in any given session. The experience of working with this model almost mandates the expectation that any intervention powerful enough to interrupt a symptomatic redundancy will elicit a countermove. The therapist must, accordingly, always be watchful to meet the challenge of the new weapon and, by coopting it, prescribing it, or reframing it, set the stage for the next round. The Milan team's case histories show how adroitly they swerve to hold fast to the protean shape that presents itself in such different forms from session to session.

This does not mean that every family offers a variety of blocking maneuvers. Very often the simple shift from child symptom to marital problem is the version encountered in child-focused settings. And sometimes the family makes a jump to a new integration without any of these intermediate steps, or goes through its own series of stages on its own. But if these shifts, tossing up new obstacles, appear, this does not mean that the therapy is not going well, or that the therapist is not a good therapist, or that the family is too "sick" to be worked with. It may actually be a sign that the therapy is having an effect.

This brings us to the next facet of this way of working. If therapy is succeeding, one is often faced with an extremely frightening escalation—a sudden worsening of the problem—or the eruption of a new and more destructive one. This can be difficult for the therapist, but it may be that without a crisis of this sort, some families will never achieve a major structural change. There is no threat so likely to make a therapist draw back from the decision to try to crack the symptom as the sudden explosion of forces which may be set loose by a powerful systemic intervention. Therapists working this way for the first time often feel that all is lost when such mayhem breaks loose. The more chronic and severe the primary system is, the more disastrous the crisis is likely to seem. And yet without this crisis, the family may never escape its deadly dance.

The Evolution of a Problem

The systemic approach, as we have seen, is deeply concerned with the evolution of a problem, which frequently means going back to previous generations and to collateral groups in the present generation as well. But the reason for focusing on the past is not to cast as wide a net as possible in the belief that understanding the whole process will help people to escape from it or change it. Rather, the idea is to be economical, and to trace out only as much as one needs for a hypothesis. If interventions based on this hypothesis do not work, or work incompletely, then explorations into a whole new branch of the family or its history are in order. This information is used to disrupt the symptomatic configurations in the present. There is no idea that "working through" an event or relationship or pattern in the past will relieve a problem or symptom, as the more historically oriented family therapist believes.

I treated one family with a boy who had always had trouble at school. He was a likable, spirited seventeen-year-old, but since his early years his mother had engaged in endless battles with him over his school work. He was not doing well during his senior year at a demanding prep school, and had been caught cheating in writing a paper. The boy's anxieties were centered mainly on academic achievement, and psychological tests revealed that he was very nervous about doing anything without exact instructions. The parents were in the process of finding a less demanding and more relaxed school, but the school psychologist had recommended family therapy because the boy's problems were "emotional."

A look at the family showed many strengths. Boy and parents were quite capable of coping with the problem of finding another school. It was hard to understand why, in this family where nonconforming brightness and originality were prized as well as conventional abilities, the son was having such a problem. He seemed like a person who did not have an academic bent but would undoubtedly find his own level of achievement if not pressured. The one who seemed to feel that pressure was necessary was, of course, the mother. There was some hint that the boy, who seemed to be repeating his artistic father's own early school difficulties, reflected the mother's disappointment with her husband, especially his choice of an artistic career, with all the financial problems that implied. But the couple's fondness for each other seemed much too genuine to require such a serious problem to keep their relationship going.

When we went back to the past, the mother disclosed that her own mother was a hard-driving perfectionist who had always made this oldest daughter the living proof of her own success. As a little girl, the mother had had to be more brilliant, more responsible, more handsome, more successful, than any other mother's little girl. She ended up with many resentful feelings about her mother, but did not outwardly rebel except in one respect: She chose for a husband a man who was an artist, not the banker or businessman her mother would have preferred. She continued to hold a high standard for herself and for everybody else in the family, especially her son.

It seemed that the only possible move would be to try to break the hold this perfectionist grandmother still had over her striving daughter, which had made her try so hard to produce the perfect son. Of course the harder she tried, the more the boy resisted (possibly also out of an identification with his father), even though consciously he was doing what he could to live up to her expectations and feeling miserable when he failed.

The therapist told the mother that, in a curious way, she was still showing her mother how hard she was trying, and would always try, to be the best in every way: the best career woman, the best wife, and the best mother. This was the greatest sign of devotion she could possibly pay her mother: that she was still trying to please her at any cost. And this was why she had to continue to pressure her son to succeed: out of loyalty for this mother whose opinion she had long since thought she did not care about.

At the same time the boy was told that by presenting himself as an academic failure, which had been his father's problem, he was not only being loyal to his father but was in some way representing his mother's resistance to her own mother's perfectionism. In this family where there was a rule that failure must never be allowed, he was a kind of pioneer.

The aim of this intervention was to activate a recoil from the strictures the mother did not realize she was laboring under; and to redefine the son's apparent disgrace as a way of helping the family, especially his father. The statement to the son would not have been sufficient if it had not been coupled with the mother-grandmother issue, making it hard for the mother to continue her effort to "perfect" her family without feeling that she was playing into the hands of her own deeply resented mother.

A number of changes followed this session. The father announced that he was quitting a poorly paid but stable job he had held for some years and going back into free-lance work. His wife, although it obviously cost her something, backed him and said she was proud that he had the courage to leave a job that was unworthy of him. The boy was placed in a school that emphasized athletics, which he was good at, rather than scholarship.

This, then, is an example of a three-generation systemic intervention. We can see how forces coiled within the past can be used as a source of momentum for change in the present. History, used in this way, is no longer dead but alive, carrying within it the means for the destruction of the very patterns it predicted and sustained. This is the systemic use of the past, very different from the older view that to understand or "work through" emotions or attitudes or patterns that are no longer appropriate to the present will eliminate them. They would not be still in use if they were not, in some way, still appropriate.

Establishing a Benevolent Contest

One aspect that differentiates the strategic/systemic approaches to therapy from many others is the seemingly less compassionate role of the therapist. Milton Erickson has spoken of the "contest" between therapist and client, and most of his therapy consists of a brilliant balancing act between bringing out positives in a client's situation and bringing out—almost eliciting—his resistance.

It is possible that a contest of some sort is a natural prerequisite for any therapeutic change. This idea goes against the helper/healer notion, whereby the therapist is a benevolent doctor of the soul, offering advice and support or acting as his client's advocate or guide. But implicit in most therapies is an adversary position, usually covert, sometimes overt. From the momentum generated by this position comes the energy for change. An ineffective therapist is like a fisherman whose line hangs limp in the water; at times there is a tug—the fish nibbles, then gets away. The therapist who is caught in the family's or client's "game" is painfully aware of this fact; the interview drags on tediously and the therapist feels confused, incompetent, and humiliated. By contrast, a systemic prescription that hits every relationship unit in the group produces an indescribable effect. It is as if the fish, thinking itself quite safe with this booby of a fisherman, suddenly finds itself with a hook in its mouth. There is a general motion of shock, surprise, rejection, as the family tugs hard on the line. A quiet period often follows, as family members try to figure out their position, much as the fish swims around with the slack line, not realizing that it has been caught. Then comes the relentless tugging as family members begin to react; one will challenge the therapist; another will laugh and insist that the therapist is joking; another may take the message very seriously and, in some cases, even weep. Bafflement, bewilderment, anger, indifference are common. But the major fact is that the therapist, perhaps for the first time with this family, feels that he has a fighting chance to catch this elusive fish, which is not any particular family member but the relentless pattern that enslaves them all.

Of course a therapeutic contest is not indicated for families whose resistance to change is low, or whose range of behaviors can readily be reset. As we have previously said, neither is it appropriate for a family that is so badly fragmented that there is no potential for recoil. The contest stance is for the family at the "consensus-sensitive" or "too richly cross-joined" end of the continuum. Here is where one finds the entrenched psychotic or neurotic behaviors that mark the family stuck in a "game without end," and where the therapist knows it is vital to harness the forces that reside within the family's resistance to change. And if in addition to the contest with himself the therapist can add elements of intense ongoing contests within the relationship system itself, there is even more momentum to draw on.

A very real problem for the therapist who works systemically, however, is that he or she may attract all kinds of hostilities and negative reactions from members of the family. Even if he escapes blame, he will not receive credit. An intervention, especially a message encouraging a problem, may by itself create a seemingly magic turn for the better, so that the symptom the family complained of will disappear. However, they will not always associate this change with the therapist or even remember it. A child with daily headaches may suddenly stop having them, but when the therapist asks how the headaches are, the mother may have complete amnesia about the complaint that brought the family into treatment, and proceed to complain about some other problem.

Sometimes it even seems as though the therapeutic relationship may have to be sacrificed in favor of accomplishing at least some minimal shift, which takes place even though the family is irritated and leaves treatment. To deliberately engineer things so that the family drops out of therapy and leaves feeling angry with the therapist is extremely uncomfortable, but it is sometimes the price of a change. If there must be a scapegoat, better that it be the professional.

More often the family, after a major shift has occurred, merely becomes cool toward the therapist or team. I have wondered sometimes whether the systemic approach may not draw on the mysterious extrusion process—the need to draw bodies in or push them out—so often noticed in families in crisis. At least one person becomes symptomatic, and there seems to be a decree that someone has to go: through hospitalization, divorce, running away, or worse. A therapist, by appearing to take the side of all the things the family is complaining about, offers himself as a substitute for extrusion. The family, in pushing the therapist away, also pushes away the behaviors they have so extravagantly attached themselves to. This would be analogous in pharmacology to giving a person with gastric acidity an aluminum gel compound that coats the offending substances and is expelled along with them. How else to account for the amazing indifference families display toward a therapist or team after the problem has dropped away, no matter how intensely all have been involved before?

In any case, a systemic approach is not for therapists who must be liked at all costs. The therapist will not get cards at Christmas or invitations to weddings. Therapists who work this way must have a cotherapist, or a team, or some kind of sympathetic professional group. This is not just for support while in braving out some hostility-arousing intervention, or to get suggestions for making a stronger impact on a family that is eluding efforts at change, but, first, to get the rewards we all need during difficult and unappreciated work and, second, to have a support group to counteract therapist extrusion.

A Graceful Exit

If this approach to therapy offers difficulties for the therapist, it also presents acute problems for the family. Termination of therapy, in particular, is an issue for the family, not just the therapist. The situation created by the therapeutic contest poses a problem in ending therapy because the family should not leave with the feeling that the therapist has defeated them and is gloating. Thus Milton Erickson speaks of supplying a graceful exit for the patient: Conventional therapy provides solemn rituals to end therapy—working through the loss, as if termination were like a death, or as if the therapist were so important a person that to lose him or her would be to lose a family member or dear friend. But this does not apply to the methods we have been describing here.

Credit must be given to the strategic-systemic schools of therapy for having organized therapy in such a manner that the sought-for change takes place out of the room, away from the therapist, and usually with a disclaimer by the therapist that anything he or she did, or anything in the therapeutic relationship, brought about the change. If anything, the therapist challenges the change or declares that it won't last: a sure sign to the patient that the therapist hasn't much stake in it. The patient can then own it, rather than having to give the therapist the credit.

A particularly nice example of a way to give a family a "graceful exit" and still get some confirmation of change is to ask each member the question: What would you personally have to do to bring things back to the way they were when you first walked into the room? This question can be asked of a family whose members have absolutely no understanding of their own contribution to maintaining the problem, or any idea of the processes that made it disappear, and yet they will answer as if they had each studied in detail the part they played in the whole event. A mother of a "behavior problem" boy will say, "I would have to think I had to solve everything by myself"; the father will say, "I would have to be away from home all the time, working late"; and a younger "good" sibling may say, "I would have to yell as if he were killing me every time he came near me."

In this therapy, termination can often be presented in the form of a recess. A therapeutic model which does not think of emotional problems as illnesses does not think in terms of cure. If a psychiatric problem is defined as evidence that a family is having difficulty negotiating a transition to a new phase, the therapist's job is to help with the transition, then get out, leaving the family to settle itself around its new integration. There is no assumption that the family will then be trouble-free, because new transitions or crises will come along and new symptoms will arise. As with the old-fashioned G.P., this new-fashioned therapist sees his or her function as being on hand when needed, any time the family is having problems as they face a change. An episodic therapy is the result: with sessions placed close together or else far apart; with recesses common when it looks as if the family can go it alone; with invitations to come back at any time for a "checkup," or for more serious things, but with a hope and expectation that this will not be necessary.

The God in the Machine

One objection to the team approach is that it seems like an enormous outlay of therapist time on comparatively few cases. How can this become a workable model when it takes four people to deal with one problem, even though the number of sessions may be relatively few? One can justify it for training purposes; there it is even rather economical. One can justify it for research, of a soft clinical nature but nevertheless breaking new ground. But how can one justify it as a major therapeutic method?

The obvious answer is that a team is forcibly called for in severe, difficult cases that do not yield to years of intensive individual treatment, or to family treatment of a more conventional type. We are talking about serious problems, the psychosomatic "killer" disorders, the class of conditions known as the psychoses, and many other stubborn, resistant symptoms which, though not always life-threatening, cripple the activities of the person and the family in which they are found. Surely, in every clinic, there should be a team following the systemic model for problems that have proved resistant to other approaches.

What is of immense interest in this team approach is that it calls upon so many sources of power. When using one of these teams for consultation, the therapist who has been stumbling along with a difficult family finds his or her own position immensely enhanced.

Call it a *deus ex machina* effect, an effect born of the expectation that goes with the fact of unseen "experts," a cheap magic trick, or what you will, the presence of the group exerts tremendous leverage. As a matter of fact, at least one therapist I know, having no group and no one-way screen, used a phone in his office and *pretended* to be in touch with a group of consultants, giving his family a message from this imaginary team which had the same effect as if the team were real.

However, it is more than an atmosphere of mystery that produces the sometimes amazing changes induced by this method; it is the synergistic effect of several minds applied to a given problem. I agree entirely with the position of the Milan Associates that the use of the therapeutic paradox, and the logic it is based on, is independent of the charismatic influence of a particular therapist. It would be incorrect to say "independent of the therapeutic relationship," but with that as a proviso, the method is indeed, if correctly applied, amazingly effective. This is true even when the family is working with a comparatively inexperienced therapist, if there are experienced practitioners behind the screen.

Peggy Papp points out an extra resource the team provides for the therapist in "The Family That Had All the Answers." She describes the team as being able to differ from or criticize the therapist in the room, thus acting as "a dissenting voice forming a triangle and forcing the family to take sides."[1] S. J. Miller, in "The Social Base of Sales Behavior," describes a similar maneuver.[2] The car salesman impresses the client with how hard it has been to convince his boss to get him to accept the supposedly low price he has worked out for his client. As he is writing up the sale the manager comes in, and the following prepackaged scene takes place. The manager "discovers" that his salesman has forgotten to charge for a number of quite expensive items, all of which were supposedly included, and he angrily criticizes his employee. He then marches out, after commiserating with the client on how shabbily he has been treated, and the salesman looks helplessly and miserably at the client. The client —better yet if it is a couple with a kindly wife—infuriated by the insolent manner of the manager, and quite sympathetic to the salesman, may agree to pay the difference or at least part of it. The object of the maneuver is to ally the client and the salesman against the manager; the client then protects the salesman against the (supposed) anger of the manager—and incidentally purchases a car.

Using a version of the same strategy, although we hope for more constructive ends, Papp prearranged for her team to call her out toward the end of the fourth session with the family, and told them when she came back in: "They feel that I am wrong again in trying to get you, Mother, to be strong and firm with John [a twelve-year-old problem child who had been in individual therapy for six futile years], because that means that father would have to be soft, and since you seem to have such a nice balance going now and your roles are clear, they're afraid it would upset the balance in your marriage to change the relationship with the children. Their feeling is, your marriage is more important than anything else, and if the children have a few problems, that's a small price to pay for maintaining the stability in your marriage."[3]

The effect was dramatic. In the following session the mother came in saying that she had completely reversed her usual role and had been telling everybody off, especially her husband. The boy had already begun to improve and, once the husband-wife issues were out in the open, began to behave well at home and do well at school too. To the parents' intense surprise, the boy was also able to tell them that he had been worried for years that they would get divorced.

In discussing the deliberate splitting of the team, Gillian Walker has written that it is most efficacious if the therapist in the room is in favor of change, and the team takes the part of the "loyal opposition." The team can be skeptical, suggest outrageous intensifications of the behaviors the family is already engaged in, and declare outright that the family can in no way succeed in making the changes "their" therapist has been working for. To go back to the story of Bateson's porpoise, the therapist is like the handler, giving the porpoise unearned fish, while the team can continue to be the cold-hearted experimenter.

Quite apart from the direct therapeutic uses of the team, there is an unlooked-for special effect that people using the Milan Associates' format discover to be of inestimable value: the combined energies and talents of a small cell of people, behind a one-way screen, seeing families in a peer or semipeer situation. Once started, these little foursomes, or sixsomes, can become a magnetic center in any agency or institution where they take root. A form of practitioner-research becomes possible without grants, immense outlays of money (except somehow to get a one-way screen), or the deployment of many people or much time. Four people can take on four families, each seen by one or two therapists once every two weeks or on a monthly basis. The effort to focus on a hypothesis and then to plan interventions for each session, whether or not "paradoxical" techniques are used, seems to stir up much enthusiasm and a lively sense of participation, an effect which is bound to make waves throughout any institution. It may be wise for these sporelike cells to keep as quiet as possible about their activities for as long as possible, for fear that too great a show of excitement will breed envy and hostility in the host, and produce efforts to extrude the too-successful spore, now rapidly growing into a large, productive mushroom.

Questions: Resolved and Unresolved

There are still, however, many questions for which there are no easy answers. We can, for example, ask whether this systemic approach is so team-bound as to be of little value to the lone clinician working with families. My own view is that it is of enormous value. Many clinicians who have worked with teams report that a subtle shift takes place that carries over to their individual work, as if the colleagues behind the screen had taken up residence in the back of the clinician's head like the tiny people children sometimes think live inside the radio. I often feel while working alone that I am consulting with these little people.

If I need to seek real advice, I will unhesitatingly use my colleagues as an ad hoc team. No therapist, no matter how independent, should ever be without access to back-up professionals. Here is where the team idea works as a blessed antidote to the notion that the therapist should always be effective alone. I tell trainees who sometimes complain about their lack of success that without more troops, without stronger ammunition, nothing will alter the situation and that they should not be ashamed about these "failures." In assessing a trainee's performance with a family, one now must add to the usual letter grades SWMH (Struggle Without Much Hope) and LLTG (Learning to Let Them Go).

Another question is whether the systemic approach, with or without a team, is applicable to individuals or couples who are less caught up in the family web, that is, to those who present themselves in smaller units and seem to have smaller problems. Of course, one must determine whether these units are not, in fact, deeply entangled in the family web, and hence whether one should either join them to other family members or else redesign the treatment to address this issue. The Milan Associates focus on problems with large, messy relationship contexts, thus automatically eliminating small units, but they will occasionally treat a couple relationship *in vitro.* It is only when they speak of their private practice that one hears of them dealing with individuals. Even then they claim that their research has changed the way they work, although they find it hard to explain the nature of this change.

There is a real question here as to what the practitioner must address: the tip of the iceberg (the problem confined to a small relationship unit) or the entire iceberg (the problem plus all relationships attached to it). The systemic approach seems to argue for addressing the entire iceberg. The strategic therapists have shown, however, that one can do very decent work even if limited to the tip. Clinicians experimenting with systemic therapy are beginning to feel that one can be limited to the tip and still treat the entire iceberg—that is, still be "systemic"—as long as one deals with the iceberg in hypotheses and interventions.

A current argument proposes that "family therapy" should be redefined as "systems therapy," and that the word "family" should be eliminated on the grounds that it limits and confuses therapeutic issues. Proponents of this argument believe that one works with problem and context as an indivisible whole, and that this indivisible whole does not have to appear all at once in one's office. (Pragmatically speaking, it never does.) It is possible that one can remain faithful to the systemic vision even if one sees only an individual or a fragment of a family. It is up to the therapist to decide whether working with this fragment provides enough leverage to bring about change.

Another objection to the systemic approach is that since it is based on work with "resistant" families, to use it on less severe problems is like using a cannon to shoot a canary. Those who harbor this reservation believe that one should first try a straightforward approach to see how change-worthy the family or person is, and should go on to "paradoxical" moves only after more conventional interventions have failed. However, the reverse could be argued. Some clinicians believe that these methods should be used *first*, to break up the log jam, so to speak, before even attempting straight-forward moves. They feel that this will shorten the therapy process and make it more effective.

A question that will not (and perhaps should not) be resolved is the relationship of the major schools of systems change to one another. Are the systemic and strategic approaches basically the same, or do they come from different conceptual universes, despite their seeming likeness and common roots? If the latter is true, does this split derive from their different ancestry, one school being primarily influenced by Bateson and the other by Erickson? Again, does the common interest in family history and kinship which links the systemic approach to the historical approaches, especially Bowen's, imply that there should be a joining? If not, what are the different premises that would prevent this?

By contrast, might the structural approach be less different from the systemic approach than it appears to be? The work of the Milan Associates seems to be moving in a more structural direction, as practitioners experiment with interventions that primarily entail a revision of the family. One could say, of course, that all systemic interventions touch the organization of the family, the "paradoxi-cal" ones indirectly, and many of the rituals directly.

Finally, one cannot help but wonder what lies ahead. Will there be a mingling of these tributaries into a mighty river? Will one approach subsume the others? Or will each accentuate its borders and harden into a sect? These issues will increasingly occupy clini-cians and researchers in this swiftly expanding field.

In pursuit of answers to these difficult questions, I am working with a number of colleagues at the Ackerman Institute for Family Therapy in New York: Olga Silverstein, Peggy Papp, Gillian Walker, Joel Bergman, Peggy Penn, John Patten, and Jeffrey Ross. In different groupings, and at different times, we have been struggling with issues such as those outlined above. In particular, we have been engaged in clinical research with both brief, strategic techniques and the Milan model.

And here we face yet one more important issue. A problem the systemic approach raises for a teaching institute is whether newcomers to family therapy should be exposed to this model from the start. Fears are voiced about hordes of inexperienced paradoxical therapists being loosed upon the world. My own sense is that some of these fears are unjustified. The approach cannot be reduced to a set of techniques, paradoxical or otherwise, but rather embodies a huge epistemological shift. Being exposed to systemic work, even without fully understanding it, can often help a beginner get to the heart of a systems view of problems without sacrificing the complexity of the matter or reducing to a blueprint what ought to be experienced as a cathedral.

But despite cautionary advice there is bound to be an increasing interest in experimenting with the systemic approach. More than any other therapeutic design, it translates Bateson's abstract and visionary formulations into an elegant pragmatics of clinical action. An influential new paradigm, deeply concerned with clinical epistemology, is beginning to justify and explain the work of the Milan Associates, and it is this paradigm and its implications for psychotherapy that I wish to talk about in the Epilogue to this book.

Epilogue

Toward a New Epistemology

The Evolutionary Paradigm

This final chapter points toward the future but builds upon the past. We have spoken of a circular or recursive epistemology. Bateson addresses this concern by stressing the self-recursive nature of living forms, choosing for his metaphor that "odd worm," Ouroborous, the snake that eats its own tail. Expanding on his meaning, he says:

We live in a universe in which causal trains endure, survive through time, only if they are recursive. They "survive"—i.e. *literally live upon themselves*— and some survive longer than others.[1]

These recursive loops, however, are never totally closed, since there is always a space for new information. Each cycle comes round to a new position, sometimes so minutely different from the previous one as to be imperceptible, but sometimes representing a major shift.

For instance, take the evolution of family therapy from 1950 until now. During these three decades the "systems" metaphor for family groups, with its emphasis on homeostasis and equilibrium, became a major model for the field. The analogy of the cybernetic machine, always returning to a presumed steady-state, was a convincing analogy for the redundancies in interaction observed not only in families with symptomatic members but in all families. It was also useful in jogging the field out of earlier analogies that applied primarily to the individual in isolation.

Recently, it has become clear that a new template is forming. A powerful group of new ideas is challenging the equilibrium model, not just for families, but for many other entities as well. During the 1970s a group of scientists in physics, chemistry, mathematics, and other fields began to question the almost sacred Second Law of Thermodynamics. This law held that all entities in the universe tend toward a state of entropy: a gray, random sameness without movement or change. Notable among researchers who began to challenge this law was the physicist Ilya Prigogine. A number of physical and chemical processes seemed exempt from it, he observed, and living forms seemed almost to flout it. Living forms moved in a negentropic direction much of the time, toward greater complexity and new and different states. In addition, in the eternal, static realm of classical physics, time, with its property of irreversibility, was ignored. Tomorrow was the same as yesterday and only that which never varied was a proper subject of study. The interesting case of *instabilities* was ignored by physics, as was much else in the natural world that changes and evolves. Prigogine says:

I often use the example of the cathedral and the brick. As long as you think "brick," you see that the brick stays the same for millions of years. But if you think "cathedral," there is the moment when it is built and the moment when it falls into ruins. And with these same bricks, you can construct cathedrals and palaces.[2]

Living forms, and how they come into being, could not be addressed by classical physics because it could only "think brick."

A central concept of Prigogine's, described in Chapter 9, is what he calls "evolutionary feedback." This means that a movement that is only a fluctuation in a system at one time can suddenly become the basis for an entirely new arrangement of the system at another time: "The evolution of the system goes spontaneously to situations that are *less probable*," Prigogine says, and this can be true for physical processes as well as life processes.[3]

Of particular relevance to family theory is the idea that living systems have the capability of mutating to more complexly organized regimes through small fluctuations, usually random ones. Two writers who have been linking family theory with this model for nonequilibrium dynamics are the psychologist Paul Dell, whose writing on this theme has been described earlier in this book, and the psychiatrist Mony Elkaim of the Institute for Family and Human Systems Study in Brussels. Both criticize the cybernetic model for family systems and systems change accepted by many family theorists. Current reasoning, according to Elkaim, states that,

> The family is caught between two forces: one force that leads toward change . . . and a force that tends to preserve internal equilibrium. The attempt was thus made to understand the symptom as having the function of protecting the homeostasis, in that it protected the family from the dangers represented by change. . . .[4]

As an alternative, both Elkaim and Dell turn to the ideas of Prigogine, who depicts all living forms as vulnerable to change, especially when driven far from equilibrium. At this point, any small instability can amplify, causing the system to pass beyond its limits and in an almost magical way reappear in quite a different state. The form that results from this process of evolutionary feedback is unpredictable, notes Prigogine. It is impossible to say which of the system's fluctuations will drive it from its former state.

Applying this model to therapy, Elkaim states that the task of the therapist is to try to push the system away from equilibrium, forcing it to search for a different solution; and above all, recognizing the importance of chance in determining which instability will be the determining one. The structure will be transformed according to its own special laws, laws that the therapist cannot possibly guess at, since they are part of what Elkaim respectfully calls the family's "singularity."[5]

It is interesting to consider that the systemic model pioneered by the Milan Associates provides a living illustration of this theoretical model, derived from such a different field. It is as if their therapeutic approach had been founded expressly on the idea of evolutionary feedback, rather than emerging separately and concurrently. The attention to small perturbations that might lead a system away from equilibrium; the expectation of discontinuous change; the concern for time and its irreversibility; the respect for the self-organizing capabilities of the system—all this suggests an unusual congruence.

An added fascination for me (as for Prigogine) is the possibility of developing theories that begin to unite living and nonliving forms.[6] To go back to Bateson's words, quoted earlier, "We might expect to find the same sort of laws at work in the structure of a crystal as in the structure of society. . . ." The development of an evolutionary model for social change that so closely parallels laws for change from the world of chemistry and physics seems to offer a hope that this prophecy might one day be fulfilled.

The Importance of Epistemology

For Bateson, the subject of epistemology was an intensely moral concern. Epistemology for him meant the rules one uses for making sense out of the world. These rules—not always conscious—determine much of our behavior and our interpretations of the behavior of others. Bateson isolates two particular villains, epistemologically speaking. One is "linear thinking," which appears to assign a cause and often ends up assigning blame. The other is any form of dualism. In this passage, Bateson is going after one of the most outstanding products of dualism, the idea of the "self":

To draw a boundary line between a part which does most of the computation for a larger system and the larger system of which it is a part, is to create a mythological component, commonly called a "self." In my epistemology, the concept of self, along with all arbitrary boundaries which delimit systems or parts of systems, is to be regarded as a trait of the local culture—not indeed to be disregarded, since such little epistemological monsters are always liable to become foci of pathology. The arbitrary boundaries which were useful in the process of analyzing data become all too easily battlefronts, across which we try to kill an enemy or exploit an environment.[7]

Bateson is always at pains to make it clear that he is talking about total circuits. To "chop up the ecology" is what one does when one takes the parts and pieces of what one is describing and decides that one part "controls" another or one part "causes" another.

Dell, applying Bateson's ideas to family therapy, points out the tendency of many family therapists to negate the epistemological revolution that the family therapy movement represents.[8] He particularly objects to the common use of the idea of homeostasis. Family therapists have taken too literally the notion that a family is like a homeostatic machine with a governor. Thus it is said that a "family needs a symptom," or "a symptom serves a homeostatic function in the family." To use this kind of language is to assume a dualism between one part of the system and another part. It is more correct to say that all parts are engaged in whatever ordering of constancy or change is in question, in an equal and coordinate fashion. To speak otherwise is to engage in what Dell describes as a kind of "fuzzy systems animism."

What must be kept in mind is the continuous recursiveness of all circuits in complex systems. It is not valid to say that the parents are "using" the child's problems to keep them together. One could just as well say that the child is using the parents' overprotectiveness to keep him from the perils of leaving home; or that without his problem, there would be no link between the mother and the father's mother; or that a valued older child keeps being drawn back home because of it; or that the problem child is the primary comforter of mother. Dell uses analogies to biology and other sciences: "DNA is not a governor of biological systems; biological functions are regulated by the total system of DNA and cytoplasm."[9]

Another Batesonian thinker, psychologist Bradford Keeney, proposes an ecosystemic epistemology.[10] This framework prohibits blaming the patient for his behavior or blaming his symptoms on etiological factors. Instead, Keeney suggests that symptoms must be seen as metaphoric communications about the ecology of the patient's relationship systems. Above all, he repeats the characteristic Batesonian warning that the therapist must never consider himself as an outside agent but rather as part of the therapeutic system, or "part of an ecosystem." This position offers an alternative to the formulations that place therapist versus patient in a power struggle or game that the patient is always trying to "win."

Dell raises one problem that epistemological purity poses for many of us: When we reject dualism, we reject most of the concepts we have been raised by, concepts that order our thinking—causality, purpose, objectivity, and the like. In fact, we cannot claim any accuracy at all for our attempts to make statements about the world, because we cannot set ourselves apart from that which we are describing. The reality "out there" is unknowable because it changes as we watch, and because our watching changes it.[11]

The end point of this thinking is, of course, rather radical. Statements cannot be made about one's own experience because we are spectators and participants at the same time, and our very grammar violates this unity. Lest we become totally mute, Bateson and those following him state that we may go on committing epistemological errors as long as we know we are committing them. Dell takes the comforting position that as long as we are aware that we are always operating in the context of a self-recursive network, it does not matter what epistemologies we use or what theories we adopt: "What matters is our awareness that both we and our chosen theory participate in a self-recursive way in the emerging, evolving flow of events. Bateson has aptly labeled this awareness 'wisdom.' "[12]

The Second Generation

The new theoretical positions, the systemic approaches linked with these positions, and the epistemological consciousness-raising that provides a context for both are beginning to have an impact on the family field, not just here but abroad. Some of the work in Europe was originally influenced by American models; Satir has heavily colonized Sweden, for instance, and Minuchin's structural model has taken hold in several countries. Italian psychiatrist Maurizio Andolfi's Institute of Family Studies in Rome offers an approach that blends the stress techniques of Minuchin with the quixotic, in-the-room binds of Whitaker. The pressure-box model that has resulted may become an alternative to the Milan approach, which otherwise seems to be sweeping Europe.

Other pioneers who have contributed to the international flowering of family therapy are figures such as John Byng-Hall, Rosemary Whiffen, and Robin Skynner in London; Philippe Caillé and Rolv Blakar in Oslo; Helm Stierlin in Heidelberg; Luc Kaufman in Lausanne; Yrjo Alanen in Helsinki; Geoffrey Goding in Melbourne; Siegi Hirsch in Paris; and many others who will have to forgive me for not mentioning them.

Even more important for Europeans, who are often more concept-oriented and less pragmatic than Americans, is the development of a body of theory for family therapy. For instance, my own observations suggest that more European clinicians interested in family therapy have read *Pragmatics of Human Communication* in the last three years than their counterparts in the United States have in the last ten. The proliferation of international conferences, in which Europeans are a very real presence, is also an indication of the increasingly important position they are taking.

In America, there is an even more interesting picture. Here and there, at universities and clinics, younger clinicians and researchers are asking about and struggling with a new kind of therapy and a new way of thinking about therapy. This new way isn't Bowenian; it isn't structural; it isn't strategic; and it isn't attached to any single therapist. It is in some sense systemic but it is not necessarily modeled on the work of the Milan Associates, even though most of the energy stream of the field seems to be emanating from that source. It is profoundly Batesonian, and yet Bateson does not explicitly address it.

What I believe we are witnessing is the emergence of a second generation of family therapists clearly distinguishable from the first. This second generation is not content with just a change in etiology. To say that "The family, not the individual, is the 'cause' of the problem" is not a real change for them. They are grasping the real meaning of Bateson's thought, and they are understanding what the strategic theorists in Palo Alto, the systemic practitioners in Milan, and other voices in the United States and Europe have been trying to convey: the need for a new epistemology. This new epistemology would influence profoundly not only the way one thought about therapy but also how one practiced it.

345

Let me address the issues that are being raised by this second generation of family and systems thinkers and therapists. I will highlight in particular the shift from a homeostatic to an evolutionary paradigm that Dell in particular has addressed, and the even more extraordinary implications of a circular epistemology. The two are in many ways entwined. Here are some of the ideas I believe will be the benchmarks of the new generation.

1. An emphasis on circular rather than linear thinking is, of course, basic. This applies very much to what used to be called diagnosis, or a guess as to what "caused" the particular illness or distress. A circular model takes one completely out of that frame. Bateson says that wisdom is awareness of how all the circuits in the system fit and are connected. This means not deciding that the family has "caused" the individual's problem, any more than the other way round. No one element takes precedence over or controls another. Brodey once described a case in exactly those terms, and with the economy of a poet:

"They never let me leave the house," the child states. "We tried but he always got lost," the parent states. And so the circle now spirals through time.[13]

2. We must change from the idea of causation to a concept that is nearer that of "fit." This concept is beautifully developed by Dell in "Beyond Homeostasis." Describing the difference, Dell says,

Without making reference to etiology or causation, fit simply posits that the behaviors occurring in the family system have a general complementarity; they fit together. *Causation,* on the other hand, is a specified type of interpretation of fit that considers the observed complementarity to have the form: A causes B. For instance, bad parents make their children sick.[14]

3. We must add positive to the usual negative interpretations of symptomatic behavior, not just as a strategy for change, but because doing so adds a layer of complexity that guards against linear thinking. Instead of assuming that a symptom is a kind of minus sign indicating a dysfunctional family, we may regard it instead as the one factor that keeps pushing the family toward a new and different state.

I first began to think of symptoms as harbingers of change when I was learning how to put together a "positive connotation." The work involved in this process amounts to finding an organizing principle for the presence of a problem at the family system level. In addition, one can often construe the symptom as a solution, however uncomfortable or destructive it may seem, to a dilemma faced by the family on its evolutionary path. This is not to say that a positive connotation is thereby "true," or that it is not just as linear as a negative one, but in this case, two "linears" can make a "circular," much as Yin plus Yang can make a round.

4. We would have to once more legitimize Time, banned for so long as a piece of useless psychotherapeutic baggage. Current thinking about living systems emphasizes that the processes of life are always irreversible. Nothing can ever go back or step in the same river twice. A shift in the entire gestalt of a system, in particular, can never be reversed, witness again the kaleidoscope.

5. We would have to accept the concept of unpredictability. It seems that major systems changes can never be foreseen, although in some cases probabilities can usefully be assessed. This means abandoning our emphasis on goals and giving more attention to chance. We will have to substitute a respect for what Elkaim calls the "singularity" of each family, with its universe of possible solutions, rather than imposing our own ideas of what a family ought to look like. Families can think up far more amazing solutions than we can.

6. We would have to abandon the idea of the therapist as a bullfighter, pushing and pulling the family to where he wanted it. If we are going to give up the notion of a Newtonian universe, with forces acting upon things, we are going to have to give up the notion of the therapist as a force, acting upon a client or a family. The careful way the Milan Associates position themselves in the therapeutic field and their emphasis on what they call "neutrality" express this idea, as does Bateson in his epistemological thinking.

7. We would have to give up the traditional idea of resistance, usually thought of as an oppositional trait residing in the client or family. The idea that the client is "resistant," or that the family

"homeostasis" causes it to resist, is totally linear. As Dell says, "the system does not 'resist,' it only behaves in accordance with its own coherence."[15]

Homeostasis is the counterpart in family therapy of the concept of resistance in individual therapy. It is more accurate to describe resistance as the place where the therapist and client or family intersect. Resistance is merely an artifact of that time and place. In addition, we can think positively about resistance, since it often generates the momentum needed to accomplish change. It is a fact that all strategic/systemic therapists use this judo technique in their work.

8. We must learn to favor instability over equilibrium. If Prigogine is right, living systems are permanent instabilities. A town, for instance, is always changing as flows of people and goods come in and out. Evolving systems might even be seen as going from a state of instability, to states characterized by relative rigidity, to new instabilities. This is the reverse of classical physics and the reverse of common sense. It also has some trying implications for therapists, let alone their clients, who may not take kindly to the message: Come in and I will get you out of this state of anxiety, nervousness, depression you are in and make you unstable again.

9. In "Beyond Homeostasis," Dell replaces homeostasis with a new concept, that of coherence. Coherence has to do with how pieces of a system fit together in a balance internal to itself and external to its environment. Homeostasis has a more rubbery, punchy feel to it than coherence, which is why I hate to give it up (and won't) but coherence is purer in the epistemological sense. I also like coherence because it has to do with the family in a field. The family has to fit with its environment, just as the individual has to fit within the family, or the separate organs have to fit together in a system that is the biological self. And all have to fit together in the ecology of the whole.

I would like to end here with an excerpt from the *Notebooks* of Paul Klee, because it so well expresses the position I myself have come to:

Formerly, artists depicted things that were to be seen on the earth, things people liked to see or would like to have seen. Now the relativity of visible

348

things is made clear, the belief expressed that the visible is only an isolated case taken from the universe, and that there are often more truths unseen than seen. . . .

A few examples: A man of antiquity, sailing a boat, quite content and enjoying the ingenious comfort of the contrivance. The ancients represent the scene accordingly. And now: What a modern man experiences as he walks across the deck of a steamer: 1. his own movement, 2. the movement of the ship which may be in the opposite direction, 3. the direction and velocity of the current, 4. the rotation of the earth, 5. its orbit, 6. the orbits of the moons and planets around it.

Result: an interplay of movements in the universe, at the centre "I" on the ship.

An apple tree in blossom, the roots, the rising sap, the trunk, a cross section with annual rings, the blossom, its structure, its sexual functions, the fruit, the core and seeds. An interplay of states of growth.

A sleeping man, the circulation of his blood, the measured breathing of the lungs, the delicate function of the kidney, in his head a world of dreams related to the powers of fate. An interplay of functions, united in rest.[16]

The epistemology of this passage is circular not linear. It is multifaceted and therefore systemic. It sets no part over any other part, so it is not dualistic. It does not chop the ecology to pieces, so it is holistic. It links the viewer of one period to the viewer of another, so it is recursive. And it is evolutionary because it highlights a shift toward greater complexity between these different times.

The above passage also represents a metaphor for the many-layered perspectives of this book. From the early 1950s, when the family movement began, to the year 1980, when its two presiding geniuses, Gregory Bateson and Milton Erickson, died, there has been the span of a generation. This Epilogue shall fittingly be dedicated to the new generation. After all, we are talking about an evolutionary paradigm.

Notes

Prologue: Behind the Looking Glass

1. Bateson, G., *Mind and Nature*. New York: E. P. Dutton, 1979.
2. Jackson, D. D., "The Question of Family Homeostasis," *The Psychiatric Quarterly Supplement* 31 (1957), 79–90.
3. Dell, P., and H. Goolishian, "Order Through Fluctuation," Speech at the Annual Scientific Meeting of the A. K. Rice Institute, Houston, Texas, 1979.
4. Bateson, *Mind and Nature*, p. 41.
5. Bateson, M. C., "Daddy, Can a Scientist Be Wise?" in Brockman, J. (ed.), *About Bateson*. New York: E. P. Dutton, 1977, p. 65.
6. Bateson, G., "The Birth of a Double Bind," in Berger, M. (ed.), *Beyond the Double Bind*. New York: Brunner/Mazel, 1978, p. 53.
7. Bateson, ibid., p. 45.
8. Hoffman, L., "Deviation-Amplifying Processes in Natural Groups," in Haley, J. (ed.), *Changing Families*. New York, Grune and Stratton, 1971.
9. Speer, A., "Family Systems: Morphostasis and Morphogenesis," *Family Process* 9 (1970), 259–278.
10. Dell, P., "Researching the Family Theories of Schizophrenia: An Exercise in Epistemological Confusion," *Family Process* 19 (1980), 321–335.

Chapter 1   Early Research on Family Groups

1. Guerin offers a history of developments and figures in the field; see Guerin, P., *Family Therapy: Theory and Practice*, New York: Gardner Press, 1978. For a clear presentation of the major shift in ideas represented by this group, see "A Review of the Family Therapy Field,"

in Haley, J., *Changing Families,* New York: Grune and Stratton, 1971. And for an excellent critique of eaarly studies on the family and schizophrenia, see Paul Dell, "Researching the Family Theories of Schizophrenia: An Exercise in Epistemological Confusion," *Family Process* 19 (1980), 321–335.

2. Watzlawick, P., D. Jackson, and J. Beavin, *Pragmatics of Human Communication.* New York: W. W. Norton, 1967.

3. Jackson, D. D., "The Question of Family Homeostasis," *Psychiatric Quarterly Supplement* 31 (1957), 79–90.

4. Haley, J., *Strategies of Psychotherapy.* New York: Grune and Stratton, 1964, p. 189.

5. Haley, J., "Research on Family Patterns: An Instrument Measurement," *Family Process* 3 (1964), 41–65.

6. Haley, J., and L. Hoffman, *Techniques of Family Therapy.* New York: Basic Books, 1968, p. 227.

7. Bateson, G., D. Jackson, J. Haley, and J. Weakland, "Toward a Theory of Schizophrenia," *Behavioral Science* 1 (1956), 251–254.

8. Haley, J., "The Family of the Schizophrenic: A Model System," *Journal of Nervous and Mental Disease* 129 (1959), 357–374.

9. Jackson, D. D., *Therapy, Communication and Change* and *Communication, Family and Marriage.* Palo Alto, Calif.: Science and Behavior Books, 1967.

10. Weakland, J., and D. D. Jackson, "Patient and Therapist Observations on the Circumstances of a Schizophrenic Episode," *A.M.A. Archives of Neurology and Psychiatry* 79 (1958), 554–574. Jackson, D. D., and I. Yalom, "Conjoint Family Therapy as an Aid to Intensive Psychotherapy," in Burton, A. (ed.), *Modern Psychotherapeutic Practice.* Palo Alto, Calif.: Science and Behavior Books, 1965, pp. 80–98. Weakland, J., and W. Fry, "Letters of Mothers of Schizophrenics," *American Journal of Psychiatry* 32 (1962), 604–623.

11. Reprinted in Sluzki, C., and D. Ransom (eds.), *Double Bind: The Foundation of the Communicational Approach to the Family.* New York: Grune and Stratton, 1976.

12. Sluzki, C., and D. Ransom (eds.), *Double Bind: The Foundation of the Communicational Approach to the Family.* New York: Grune and Stratton, 1976.

13. Ibid., pp. 23–37.

14. Bateson, G., D. Jackson, J. Haley, and J. Weakland, "A Note on the Double Bind— 1962," *Family Process* 2 (1963), 154–161.

15. Watzlawick, P., "A Review of the Double Bind Theory," *Family Process* 2 (1963), 132–153.

16. Weakland, J., "The Double Bind Theory by Self-Reflexive Hindsight," *Family Process* 13 (1974), 269–277. Bateson, G., "The Birth of a Matrix or Double Bind and Epistemology," in Berger, M. (ed.), *Beyond the Double Bind.* New York: Brunner/Mazel, 1977.

17. Bateson, G., *Steps to an Ecology of Mind.* New York: Ballantine Books, 1971, p. 241.

18. Neumann, J. von, and O. Morgenstern, *Theory of Games and Economic Behavior.* Princeton, N.J.: Princeton University Press, 1947.

19. Bateson, *Steps to an Ecology of Mind,* p. 240.

20. Haley, J., "Development of a Theory," in Sluzki, C., and D. Ransom (eds.), *Double Bind.*

21. Bateson, *Steps to an Ecology of Mind,* p. 236.

22. Paul Dell. Personal communication.

23. Haley, J., "Development of a Theory," in Sluzki, C., and D. Ransom (eds.), *Double Bind,* p. 78.

24. Haley, J., *Strategies of Psychotherapy.* New York: Grune and Stratton, 1963.

25. Lennard, H., and A. Bernstein, *Patterns in Human Interaction.* San Francisco, Calif.: Jossey-Bass, 1970, p. 134.

26. Whitehead, A. N., and B. Russell, *Principia Mathematica.* Cambridge: Cambridge University Press, 1910.

27. Riskin, J., and E. Faunce, "An Evaluative Review of Family Interaction and Research," *Family Process* 11 (1972), 365–455.

28. Bowen, M., *Family Therapy in Clinical Practice.* New York: Jason Aronson, 1978.

29. Bowen, M., "The Use of Family Theory in Clinical Practice," *Clinical Psychiatry* 7 (1966), 345–374.

30. Wynne, L. C., "The Study of Intrafamilial Splits and Alignments in Exploratory

NOTES

Family Therapy," in Ackerman, N. (ed.), *Exploring the Base for Family Therapy.* New York: Family Service Association of America, 1961, pp. 95–115.

31. Ibid.

32. Wynne, L. C., et al., "Pseudo-Mutuality in the Family Relations of Schizophrenics," *Archives of General Psychiatry* 9 (1963), 161–206.

33. Ibid., p. 206.

34. Laing, R. D., and A. Esterson, *Sanity, Madness, and the Family.* New York: Basic Books, 1971.

Chapter 2   *The Dynamics of Social Fields*

1. Bateson, G., *Steps to an Ecology of Mind.* New York: Ballantine Books, 1972, p. 74.

2. Bateson, G., *Naven.* Stanford, Calif.: Stanford University Press, 1958 (rev. ed.).

3. Bateson, *Steps to an Ecology of Mind,* p. 77.

4. Bateson, *Naven,* p. 175.

5. Boulding, K., *Conflict and Defense.* New York: Harper and Row, 1963.

6. Bateson, *Steps to an Ecology of Mind.,* pp. 107–112.

7. Bateson, *Naven,* p. 194.

8. Barth, F., "Segmentary Opposition and the Theory of Games: A Study of Pathan Organization," *Journal of the Royal Anthropological Institute* 89 (1959), 5–21.

9. Bateson, *Steps to an Ecology of Mind,* p. 110.

10. Bateson, *Naven,* p. 289.

11. Ashby, W. R., *Design for a Brain.* New York: Wiley, 1952.

12. Nett, R., "Conformity-Deviation and the Social Control Concept," in Buckley, W. (ed.), *Modern Systems Research for the Behavioral Scientist.* Chicago: Aldine, 1968.

Chapter 3   *The Second Cybernetics*

1. Maruyama, M., "The Second Cybernetics: Deviation-Amplifying Mutual Causal Processes," in Buckley, W. (ed.), *Modern Systems Research for the Behavioral Scientist.* Chicago: Aldine, 1968, p. 304.

2. Wiener, N., *The Human Use of Human Beings.* New York: Anchor Books, 1954, p. 25.

3. Hardin, G., "The Cybernetics of Competition: A Biologist's View of Society," in Shepard, P., and D. McKinley (eds.), *The Subversive Science: Essays Toward an Ecology of Man.* Boston: Houghton Mifflin, 1969, pp. 275–295.

4. Schroedinger, E. *What Is Life?* Cambridge: Cambridge University Press, 1945.

5. Buckley, W., "Society as a Complex Adaptive System," in Buckley, W. (ed.), *Modern Systems Research for the Behavioral Scientist.* Chicago: Aldine, 1968, p. 491.

6. Reiss, D., "The Working Family: A Researcher's View of Health in the Household." Distinguished Psychiatrist Lecture, Annual Meeting, American Psychiatric Association, San Francisco, Calif., 1980.

7. Buckley, "Society as a Complex Adaptive System," p. 500.

8. Maruyama, "The Second Cybernetics," p. 312.

9. Minuchin, S., and A. Barcai, "Therapeutically Induced Family Crisis," in Masserman, J. H. (ed.), *Science and Psychoanalysis.* New York: Grune and Stratton, 1969.

10. Bateson, G., *Naven.* Stanford, Calif.: Stanford University Press, 1958 (rev. ed.), p. 197.

11. Simon, H., "Comments on the Theory of Organization," *American Political Science Review* 46 (1952), 1130–1139.

12. Ruesch, J., and G. Bateson, *Communication: The Social Matrix of Society.* New York: W. W. Norton, 1951, p. 287.

13. Ibid., p. 289.

14. Merton, R., *On Theoretical Sociology.* Glencoe, Ill.: Free Press, 1967, p. 115.

15. Haley, J., *Strategies of Psychotherapy.* New York: Grune and Stratton, 1963, Ch. 1.

16. Wilkins, L. T., "A Behavioral Theory of Drug Taking," in Buckley, W. (ed.), *Modern Systems Research for the Behavioral Scientist.* Chicago: Aldine, 1968, pp. 421–427.

17. Vogel, E. F., and N. W. Bell, "The Emotionally Disturbed Child as the Family Scapegoat," in Bell, N. W., and Ezra F. Vogel (eds.), *The Family.* Glencoe, Ill.: Free Press, 1960, pp. 382–397.

18. Dentler, R. A., and K. T. Erikson, "The Functions of Deviance in Groups," *Social Problems* 7 (1959), 98–107.

19. Daniels, A., "Interaction Through Social Typing: The Development of the Scapegoat in Sensitivity Training Sessions." Mimeographed manuscript.

20. Haley, J., and L. Hoffman, *Techniques of Family Therapy.* New York: Basic Books, 1967, p. 205.

21. Haley, J., "Toward a Theory of Pathological Systems," in Zuk, G. H., and I. Boszormenyi-Nagy (eds.), *Family Therapy and Disturbed Families.* Palo Alto, Calif.: Science and Behavior Books, 1969, pp. 11–27.

22. Lederer, W. J., and D. D. Jackson, *The Mirages of Marriage.* New York: W. W. Norton, 1968, pp. 161–173.

23. Jackson, D. D., "The Role of the Individual." Address to Conference on Mental Health and the Idea of Mankind, Annual Meeting, Council for the Study of Mankind, Chicago, 1964.

24. Taylor, W., "Research on Family Interaction I: A Methodological Note," *Family Process* 9 (1970), 221–232.

25. Bales, R., "In Conference," in Etzioni, A. (ed.), *Readings on Modern Organizations.* Englewood Cliffs, N.J.: Prentice-Hall, 1969, p. 150.

26. Reiss, "The Working Family."

Chapter 4   Typologies of Family Structure

1. Singer, M. T., and L. C. Wynne, "Differentiating Characteristics of Parents of Childhood Schizophrenics, Childhood Neurotics, and Young Adult Schizophrenics," *American Journal of Psychiatry* 120 (1963), 234–243.

2. Jackson, D. D., "Family Interaction, Family Homeostasis and Some Implications for Conjoint Family Therapy," in Masserman, J. (ed.), *Individual and Familial Dynamics.* New York: Grune and Stratton, 1959.

3. Jackson, D. D., *The Mirages of Marriage.* New York: W. W. Norton, 1968.

4. Watzlawick, W., D. D. Jackson, and J. Beavin, *Pragmatics of Human Communication.* New York: W. W. Norton, 1967, p. 110.

5. Ibid., pp. 110–117.

6. Ibid., pp. 107–108.

7. Minuchin, S. et al., *Families of the Slums.* New York: Basic Books, 1969.

8. Ibid., p. 352.

9. Ibid., p. 358.

10. Minuchin, S., *Families and Family Therapy.* Cambridge, Mass.: Harvard University Press, 1974.

11 Ibid., pp. 248–249.

12. Ashby, W. R., *Design for a Brain.* London: Chapman and Hall, Science and Behavior Books, 1969, p. 79.

13. Ibid., p. 154.

14. Ibid., p. 155.

15. Ibid., p. 207.

16. Ibid., p. 208.
17. Ibid., p. 210.
18. Bowen, M., "The Use of Family Theory in Clinical Practice," *Comprehensive Psychiatry* 7 (1966), 345–374.
19. Stierlin, Helm, *Separating Parents and Adolescents.* New York: Quadrangle/New York Times Book Co., 1972.
20. Thomas, Lewis, *Lives of a Cell.* New York: Bantam Books, 1974, pp. 62–63.
21. Minuchin et al., *Families of the Slums,* p. 355.
22. See Aponte, H., "Underorganization in the Poor Family," in Guerin, P., *Family Therapy: Theory and Practice,* New York: Gardner Press, 1976, for a more general discussion of this type of family.

Chapter 5   The Concept of Family Paradigms

1. Dell, P., "Researching the Family Theories of Schizophrenia," *Family Process* 19 (1980), 321–335.
2. Reiss, D., "Varieties of Consensual Experience," *Family Process* 10 (1971), 1–35.
3. Ibid., p. 6.
4. Ibid., p. 4.
5. Hess, R., and G. Handel, *Family Worlds.* Chicago: University of Chicago Press, 1959.
6. Wertheim, E., "Family Unit Therapy and the Science and Typology of Family Systems," *Family Process* 12 (1973), 361–376.
7. Beavers, W. R., "A Systems Model of Family for Family Therapists." Unpublished manuscript. See also Beavers, W. R., *Psychotherapy and Growth,* New York: Brunner/Mazel, 1977.
8. Haley, J., *Leaving Home.* New York: McGraw-Hill, 1980.
9. Kantor, D., and W. Lehr, *Inside the Family.* San Francisco, Calif.: Jossey-Bass, 1975.
10. Reiss, D., "The Working Family: A Researcher's View of Health in the Household." Distinguished Psychiatrist Lecture, Annual Meeting, American Psychiatric Association, San Francisco, Calif., 1980.
11. Ibid., p. 32.
12. Fivaz, R., "Une Evolution Vers l'Impasse?" *Polyrama* (Ecole Polytechnique Fédérale de Lausanne), January 1980, no. 45, pp. 9–11.

Chapter 6   The Pathological Triad

1. Weakland, J., "The Double Bind Hypothesis of Schizophrenia and Three-Party Interaction," in Sluzki, C., and D. Ransom (eds.), *Double Bind: The Foundation of the Communicational Approach to the Family.* New York: Grune and Stratton, 1976.
2. Ibid., p. 29.
3. Wynne, L. C., and Singer, M. T., "Thought Disorder and Family Relations of Schizophrenics: I. A Research Strategy. II. A Classification of Forms of Thinking," *Archives of General Psychiatry* 9 (1963), 191–206.
4. Lidz, T., A. R. Cornelison, S. Fleck, and D. Terry, "Schism and Skew in the Families of Schizophrenics," in Bell, N. W., and E. F. Vogel (eds.), *A Modern Introduction to the Family.* Glencoe, Ill.: Free Press, 1960, pp. 595–607.
5. Stanton, A., and M. Schwartz, *The Mental Hospital.* New York: Basic Books, 1954.

6. Haley, J., "The Family of the Schizophrenic: A Model System," *Journal of Nervous and Mental Disease,* 129 (1959), 357–374.

7. Haley, J., "Development of a Theory," in Sluzki, C., and D. Ransom (eds.), *Double Bind.*

8. Haley, J., "Toward a Theory of Pathological Systems," in Watzlawick, P., and J. Weakland (eds.), *The Interactional View.* New York: W. W. Norton, 1977.

9. Ibid., p. 37.

10. Caplow, T., *Two Against One.* Englewood Cliffs, N.J.: Prentice-Hall, 1968.

11. Haley, "Pathological Systems," p. 38.

12. Haley, "Pathological Systems," p. 41.

13. Davis, J., "Structural Balance, Mechanical Solidarity, and Interpersonal Relations," *American Journal of Sociology* 68 (1963), 444–462.

14. Boulding, K., *Conflict and Defense: A General Theory.* New York: Harper and Row, 1963, p. 83.

15. Caplow, *Two Against One,* p. 78.

16. Haley, "Development of a Theory," p. 81.

17. Ruesch, J., and G. Bateson, *Communication: The Social Matrix of Psychiatry.* New York: W. W. Norton, 1951, p. 193.

18. Ibid., p. 196.

19. Haley, J., *Strategies of Psychotherapy.* New York: Grune and Stratton, 1963, Ch. 5.

20. Haley, "Pathological Systems," pp. 42–44.

21. Ibid., p. 44.

22. Haley, J., *The Power Tactics of Jesus Christ.* New York: Grossman, 1969.

23. Wynne, L., "Intrafamilial Splits and Alignments in Exploratory Family Therapy," in Ackerman, N., et al. (eds.), *Exploring the Base for Family Therapy.* New York: Family Service Association of America, 1961.

24. Haley, "Pathological Systems," p. 40.

25. Caplow, *Two Against One,* p. 106.

26. Haley, "Pathological Systems," p. 39.

27. Hsu, F., "Kinship and Ways of Life: An Explanation," in *Psychological Anthropology: Approaches to Culture and Personality.* Homewood, Ill.: Richard D. Irwin, 1961.

28. Ross, A., "The Substructure of Power and Authority," in Barash, M., and A. Scourby (eds.), *Marriage and the Family.* New York: Random House, 1970, p. 86.

29. LeVine, R., "Intergenerational Tensions and Extended Family Structures in Africa," in Barash and Scourby, *Marriage and the Family,* pp. 144–164.

Chapter 7   The Rules of Congruence for Triads

1. Cartwright, C. and F. Harary, "Structural Balance: A Generalization of Heider's Theory," *Psychological Review* 63 (1956), 277–293.

2. Taylor, W., "Research on Family Interaction: Static and Dynamic Models," *Family Process* 9, 1970, 221–232.

3. Caplow, T., *Two Against One: Coalitions in Triads.* Englewood Cliffs, N.J.: Prentice-Hall, 1968, p. 59.

4. Davis, J., "Clustering and Structural Balance in Graphs," *Human Relations* 20 (1967), 181–187.

5. Wolff, Kurt H., *The Sociology of Georg Simmel.* New York: Free Press, Collier-Macmillan, 1950, p. 141.

6. Coser, L., *The Functions of Social Conflict.* New York: Free Press–Collier, 1969, Ch. 4.

7. Davis, "Clustering," p. 187.

8. Apple, D., "The Social Structure of Grandparenthood," *American Anthropologist* 53 (1956), 656–663.

9. Bott, E., *Family and Social Network.* London: Tavistock Publications, 1957.

NOTES

10. Flomenhaft, K., and D.M. Kaplan, "Clinical Significance of Current Kinship Relationships," *Social Work,* Jan. 1968, 68–74.
11. Taylor, H. F., *Balance in Small Groups.* New York: Van Nostrand–Reinhold, 1970.

Chapter 8   Triads and the Management of Conflict

1. Freilich, M., "The Natural Triad in Kinship and Complex Systems," *American Sociological Review* 29 (1964), 529–540.
2. Stanton, A., and M. Schwartz, *The Mental Hospital.* New York: Basic Books, 1964.
3. Ibid., p. 345.
4. Ibid., p. 363.
5. Minuchin, S., B.L. Rosman, and L. Baker, *Psychosomatic Families.* Cambridge, Mass.: Harvard University Press, 1978.

Chapter 9   The Simple Bind and Discontinuous Change

1. Bateson, G., *Mind and Nature.* New York: E. P. Dutton, 1978, p. 194.
2. Dell, P., and H. Goolishian, "Order Through Fluctuation: An Evolutionary Epistemology for Human Systems." Presented at the Annual Scientific Meeting of the A. K. Rice Institute, Houston, Texas, 1979.
3. Bateson, G., *Mind and Nature,* pp. 47–48.
4. Dell and Goolishian, "Order Through Fluctuation," p. 10.
5. Platt, J., "Hierarchical Growth," *Bulletin of Atomic Scientists* (November 1970), 2–4, 14–16.
6. Ashby, W. R., *Design for a Brain.* London: Chapman and Hall, Science Paperbacks, 1960.
7. Bateson, *Mind and Nature,* p. 98.
8. Erikson, E., *Childhood and Society.* New York: W. W. Norton, 1963.
9. Lindemann, Eric, "Symptomatology and Management of Acute Grief," in Parad, H. J., and G. Caplan (eds.), *Crisis Intervention: Selected Readings.* New York: Family Service Association of America, 1969, p. 18.
10. Rapoport, L., "The State of Crisis: Some Theoretical Considerations," in Parad and Caplan, *Crisis Intervention,* p. 23.
11. Hill, Reuben, *Families Under Stress.* New York: Harper and Bros., 1949.
12. Solomon, M., "A Developmental Premise for Family Therapy," *Family Process* 12 (1973), 179–188.
13. Eliot, Thomas D., "Handling Family Strains and Shocks," in Becker, Howard, and Reuben Hill (eds.), *Family, Marriage and Parenthood.* Boston: Heath and Co., 1955.
14. LeMasters, E. E., "Parenthood as Crisis," in Parad and Caplan, *Crisis Intervention,* pp. 111–117.
15. Holmes, T. H., and R. H. Rahe, "The Social Readjustive Rating Scale," *Journal of Psychosomatic Research* 11 (April 1967), 213–218.
16. Ibid., p. 215.
17. Haley, J., "The Family Life Cycle," in *Uncommon Therapy: The Psychiatric Techniques of Milton Erickson, M.D.* New York: W. W. Norton, 1973.
18. Ashby, *Design for a Brain.*

19. Ibid., pp. 87–89.
20. Gramsci, Antonio, *Prison Notebooks: Selections,* trans. Quintin Hoare and Geoffrey N. Smith. New York: International Publishing Co., 1971, p. 71.
21. Reiss, D., "The Working Family: A Researcher's View of Health in the Household," Distinguished Psychiatrist Lecture, Annual Meeting of the American Psychiatric Association, San Francsco, 1980.
22. Rabkin, R., "A Critique of the Clinical Use of the Double Bind," in Sluzki, C., and D. Ransom (eds.), *Double Bind: The Communicational Approach to the Family.* New York: Grune and Stratton, 1976, pp. 287–306.
23. Sluzki, C., et al., "Transactional Disqualification: Research on the Double Bind," in Watzlawick, P., and J. Weakland (eds.), *The Interactional View.* New York: W. W. Norton, 1977, p. 217.
24. Rabkin, "Critique of the Double Bind," in Sluzki and Ransom, *Double Bind,* p. 297.
25. Bateson, G. *Steps to an Ecology of Mind.* New York: Ballantine Books, 1972, p. 277.
26. Wynne, L., "On the Anguish and Creative Passions of Not Escaping the Double Bind," in Sluzki and Ransom, *Double Bind,* pp. 243–250.

Chapter 10   *The Thing in the Bushes*

1. Bateson, G., *Mind and Nature.* New York: Holt, Rinehart, and Winston, 1979, p. 103.
2. Ravich, R., *Predictable Pairing.* New York: Peter H. Wyden, 1974, p. 269.
3. Wild, C., L. Shapiro, L. Goldenberg, "Transactional Disturbances in Families of Male Schizophrenics," *Family Process* 14 (1975), 131–160.
4. Lidz, T., et al., "The Intrafamilial Environment of Schizophrenic Patients: II. Marital Schism and Marital Skew," *American Journal of Psychiatry* 114 (1957): 241–248.
5. Lederer, W., and D. D. Jackson, *Mirages of Marriage.* New York: W. W. Norton, 1968.
6. Ravich, *Predictable Pairing,* Ch. 7.
7. Steinglass, P., I. D. Davis, and D. Berenson, "Observations of Conjointly Hospitalized 'Alcoholic Couples' During Sobriety and Intoxication," *Family Process* 16 (1977), 1–16.
8. Berman, E., C. Pittman, and V. Ratliffe, "A Relational Approach to Spouse Abuse." Unpublished manuscript.
9. Sampson, H., S. L. Messinger, and R. D. Towne, "Family Processes and Becoming a Mental Patient," *American Journal of Sociology* 68 (1962), 88–96.
10. Sluzki, C. "Marital Therapy from a Systems Therapy Perspective," in Paolino, T. J., and B. S. McCrady (eds.), *Marriage and Marital Therapy.* New York: Brunner/Mazel, 1978; Papp, P., "The Use of Fantasy in a couples Group," in Andolfi, M., and I. Zwerling (eds.), *Dimensions of Family Therapy.* New York: Guilford Press, 1980; Paul, N. and B. Paul, *A Marital Puzzle.* New York: W. W. Norton, 1975; Sager, C., *Marriage Contracts and Couple Therapy.* New York: Brunner/Mazel, 976.
11. Erikson, Kai T., *Everything in Its Path.* New York: Harper & Row, 1978.
12. Chapple, E. D., *Culture and Biological Man.* New York: Holt, Rinehart, and Winston, 1970.
13. Ibid., p. 48.
14. Raush, H., et al., *Communication, Conflict and Marriage.* San Francisco, Calif.: Jossey-Bass, 1974.

NOTES

Chapter 11 Breaking the Symptomatic Cycle

1. Watzlawick, P., J. Weakland, Jr., and R. Fisch, *Change: Problem Formation and Problem Resolution.* New York: W. W. Norton, 1974, p. 9.
2. Dell, P., and H. Goolishian, "Order Through Fluctuation: An Evolutionary Epistemology for Human Systems." Presented at the Annual Scientific Meeting of the A. K. Rice Institute, Houston, Texas, 1979.
3. Minuchin, S., *Psychosomatic Families.* Cambridge, Mass.: Harvard University Press, 1978.
4. Ibid., pp. 165–66.
5. Haley, J., and L. Hoffman, *Techniques of Family Therapy.* New York: Basic Books, 1967, p. 6.
6. Ibid., p. 63.
7. Haley, J., "Strategic Therapy when a Child is Presented as the Problem," *Journal of the American Academy of Child Psychiatry* 12 (1973), 64–74.

Chapter 12 Family Therapy and the Great Originals

1. Madanes, C., and J. Haley, "Dimensions of Family Therapy," *Journal of Nervous and Mental Disease* 165 (1977), 88–98.
2. Satir, V., *Conjoint Family Therapy.* Palo Alto, Calif.: Science and Behavior Books, 1964.
3. Haley, J., and L. Hoffman, *Techniques of Family Therapy.* New York: Basic Books, 1967. Ch. 2.
4. Ackerman, N. "The Family as a Social and Emotional Unit," *Bulletin of the Kansas Mental Hygiene Society,* October, 1937.
5. Ackerman, N. and P. Franklin, "Family Dynamics and the Reversibility of Delusional Formation: A Case Study in Family Therapy," in Boszormenyi-Nagy, I. and J. Framo (eds.), *Intensive Family Therapy.* New York: Harper and Row, 1965, Ch. 6.
6. Ackerman, N., *Treating the Troubled Family.* New York: Basic Books, 1966.
7. Whitaker, C., "Power Politics of Family Psychotherapy." Presented at the American Group Psychotherapy Association Conference, February 1973.
8. Ibid.
9. Whitaker, C., "Psychotherapy of the Absurd," *Family Process* 14 (1975), 1–16.
10. Napier, A. Y., with Carl Whitaker, *The Family Crucible.* New York: Harper and Row, 1978.
11. Whitaker, C., "Psychotherapy of the Absurd," p. 11.
12. Haley, J., *Uncommon Therapy: The Psychiatric Techniques of Milton H. Erickson, M.D.* New York: W. W. Norton, 1973.
13. Erickson, M., in Haley, J. (ed.), *Advanced Techniques of Hypnosis and Therapy.* New York: Grune and Stratton, 1967, pp. 395–397.
14. Ibid., p. 396.
15. Ibid., pp. 393–395.
16. Grinder, J., et al., *Patterns of the Hypnotic Techniques of Milton H. Erickson, M.D.* Cupertino, Calif.: Meta Publications, 1977.
17. Haley and Hoffman, *Techniques of Family Therapy,* Ch. 3.
18. Weakland, J., and D. D. Jackson, "Patient and Therapist Observations on the Circumstances of a Schizophrenic Episode," *A.M.A. Archives of Neurology and Psychiatry* 79 (1958), 554–574.
19. Bateson, G., D. D. Jackson, J. Haley, and J. Weakland, "Toward a Theory of Schizophrenia," *Behavioral Science* 1 (1956), 251–264.

20. Watzlawick, P., J. Beavin, and D. D. Jackson, *Pragmatics of Human Communication.* New York: W. W. Norton, 1967, pp. 243–244.

21. Ibid., pp. 74–75.

22. Jackson, D. D., and I. Yalom, "Conjoint Family Therapy as an Aid to Intensive Psychotherapy," in Jackson, D. D. (ed.), *Therapy, Communication and Change.* Palo Alto, Calif.: Science and Behavior Books, 1968.

23. Haley and Hoffman, *Techniques of Family Therapy,* p. 180.

24. Ibid., p. 174.

25. Ibid., p. 177.

Chapter 13 Historically Oriented Approaches to Family Therapy

1. Bowen, M., *Family Therapy in Clinical Practice.* New York: Jason Aronson, 1978.

2. Anonymous, "Towards the Differentiation of a Self in One's Own Family," in Framo, J. (ed.), *Family Interaction.* New York: Springer Publishing Co., 1972.

3. Guerin, P., and K. Guerin, "Theoretical Aspects and Clinical Relevance or the Multi-Generational Model of Family Therapy," in Guerin, P. (ed.), *Family Therapy: Theory and Practice.* New York: Gardner Press, 1976.

4. Carter, E., and M. Orfanides, "Family Therapy With One Person and the Therapist's Own Family," in Guerin (ed.), *Family Therapy,* p. 207.

5. Guerin (ed.), *Family Therapy,* p. 104.

6. Paul, N., "The Role of Mourning and Empathy in Conjoint Marital Therapy," in Zuk, G., and I. Boszormenyi-Nagy (eds.), *Family Therapy and Disturbed Families.* Palo Alto, Calif.: Science and Behavior Books, 1969.

7. Framo, J., "Family of Origin as Therapeutic Resource for Adults in Marital and Family Therapy," *Family Process* 15 (1976), 193–210.

8. Papp, P., "Family Sculpting in Preventive Work with 'Well' Families," *Family Process* 12 (1973), 197–212.

9. Boszormenyi-Nagy, I., and G. Sparks, *Invisible Loyalties.* New York: Harper and Row, 1973.

10. Ibid., p. 6.

11. Ibid., pp. 47–48.

Chapter 14 Ecological, Structural, and Strategic Approaches

1. Minuchin, S., et al., *Families of the Slums.* New York: Basic Books, 1968.

2. Rabkin, R., *Inner and Outer Space.* New York: W. W. Norton, 1970.

3. Auerswald, E. H., "Interdisciplinary versus Ecological Approach," *Family Process* 7 (1968), 205–215.

4. Hoffman, L., and L. Long, "A Systems Dilemma," *Family Process* 8 (1969), 211–234; Hetrick, E., and L. Hoffman, "The Broome Street Network," in Sanders, D. S., J. Fischer, and O. Kurken (eds.), *Fundamentals of Social Work Practice.* North Scituate, Mass.: Duxbury Press, 1981.

NOTES

5. Langsley, D., and D. Kaplan, *Treating Families in Crisis.* New York: Grune and Stratton, 1968.

6. Haley, J., and L. Hoffman, *Techniques of Family Therapy.* New York: Basic Books, 1967, Ch. 5.

7. Speck, R., and C. Attneave, *Family Networks.* New York: Vintage Books, 1974.

8. Aponte, H. "The Family-School Interview: An Eco-Structural Approach," *Family Process* 15 (1976), 303–311. Aponte, H. "Under-organization in the Poor Family," in Guerin, P. (ed.), *Family Therapy: Theory and Practice.* New York: Gardner Press, 1976.

9. Minuchin, S., *Families and Family Therapy.* Cambridge, Mass.: Harvard University Press, 1974.

10. Minuchin, S., *Psychosomatic Families.* Cambridge, Mass.: Harvard University Press, 1978.

11. Ibid., Ch. 5.

12. Aponte, H., and L. Hoffman, "The Open Door: A Structural Approach to a Family with an Anorectic Child," *Family Process* 12 (1973), 1–44.

13. Malcolm, Janet, "A Reporter at Large: The One-Way Mirror," *The New Yorker* (May 1978,) 40.

14. Weakland, J., R. Risch, P. Watzlawick, and A. Bodin, "Brief Therapy: Focused Problem Resolution," *Family Process* 13 (1974), 141–168. Watzlawick, P., J. Weakland, and R. Fisch, *Change: The Principles of Problem Formation and Problem Resolution.* New York: W. W. Norton, 1974.

15. Haley, J., *Uncommon Therapy: The Psychiatric Techniques of Milton H. Erickson, M.D.* New York: W. W. Norton, 1973.

16. Haley, J., *Problem-Solving Therapy.* San Francisco, Calif.: Jossey-Bass, 1977.

17. Haley, J., *Leaving Home.* New York: McGraw-Hill, 1980.

Chapter 15   The Systemic Model

1. Selvini Palazzoli, M., *Self-Starvation.* New York: Jason Aronson, 1978, p. 19.

2. Selvini Palazzoli, M., et al., *Paradox and Counterparadox.* New York: Jason Aronson, 1978, p. 8.

3. Selvini Palazzoli, M., "Why a Long Interval Between Sessions," in Andolfi, M., and I. Zwerling (eds.), *Dimensions of Family Therapy.* New York: Guilford Press, 1980.

4. Selvini Palazzoli et al., *Paradox and Counterparadox,* p. 55.

5. Selvini Palazzoli, *Self-Starvation,* p. 208.

6. Selvini Palazzoli et al., *Paradox and Counterparadox,* p. 56.

7. Madanes, C., "Protection, Paradox and Pretending," *Family Process* 19 (1980), 73–85.

8. Selvini Palazzoli, M., et al., "Hypothesizing—Circularity—Neutrality," *Family Process* 19 (1980), 3–12.

9. Selvini Palazzoli, *Self-Starvation,* p. 231.

10. Selvini Palazzoli, M., et al., "The Problem of the Referring Person," *Journal of Marital and Family Therapy,* 6 (1980), 3–9.

11. Ibid., p. 4.

12. Selvini Palazzoli et al., "Hypothesizing—Circularity—Neutrality," pp. 3–12.

13. Ibid.

Chapter 16   Theories About Therapeutic Binds

1. Watzlawick, P., D. Jackson, and J. Beavin, *Pragmatics of Human Communication.* New York: W. W. Norton, 1967, Ch. 7.

2. Stanton, M. D., "Strategic Approaches to Family Therapy," in Gurman, A., and D. Kniskern (eds.), *Handbook of Family Therapy.* New York: Brunner/Mazel, 1981.

3 Bateson, G., *Mind and Nature.* New York: E. P. Dutton, 1979, p. 62.

4. Haley, J., *Strategies of Psychotherapy.* New York: Grune and Stratton, 1963, p. 159.

5. Hoffman, L., " 'Enmeshment' and the Too Richly Cross-Joined System," *Family Process* 14 (1975), 457–468.

6. Selvini Palazzoli, M. "Why a Long Interval Between Sessions," in Andolfi, M., and I. Zwerling (eds.), *Dimensions of Family Therapy.* New York: Brunner/Mazel, 1980.

7. Ashby, *Design for a Brain,* p. 207.

8. Dell, P., "Beyond Homeostasis," *Family Process* (forthcoming).

9. Ibid.

Chapter 17   Issues on the Cutting Edge

1. Papp, P., "The Family That Had All the Answers," in Papp, P., (ed.), *Family Therapy: Full Length Case Studies.* New York: Gardner Press, 1977, Ch. 9.

2. Miller, S. J., "The Social Base of Sales Behavior," *Social Problems* 12 (1964), 15–24.

3. Papp, "The Family That Had All the Answers," p. 152.

Epilogue   Toward a New Epistemology

1. Bateson, G., "Afterword," in Brockman, J., (ed.), *About Bateson.* New York: E. P. Dutton, 1977, p. 242.

2. Salomon, M., "Entretien avec Prigogine," *Prospective et Santé* 13 (June 1980), 41–58.

3. Prigogine, I., "L'ordre a partir du chaos," *Prospective et Santé* 13 (June 1980), 29–39.

4. Elkaim, M., "Debat entre Ilya Prigogine, ses collaborateurs, Felix Guattari et Mony Elkaim," *Cahiers Critiques de Therapie Familiale et de Pratiques de Reseaux* 3 (Paris: Editions Gamma, 1980) 6–17.

5. Elkaim, M., "Non-Equilibrium, Chance and Change in Family Therapy," to be published in "Models of Therapeutic Intervention with Families: A Representative World View," special issue of the *Journal of Marital and Family Therapy* (summer 1981).

6. Prigogine, I., "Structure, Dissipation and Life," in *Theoretical Physics and Biology.* Amsterdam, Holland: North-Holland Publishing Co., 1969, pp. 23–32.

7. Bateson, G., "The Birth of a Matrix or Double Bind and Epistemology," in Berger, M., (ed.), *Beyond the Double Bind.* New York: Brunner Mazel, 1977, p. 53.

8. Dell, P., and H. Goolishian, "Order Through Fluctuation: An Evolutionary Paradigm for Human Systems." Presented at the Annual Scientific Meeting of the A. K. Rice Institute, Houston, Texas, 1979.

9. Dell and Goolishian, "Order Through Fluctuation."

NOTES

10. Keeney, B., "Ecosystemic Epistemology: An Alternative Paradigm for Diagnosis," *Family Process* 18 (1979), 117–129.

11. Dell, P., "Beyond Homeostasis," *Family Process* (forthcoming).

12. Dell and Goolishian, "Order Through Fluctuation."

13 Brodey, W., "Some Family Operations and Schizophrenia," *Archives of General Psychiatry* 1 (1959), 379–402.

14. Dell, P., "Beyond Homeostasis."

15. Ibid.

16. Paul Klee, *Notebooks,* vol. 2, trans. Ralph Manheim, ed. Jürg Spiller. New York: George Wittenborn, 1973, pp. 78–79.

Index